No Strings Attached

No Strings Attached

Boundary Lines in Pleasant Places

A History of Warren Street / Pleasant Oaks Mennonite Church

Rachel Nafziger Hartzler

with contributions by
Sara Yoder VonGunten
and **Leona Doell Yoder**

RESOURCE *Publications* · Eugene, Oregon

Resource Publications
An Imprint of Wipf and Stock Publishers
199 W. 8th Ave., Suite 3
Eugene, OR 97401

www.wipfandstock.com

ISBN 13: 978-1-62032-179-9

Manufactured in the U.S.A.

The boundary lines have fallen for me in pleasant places;
surely I have a delightful inheritance.

Psalm 16:6 (NIV)

Dedicated to the glory of God
and to the memory of
Warren Street Mennonite Church (1923–1965)
and Pleasant Oaks Mennonite Church (1965–2009)

Contents

Foreword

THIS EXCEPTIONALLY WELL-RESEARCHED AND written book begins with a story of conflict and division very early in the twentieth century in a Mennonite church in Middlebury, Indiana. The specific issue was whether or not the bonnets that women wore when out in public had to have ribbons attached to them. The church authorities said that they must; the women refused, and they were excommunicated by the church. One of these women was my mother, Ferne Yoder Ramseyer.

With this story as the starting point, Rachel Nafziger Hartzler and Sara Yoder VonGunten lead us into Part I of this book, which is a careful study of how Anabaptist Mennonites adjusted to society and culture in North America, particularly to life in northern Indiana in the late nineteenth and early twentieth centuries. Special focus here is on the contrast between those with a congregational understanding of church polity, especially the Amish Mennonites, and those with a more hierarchical view of authority in the church, that is the "old" Mennonites.

Although the immediate focus for this study is the congregation in Middlebury, Indiana, we are treated here to a much broader study of authority in two groups, groups which came to be known as the General Conference Mennonite Church and the "old" Mennonite Church.

Part I has a wealth of background material and resources. Anyone interested in Anabaptist-Mennonite church polity will find Part I an extremely valuable resource.

Part II of this book is a careful history of the congregation that was formed when the young women were expelled from the Mennonite Church in 1923. Their supporters organized what came to be called the Warren Street Mennonite Church, later the Pleasant Oaks Mennonite Church. The history of the congregation is given in detail from the beginning in 1923 until it re-united in 2009 with the congregation it had left in 1923. This is probably the first time that an unhappy church schism ended with re-unification and a time of joyous celebration.

This account then leads naturally to Part III and the last chapter of this study: What can we learn from this experience? Here I found the discussion of strings and boundaries very helpful, especially as the author suggests that homosexuality and peace and non-resistance are two divisive issues which need to be dealt with in congregations today. How can we keep our central focus on Jesus? How can we have real unity without insisting on uniformity?

Finally, I found the rich resources in the appendices of this volume also very helpful. I strongly recommend this book, not only for people interested in the history of Pleasant Oaks Church in Middlebury, but for anyone concerned about the future of the Anabaptist-Mennonite church here in North America.

Robert L. Ramseyer
Bluffton, Ohio

Preface

THE FIRST TIME THAT I engaged in a significant conversation with someone about the General Conference Mennonite Church (GCMC) and the "old" Mennonite Church (MC) was in the autumn of 1969 when I was learning to know my new college roommate. I was a senior at Goshen College and Jean Schrag (later Lauver) had just arrived on campus, transferring from Freeman Junior College in Freeman, South Dakota. Jean had grown up in rural Freeman and her extended family was fully engaged in the General Conference Mennonite congregations there.

I grew up in Fulton County of Northwestern Ohio where all the Mennonite congregations in the area were part of the "old" Mennonite Church except for two Evangelical Mennonite Churches.[1] Although I had friends who were members of these congregations, I knew little about the theology of those groups except that their women didn't wear head "coverings," and in my church they did. My maternal grandmother (Carrie Rupp King) had grown up in this group, then called the Defenseless Mennonite Church of Archbold, Ohio. All I knew about Carrie's transition to the "old" Mennonite Church is that when she married my grandfather (Harvey King) in 1905, she took off her fancy hat and put on a covering—with strings!

In the Ohio Mennonite Church of my youth (1960s), girls and women who had been baptized wore head coverings made of white netting when attending church services. The older women of my grandmothers' generation wore their coverings during most of their waking hours, and some of these had strings. My mother (Doris King Nafziger), as a member of the Central Mennonite Church in Archbold, Ohio, had strings on her covering when she got married in 1944, but she soon changed to a covering without strings. Her generation of Mennonite women put on their coverings for meals—and other times when they prayed at home—and always wore them

---

1. These congregations in Archbold and Wauseon, Ohio, were part of the Evangelical Mennonite Conference, although the conference has since been renamed Fellowship of Evangelical Churches. It is stated on the Archbold Evangelical Church website that the "reasoning behind the name change was not to distance ourselves from our Anabaptist background, but to better communicate to the next generation who we are." The Archbold Evangelical Mennonite congregation split from the Central Mennonite Church in rural Archbold in 1870. They were also referred to as the Egly/Defenseless Mennonites. http://www.archboldevan.org/about-us/history/?view=mobile; Umble, John S. "Central Mennonite Church."

to church meetings. Most of my peers and I wore our coverings only during worship services. Mine was a fairly small white net cap.

In our dorm room in Kratz Hall in 1969, Jean and I were learning to know each other. Jean had not had much experience with the "old" Mennonite Church, so I attempted to give a simple introduction to my branch of the faith. I said that I thought MCs (Mennonite Church people) were more concerned about following the teachings of Jesus and that GCs (General Conference Mennonites) were more concerned about the "social gospel."

"Aren't those the same?" Jean wisely asked, and I was stumped! That was the beginning of my inquiry into the similarities and differences between these two groups, leading to my coming to claim both groups as "my people." Of course I had no idea that these two denominations would become one denomination three decades later or that thirty-seven years later I would pastor a former General Conference Mennonite Church. But thanks be to God, that has happened. Both of these are factors in the way in which my part of this book is written.

A few technical explanations are in order. A climatic event in the primary story of this book is the re-uniting of two congregations after they had divided eighty-six years earlier. This new union is described as a *re-union*, using the hyphenated form of the word to accent that it was not an ordinary reunion, but a unique, positive, and hopeful happening in the advancing of God's reign. Also, because of the tendency toward humility among Mennonites and the belief in the "priesthood of all believers," church leadership titles are often not highlighted in Mennonite circles. Therefore, when a name herein is preceded by *bishop, minister,* or *pastor,* these are not capitalized, making them adjectives rather than titles. In addition, the term *Reverend* is seldom used except in quotations. On the other hand, recognizing that people are shaped by their heritage, educational experiences, and other life choices, biographical information is provided about many key players in the stories included in this book.

The first Mennonite church in Middlebury was known as Middlebury Mennonite Church when it formed in 1904. After Warren Street Mennonite Church began a few blocks away in 1923, the "first" church was often referred to as Lawrence Street. In 1962, the name was changed to First Mennonite Church of Middlebury. Attempts are made to avoid confusion regarding this congregation that has been known by three different names.

A guiding foundation for this project has been the mission statement of the Historical Committee of Mennonite Church USA: "God calls us to preserve our heritage, to interpret our faith stories, and to proclaim God's work among us." Along with this call, it has sometimes been said that for Mennonites, "their history is their theology."[2] We explore our history to better know ourselves today and hopefully more clearly hear God's voice in the present and in the future.

---

2. Loewen, *One Lord,* 17.

Acknowledgments

SARA YODER VONGUNTEN AND Leona Doell Yoder were major contributors to this book. A significant amount of the historical data was collected by Sara and put into writing in 1984 to meet the requirements for an Indiana University class: Graduate Readings in History. Sara gathered information about Pleasant Oaks Mennonite Church and its predecessor, Warren Street Mennonite Church. Her finished project, *Warren Street Mennonite Church, 1923–1964; Pleasant Oaks Mennonite Church, 1965–1984*, is the foundation for part of chapter 4, much of chapter 5, and portions of chapter 6.

In addition to presenting factual information, Sara has written as one with inside connections and a special vantage point: Sara's mother (Lillian Litweiler Yoder[1]) was one of the twelve young women at the Mennonite Church in Middlebury who wore a hat without strings in 1923. These women were consequently denied communion, the event that prompted the beginning of the Warren Street Mennonite Church. After marrying Sara's father (Noble E. Yoder from Mahoning County, Ohio) and eventually moving to Goshen, Lillian and her family became members of a sister congregation, Eighth Street Mennonite Church, where Sara was nurtured in her childhood and youth. Sara graduated from Bluffton College (now Bluffton University) with a degree in elementary education. After Sara married Ken VonGunten, they moved to Middlebury to both teach school and they became members of Pleasant Oaks. Sara and Ken raised their three children at Pleasant Oaks and were both very active lay leaders throughout the years of their marriage. After Ken's death in 2002, Sara returned to the Eighth Street congregation. Sara now lives in Goshen, Indiana, with her husband, Evan Miller.

Leona Doell Yoder also offered extremely valuable resources for this project. Leona is a natural collector of stories. She grew up in a General Conference congregation in Henderson, Nebraska, in a family deeply rooted in the Russian Mennonite tradition. After attending Bethel College (in North Newton, Kansas) and becoming a registered nurse, Leona worked as the camp nurse at Camp Friedenswald in rural Cassopolis, Michigan, where she and Junior Olen (J. O.) Yoder met. After Leona and J. O. married, Leona joined Warren Street Church in 1956 and remained an active member for the remainder of the congregation's life. She personally collected historical data that greatly

---

1. Lillian Litwiller/Litweiler (born in 1901) and a brother changed the spelling of their family name from Litwiller to Litweiler.

supplement the congregation's sometimes scant historical records. Leona is an able and dedicated historian without whom Warren Street and Pleasant Oaks congregations would have lost much valuable information. Her preservation of historical materials, her outstanding memory of people and events, and her numerous lists of factual data are gifts to the memory of Warren Street/Pleasant Oaks Mennonite Church. Leona and J. O. continue living adjacent to their family farm near Middlebury, Indiana.

Other significant contributions have been made by: J. O. Yoder, life-long member of this congregation who was at the Mennonite Church in Middlebury as a three-year-old in the spring of 1923; and Robin Tahara Miller, also a life-long member of the congregation, great-granddaughter of founding members of the congregation (Freed and Nina Hershberger), and longtime chair of the Pleasant Oaks Preschool Board. Don and Doris Hershberger and many other members and former members added appreciably to this project. Bill Swartzendruber has been an excellent proofreader throughout the project.

Many other people, too numerous to mention, have helped in the writing of this book, which grew into a project of more than four years. Librarians, historians, pastoral colleagues, interested friends, prayer partners, and family members have supported my writing with questions, kind words, and various kinds of encouragement. The members of my Writers' Circle reviewed much of the book in sections, asked probing questions, and offered crucial critique. I am grateful for each of these individuals.

I must name a few friends who have given me outstanding support throughout the past years. To these I owe and express my deep gratitude. John D. Rempel, former Professor of Historical Theology and Anabaptist Studies at Associated Mennonite Biblical Seminary[2] and present Director of the Toronto Mennonite Theological Centre at the Toronto School of Theology, has been a superb consultant on many theological and historical questions throughout the book. Theron Schlabach, Goshen College Professor of History Emeritus and editor and one of the writers of Studies in Anabaptist and Mennonite History Series and The Mennonite Experience in America Series, read historical sections of the book and gave valuable critiques on historical and textual issues. Leonard Gross, Executive Director Emeritus of the Historical Committee of the Mennonite Church and consulting archivist at the Archives of the Mennonite Church in Goshen, also read and responded to historical chapters. Joe Springer, Curator of the Mennonite Historical Library at Goshen College, and his staff were extremely helpful in assisting with historical information and a display of bonnets. And how exciting it has been to have a conversation partner in Rachel Weaver Kreider, someone who has memories longer than the life of Warren Street and Pleasant Oaks combined! Myra Oswald and Kathy and Rick Stiffney provided spaces for writing retreats. And my small group of supportive brothers and sisters has walked with and prayed for me throughout these years of writing and other life challenges:

2. Associated Mennonite Biblical Seminary became Anabaptist Mennonite Biblical Seminary in August 2012.

Ruth and Ron Guengerich, Judy and Ron Kennel, and John D. Rempel. Words of thanks are inadequate to express my great appreciation.

In addition, I am very pleased that Robert Ramseyer, Mennonite Church elder statesman, agreed to write a foreword. Bob is a grandson of Simon S. Yoder, the first pastor of Warren Street Mennonite Church; son of Fern Yoder Ramseyer, one of the young women who wore a bonnet without strings in 1923, and Lloyd Ramseyer, president of Bluffton College (now University) from 1938 to 1965; ordained minister in Mennonite Church USA; missionary in Japan (along with his wife, Alice, also an ordained minister in MC USA) for many years between 1952 to 1995; professor at AMBS (1972–78 and 1982–87) and now AMBS professor emeritus of mission and anthropology; regular visitor to Warren Street and Pleasant Oaks; and life-time active participant in Central District Conference.

I am also grateful to Christian Amondson, editor at Wipf and Stock, and Matthew Wimer, typesetter at Wipf and Stock, who helped to see this book through to publication. Even with the support of so many people, I expect errors remain. I take responsibility for these and ask forgiveness if I have misquoted, misrepresented, or misunderstood any individuals or groups. My intentions have always been to give accurate information in the most interesting way possible, hoping that those who read these pages will be prompted to engage more fully in the church and help bring about the reign of God.

Perhaps only family members of writers (who undertake a project such as this) have an idea of how much time it takes, time sometimes taken away from family activities. I am grateful for the patience and encouragement of my mother and siblings and especially my children and their spouses: Dori Hartzler, Carrie Hartzler Bhandari and Suman Bhandari, Aaron Jon Hartzler and Nakeisha Miller, and Joel Hartzler and Tarah Nimz Hartzler. And I suppose my darling and inquisitive grandchildren (Juna, Rowan, Curran, Oliver, Harold, and Ellis) have wondered why "Nana" so often spends time on her computer! For my part, I am pleased that my older grandchildren are already writers!

I acknowledge that most people will not read this book in its entirety. Some will be more curious about the history of the congregation, and others will be interested in the 150-year scan of Mennonite history. Perhaps it should have been two books, as Sally Weaver Glick and Peggy Reiff Miller imagined, but it is what it is.

Finally, I want to acknowledge that I have numerous conservative Mennonite and Amish friends whom I highly respect. I sincerely hope that I have not offended those who continue to hold that a literal understanding of the teachings of the Apostle Paul about women wearing special coverings is the most faithful interpretation of the Bible. And may those dear women who continue to wear coverings with strings attached be assured that their faithfulness to their traditions and understandings of scripture can be an inspiration, even to those of us who no longer wear coverings, with or without strings!

Rachel Nafziger Hartzler
Goshen, Indiana
Advent 2012

Abbreviations

AM	Amish Mennonite
CDC	Central District Conference (of Mennonite Church USA)
CO	Conscientious Objector
CPS	Civilian Public Service
FMC	First Mennonite Church
GAMEO	*Global Anabaptist Mennonite Encyclopedia Online*
GC or GCMC	General Conference Mennonite Church
IM	Indiana-Michigan
LWF	Lutheran World Federation
MBE	Mennonite Board of Education
MC	Mennonite Church, also known as "old" Mennonite Church
MC USA	Mennonite Church, United States of America
MCC	Mennonite Central Committee
OM	"Old" Mennonite
PAX	A Mennonite-based service program from 1951 to 1975
POMC	Pleasant Oaks Mennonite Church
UNRRA	United Nations Relief and Rehabilitation Administration
WSMC	Warren Street Mennonite Church
YMCA	Young Men's Christian Association
YPCA	Young People's Christian Association
YWCA	Young Women's Christian Association

Introduction

A Time to be Born and a Time to Die

> There is a time for everything . . .
> a time to be born and a time to die,
> a time to plant and a time to uproot . . .
> a time to weep and a time to laugh,
> a time to mourn and a time to dance,
> a time to scatter stones and a time to gather them . . .
>
> ECCLESIASTES 3:1–5a (NIV)

"BEFORE WE PROCEED WITH the ordinance of the Lord's Supper, I will read the names of twelve young women who have not been conforming to the regulations for proper attire as set forth by the Indiana-Michigan Mennonite Conference. These young women are asked to stand and make confession for their sin of not abiding by church regulations before they receive the elements of this Supper. Please stand: Lillian Litweiler, Ferne Yoder, Violet Karch, Lucile Schrock, Ruby Yoder[1] . . ."

One could likely have heard a pin drop in the Middlebury Mennonite Church in Indiana on that spring Sunday morning in 1923 when bishop Daniel D. Miller spoke. It's easy to imagine silence as the young women, ages sixteen to twenty-three, remained seated with heads bowed. Those seated beside them might have noticed that their downturned eyes moved side to side as they each wondered if anyone would dare to stand. Eventually, the bishop continued with the ordinance of the Lord's Supper (communion), serving those who had been baptized—that is, those baptized members who had confessed any sins that had been made public. By not

---

1. This is the way the story was remembered in 1984 by Lillian (Litweiler) Yoder, one whose name was called out. Lillian's daughter, Sara Yoder VonGunten, recorded this story in her 1984 document, *Warren Street Mennonite Church, 1923–1964; Pleasant Oaks Mennonite Church, 1965–1984*. Additional names have been suggested by Rachel Weaver Kreider (born in 1909). Interview with Kreider at Greencroft, Goshen, March 8, 2011.

standing when the bishop read their names, the young women were effectively ex-communicated, silenced in the silence.[2]

Their sin? They had been seen wearing hats without strings. The regulation head-wear or "covering" for women in worship in the "old" Mennonite churches of Indiana in 1923 was a white net cap with strings or ribbons hanging down from the square corners beside the ears.[3] Regulation *outerwear* included a black bonnet with strings to tie under the chin. It is presumed that the young women were wearing their white net coverings for the worship service as all baptized "old" Mennonite women did at that time. However, outside the worship service these "rebellious" women had been wearing modern headwear, felt turban-style hats, instead of what had become known as the "Mennonite bonnet."[4]

It was a time of rapid change in the Mennonite Church in Indiana and beyond. There was much disquiet among Mennonite folks who had earlier been known as "the quiet in the land" and whose theology held "nonresistance" or the "peace posi-tion" as a core doctrine. Earlier there had been intense conflicts about whether to hold Sunday schools in Mennonite churches and about formal education in general. Questions of authority also threatened peace among Mennonites. For example, who had the authority to make decisions about what church materials to publish and who was in charge of Mennonite schools? And a huge question was *who* decides what women wear on their heads!

Winds of change were blowing throughout US religious and secular culture in the early 1920s, and at least a heavy draft from the winds was felt in Mennonite con-gregations. Changes in the Mennonite Church were most dramatically expressed in northern Indiana. In some ways, the city of Goshen, in the center of Elkhart County, was the hub of a whirlwind of churchly discontent, and tornado-like activity occurred there and in rural areas and small towns surrounding Goshen. The decision to close Goshen College for a year was made in 1923, the same spring that communion was

---

2. The Mennonite Church in 1923 and in 2012 is part of the Anabaptist tradition where "believ-ers baptism" is practiced. Rather than observing infant baptism, the church community surrounds parents of babies and together with them promise or "dedicate themselves" to nurture the child in faith in Jesus Christ. Children and youth are encouraged to participate in believers baptism when they reach the "age of accountability," which ranges from age 10 to 21 in the various Anabaptist traditions.

3. Terms for the regulation headwear were "devotional covering," "prayer covering," "prayer head covering," "head covering," "prayer veiling," and "prayer veil," and, in ordinary speech, usually just the "covering." Wearing the covering was in keeping with Paul's admonition to the Corinthian church in 1 Corinthians 11. The covering with strings was the regulation headwear for women within some groups of Mennonites. In addition to coverings, women also wore bonnets as outer, weather-protect-ing headgear. More information about headgear for women is in chapter 2.

4. Sara VonGunten has in her possession her mother's hat "that caused the trouble" in 1923. It is a black felt turban style with decorative bands of the same fabric. It is not totally clear whether this is the hat that Lillian Litweiler wore instead of a more conservative bonnet, or if this is the hat that was the prescribed headwear of the Mennonite Church and Lillian had removed the strings or ribbons.

denied to the young women in Middlebury. Two main issues at Goshen were authority and conformity to a prescribed dress code.[5]

In the years around 1923, Daniel D. (D. D.) Miller was thought by some, especially the families affected by the excommunications of the Middlebury women, to be a rigid and strict church leader, inconsiderate, and lacking a Christian world view. However, bishop Miller was responding to a growing concern among conservative Mennonite leaders, that allowing the young members to follow fashions of the world would lead to their becoming more and more assimilated into the "worldly" culture, and the important distinctives (some of which had become restrictions) of the Mennonite Church would be lost.

It wasn't easy being a Mennonite minister or bishop in Indiana in the 1920s. Bishop D. D. Miller was also a school teacher (having begun teaching school at age seventeen) and a family man with five sons and six daughters.[6] Before the spring of 1923, he had struggled with one of the pressing issues at hand, that of the bonnet for women. While his sons were milking the cows one evening, D. D. came to the barn. He stood watching his sons continue with the milking before finally saying something like, "Boys, I don't know what to do about the matter of the bonnet and strings. What do you think?" The young sons did not have a ready answer, so after a pause, the bishop continued. "If I am lenient, some will disapprove and I'm afraid it will split the church." After another pause, and perhaps a clearing of the throat, he went on. "If I strictly uphold the church regulations, others will be upset and I fear that that will also split the church."[7]

One of Menno Simon's favorite Bible passages was from Ephesians 5, which refers to Christ loving the church and wanting to present the church to himself in splendor, without a spot or wrinkle or anything of the kind—yes, so that she may be holy and

5. More information on the closing of Goshen College for one academic year (1923–1924) is in chapter 3 and details are described in many places, including Susan Fisher Miller's *Culture for Service: A History of Goshen College 1894–1994* and *College Mennonite Church 1903–2003* edited by Ervin Beck.

6. Daniel D. Miller (December 10, 1864–January 19, 1955), a son of Daniel P. and Anna Hershberger Miller, was born in LaGrange County, Indiana. After his childhood in Missouri, the family returned to Indiana and he taught school for twenty years. On May 26, 1889, he married Jeanette "Nettie" Hostetler and they had thirteen children, of whom eleven grew to maturity: Orie O., Ernest E., Truman T., Ida, Clara, Wilbur W., Kathryn, Bertha, Alice, Samuel S., and Mabel. All became schoolteachers for longer or shorter periods. Miller became a member of the Forks Amish Mennonite Church where he was chosen deacon in 1890, preacher in 1891, and bishop in 1906 with bishop Daniel J. Johns performing all three ordinations. He voluntarily adopted the "plain coat" so that his ministry would be more effective among the "old" Mennonites although his Amish Mennonite Church did not require it. He traveled far and wide in the Amish Mennonite and Mennonite churches and helped to bring about the merger of the Amish Mennonite and Mennonite churches. He served on many church boards throughout his long life, including the Mennonite Board of Missions and Charities, of which he was president from 1920 to 1936. J. C. Wenger said, "His sermons were well prepared, his voice was strong and clear, his thought processes clear and direct. As a disciplinarian he was somewhat strict, yet not a legalist." Wenger, *Mennonite Encyclopedia, Vol. III*, 691.

7. This story was told to Rachel Nafziger Hartzler by D. D. Miller's grandson Donald Miller, son of Ernest E., on March 27, 2010, at College Mennonite Church, Goshen, Indiana.

without blemish. As an early Dutch Mennonite leader, Menno had been caught in various disputes about keeping the church pure and enforcing church discipline. Before his death in 1561, Menno admitted that the matter of church discipline was the most difficult part of his ministry. We might wonder if D. D. Miller said the same thing.

And indeed there was a split in the Mennonite Church of Middlebury in 1923 when the families of the young women who didn't have strings attached to their outer headwear left to form another Mennonite congregation, first referred to as West Side Church, and then as Warren Street Mennonite Church (WSMC) because of its location on Warren Street. Forty-two years later (in 1965) a new meetinghouse was constructed and the name Pleasant Oaks Mennonite Church (POMC) was chosen for this congregation. (When referring to the group of people who made up this congregation over the years, the acronym WSMC/POMC will be used.)

Following is a story of God's faithfulness to that new Mennonite congregation in Middlebury that spanned the years from 1923 to 2009. This is also a story of a people committed to following Jesus Christ, with a focus on his Sermon on the Mount. These stories are similar to those of many congregations, especially Mennonite congregations in the United States and Canada, who take seriously Jesus' call to voluntary discipleship, which includes love, even for an enemy.

Stories, such as this tale of one congregation, beg deeper questions about strings, boundaries, and fences. Why do people committed to following the same Jesus vary so much in their understandings of how to live? How can divisions happen in a denomination with a strong peace theology? Are the issues and questions facing the church today similar to issues and questions that erupted throughout the twentieth century? What can we learn from history? We *do* have a good inheritance, delightful in many ways. But we might wonder if boundary lines are in pleasant places today, as the Psalmist declares in Psalm 16:6 (NIV): "The boundary lines have fallen for me in pleasant places; surely I have a delightful inheritance."

There are many "pleasant" places in northern Indiana and many of them are places of Christian worship. In 2009, within a ten-mile radius of Pleasant Oaks Mennonite Church were Pleasant View Mennonite Church, Pleasant Grove Conservative Mennonite Church, Pleasant Ridge Missionary Church, and Pleasant Valley Church of the Brethren. There are likely both pleasant and unpleasant stories in each of these congregations. Pleasant threads have been underlying themes throughout the eighty-six years of the life of WSMC/POMC—God's faithfulness to all generations, and people of God attempting to follow Jesus Christ with the guidance of the ever-present Spirit of God.

The beginnings of the congregation were not altogether pleasant. But God was at work, helping faithful followers of Jesus to name their differences and discover how to continue to worship the God who was faithful to both congregations—the group from which the new congregation emerged and the new fledging group.

Part 1 of this book is background information about the two groups that had been the two largest Mennonite denominations in the United States, the two denominations in which First Mennonite Church of Middlebury and Pleasant Oaks Mennonite Church were rooted, that is, the Mennonite Church and General Conference Mennonite Church. These two denominations merged in 2002 to become Mennonite Church USA (MC USA). The official name of the former Mennonite Church denomination had the risk of inaccurately implying that its members thought they were *the* Mennonite Church. To avoid that implication, this text (along with the writings of many Mennonite historians) uses the longtime popular phrase "old" Mennonite Church, with *old* in quotation marks since it is not part of the official name.[8]

Considering the historical background and theological development (in the form of confessions) of Mennonites is beneficial for understanding the Middlebury story. In addition, the beginnings and developments within other area Mennonite congregations and institutions impacted Mennonites in Middlebury. Part 1 also includes snippets from the lives of numerous people and institutions whose stories parallel or feed into the WSMC/POMC story.

Part 2 traces the life of WSMC/POMC through its cycles of growth and decline to its ending as a congregation in 2009. In a unique development, the congregation ended its life as it had been and there was grief, but not a burial. Instead, it was a time of transformation into a new phenomenon that includes more than 200 people, a thriving preschool, a forty-five-year-old well-maintained church building on six acres, and a ninety-nine-year-old land-locked meetinghouse with numerous additions. The new phenomenon is a new congregation consisting of members of the former Pleasant Oaks Mennonite Church and First Mennonite Church of Middlebury, the congregation from which WSMC/POMC had come in 1923. In some ways it was like a marriage. As far as is known, no other congregations that split over differences have re-united into a new congregation, although it is hoped that this will be the first of many!

In brief, in 1923 about eighty people became Warren Street Church (which in 1965 became Pleasant Oaks Mennonite Church), leaving Middlebury Mennonite Church (which later became Lawrence Street Mennonite and then First Mennonite) because of different understandings of scripture and tradition and authority. Middlebury Mennonite remained with the Indiana-Michigan Mennonite Conference, which was part of the "old" Mennonite Church,[9] and in 1926 Warren Street

8. The phrase "old" Mennonite Church, sometimes shortened to MC, is at times inclusive of the Amish Mennonite Church of the nineteenth and early twentieth centuries. The word conference is used repeatedly throughout this story. When used with a lower case "c" it often refers to a meeting or series of meetings, a convention. When used with a capital "C" it usually is part of the official name of a structure or organization, such as the General Conference Mennonite Church, the Central District Conference or the Indiana-Michigan Conference. Such organizations are sometimes referred to as "conferences," meaning associations. Most confusing is that the "old" Mennonite Church had an organizational structure called the Mennonite Church General Conference, an association of leaders of the denomination. Attempts will be made to clearly differentiate that organization from the General Conference Mennonite Church.

9. This denomination began in Pennsylvania in 1683, making it the oldest Mennonite denomination in North America. However, the group was not formally organized until 1898 at Wakarusa,

joined the Central Conference of Mennonites, which in 1946 joined the General Conference Mennonite Church.[10]

WSMC/POMC was fully alive for eighty-six years, nurturing children, youth, and adults, providing a place for worship, and engaging in God's mission in the world. Perhaps the stories of this congregation are not unusual, but they are unique, having emerged from a distinctive group of people, some of whom forged a new identity in Middlebury in 1923, many of whom joined with the congregation for periods of time along the way, and thirty of whom remained active members until the final worship service on November 22, 2009.

Three of those thirty members were present in 1923 when WSMC/POMC began: Junior Olen (J. O.) Yoder, Donald Hershberger, and Doneta Hershberger Burkhardt.[11] Four more of the remaining members were born into and nurtured within the congregation throughout their lives until November 2009: Grant Tetsuo Miller, Robin Tahara Miller, Brian Yoder, and Richard Yoder.

Part 3 of this book grows out of three and one-half years of pastoral engagement with this congregation in addition to reflections on the stories collected. These stories illustrate the creative tension within which one congregation lived for eighty-six years. There is, and perhaps has always been, a creative tension between which strings to leave attached and which to cut, and where to draw the boundary lines, if we indeed do need boundaries. These stories illuminate times to be born, times to grow and thrive, and times to come to an end. These stories invite dreams and visions for the future of the Christian Church and particularly Mennonite Church USA, where this author and Mennonites in Middlebury continue to be at home.

The last members of Pleasant Oaks fervently hope and pray that this re-uniting of two congregations will be a testimony to all who hear the story, as Jesus himself prayed in John 17:20–21. "I ask not only on behalf of these [my disciples], but also on behalf of those who will believe in me through their word, (referring to Christians today) that they may all be one. As you, Father, are in me and I am in you, may they also be in us, so that the world may believe that you have sent me."

Indiana. It dissolved in 2002 when it merged with the General Conference Mennonite Church to form Mennonite Church USA. In this book the denomination will be referred to as the "old" Mennonite Church or MC (or OM in some citations).

10. The General Conference Mennonite Church denomination (known as the General Conference of the Mennonite Church in North America until 1950) was organized in 1860 at West Point, Iowa. It existed until 2002 when it merged with the "old" Mennonite Church to form Mennonite Church USA. In this book it will be referred to as the General Conference Mennonite Church, GCMC, or simply GC.

11. Donald and Doneta were twins, born to Freed and Nina (Horner) Hershberger on January 13, 1924. The first meetings of the congregation were in the fall of 1923, so both Donald and Doneta enjoyed saying that they were present (*en utero*) when the church began. Doneta was a member of the church when the last service was held, but she died on February 5, 2010, before the legalities of re-uniting with First Mennonite Church were complete.

PART I

A Summary of Growth and Schisms among Mennonites

In Essentials, Unity;
In Nonessentials, Liberty;
In All Things, Charity

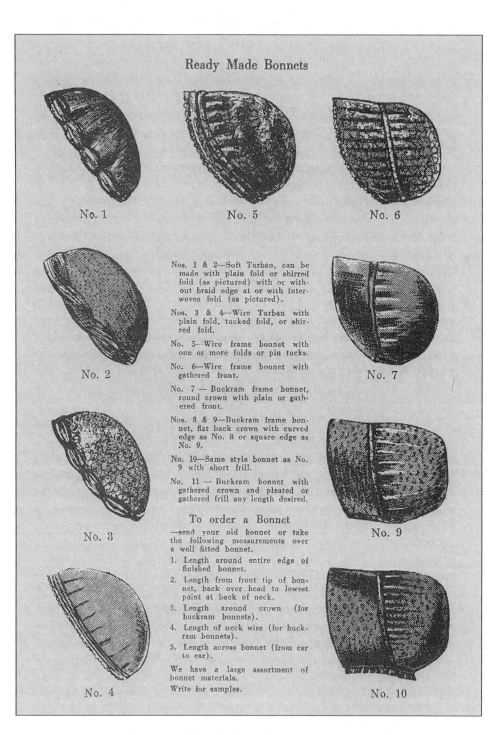

Ready Made Bonnets

No. 1

No. 5

No. 6

No. 2

Nos. 1 & 2—Soft Turban, can be made with plain fold or shirred fold (as pictured) with or without braid edge at or with interwoven fold (as pictured).

Nos. 3 & 4—Wire Turban with plain fold, tucked fold, or shirred fold.

No. 5—Wire frame bonnet with one or more folds or pin tucks.

No. 6—Wire frame bonnet with gathered front.

No. 7 — Buckram frame bonnet, round crown with plain or gathered front.

Nos. 8 & 9—Buckram frame bonnet, flat back crown with curved edge as No. 8 or square edge as No. 9.

No. 10—Same style bonnet as No. 9 with short frill.

No. 11 — Buckram bonnet with gathered crown and pleated or gathered frill any length desired.

No. 7

To order a Bonnet

—send your old bonnet or take the following measurements over a well fitted bonnet.

1. Length around entire edge of finished bonnet.
2. Length from front tip of bonnet, back over head to lowest point at back of neck.
3. Length around crown (for buckram bonnets).
4. Length of neck wire (for buckram bonnets).
5. Length across bonnet (from ear to ear).

We have a large assortment of bonnet materials.

Write for samples.

No. 3

No. 9

No. 4

No. 10

A 1960s advertisement from the Hager Store in Lancaster, Pennsylvania.

1

Early Anabaptist Life and History

From Europe to North America

I . . . beg you to lead a life worthy of the calling to which you have been called,
with all humility and gentleness, with patience, bearing with one another in love,
making every effort to maintain the unity of the Spirit in the bond of peace.

EPHESIANS 4:1–3

RACHEL WEAVER KREIDER REMEMBERS that in 1918 the bishop came to their home
between Shipshewana and Middlebury, just around the corner from the Pashan cemetery. Being a curious nine-year-old, she wondered why he had come calling. She
knew bishop Daniel D. Miller from his presence at the Sunday meetings at the Forks
church, especially when there was baptism or communion.[1] It was bishop Daniel J.
Johns who had ordained her father preacher in 1904, five years before she was born,
because at that time D. D. Miller was not yet a bishop. Rachel remembers that when
D. D. Miller came in 1918, her mother, Laura, and father, Sam Weaver, met him on the
porch. Rachel and her older brother, Stahly, knew that they were to stay in the house.

Stahly was six years older than Rachel and he seemed to know something that
she didn't. He was usually quiet and relaxed and patiently explained things to Rachel.
That day Stahly was different. He walked back and forth between the kitchen and the
front room, shuffled through magazines, and didn't sit down. Rachel wondered what
was being discussed on the porch and why Stahly seemed restless.

In due time, Rachel learned that the bishop came to visit her mother "to let her
know she was in need of a warning and of enough discipline to make the warning

1. Both of these ordinances, baptism of new believers and communion of existing members, could
be presided over by only a bishop at that time.

stick." She had taken the ribbons off her bonnet. Because of this, she was not allowed to take communion when that Sunday came.[2]

The ordained men in the church had the responsibility to try to keep church members from straying across that boundary that separated them from the ways of the world. Some people would have expected a husband to reprimand his wife on matters like this. After all, as heads of households, husbands were to "keep their wives in line." Sam Weaver, however, was a progressive-thinking man and "he was apt to stray as well"!

Husbands were to keep their wives in line, and ministers were expected to keep the whole congregation in line, and the challenge seemed to be getting greater. In addition to Laura Weaver, "there was the young Orpha who was caught on the streets of Goshen wearing a hat." Orpha was also banned from communion, and her response was to be absent on communion Sunday. Mrs. Weaver, on the other hand, went to church as usual on communion Sunday but sat quietly on the bench when the others rose to partake of the elements.

One might imagine the bishop sighing, wondering if church discipline would always be such a problem. How long would the people of the church need to be admonished "to resist the continual temptations of accepting more and more of the secular culture surrounding them?"[3]

It's an oversimplification to say that the trouble in Middlebury in 1923 and what happened on the Weaver farm in 1918 had to do with conflicts about the essentials for being in fellowship with the church, but that is one way to look at what happened. A motto often used during the years of the denomination of General Conference (GC) Mennonite Church (1860 to 2002) is that in essentials there should be unity; in nonessentials, liberty; and in all things, charity.[4]

Although there is some agreement on essentials among the various groups of Mennonites, historically there has been much disagreement. Differences tend to be not so

---

2. These thoughts and quotations are from a four-paragraph essay typed by Rachel Weaver Kreider (born May 28, 1909) and given to Rachel Nafziger Hartzler on March 7, 2012. Additional information from Rachel Kreider came through conversation with Hartzler in Kreider's apartment at Greencroft Retirement Center, Goshen, Indiana, on September 10, 2010. Rachel's mother was Laura Johns (December 28, 1883–January 30, 1975), and her father was Samuel E. Weaver (February 26, 1880–November 16, 1935). Sam studied at Valparaiso University and received a BA from Goshen College and was a school teacher/superintendent and preacher at Forks Amish Mennonite Church. Sam was ordained preacher at Forks Amish Mennonite Church in 1904 by bishop Daniel J. Johns. He resigned in 1916, an unusual move for an Amish Mennonite minister. Sam was a brother of William B. Weaver, author of History of the Central Conference; these Weavers were first cousins of Simon S. Yoder, first pastor of Warren Street Mennonite Church.

3. Rachel Kreider conversation and memo, September 10, 2010, and March 7, 2012.

4. This motto did not originate with General Conference Mennonites; numerous people over the ages have been given credit for this expression, including St. Augustine, with whom it likely did *not* originate. It appears in literature for the first time in Germany in 1627. It was the motto of the General Conference of Mennonite Churches in Russia when it was founded in 1882. See http://www9.georgetown.edu/faculty/jod/augustine/quote.html.

much about doctrine—core beliefs—as they are about practice—how Christians live out their faith. Being faithful in practical matters has always been an Anabaptist value.

For readers not familiar with the beginnings of Anabaptism as a part of the Radical Reformation in the 1500s, a brief summary is in appendix A. There are many good sources of further reading on this subject.[5] In the past generation, Christians with no former ties to a Mennonite church have been drawn to the sixteen-century Anabaptist vision. One example is Stuart Murray who in *The Naked Anabaptist* describes Anabaptism as a "way of following Jesus that challenges, disturbs, and inspires us, summoning us to wholehearted discipleship and worship."[6]

THE CHURCH AS THE PURE BRIDE OF CHRIST

A basic biblical passage for Anabaptists is Ephesians 5:21–27:

> Be subject to one another out of reverence for Christ. . . . Husbands, love your wives, just as Christ loved the church and gave himself up for her, in order to make her holy by cleansing her with the washing of water by the word, so as to present the church to himself in splendor, without a spot or wrinkle or anything of the kind—yes, so that she may be holy and without blemish.

Without Spot or Wrinkle: Treasure in Clay Jars

Anabaptist theology has an underlying belief about the church being the pure bride of Jesus Christ. In the "household codes" (Ephesians 5:21—6:9), the writer to the Ephesians calls for relationships between husbands and wives to be loving, as is the relationship between Christ and the church, the church being "the bride of Christ." Jesus Christ's love was so great that he gave his life for the church so that the church would be cleansed. Consequently, the church is presented to Christ in "splendor, without a spot or wrinkle or anything of the kind—yes, so that [the church] may be holy and without blemish" (Ephesians 5:27).

The Anabaptist-Mennonite quest to be a church "without stain or wrinkle" has sometimes resulted in unhealthy practices of legalism and unloving exclusion. However, the goal of church discipline is to restore those who have gone astray, not to punish

---

5. There are two academic versions of *Anabaptist History and Theology* by C. Arnold Snyder. Less academic and very readable accounts of Mennonite history are presented by John D. Roth in *Stories: How Mennonites Came to Be* and Harry Loewen and Steven Nolt in *Through Fire and Water: An Overview of Mennonite History*. An older volume still recommended is *An Introduction to Mennonite History: A Popular History of the Anabaptists and the Mennonites* by Cornelius Dyck.

6. Murray, *Naked Anabaptist*. Murray, from Great Britain, addresses what Anabaptism looks like when not clothed in Mennonite or Amish traditions. Murray peels back the layers to reveal the core components of Anabaptism.

them. Ideally, discipline will gently lead a wayward member to a fuller understanding of faith, discipleship, and relationships within the fellowship of a believing community.[7]

Can a group of fallible, imperfect women and men become holy, and remain without blemish, spot or wrinkle? No, not on their own, for even though created in the image of God, it is only by the grace of God extended through Jesus Christ that humanity can even approach holiness.

On the other hand, Jesus said, "Be perfect, therefore, as your heavenly Father is perfect" (Matthew 5:48). The writer to the church at Ephesus confirms that "the *holiness* and *blamelessness* of the church is *Christ's* work . . ." In *Ephesians: Believers Church Bible Commentary*, Tom Yoder Neufeld says that the fundamental intent in Ephesians 5 is not to reinforce unrealistic and impossible expectations on one another, but to be reminded of the "infinitely gracious work of salvation in and through Christ" for humanity.[8] It is not what people think, believe, or do that brings us into Christ's perfection; it is what God has already done through Christ.[9]

The church and its ministry is a treasure entrusted to jars of clay, earthen vessels, as both first and twenty-first-century Christians can be described. Illumination is in 2 Corinthians 4:5–7.

> For we do not proclaim ourselves; we proclaim Jesus Christ as Lord and ourselves as your slaves for Jesus' sake. For it is the God who said, "Let light shine out of darkness," who has shone in our hearts to give the light of the knowledge of the glory of God in the face of Jesus Christ. But we have this treasure in clay jars, so that it may be made clear that this extraordinary power belongs to God and does not come from us.

Identity: More than Conforming to Nonconformity

Historically, being and behaving differently from "the world" have been strong emphases in Amish and Mennonite groups. A key scriptural instruction for these values is Romans 12:2: "Do not be conformed to this world, but be transformed by the renewing of your minds, so that you may discern what is the will of God—what is good and acceptable and perfect." In the notorious year of 1923, a visiting preacher from Ontario, Samuel (S. F.) Coffman, preached at College Mennonite Church in Goshen on the Romans 12 text. He "urged that we too often err in our effort not to conform to 'this world' because we stop short of the transformation that is accomplished by 'the renewing of our minds'— making our religion externalistic."[10]

---

7. Roth, *Beliefs*, 139.

8. Yoder Neufeld, *Ephesians*, 262–63.

9. Another understanding of Jesus' meaning of "be perfect" is "be mature."

10. Springer, *Centennial Chronicles*, 25. Samuel Frederick (S. F.) Coffman (1872–1954) was a son of John S. Coffman whose story is in chapter 3.

There has been great curiosity about "nonconformed" people, evidenced by thousands of tourists flocking to locations highly populated with Amish folk, particularly in Lancaster, Pennsylvania; Berlin, Ohio; and Shipshewana, Indiana. Those tourists who take time to learn more about the Amish and their Mennonite cousins, for example, at an interpretive visitors' center such as Menno-Hof in Shipshewana,[11] will realize that although there are some differences, there are many specific beliefs and practices that the various Amish and Mennonite groups have in common. These are especially the following four foundational practices:

1. *Believers Baptism* is an essential belief that Anabaptist groups hold in common; it includes voluntary entrance into the community of faith followed by a life of discipleship. Baptism was a major issue in the sixteenth century Radical Reformation when the "left wing" reformers were confident that infants neither could be saved from sin by baptism, nor needed to be saved.

2. *Nonresistance* calls for loving nonviolent behavior in all of life. Nonresistance was a clearly-articulated doctrine of almost all early Anabaptists. By the time the Anabaptist movement had coalesced in the 1540s, nonresistance had almost the status of baptism in defining the movement.

3. *Community* is highly valued among Anabaptists. Upon becoming members of Mennonite Church (MC) USA congregations, whether by baptism or confession of faith, candidates are asked if they are willing to give and receive counsel in the congregation.[12] At times, this practice is at tension with individualism.

4. *Separation from the world,* or *nonconformity to the world,* are traditional Mennonite expressions of how to relate to people, things, and ideas outside the faith community.

In 1925, two years after the schism in Middlebury occurred, and 400 years after Anabaptism was initiated, John E. Hartzler, an influential, well educated, progressive Mennonite leader, wrote the following about separation from the world:

> During the past 100 years in particular the attitude was expressed in some cases by the adoption of peculiar forms of dress, while in other cases the mark of separation was the German language. . . . As a result of overemphasis on this point many sections of the denomination drifted into "isolationism," or perhaps "insulation." The community was content to move along with its own interests with little concern as to how or where the "world" was going.
>
> It should be said, however, in fairness to a large and rapidly growing group within the denomination, that since the establishment of colleges by the denomination there has come a very great change in the matter of "separation"; not that the doctrine has been discarded, but that it is being given a

11. Menno-Hof offers a virtual tour that can be accessed online at www.mennohof.org.
12. John Rempel, *Minister's Manual*, 48.

new and vital interpretation. "Separation" is coming to mean and imply the maintenance of identity and the giving of [oneself] in sacrificial service to the "world", Jesus himself being the ideal example.[13]

Which aspects of Mennonite identity would be maintained and which would change? Indeed, what are the essentials?

Church Discipline, the Ban, and Shunning: Matthew 16 and 18

From the beginning of Anabaptism there has been disagreement on the idea of perfection in the church and how to respond to members who fall short or with whom there is difference of opinion. The ban, an instrument of church discipline, is the term used to indicate either exclusion from communion or exclusion from membership. Indeed, how to interpret the Matthew 18 passage has been the cause of significant schisms, and the implementation of the ban resulted in other schisms. The verb "to disfellowship," rather than "to ban," is used in some circles.

The words of Jesus from Matthew 18:15–17 are:

> If another member of the church sins against you, go and point out the fault when the two of you are alone. If the member listens to you, you have regained that one. But if you are not listened to, take one or two others along with you, so that every word may be confirmed by the evidence of two or three witnesses. If the member refuses to listen to them, tell it to the church; and if the offender refuses to listen even to the church, let such a one be to you as a Gentile and a tax collector.

In this passage Jesus pronounces that it is the duty of the church to exercise discipline. He gave the authority to discipline in Matthew 16:19, "I will give you the keys of the kingdom of heaven, and whatever you bind on earth will be bound in heaven, and whatever you loose on earth will be loosed in heaven."[14] Only the church (not an

13. John Ellsworth (J. E.) Hartzler (February 2, 1879–May 24, 1963) was a Mennonite Church leader who was somewhat of a controversial character. He was born near Ligonier, Indiana, to Old Order Amish parents, Joseph and Mary (Beyler) Hartzler and grew up in Cass County, Missouri. He studied at the Elkhart Institute, Moody Bible Institute, Hamilton College of Law, and McCormick Theological Seminary. He received the BA (Goshen College), BD (Union Theological Seminary, New York), MA (U. of Chicago), law degree (Hamilton College), and PhD (Hartford Theological Seminary) degrees. He served as pastor at Prairie Street Mennonite Church (1910–13) and dean (1911–13) and president (1913–18) of Goshen College. In 1918 he became a professor of Bible at Bethel College (Kansas) and served as president, 1920–21. "As an early advocate of an all-Mennonite seminary, Hartzler became president of Witmarsum Theological Seminary when it opened in 1921 at Bluffton College. At Witmarsum, Hartzler and others incurred frequent charges of modernism. Hartzler defended his loyalty to the essence of Mennonite faith, but a faith defined more in terms of individual rights than Anabaptist tradition." Hartzler was on the faculty at Hartford Theological Seminary 1936–47 then retired in Goshen where he renewed relationships with Goshen College and interacted with younger Mennonite leaders. J. Denny Weaver. "Hartzler, John Ellsworth."

14. See also John 20:23, 1 Thessalonians 5:14, and James 5:16. In a sense, loosing is done in baptism

individual *leader*) has the authority to pronounce the ban—after proper discernment within the community of believers.

Two crucial points are that the ban is only for church members (not seekers), and those banned are to be treated in the way that Jesus treated Gentiles and tax collectors. Gentiles and tax collectors were Jesus' friends; he ate with them, accepted water from them, and healed them, all the while wanting to win them to his vision of the Kingdom of God. Jesus did not cast them out into darkness and reject them as the word *ban* may seem to imply. Likewise, these verses are not about punishing those who believe or behave differently. The Matthew 18 imperative is to treat those who are outside the circle and those with whom there is disagreement as friends, welcoming them into the circle and/or seeking reconciliation in the event of offense.

John D. Roth clarifies that to be a "Believers Church," discipline is necessary, making the following points: 1. "The practice of church discipline is biblical," with Matthew 18 being the cornerstone text. 2. "Church discipline was not to be punitive." It is an expression of love for the member who has strayed from the practice of the group. 3. "Church discipline is an essential corollary to the Anabaptist principles of voluntary baptism and pacifism."[15]

Regarding baptism and pacifism, Roth further says:

> Baptism: The Anabaptists rejected infant baptism, insisting that membership in the congregation was the result of a voluntary choice. The individual joined the group freely, knowing in advance the doctrines and standards of the group. Therefore, the integrity of both the voluntary choice and the moral character of the congregation could be preserved only if the community exercised discipline in relation to members' whose beliefs or actions later proved to be at odds with those of the congregation. Otherwise . . . the baptismal choice was meaningless. A church without discipline might just as well baptize babies since, to their way of thinking, moral or theological standards are ultimately meaningless in such a congregation. Discipline guaranteed that the voluntary decision to become a member of the church remained ongoing.[16]

> Pacifism: In a related fashion, discipline practiced in accordance with Matthew 18 was also a clear testimony to the nonviolent rule of Christ. In sharp contrast to the state churches, whose unity was preserved by the coercive practices of

---

and binding is done in implementing the ban. There is guidance in the current Mennonite *Minister's Manual* for binding and loosing with the following introduction: "It is perhaps the most awesome part of the church's calling to bind and loose, to hold someone responsible for a transgression of commission or omission or to release someone from repented sin (John 20:21–23). Mostly this discipline happens in everyday ways as we . . . give and receive counsel. . . . Self-righteousness is only a hair's breadth away from righteousness . . . . There are occasions when people end up in the grip of sin or of guilt . . . . The congregation can become the medium of God's grace in binding and loosing." John Rempel, *Minister's Manual*, 225.

15. Roth, "Without Spot or Wrinkle," 12–13.

16. Ibid., 13–14.

intimidation, torture, and executions, the Anabaptists insisted that the conscience could not be swayed by physical force. The biblical model of the ban and shunning was consistent with Christ's teaching of nonviolent active love.[17]

As noted above, there has been unity among Anabaptists on the principle of voluntary baptism. There have been differences in the mode of baptism (sprinkling, pouring, immersing, and with immersion, whether forward or backward and how many times), and also on the "age of accountability,"[18] but evidence of "agreeing and disagreeing in love"[19] has occurred, for instance, at Menno-Hof in Shipshewana in 2010, when four different groups of Mennonites (Amish, Beachy Amish Mennonite, Conservative Mennonite, and MC USA) gathered and had an open and congenial discussion about similarities and differences in baptism practices.[20]

Different Anabaptist Perspectives on the Ban

Early Anabaptists understood that the church must reject wayward members as the human body rejects foreign objects, such as a sliver under the skin. The doctrine and practice of the first Anabaptists was to apply the ban only to coarse, notorious sinners. As time went on, however, there was not unity among Anabaptists on how strictly to enforce the ban. The Swiss and South German Anabaptists agreed that they were to fulfill the Biblical demands of the ban "earnestly, and yet with love, strictly, and yet with justice." There was a different approach among some of the Dutch Anabaptists. Here a harsh use of the ban was the cause of "lamentable quarrels and regrettable divisions."[21]

The Amish group began in Switzerland in 1693 over different understandings of the ban. The Swiss Anabaptists led by Hans Reist practiced church discipline, but the most severe punishments were excommunication and exclusion from the Lord's Supper. A young Swiss minister, Jakob Ammann, wanted stricter rules concerning attire and other matters. To encourage repentance on the part of those who strayed, Amman called for more rigorous use of the ban and also shunning, or systematic social avoidance.[22] The rationale was that while shunning emphasized the purity of the church and the seriousness of sin, it also encouraged excommunicated members to repent and

---

17. Ibid., 14.

18. There have long been debates on what is the age of accountability, the point reached in life at which a person becomes morally responsible to God and is a candidate for baptism. This age is not the same for all people and has certainly varied among Anabaptist groups. Some groups expect children to make the baptism decision in early adolescence and others prefer them to wait until later adolescence or marriage to make this decision. Mennonite Church, "Nurture and Evangelism of Children."

19. A document titled "Agreeing and Disagreeing in Love" is used in MC USA and is available at http://mennoniteusa.org/resources/agreeing-and-disagreeing-in-love.

20. For a description of this event and more information on believers baptism, see Menno-Hof *Reunion* at http://www.mennohof.org/pdf/Reunion_Winter_2010.pdf.

21. Neff, "Ban."

22. Theron Schlabach, *Peace, Faith, Nation*, 21.

return to the church. In sum, the greatest difference between the seventeenth century Anabaptists who became Amish (followers of Ammann) and those who did not, was in the way that wayward members were treated. The separation was not over theology but about degrees of discipline and separation. Even though Swiss and South German, the Amish took a position similar to the Dutch Anabaptists but they applied it with differing degrees of firmness or harshness.

The theology of early Anabaptist Pilgram Marpeck regarding the ban is noteworthy as a middle way. Marpeck was born about 1495 to a devout Catholic family in western Austria. He trained and worked as an engineer, and served on the city council. At one time Marpeck was the mayor of Rattenberg. He converted to Anabaptism in 1528 and became a minister, theologian, prolific writer, and a leader of the South German Anabaptists from 1530 to 1556. His theology included the "general Anabaptist convictions that belief cannot be coerced and the Church cannot be one with the state." He is considered by some Anabaptist historical theologians and scholars to be the most important voice of the German Anabaptists in the middle of the sixteenth century and perhaps the most important early Anabaptist voice for the twenty-first century. Marpeck insisted that the Bible is properly understood only in the context *of* and *by* the whole community of believers.[23]

Inspired by the love of Christ, Marpeck addressed the problem of persistent sin among those claiming to live a life of discipleship to Christ. John D. Rempel elaborates on Marpeck's letter, "Concerning hasty judgments and verdicts."

> Marpeck argues that the most essential trait of love is patience. He makes his point by means of the image of a tree: first there are blossoms, then there are leaves, and finally there is fruit. Blossoms and leaves do not show what the actual fruit will be like. So it is with the Christian's walk. Our motives are mixed; in fact God can draw them into a higher purpose. For that reason, we cannot pass judgment on fellow believers before the fruit of their life—a consistent pattern of behavior—appears. We can advise and even warn, but if we come to a premature verdict, we are meddling in the hidden counsel of God.[24]

Rempel describes Marpeck's pastoral theology as standing on the following two pillars:

> The body of Christ thrives only in its interdependence. In other words, members owe it to one another to give and receive counsel; they mutually discern the Holy Spirit's work. The goal of this interdependence is the unity of the church, in each congregation but also among all of like faith. . . . Christ's love is the end of the law. The cornerstone of Marpeck's thought is freedom, the liberty in which Christ acted and in which we act. The mark of the free person is the desire to

23. John D. Rempel, Kunstbuch, 9–10. Alternate spelling of Marpeck is Marbeck, used at Bluffton University as the name of the student center.

24. Ibid., 138.

please God; the prayer of the free person is "Your Kingdom come to us." The only command freedom gives is the command to love nonresistantly.[25]

With these characteristic teachings, Marpeck effectively steered Anabaptists between two extremes of focusing on only the inner life on one hand, and giving great attention to following outward rules on the other hand, a "middle way between legalism and license."[26] He emphasized freedom in Christ, the leading of the Holy Spirit, and the necessity of the visible church for modeling Christian faith. Marpeck and his followers made fervent attempts to be the body of Christ with integrity. John Rempel points out that in their struggle to totally trust God in the midst of terrifying insecurity, "Marpeck's people are not far from us."[27] Some scholars, including Walter Klaasen, think Marpeck was the most imaginative and original of all Anabaptist theologians.[28] Marpeck's theology of finding a way between the extremes seems very relevant for the Church today.

We must be careful to not throw out Matthew 18 with the dirty bathwater of divisive shunning. Matthew 18 is not only about a process for a community to restore a wayward member, but it is also about a community of Christ engaging in spiritual discernment.[29]

CONFESSIONS OF FAITH

Mennonites have generally affirmed the early Christian creeds (Apostles', Nicene, and Chalcedonian) in their confession of God's triune being and the two natures of Christ. However, the focus of most Mennonite confessions of faith has been on interpreting the Bible's relevance for the life of discipleship. The New Testament has been the ultimate guide for Mennonites, especially Jesus' Sermon on the Mount. Confessions of faith have helped to guide Mennonite thought and practice over the centuries. The difference between creeds and confessions has not always been clear. Some would say "A creed excludes, and a confession includes. A creed tells you what you must believe, and a confession affirms what you do believe."[30]

Confessions are marks along the path of Anabaptist history. Confessions have been attempts to find a common base for unity among scattered and divided groups.

25. Ibid.

26. Klaassen and Klassen, *Marpeck*, 18.

27. John Rempel in email attachment to Hartzler, November 27, 2008.

28. Klaassen, "Church Discipline," 180.

29. This idea comes from Kent McDougal, pastor of Christ Community Church, a Mennonite congregation in Des Moines, Iowa. http://www.centralplainsmc.org/:/Events/TheRuleofChristKentMcDougal.pdf.

30. http://www.baptiststandard.com/2000/6_26/pages/confessions.html. An excellent scholarly book that addresses differences between creeds and confessions and then summarizes the most significant Mennonite confessions is Loewen's *One Lord, One Church, One Hope, and One God: Mennonite Confessions of Faith in North America.*

An important understanding is that the Anabaptist/Mennonite confessions are fluid and dynamic. They are, in some ways, consensus documents. Specifically *how* Mennonites live out faith changes over time. This is in contrast to the Lutheran Church's Augsburg confession that has been unchanged since it was submitted to His Imperial Majesty Charles V at the Diet of Augsburg in the year 1530.

Confessions of faith serve the church in the following ways:

1. Mennonite confessions provide guidelines for the interpretation of Scripture. At the same time, the confession itself is subject to the authority of the Bible.

2. Confessions of faith provide guidance for belief and practice. In this connection, a written statement should support, but not replace, the lived witness of faith.

3. Confessions build a foundation for unity within and among churches.

4. Confessions offer an outline for instructing new church members and for sharing information with inquirers.

5. Confessions give an updated interpretation of belief and practice in the midst of changing times.

6. Confessions help in discussing Mennonite belief and practice with other Christians and people of other faiths.[31]

The Schleitheim Confession

Schleitheim is the village in Switzerland where the seven articles of the *Schleitheim Confession* were written by Michael Sattler (most likely) in 1527. The literal translation of the title is *Brotherly Union of a number of children of God concerning Seven Articles*. The story of this 1527 event is dramatically portrayed in *The Radicals*, a full length movie about early Anabaptists.[32]

This is the first known Anabaptist confession of faith and it has received renewed attention in recent decades, especially regarding its teaching on "the sword," that is, on the principle of pacifism and nonresistance. The seven topics addressed are baptism, discipline, communion, separation from the world, shepherds, nonresistance, and the oath. *Schleitheim* treats each of these topics with a biblically-based brief discussion. Brief descriptions of each article follow:

1. Baptism is a symbol of becoming a disciple in the Christian community and of one's intention to live a life of discipleship, united with Christ in his death and resurrection.

2. Giving and receiving counsel, including encouragement and admonishment, is

31. *Confession of Faith in a Mennonite Perspective*, 8 and www.mennolink.org/doc/cof.

32. The historical fiction movie *The Radicals* is based on Augsburger's book *Pilgrim Aflame*. The setting is in Germany and Switzerland, 1525.

13

expected within the believing community. Following Matthew 18 is the way to maintain a disciplined church.

3. Communion is for those who have been united through Christian baptism.

4. Christians should separate themselves from the world and all evil. (Modern scholars have called Schleitheim's a "two kingdom" theology.)

5. A shepherd (or pastor), one who has a good report of those outside the faith, leads the congregation in teaching, prayer, discipline, and communion and is supported by the congregation.

6. Christians are to follow absolutely the law of love as taught by Jesus, renouncing warfare and other types of physical force and living a life of nonresistance, based on Jesus' teaching in Matthew 5:29: "Do not resist an evildoer." The sword is "outside the perfection of Christ."

7. A Christian's yes should clearly be yes and no should clearly be no; therefore it is unnecessary to swear an oath, and Jesus forbids it in Matthew 5:37. When asked to swear in a legal setting, many Christians respond with, "I affirm."[33]

The *Schleitheim Confession* does not give a complete summary of Christian faith, but addresses emphases of the early Swiss Brethren, or perhaps the points that were most challenged, either by opponents or members of the group. The writers did not consider these articles to be distinctives, but rather the marks of a true believers church. These seven points remain central for all three major Anabaptist groups (Mennonites, Amish, and Hutterites) to this day, although the understanding of nonresistance has broadened to mean "Christ's way of peace."[34]

The Dordrecht Confession

Dordrecht is the location in Holland where, at a Dutch Mennonite conference in 1632, a confession was agreed upon by fifty-one delegates from seventeen Dutch congregations. The *Dordrecht Confession of Faith* has been more generally accepted among Anabaptists of Europe and America than any other. It was more strict than other Dutch confessions at the time, holding a strict view of shunning.

In 1660, six preachers and seven deacons from Alsace adopted the Dordrecht Confession "as our own." Later it was adopted by the Mennonites in the Palatinate and North Germany; the Swiss Mennonites never officially accepted it, perhaps because it teaches shunning (Article 17), which only the Swiss *Amish* practiced, not the Swiss *Mennonites*. Probably through the influence of the Dutch Mennonites of Germantown, Pennsylvania, the Mennonites of southeastern Pennsylvania adopted the Dordrecht Confession in 1725 "in order to build unity and clarify the Mennonite

---

33. Wenger and Snyder, "Schleitheim Confession"; Friesen, *Reformers, Radicals*, 208–9. Leonard Gross in conversation with Hartzler, July 19, 2012.

34. Ibid.

theological identity and witness, particularly the Mennonite position on nonresistance, to the new society."[35] Today it is held/recognized by Amish groups and many traditional Mennonite groups.

There are numerous editions of the *Dordrecht Confession* in English. The oldest, *The Christian confession of the faith of the harmless Christians, in the Netherlands known by the name of Mennonists*, was printed in Amsterdam in 1712 at the request of the Pennsylvania churches. The language of the *Dordrecht Confession* is simple and direct, with many biblical quotations, and follows the general emphases of evangelical Protestant churches, except that it teaches the baptism of believers only, the washing of the feet as a symbol of servanthood, church discipline, the shunning of the excommunicated, the non-swearing of oaths, marriage within the same church, strict nonresistance, and in general, more emphasis on true Christianity involving being Christian and obeying Christ rather than merely holding to a correct system of doctrine.[36] Dordrecht articles 16 and 17 on the Ban and Shunning are in appendix B.

Our Common Confession

A short statement included in the 1896 constitution of the General Conference (GC) Mennonite Church[37] is *Our Common Confession*:

> The Conference recognizes and acknowledges the Sacred Scriptures of the Old and New Testament as the Word of God and as the only and infallible rule of faith and life; for "other foundation can no man lay than that is laid which is Jesus Christ" (1 Corinthians 3:11). In the matter of faith it is therefore required of the congregations which unite with the Conference that, accepting the above confession, they hold fast to the doctrine of salvation by grace through faith in the Lord Jesus Christ, baptism on confession of faith, the avoidance of oaths, the Biblical doctrine of nonresistance, and the practice of a Scriptural church discipline.[38]

Christian Fundamentals

Christian Fundamentals (also known as the *Garden City Statement*) appeared in 1921 as a confessional supplement during a time of tensions over Fundamentalism within the MC ("old" Mennonite Church).[39] It was adopted at Garden City, Missouri, and

35. Neff et al., "Confessions."

36. "Dordrecht Confession of Faith."

37. The General Conference Mennonite Church did not adopt a formal confession in 1860 when the denomination formed.

38. General Conference Mennonite Church, "Our Common Confession."

39. Neff, "Confessions."

contains eighteen articles. This was the operative confession of the Mennonite Church in Middlebury when the split occurred in 1923. Article XI on discipline follows:

> We believe that the Lord has vested the Church with authority in accordance with Scriptural teaching: (1) to choose officials, (2) to regulate the observance of ordinances, (3) to exercise wholesome discipline, and (4) to organize and conduct her work in a manner consistent with her high calling and essential to her highest efficiency. (Acts 6:1–6; Acts 13:1–3; 2 Timothy 2:2; Titus 1:5–9; Titus 2:15; Matthew 28:19, 20; Matthew 18:15–18; Ephesians 4:11–16; Hebrews 13:17; Acts 14:21–23; Acts 2:15.)[40]

The preface to the statement clarifies that it "does not supersede the eighteen articles of the Dort Confession, which the Church still confesses and teaches. It is rather a restatement of that confession in the light of present religious contentions and teachings."[41]

The Statement of Doctrine

The GC Mennonite Church was presented the *Statement of Doctrine* at its delegate session held at Souderton, Pennsylvania, during the August 17–22 conference in 1941. According to Howard John Loewen, the statement was written as a defense of the faith in the context of theological fundamentalism. It was written with seminary education in mind, as part of an effort to have local congregations more closely identify with seminary trained pastors. The board for the new Mennonite Biblical Seminary in Chicago approved this statement in July 1945, but the statement was not officially adopted by the denomination. It contains nine doctrinal statements; these were apparently highly valued at Warren Street Mennonite Church as they are included in the yearbooks of 1963 and 1964.[42]

The 1995 Confession of Faith in a Mennonite Perspective

Leaders in the GC and MC denominations worked together to prepare the *Confession of Faith in a Mennonite Perspective* that was accepted by both denominations in 1995.[43]

40. Mennonite Church, "Christian Fundamentals."

41. Ibid.

42. Loewen, One Lord, 29, 112; Neff, "Confessions." See appendix C for *Statement of Doctrine.*

43. There was also an MC (or "old" Mennonite) confession that was adopted in 1963. The preamble follows: "The Mennonite Church, begun in Switzerland in 1525, was a part of the Reformation that attempted to restore the New Testament church. We conceive the church to be a body of regenerated believers, a fellowship of holy pilgrims baptized upon confession of faith in Christ. As committed believers we seek to follow the way of Christian love and nonresistance, and to live separate from the evil of the world. We earnestly endeavor to make Christian disciples of all the nations. In its beliefs the Mennonite Church is bound ultimately to the Holy Scriptures, not to any human formulation of doctrine. We regard this present confession as a restatement of the . . . Dordrecht [Confession] and of the other statements adopted by our church. In this expression of our faith we sincerely accept the

The historic creeds of the early Christian church, which were assumed as foundational for Mennonite confessions from the beginning, are also basic to this confession. This document, readily available in a booklet and online, anticipated the likelihood of a merger of the two Mennonite denominations, which was then finalized in 2002.[44]

The 1995 *Confession of Faith in a Mennonite Perspective* appears as a list of articles as have the confessions of the past. There are four sets of articles. The first eight (articles 1–8) deal with themes common to the faith of the wider Christian church. The second set (articles 9–16) deals with the church and its practices, and the third set (articles 17–23) with discipleship. The final article (24) is on the reign of God. Summary statements are in appendix D.

Because the WSMC/POMC congregation began as a result of discipline in the church, Article 14, "Discipline in the Church" is included here.

> We believe that the practice of discipline in the church is a sign of God's offer of forgiveness and transforming grace to believers who are moving away from faithful discipleship or who have been overtaken by sin. Discipline is intended to liberate erring brothers and sisters from sin, to enable them to return to a right relationship with God, and to restore them to fellowship in the church. It also gives integrity to the church's witness and contributes to the credibility of the gospel message in the world.
>
> According to the teaching of Jesus Christ and the apostles, all believers participate in the church's mutual care and discipline as appropriate. Jesus gave the church authority to discern right and wrong and to forgive sins when there is repentance or to retain sins when there is no repentance. When becoming members of the church, believers therefore commit themselves to give and receive counsel within the faith community on important matters of doctrine and conduct.
>
> Mutual encouragement, pastoral care, and discipline should normally lead to confession, forgiveness, and reconciliation. Corrective discipline in the church should be exercised in a redemptive manner. The basic pattern begins with "speaking the truth in love," in direct conversation between the erring person and another member. Depending on the person's response, admonition may continue within a broader circle. This usually includes a pastor or congregational leader. If necessary, the matter may finally be brought to the congregation. A brother or sister who repents is to be forgiven and encouraged in making the needed change.
>
> If the erring member persists in sin without repentance and rejects even the admonition of the congregation, membership may be suspended. Suspension of membership is the recognition that persons have separated themselves

lordship of Jesus Christ and the full authority of the written Word of God, the Bible, and seek to promote the unity of the brotherhood, to safeguard sound doctrine and life, and to serve as a testimony to others." The document is available at http://www.gameo.org/encyclopedia/contents/M4663.html.

44. *Confession of Faith in a Mennonite Perspective*, http://www.mennolink.org/doc/cof.

from the body of Christ. When this occurs, the church continues to pray for them and seeks to restore them to its fellowship.

We acknowledge that discipline, rightly understood and practiced, undergirds the integrity of the church's witness in word and deed. Persistent and uncorrected false teaching and sinful conduct among Christians undermine the proclamation and credibility of the gospel in the world. As a sign of forgiveness and transforming grace, discipline exemplifies the message of forgiveness and new life in Christ through the power of the Holy Spirit. As a means of strengthening good teaching and sustaining moral conduct, it helps to build faithfulness in understanding and practice.[45]

It seems the events leading to the schism in Middlebury in 1923 did not strictly follow the confession in use at the time ("Christian Fundamentals") or the current understanding of discipline in the church.

While the above confessions have been considered consensus statements, it is clear that not everyone involved agreed on the wording or even underlying principles. After studying schisms in the "old" Mennonite Church in Indiana, Ohio, Pennsylvania, and Virginia, sociologist Fred Kniss says that "we need to view any institutional statement of religious or cultural consensus as the product of social conflict, the triumph of one party over another in gaining the ability to define reality."[46] History has shown that often some faction of a group leaves the group after an attempt to summarize beliefs into confession statements. In this sense, confessions can be divisive.

THE TRADITIONAL ANABAPTIST PEACE POSITION

Many books have been written to describe and defend a nonresistant peace position based on the teachings of Jesus, particularly the Sermon on the Mount. Some books are very scholarly such as *The Politics of Jesus* by outstanding Mennonite theologian and ethicist, John Howard Yoder.[47] Books for teens and lay readers include the highly recommended John D. Roth's *Choosing against War: A Christian View*[48] and Susan Clemmer Steiner's *Joining the Army That Sheds No Blood*.[49] Perhaps the brief-

45. *Confession of Faith in a Mennonite Perspective*, 55–56 and www.mennolink.org/doc/cof. Additional commentary on this article is in appendix E.

46. Kniss, *Disquiet in the Land*, 189.

47. Yoder, *Politics of Jesus*.

48. Roth, *Choosing Against War*. "John Roth has written a theologically sophisticated and yet wonderfully readable book about pacifism as a Christian response to war. While John Howard Yoder is probably the most powerful advocate of the pacifist position, his books are not always accessible to the ordinary reader. . . . This book balances careful theological thought, effective stories and illustrations, a historic survey, and questions of practical application. Roth works hard to support pacifism while rejecting the elitism that often colors many anti-war manifestos." From a review by J. Mulholland on Amazon.com.

49. Steiner, *Joining the Army That Sheds No Blood*. This book reviews what the Bible says about peacemaking and tells the stories of Christian peacemakers through the centuries. http://wipfandstock.

est summary is to say that the peace position is based on the Sermon on the Mount, particularly Jesus' words in Matthew 5:39 and 44: ". . . do not resist an evildoer. But if anyone strikes you on the right cheek, turn the other also. . . . Love your enemies and pray for those who persecute you."

The teaching and practice of nonresistance has not been uniform throughout Mennonite churches in North America. Article 22 of the 1995 *Confession of Faith in a Mennonite Perspective* (for members of MC USA), "Peace, Justice and Nonresistance," follows:

> We believe that peace is the will of God. God created the world in peace, and God's peace is most fully revealed in Jesus Christ, who is our peace and the peace of the whole world. Led by the Holy Spirit, we follow Christ in the way of peace, doing justice, bringing reconciliation, and practicing nonresistance even in the face of violence and warfare.
>
> Although God created a peaceable world, humanity chose the way of unrighteousness and violence. The spirit of revenge increased, and violence multiplied, yet the original vision of peace and justice did not die. Prophets and other messengers of God continued to point the people of Israel toward trust in God rather than in weapons and military force.
>
> The peace God intends for humanity and creation was revealed most fully in Jesus Christ. A joyous song of peace announced Jesus' birth. Jesus taught love of enemies, forgave wrongdoers, and called for right relationships. When threatened, he chose not to resist, but gave his life freely. By his death and resurrection, he has removed the dominion of death and given us peace with God. Thus he has reconciled us to God and has entrusted to us the ministry of reconciliation.
>
> As followers of Jesus, we participate in his ministry of peace and justice. He has called us to find our blessing in making peace and seeking justice. We do so in a spirit of gentleness, willing to be persecuted for righteousness' sake. As disciples of Christ, we do not prepare for war, or participate in war or military service. The same Spirit that empowered Jesus also empowers us to love enemies, to forgive rather than to seek revenge, to practice right relationships, to rely on the community of faith to settle disputes, and to resist evil without violence.
>
> Led by the Spirit, and beginning in the church, we witness to all people that violence is not the will of God. We witness against all forms of violence, including war among nations, hostility among races and classes, abuse of children and women, violence between men and women, abortion, and capital punishment. We give our ultimate loyalty to the God of grace and peace, who guides the church daily in overcoming evil with good, who empowers us to do justice, and who sustains us in the glorious hope of the peaceable reign of God.[50]

---

com/store/Joining_the_Army_That_Sheds_No_Blood.

50. *Confession of Faith in a Mennonite Perspective*, 81–82. The accompanying commentary for this article is in appendix F.

There have been different interpretations of nonresistance and the peace position in the Mennonite Church, especially in the past century. The early Swiss Brethren and the early Dutch Mennonites did not participate in combat. Historically, Anabaptist folk were people on the move. In the earliest years many hid, fearing persecution because of their beliefs regarding baptism and pacifism. Many were severely persecuted and executed in the sixteenth and seventeenth centuries.[51] When US Mennonites began to see war clouds in the 1740s they were concerned that their young people did not adequately understand nonresistance, so they arranged to print the *Martyrs Mirror.*[52]

Anabaptists have often moved to avoid forced military conscription. One dramatic story is of the Russian Mennonite Group—people from the North German/Dutch group that went to Prussia and then on to Russia at the invitation of Catherine the Great. That story will be addressed below after tracing earlier groups who migrated to the Americas.

MENNONITE MIGRATIONS TO NORTH AMERICA

North American Mennonites have traditionally been thought of as conservative, conscientious, and industrious people. One explanation might be that the early migrations of Mennonites to America in the middle of the nineteen century were prompted largely by both economic and religious reasons. Some came because they were poor or landless in Europe. Others came because they were very conscientious and unwilling to participate in military service.[53] The most passionate Anabaptist pacifists came to North America, which may explain why European Mennonites had become more lax about the peace position over the years.

Anabaptism emerged in three specific areas in Europe in the 1500s. There was the Swiss Anabaptist group (which quickly spread as far as Moravia to the east and Cologne to the north), South German/Austrian Anabaptist folk, and North German/Dutch Anabaptists.[54] From these areas other smaller groups spread out across Europe.

In general, each of these groups had migrations at specific times to specific areas in North and South America. There are many excellent books that describe these migrations in detail. A brief look at the major waves of Mennonite migrations leaving Europe follows.

---

51. Many of these stories are in *Martyrs Mirror*, the classic 1660 Dutch religious history by Thieleman Van Bragt, which memorializes the godly lives and deaths of thousands of early Christians, especially European Anabaptist martyrs between 1524 and 1660. The book shines a mirror on ordinary people who experienced a nearly unimaginable spiritual reality. *Martyrs Mirror* traces the history of those through the centuries, beginning with the martyrdom of Christ's apostles, who were willing to stand alone for a simple, obedient faith. It is available online at: http://www.homecomers.org/mirror/index.htm.

52. MacMaster, *Land, Piety, Peoplehood*, 143–46.

53. Pannabecker, *Open Doors*, 7.

54. This is an oversimplification of the three groups as there was diversity within each group as well as between the groups.

First Mennonite Immigrants to North America

The first Mennonite settlers to establish a functioning and lasting congregation arrived in North America from the Netherlands on October 6, 1683. A group of Dutch and German Mennonites began meeting for regular worship services about 1690 in Germantown, north of Philadelphia, Pennsylvania, under the leadership of William Rittenhouse (1644–1708) from Amsterdam. Between 1683 and 1705 about one hundred Mennonites came from Germany to the Germantown area in America.[55]

Eighteenth-century Swiss and German Migrations

A trickle of German immigrants continued to come to Pennsylvania until 1709 when larger groups of immigrants began arriving. Approximately 2000 Mennonites and 500 Amish came between 1709 and 1754,[56] migrating from Switzerland and the German Palatinate to Southeastern Pennsylvania. They were part of the approximate 100,000 Germans (Mennonites and others) who migrated from the Palatinate. Many of these immigrants were educated people and brought some aspects of European culture with them. The men and women born in early colonial America attempted to maintain traditions of the educated immigrants without the benefit of formal education.

Mennonites were attracted to Pennsylvania in part because the land was governed by English Quaker William Penn. As a pacifist, Penn had promised that his colony would not have an army. Mennonite immigrants spread out through eastern Pennsylvania. These people were (and still are) sometimes referred to as Pennsylvania Dutch even though there were only a few Dutch among the group; the name was basically a misnomer. However, many of these German and Swiss immigrants came to America by way of the Netherlands where Dutch Mennonites assisted them.

The heritage of these Swiss and German Anabaptist immigrants was saturated with the theme of being separate from the world, and many continued that stance in North America. Almost all Mennonites in America during that time were committed to nonresistance and the peace position. When they were pressured to take sides in the American Revolutionary War, most of them refused and some were persecuted. Others, who wanted to keep the pledge they had made to the British crown, migrated to Ontario.[57]

Many of the Amish and Mennonite folks who settled in Elkhart and LaGrange counties of Indiana in the nineteenth century were descendents of these eighteen century immigrants.

---

55. Wenger, *Mennonite Church in America*, 67.

56. Loewen, *Through Fire and Water*, 147–50.

57. A 2011 engaging historical novel about the crossing to Pennsylvania and immigrant life in a Mennonite family is *Johann* by Everett Thomas.

Nineteenth-Century Swiss and German Migrations

Immigration rose dramatically after 1815 when there was a time of relative peace in North America and travel across the Atlantic became safer. Those who came later tended to go farther west. In the 1840s and 1850s German Mennonites went to southern and western Illinois and into Iowa.

The later immigrants had decades (and in some cases more than a century) of European cultural influence that those living in the forests of North America hadn't experienced. Some of the religious restrictions among European Mennonites had been lifted. Church buildings and trained, salaried pastors were common in the South German Mennonite churches after 1820. One German congregation even installed an organ in 1822.

The groups from different areas of Europe, and even those from the same areas that came at different times, didn't always get along well in America. Later immigrants had difficulty understanding why the earlier immigrants were "backward." In 1841, the newly-arrived Palatinate preacher Jacob Krehbiel sent the following letter from New York State to friends in Germany:

> I do not wish to deny that in some American Mennonite congregations too much emphasis is placed on outward forms and at times, therefore, some points seem exaggerated. But this is admitted by most of the preachers here themselves, and I would not want to say that there is no good intention at heart. Rather it is the case with a good many that they possess only to a small degree the gift of differentiating between the greater and the less, wherefore nonessentials are made to be essentials and consequently too much strictness is laid upon these matters, forgetting that Paul laid the first emphasis on "new creation in Christ . . ."[58]

German Mennonites who in the nineteenth century went directly from Europe to Illinois and Iowa were known as German Evangelical Mennonites. They were more progressive than most of the Pennsylvania Mennonites. They did not have requirements for clothing styles, but they did hold to fundamental Mennonite positions on baptism, discipline, and authority of the Bible. Other Mennonites and Amish in Iowa, whose ancestors had first lived in Pennsylvania before moving west, had little association with the German Evangelical Mennonites.

An estimated 1,200 Swiss Mennonites came to North America between 1817 and 1874, some first sojourning in French or German provinces, in some cases even learning the local languages. Because of greater restrictions and poverty, these Swiss brothers and sisters had less education, cultural contacts, and acquaintance with other Anabaptists than their German counterparts did. They tended to be conservative and lived with integrity, industry, frugality and simplicity. These hardy Swiss Mennonites

---

58. Pannabecker, *Open Doors*, 14.

settled between eastern Ohio and Missouri, with eleven congregations developing. Of these, seven eventually joined the GC Middle District and three joined the "old" Mennonite Church. Two of these three are Kidron Mennonite Church near Dalton, Ohio, and Crown Hill Mennonite Church near Marshallville, Ohio.[59]

The GC congregations include First Mennonite in Berne, Indiana, who joined the GCs in 1887; Bethel near Fortuna, Missouri, who joined in 1881; Salem near Dalton, Ohio, who joined in 1887; and the large Swiss congregation between Bluffton and Pandora, Ohio, who joined GCMC in 1893. (The latter congregation divided into Ebenezer near Bluffton, St. John near Pandora, and First Mennonite in Bluffton.)[60]

The Wadsworth Institute, although operating from only 1868 to 1878, was influential in all these congregations of Swiss immigrants, as all had leaders who had trained at Wadsworth. The emphases at Wadsworth were rebirth, prayer, Sunday school, missions, and trained leadership.[61]

The Russian Mennonite Story

The Russian Mennonite story may seem out of place in the history of WSMC/POMC, but a brief summary is included here for two reasons. One, many former GC Mennonite Church members were immigrants or descendents of immigrants from Russia, including numerous members and leaders of WSMC/POMC. In addition, this is an important story that is not well known among people of the former "old" Mennonite Church, and it's an important story to be known as MC USA continues the integration process.

One of the gifts of the Russian Mennonite story for the North American Mennonite church today is that it broadens the understandings of persecution in Mennonite history. Those Mennonites whose ancestors came primarily from Germany and Switzerland[62] may be well-informed of the persecution their forebears experienced in the 1500s and 1600s, but are likely not as familiar with the widespread severe persecution and deprivation experienced by the Mennonites in Russia after the communist revolution of 1917, and the ongoing effects of that persecution on descendants of Russian Mennonites today. It was particularly poignant when one POMC person who has the Russian Mennonite story in her blood—both literally and figuratively—pointed to the extreme contrasts between the early twentieth-century concerns of her ancestors and her husband's ancestors. "While my people were dying in Russia, people here were bickering about buttons and bows," she said with tear-filled eyes.

59. Ibid., 78.

60. Pannabecker, *Faith in Ferment*, 46.

61. Pannabecker, *Open Doors*, 78.

62. The majority of WSMC/POMC participants who have Mennonite ancestors can trace their heritage to Germany and/or Switzerland. This would also be true of Middlebury First Mennonite Church members.

PART I: A Summary of Growth and Schisms among Mennonites

Those who didn't hear Russian Mennonite stories from the quivering lips of parents or grandparents can probably never fully grasp the effect of such severe persecution on one's life. However, there are many well-written stories from that era that open windows into the horrors of that period and the events of Russian Mennonite emigrations to the Americas.

The Russian Mennonites were not ethnic Russians. Most of them went to Russia from Prussia, but neither were the majority ethnic Prussians. Earlier generations of Mennonites had gone to Prussia from the Netherlands and Northern Germany for two primary reasons—fleeing persecution and escaping enforced military service.

In the 1760s Catherine II, Empress of Russia (1762–96), invited German farmers from minority groups like Jews and Mennonites to settle newly acquired lands (by conquest from Turkey) in the South of the Russian empire, north of the Black Sea (present-day Ukraine). "Catherine the Great" specifically invited the Mennonites in West Prussia to immigrate to Russia, promising them complete freedom "for all time," and 165 acres of land for each family.[63] In the 1780s, under the pressure of new Prussian restrictions on buying land and a severe limiting of conscientious objection, several hundred Prussian Mennonites migrated to the Russian steppes in the Ukraine.[64]

These Mennonites lived together in villages and farmed the lands surrounding the villages. Slowly but surely they tilled the land and became highly productive. There were more and more prosperous Russian Mennonites, although at the same time, more poor and landless people in the group. By the 1850s there were 35,000 Mennonite immigrants in Russia.[65]

One of the concerns of the Russian government (and the Russian Orthodox Church) was that the Mennonites might try to evangelize the Orthodox Russians. In most ways Mennonites were free to create a religious culture that expressed their convictions, but they were forbidden to proselytize. The Russian government gave the Mennonites significant control over local governance. They had their own municipal government, their own church courts, and their own schools.

Because the inheritance of land depended on being a church member, there arose great pressure to baptize all the young people who were of age. One of the currents of reform focused particularly on the question of a pure church and baptism only for people who showed evidence of a personal faith. The reformers and the religious and civic leaders among the Mennonites antagonized each other. Out of this struggle, the Mennonite Brethren Church was born in 1860.

This development was part of a larger ferment in favor of higher education and modern agriculture. The original two colonies (Chortitza, established in 1789 on the

63. The empress remained friendly to the Mennonites throughout her life. She died in 1796.

64. The Russian government wanted more settlers with the valuable agricultural and craft skills of the Mennonites. In 1800 Paul I of Russia enacted a Privilegium (official privileges) for Mennonites, granting them exemption from military service "for all time."

65. Kroeker, *Introduction to the Russian Mennonites*, 22.

bank of the Dnieper River, and Molotschna, founded in 1803 approximately 100 miles southeast of Chortitza) and increasingly, smaller new colonies prospered.

Following the withdrawal of some of the privileges granted the first Mennonite arrivals in Russia (such as the freedom to use the German language in their schools), a first wave of emigrations to North America began in 1873. Around 10,000 of these Mennonites went to the United States (Kansas, Nebraska, Dakota, and Minnesota) and 8,000 to Manitoba. This was about one third of the Russian Mennonites at that time.

The years from 1870 to 1917 have been called the "Golden Era" of the Mennonites of southern Russia.[66] By the beginning of the twentieth century the two large colonies boasted secondary and vocational schools, hospitals, orphanages, publishing houses, and large industry, especially the manufacturing of farm implements. Some became extremely wealthy. Many well-to-do Mennonites seemed oblivious to the poverty in their midst and to the even more acute poverty among their Ukrainian neighbors.

By 1917 at the onset of the Russian Revolution, the Russian Mennonites had grown in number to 120,000. Most Mennonites were spiritually and morally unprepared for the revolution. In the power vacuum following the revolution, anarchist Nestor Machno rallied hundreds of thousands of peasants to take over power. Initially the anarchists concerned themselves with avenging themselves on oppressive landlords. Before long the blood-letting became indiscriminate. Even in this extreme situation, the majority of Mennonites remained nonresistant, but a minority formed self-defense units, sometimes colluding with the "White Army" of the old regime. When the self-defense units became part of the larger torrents of violence in the society, some of their proponents returned to a pacifist position.

When Soviet power was asserted in the Ukraine in 1921, all the Ukrainians, including the Mennonites, worked to overcome the trauma. Many Mennonites concluded that there would be no place for them in the emerging political order. Twenty thousand migrated to Canada and several thousand each to the United States and Paraguay.

Those who remained underwent the naked brutality of the Stalinist regime. Farms were confiscated, churches were closed, and many men were sent to hard labor in Siberia. Many Mennonites died in the Gulag, the Russian political repressive system from 1929 to 1953 that oppressed millions of people and in which between one and two million people died from persecution, starvation, and other kinds of oppression. This included not only European Mennonites, but also Jews, other Christians from Europe, and Russian peasants.

In the chaos of World War II, thousands of Mennonites escaped from the Soviet Union under the protection of the retreating German army. They settled in Germany, Canada, the United States, Paraguay, and Brazil. However, tens of thousands

---

66. John D. Rempel helped to assemble a collection of tableaux that depict highlights of the Golden Era. The tableaux suggest "a collective wish of the Mennonites of Russia to project an image of themselves as individuals who had come to adopt comfortably the conventional manners and dress of European society." Peter Gerhard Rempel, *Forever Summer, Forever Sunday.*

of Mennonites remained in the Soviet Union. After 1953 when Stalin died, their lot became more bearable.

Starting in the 1970s, the Soviet Union slowly acknowledged the West German government's law of return for ethnic Germans living in other societies. Very modest emigration to East and West Germany continued until the collapse of the Soviet Union in 1991. Then tens of thousands of Mennonites and people with historical Mennonite connections migrated to a newly unified Germany. A minority of Mennonites decided to remain in the former Soviet Republics because they saw the changes as an opportunity for evangelistic and social mission such as they had never had. In many cases they continued a long-standing cooperation with Baptists, injecting certain of their beliefs including nonresistance into their new missional identity.[67]

Life in the Americas for Russian Mennonite immigrants has varied greatly. For some the nostalgia of the "Golden Age" in Russia clouded the realities of immigrant life. There were differences among Russian Mennonite immigrants just as there had been differences in the people from Switzerland and Germany that came to North America in different time periods. A Canadian Mennonite told the story of when his parents announced their plans to marry. Some members of his mother's family, who had come from Russia to Canada in the 1870s (nicknamed "Kanadiers"), were very unhappy that Miss Reimer would marry a man whose family had arrived in Manitoba from Russia in the 1920s (referred to as "Russlanders"). Likewise, some relatives of Mr. Hildebrand begged him to not marry a woman from the earlier immigrant group.

The Hildebrand marriage is an example of Mennonites living together harmoniously in spite of differences. They had a sincere commitment and enough in common to form a lasting union. What will it take for Mennonite congregations throughout North America to form lasting unions in spite of differences? What are essentials and what are nonessentials?

67. This summary of the Russian Mennonite Story is based on reflections from John D. Rempel, November 18, 2010.

2

Practices, Growth, Schisms, and Unions in Mennonite Groups

Disfellowshiping and Reconciliation

> Blessed are the poor in spirit, for theirs is the kingdom of heaven.
> Blessed are those who mourn, for they will be comforted.
> Blessed are the meek, for they will inherit the earth.
> Blessed are those who hunger and thirst for righteousness,
> for they will be filled.
> Blessed are the merciful, for they will receive mercy.
> Blessed are the pure in heart, for they will see God.
> Blessed are the peacemakers, for they will be called children of God.
> Blessed are those who are persecuted for righteousness' sake,
> for theirs is the kingdom of heaven.
> Blessed are you when people revile you and persecute you
> and utter all kinds of evil against you falsely on my account.
> Rejoice and be glad, for your reward is great in heaven . . .
>
> MATTHEW 5:3–12

"WHAT'S THAT HAT YOU'RE wearing?" Linford Martin asked. "You can't wear that. The church says you can't." He was talking to Rachel Nafziger Hartzler who was wearing a dark-colored felt turban hat, not unlike the fashionable hats of the early twentieth century.

"Come on, Linford," Rachel replied. "It's 2009, not 1923." This conversation was happening at the Middlebury Memorial Park on September 21, 2009.

A few minutes earlier, Pleasant Oaks Preschool children had sung, "This little light of mine, I'm going to let it shine," as they held up their (as yet un-lit) candles. With guitar and banjo in the background, they continued, "Hide it under a bushel—No! I'm going to let it shine," along with preschool alumni in the crowd of seventy-five people. All were invited to conclude with, "All over Middlebury, I'm going to let it shine" before the children playfully danced back to their parents.

Eleven days earlier the church council of the First Mennonite Church of Middlebury had released the following statement:

1. We at First Mennonite Church want to welcome individuals from Pleasant Oaks Mennonite Church into our worship services and church body. We commit to being intentionally welcoming and will make the extra effort to be inclusive at all church gatherings as well as being willing to combine our future vision.

2. Pleasant Oaks has prioritized and supported their preschool program for thirty-eight years. In the past First Mennonite has expressed the desire to increase our local mission (ministry) outreach and we are therefore excited about taking a more active role in supporting this local ministry in a variety of ways.

In 1981 the United Nations designated September 21 as the "International Day of Peace." In 2004 Christians organized it to be an "International Day of *Prayer* for Peace."[1] Three Middlebury historic peace churches (First Mennonite, Middlebury Church of the Brethren, and Pleasant Oaks) began working together in 2006 to host annual candlelight walks and peace vigils in the park on each September 21.

By 2009 the planning committee represented more congregations (Bonneyville Mennonite and Forks Mennonite), and the Middlebury community was again invited. Titled "Celebrating a Harvest of Peace," the event was to celebrate peace and reconciliation efforts of the community and its churches. Thousands of people on five continents were also praying for peace.

With a focus on reconciliation, Pastors Linford Martin from First Mennonite and Rachel Nafziger Hartzler from Pleasant Oaks stepped onto the stage in front of the small crowd that evening. Pretending surprise, Linford exclaimed, "You can't wear that hat!"

The plastic flowers on her hat prompted raised eyebrows as Rachel reminded Linford of the century in which they were living and then went on to say, "In the past, what people wore in some Mennonite churches mattered a lot. The church was taking seriously the biblical call to not be conformed to the world, which meant that there was a dress code for church members, especially for women!"

The dialogue continued with the pastors reflecting on the previous eighty-six years. "About 40 percent of what was Middlebury Mennonite left the church and started what

1. The International Day of Prayer for Peace was established by and is resourced by the World Council of Churches.

was first called Warren Street Mennonite Church, then eventually Pleasant Oaks. Now eighty-six years later, our two congregations are in dialogue about getting back together. Pleasant Oaks, which at one time had a high attendance of 135, and First Mennonite, which once had a high attendance of 430, have both diminished in size over the years. And with the economy being what it is, we are facing challenging times."

"During the past three years we have had ups and downs at Pleasant Oaks," Rachel stated. "The attendance was slowly dwindling. God sent us new members, but then some died and others moved away. In February of this year, we realized that we needed to make some financial changes. We considered various options, and as we listened to each other, we agreed that maintaining our preschool is a high priority. Pleasant Oaks members looked at the facts and decided that a broader base of support was needed for the preschool. And we were pleased that First Mennonite leaders and members expressed interest in helping."

Linford added, "First Mennonite had recognized that Pleasant Oaks, a sister congregation, was struggling, and one attitude expressed was, 'Why wouldn't we help them?'"

"That was really good news to Pleasant Oaks," Rachel responded. "However, there was still a tinge of the painful memories from the 1920s that was quietly expressed. We listened to each other, prayed with and for each other, and some of those feelings diminished. One Pleasant Oaks member who at one time said he couldn't worship at First Mennonite began to reconsider, and after we had been together for worship and fellowship, he changed his mind. Now that is reconciliation!"

"God is surely at work!" Linford agreed. "We are moving toward coming together into one new body, and meeting at the First Mennonite building for the time being. Some have even suggested that now may be a good time for a name change to represent this union, or re-union."

"This re-uniting is still in process" added Rachel, "and it has been a good experience in listening and dialoguing."

Linford confirmed, "We continue to listen to each other and to the Holy Spirit as God guides us in this process."

Rachel concluded, "You know, since most of the women in our congregations today don't wear hats, I'm taking off this hat!"

Those gathered then joined together in singing, "Unity: Jesus, help us live in peace."[2] At the end of the evening service, all were invited to light candles and carry them as they went into the darkness, inspired to be better peacemakers and reconcilers.

The re-uniting of these two congregations is one unique incident in a 160-year history of conflicts over belief and practices among Mennonite folk in Indiana. Many of the conflicts of the later nineteenth and early twentieth century were between "progressives" and "conservatives." Progressives were more accepting of

---

2. Lyrics and tune by Jerry Derstine Martin, 1971. "Unity" was the final song every Sunday at Pleasant Oaks for an extended period of time. "Unity" has also been sung at First Mennonite.

outside innovations like revivals, Sunday schools, and higher education, setting them apart from traditionalists who tended to resist change. Ervin Stutzman has given historical definitions to the somewhat unclear and confusing terms often used to describe theological positions in the church. He defines *conservatives* as those who seek to conserve the values and practices of the past, perceiving the dangers of change. Conservative people have sometimes called themselves fundamentalists, especially in the first half of the twentieth century.[3]

Progressives value progress, even to the extent of giving up some values for the promises of a better future. Progressives may pick up historical threads to weave into working for a better future. Progressive folk are not necessarily liberals; however, conservative folk often think of progressives as liberals. In 1918 Mennonite Church leader Daniel Kauffman described *liberals* as those who put a "flexible construction upon the teaching of the Bible as God's Word."[4] Liberal folk tend to place a high value on the insights of social science and align themselves with progress.

The world is constantly changing, and, as sociologist Fred Kniss clearly illustrates in *Disquiet in the Land*, traditional religious communities do not provide "shelter from the winds of change." He goes on to say that while there may be good reasons to be part of religious communities, "a desire for calm consensus, shared values, and a retreat from uncertainty is not among them."[5]

CONTESTED INNOVATIONS AND TRADITIONS

Disagreement ran deep among Mennonites in Middlebury in the early 1900s. John C. Wenger described underlying reasons for the 1923 schism in Middlebury as "the issue of how strict the discipline of the church ought to be, and how much direction conference ought to give its constituent congregations." He called it as a "lamentable division."[6]

Fred Kniss, who has identified the sources of conflicts within MC ("old" Mennonite) congregations from 1870 to 1985, concludes that reaction to authority was the

---

3. Stutzman, *Nonresistance,* 24. Stutzman became executive director of Mennonite Church USA in 2010.

4. Kauffman, *Conservative Viewpoint*, 8.

5. Kniss, *Disquiet in the Land*, 18.

6. Wenger, "First Mennonite Church"; Wenger, *Mennonites in Indiana and Michigan*, 182. John Christian Wenger (December 25, 1910–March 26, 1995) grew up in Eastern Pennsylvania and lived all his adult years in Elkhart County. He taught at Goshen Biblical Seminary starting in 1938, and served as deacon, preacher, and bishop in the Indiana-Michigan Conference; BA from Goshen College, MA from University of Michigan, ThD from the University of Zurich; ordained as Mennonite deacon in 1943, preacher in 1944, and bishop in 1951; served on the Committee on Bible Translation that supervised the preparation of the NIV Bible; served on the Mennonite Historical Committee, Board of Education, Publication Board, executive committees of the Indiana-Michigan Conference, the denominational conference, and Mennonite World Conference; wrote numerous books and articles and contributed many entries to the *Mennonite Encyclopedia*. A short autobiography is *J. C.: A Life Sketch*.

most frequent cause of church conflicts, especially between 1907 and 1934. During the earlier period that Kniss considered, 1870 to 1906, resistance to innovations was by far the greatest source of Mennonite conflicts.[7]

Between 1800 and 1850 there was also a lot of activity among North American Christians in general. Church groups were forming various kinds of agencies. The first foreign mission board (the American Board of Commissioners for Foreign Missions), was established in 1815; the American Bible Society in 1816; the American Sunday School Union in 1824; the American Tract Society in 1825. By 1830 the Bible Society, the Sunday School Union, and the Tract Society were cooperating in a tremendous campaign, using aggressive evangelical methods to Christianize America, and they were doing it outside the regular denominational organizations. In response, around 1850 many denominations, including some Mennonites, began to form their own organizations to promote Sunday schools, publications and missions.[8]

The years from 1840 to 1890 were times of strain and stress among some Anabaptists, with major schisms occurring among "old" Mennonite and Amish groups. Outside influences put great pressure on the tradition-minded Anabaptist communities. Significant conflicts occurred over Sunday schools, revivalism, the Methodist and United Brethren and Evangelical evangelists, and a pietistic type of literature. These resulted in the loss of many Mennonites to the more "aggressive and progressive" denominations.[9]

Lightning rods, life insurance, business insurance, and lodge membership were other issues that prompted disagreements. Many Mennonite leaders, pressured by conservative church members, tended to resist most innovations, and often those who wanted progress had great difficulty making their influence felt and then tended to become seriously dissatisfied. The struggle over maintaining the German language and the gradual change to English added to the friction.[10]

Interestingly, from his vantage point as a twentieth-century General Conference (GC) Mennonite leader, Samuel F. Pannabecker describes the period from 1850 to 1925 as a "time of reorientation in the faith and reinterpretation of essentials" within the conference.[11] There were significant differences between the MCs and GCs. In general, the change to the English language in community life and worship services came much earlier to MCs. Many GCs (Russian Mennonites and Swiss Mennonites) had arrived in North America later than many of the MCs. Maintaining the German language was part of what kept these later arrivals nonconformed to the world. One

---

7. Kniss, *Disquiet in the Land*, 13.

8. Bender et al., "Sunday School."

9. Bender and Hostetler, "Mennonite Church (MC)."

10. Ibid.

11. Pannabecker, *Open Doors*, 16. Pannabecker (April 15, 1896–September 14, 1977) received his PhD from Yale University and taught at Bluffton College, was a missionary in China (1923–41) and served in many capacities, including dean and president at Mennonite Biblical Seminary and Associated Mennonite Biblical Seminaries.

might wonder if that is part of the reason why distinctive clothing was not as important for GC Mennonites as for MCs.

Sunday Schools

The split in the Middlebury Mennonite congregation that created the Warren Street Church had its roots in longtime controversies in Mennonite churches throughout North America. One significant conflict was over Sunday schools. Before 1840 (and later in some areas), some Mennonite children attended Sunday schools that were conducted by the American Sunday School Union[12] or other denominations, because Sunday schools began later in most Mennonite churches. Because of this, many Mennonite children and young people were drawn away from the Mennonite Church into other denominations.[13]

The opposition to Sunday schools in the 1800s was deeply rooted and widespread, not only in the Mennonite churches, but in many Protestant churches. Sunday school was a new concept and evoked deep suspicion, as were (and perhaps still are) most innovative initiatives in the church. It may be difficult for twenty-first century people to understand how Christian education in churches could have been a divisive issue, but in the 1800s, it was.

Sunday schools had been started in at least two Mennonite congregations in Virginia around 1870, followed by the circulation of a list of twenty-five reasons to oppose Sunday schools. Some of the reasons given for this opposition were that Sunday schools were patterned after the Sunday schools of other denominations, placed teaching responsibility into the hands of the laity and often women, and were unsupported by the Bible. In addition, they were "worldly" and fostered "pride" by devices such as prizes for Bible memory.[14]

Reasons for supporting Mennonite Sunday schools were that the schools might help Mennonite and Amish Mennonite children retain the German language (other Sunday schools were taught in English), would increase Bible knowledge among Mennonites, and would hopefully stop the exodus of young people to other denominations who offered Sunday schools. The debates were vigorous, and sadly, some congregations and conferences suffered painful divisions.

The first "old" Mennonite Sunday school in North America was probably the one established in 1840 in Waterloo County, Ontario. The first Sunday school instruction in a congregation that eventually became part of the General Conference Mennonite

12. Union events and organizations include more than one church body, that is, more than one denomination or conference or congregation.

13. Wenger, *Mennonite Church in America*, 147.

14. Kniss, *Disquiet in the Land*, 37; Bender et al., "Sunday School"; Theron Schlabach in email correspondence with Hartzler, April 15, 2011. Theron Schlabach is Goshen College Professor Emeritus of History and the author/editor of numerous books and scores of articles on Mennonite history. He is a brother of Dale Schlabach, long time member of POMC.

Church began in 1847 at the West Swamp Creek Mennonite Church in Bucks County, Pennsylvania, by John H. Oberholtzer.[15] The first two *Amish Mennonite* congregations in Indiana to hold Sunday schools were Haw Patch (later Maple Grove) in Topeka in 1868, and Clinton Frame, east of Goshen, in 1876. The first "old" Mennonite Sunday school in Indiana began in 1887 under the influence of John F. Funk in the Olive Mennonite Church meetinghouse.[16]

John F. Funk, himself a product of the American Sunday School Union in his home community in Bucks County, Pennsylvania, founded and edited the *Herald of Truth* beginning in 1864. This unofficial publication of the Mennonite Church was a forum for debating the Sunday school movement and other issues. An example of the arguments against Sunday school is given in an excerpt from an 1870 letter: "We find no scripture for lay members to speak publicly in our churches . . . . It is a violation of the gospel for women to teach in our churches."[17]

During the last decades of the 1800s, Sunday schools gradually became accepted in Mennonite churches. With the development of Sunday schools, more lay leadership was needed in congregations. Teachers, song leaders, superintendents, and librarians were needed to successfully run the Sunday school program. Even those who did not participate in the preparatory and administrative aspects of the Sunday school were given opportunity to express themselves during class time. Gradually, all this activity among the lay membership made a significant contribution to spiritual growth and new life within the church.[18]

Conservative Attire and Head Coverings

A significant MC conference took place in 1880 in Allen County, Ohio. Six bishops, seven deacons, and twenty ministers were present. A lengthy resolution was adopted that affirmed "Christian people are to be a separate people and not conformed to the world." The following quote is only a sample of the many admonitions that this conference presented: "Men members were to dress plainly and not cut their hair after the fashions. . . . Women were to wear the devotional covering as a token of subjection[19] and were to abstain from wearing jewelry, gold, pearls, laces, unnecessary buttons, breastpins, or bracelets. . . . Our tables should be set plainly at all times—not adorned with ornamental dishes, flowered cakes, etc."[20]

---

15. John H. Oberholtzer is considered a major leader in the beginning of the General Conference Mennonite Church. More about Oberholtzer follows later in this chapter.

16. Wenger, *Mennonites in Indiana and Michigan*, 75.

17. Wenger, *Mennonite Church in America*, 158.

18. Ibid., 176.

19. Subjection meant "submission to men."

20. Stoltzfus, *Ohio and Eastern Conference*, 153–54.

Many similar attempts to regulate dress and possessions were made in succeeding conferences. Menno (M. S.) Steiner[21], an MC progressive leader who attended the conference in Ohio, wrote in his diary on May 13, 1895, "Our conferences are not what they ought to be. They are poorly managed. The bishops have too much power and usually usurp authority . . ." Further diary entries show that he thought the conference was guilty of being preoccupied with restrictions and resolutions. He wrote, "We discourage the essentials and encourage the nonessentials."[22]

The storm clouds of controversy seemed to hover as the Mennonite Church entered the twentieth century. Paul Whitmer[23] spoke of the discord in his unpublished autobiography: "I heard a prominent churchman at a board meeting at Goshen College say 'we want to organize our church on the pattern of the International Harvester Company with a powerful board of directors which can hold things where they should be held.'"[24] There was certainly not agreement about church polity.[25]

Although the biggest issues regarding conservative dress seemed to focus on women's apparel, the issue of the "plain coat" for men is also noteworthy. In Colonial America the dress coat for men was a long-tailed coat, with split tails for horseback riding. This "frock" coat buttoned up to the top in front and had no lapels. By the end of the eighteenth century, the collar had risen as high as it could on the back and had turned over to make the modern lapel. During the nineteenth century, the frock coat slowly passed out of general use in American society and some Mennonites followed these changes. However, in parts of the "old" Mennonite Church, ministers were required or expected to wear a "regulation" coat without lapels, the style that had earlier been popular. This "plain" coat of the late nineteenth and twentieth centuries is shorter (without tails) but still has the collar of the Colonial coat.[26]

In the early twentieth century some MC ministers and college professors did not wear the "plain" coat, and that became a divisive issue in some circles. Mennonite

21. Menno Simon (M. S.) Steiner (April 30, 1866–March 12, 1911) was ordained at Prairie Street in 1893 and then helped to start a mission in Chicago, making him the first missionary of the "old" Mennonite Church in America. Moved to Ohio in 1894. Wenger, *Mennonites in Indiana and Michigan*, 27, 331–32.

22. Ibid.

23. Paul E. Whitmer (January 2, 1876–August 12, 1966), a native of North Lima, Ohio, attended the Elkhart Institute, Goshen College, Oberlin College, Oberlin School of Theology and the University of Chicago. He was professor of English and Bible at Goshen College, 1908–16; during that time he was also pastor of College Mennonite Church periodically: 1905–06, 1910–13, and 1916–17; he was professor of Bible at Bluffton College 1917–21; dean of the Witmarsum Theological Seminary 1921–31; pastor of the Grace Mennonite Church, Pandora, 1928–41. He preached numerous times at Warren Street Mennonite Church, including the dedication service on May 24, 1924.

24. Whitmer, *Autobiography*, 91.

25. Church polity is the system of government used by a given church. There are three primary types of church polity: *episcopal*, *presbyterian*, and *congregational*. These are roughly similar to types of national governments: absolute monarchy, democratic republic, and pure democracy.

26. Wenger, "Plain Coat." In some conservative Mennonite groups, the plain coat continues to be worn by ministers and some lay men in the twenty-first century.

clothing distinctives as compared with the conventions of surrounding culture were symbols of nonconformity to the world. Nonconformity was an important value, but opinions varied as to how to express nonconformity.

The plain black bonnet became a symbol of nonconformity for women in the late 1800s and early 1900s, just as the "plain coat" had become that symbol for men. Why and how did conservative dress and head coverings become divisive issues in Amish Mennonite (AM) and "old" Mennonite (MC) churches in northern Indiana? Different structures, procedures, and restrictions of these two groups compared with the General Conference (GC) groups give a clue. In the AM and MC churches there were long lists of doctrine and practices that were spelled out and preached about. Far fewer regulations were specified in the GC Mennonite Church. A dramatic illustration of this is Daniel Kauffman's 639-page *Doctrines of the Bible: A Brief Discussion of the teachings of God's Word* published by order of the General Conference of the "old" Mennonite Church in 1928,[27] compared with William B. Weaver's 1926 twelve-page summary of the doctrines of the Central Conference of Mennonites (which in 1946 became part of the General Conference Mennonite Church).[28]

What became the traditional Mennonite bonnet began as ordinary headwear for women in the general culture. In *Mennonite Attire through Four Centuries*, Melvin Gingerich clearly describes the taking on of certain cultural customs and then maintaining these customs rather than changing as cultures continually changed. For example, bonnets came into popularity for women in the early 1800s in England, France, and North America. American Mennonite women of the early 1800s began wearing bonnets as was the custom of the day, although without lace, ruffles, and frills.[29] Variations of the simple bonnet became the standard for Amish and Mennonite women for wearing out of doors.

Before the bonnet had come into popularity, Mennonite women had worn a "flat hat" for outdoor wear. The flat hat had a small crown about one inch deep and a wide brim turned down on both sides and was held down by strings tied under the chin. This headgear was popular in the 1600s and still worn by some Amish women in Mifflin County, Pennsylvania, and in Switzerland, Alsace, and the Palatinate in the mid 1800s.[30]

---

27. Earlier editions were published in 1898 and 1914. These are described in more detail in chapter 3.

28. W. Weaver, *Central Conference*, 187–98. Weaver (January 24, 1887–December 12, 1963) wrote this for his master's degree at Garret Biblical Institute (now Seminary). Weaver was a first cousin of Simon S. Yoder, had grown up in LaGrange County, graduated from Goshen College in 1914, and taught at Goshen College for eight years. He was licensed to preach in the spring of 1913; preached for one year at Barker Street Mennonite Church; was ordained on September 14, 1914; was pastor of Prairie Street Mennonite Church in Elkhart until 1920; was pastor at North Danvers Mennonite Church 1922–52.

29. Melvin Gingerich, *Mennonite Attire*, 109–38.

30. Ibid., 110–11.

Two stories illustrate the dilemma with the transition from flat hat to bonnet, evocative of the difficulties in discontinuing the bonnet many years later. A granddaughter of Amish preacher Jacob Marner (1789–1881) from Kalona, Iowa, reported that her grandmother wore the broad flat hat. Because she was the preacher's wife, she continued wearing the conservative hat while the other women were allowed to wear bonnets. Closer to Middlebury is the story of a woman from the Forks Amish Mennonite Church who, when on her deathbed, begged her daughters to promise that they would never wear bonnets, presumably sticking with the flat hat. As the story goes, one daughter kept her promise and the other did not. She later wore a stylish bonnet![31]

There are more hat and bonnet stories in Mary Jane Hershey's 1958 article, "A Study of the Dress of the (Old) Mennonites of the Franconia Conference 1700–1952." It was reported that women in the Vincent congregation in Chester County, Pennsylvania, were received as members not wearing coverings, but wearing hats, some of which had ribbons and feathers. Hettie Kulp Mininger (1874–1965) remembered that when she was a little girl in the Doylestown Mennonite Church in Bucks County, Pennsylvania, half of the women wore hats while the other half wore fancy bonnets.[32]

While the bonnet was the headwear of fashion in America (from 1810 to about 1870), some Mennonites were slow to accept the bonnet. However, as the 1800s came to a close, most Amish and Mennonite women wore black bonnets when going out of the house. The bonnets were tied under the chin and had no ornamentation; during the early 1900s they kept getting smaller. Not only did the bonnets get smaller; the tie ribbons gradually got shorter and narrower.[33]

References to bonnet regulations are not found in Mennonite Church records before 1913, at which time the General Conference of the "old" Mennonite Church ruled against "any form of the bonnet which indicates that it is being worn for display rather than service." The Indiana-Michigan Amish Mennonite Conference (of which the Middlebury Mennonite Church was a part) clarified in 1916 that women should "wear only plain bonnets or veils (for those who prefer such for winter)." The bonnet was to have "dimensions and proportions to properly cover the head and fastened with tie ribbon."[34]

Bonnets with draping fabric attached at the back of the headpiece were sometimes called hoods. Women's hoods varied from close-fitting, soft headgear to stiffened, structured hoods or very large coverings made of fabric over a frame that fashionable women wore over towering hairstyles to protect them from the elements.

---

31. The date of the Forks woman's story is unknown, but it was told to Gingerich in 1965 by Clara Hershberger who was a relative of the Forks woman. Melvin Gingerich, *Mennonite Attire*, 111–12.

32. Hershey, "Study of the Dress," 26–27.

33. See the photo of the Mennonite Historical Library collection of Elkhart County bonnets.

34. Gingerich, *Mennonite Attire*, 118.

Bonnets in the Mennonite Historical Library, Goshen, Indiana, arranged by curator Joe Springer. The two larger bonnets belonged to Salome Kratz Funk, 1839–1917, wife of John F. Funk, presumably from the last decades of her life when she was a member at Prairie Street Mennonite Church. The middle bonnet belonged to Minnie Pearl Miller Hooley, 1885–1965, member of Forks Mennonite Church and wife of Levi F. Hooley. The two "newer" bonnets belonged to Elsie Kolb Bender, 1875–1949, widow of George L. Bender and mother of Harold S. Bender. These were likely worn after 1925 when she lived with Harold and Elizabeth in Goshen and attended College Mennonite Church. Earlier Elsie had been a member at Prairie Street. Photo by Dottie Kauffmann.

To clarify, the bonnet and the covering are not the same. The covering is usually made of white lightweight fabric (although sometimes black) and is worn during times of worship and in some groups, during all waking hours. Bonnets or hats are outerwear, worn when going out of doors. The covering or prayer veil is not necessarily considered an article of clothing, but it is a religious symbol. Mennonite and Amish coverings are usually white caps in varying sizes made of organdy, rayon, or nylon netting or mesh. The Biblical foundation of the covering is in 1 Corinthians 11:5: . . . "any woman who prays or prophesies with her head unveiled disgraces her head (husband)." Some understand the covering to be a sign of women being subordinate to men.

During most of Christian history, women have covered their heads to pray and worship. Gingerich carefully documents this in his chapter "Women's Headdress and Footwear." There is not much reference to the covering in early American Mennonite literature (from the early 1800s), perhaps in part because the casual observer would have likely not noticed a difference between "Mennonite caps" and those worn by the typical North American woman. Mennonite caps usually were unadorned while other women typically wore caps with lace or ruffles. In the German Palatinate women didn't wear *Häubchen* (translated "caps") until they were married or past age forty. The expression *unter die Haube kommen* literally means "to come under the cap," but the expression was used to mean "to get a husband" or "to get married."[35]

Women from Prairie Street Mennonite Church, dressed in clothing typical of Mennonite women in the early 1900s, posed for this photo taken for the Chicago Chronicle in 1903: Lavona Berkey Ebersole, Barbara Blosser Steiner, Minnie Stauffer, Adeline Brunk, Anna Holdeman Miller, and Elsie Kolb Bender. Mennonite Church USA Archives: Phoebe Mumaw Kolb Photograph Collection (HM4-162 Box 2 Folder 3-1903 Plain Clothes). Used with permission.

During Queen Victoria's time (1819–1901) women in secular culture gradually stopped wearing the cap. However, Mennonite women continued to wear the cap/covering, at least at church. Surprisingly, in some areas Mennonite women wore their caps only at church during the late 1800s and early 1900s. In certain congregations, the caps were kept in boxes at the church building and were not worn at home.[36]

35. Ibid., 119–23, 126.
36. Ibid., 126.

Some Mennonites paid little attention to the biblical basis for women covering their heads for worship as long as it was the general practice of Christian women to do so. Teacher and minister Jonas S. Hartzler[37] remembered that at the time of his ordination in 1881, he was not aware that there was a scriptural basis for the cap. However, when other Protestant women began to worship bareheaded, conservative Mennonites began to stress the biblical argument for women covering their heads.[38]

Eventually the cap came to be more than a religious symbol; the Mennonite practice of wearing the cap was elevated to the level of ordinance near end of the nineteenth century. In the 1880s the cap gradually became called the "prayer head-covering" or "devotional covering." In his 1970 book, Gingerich explains:

> When this practice was first referred to as a church ordinance is not clear. Perhaps the first written reference to it came in 1891 when the Indiana-Michigan Conference minutes mentioned that in one of the congregations some of the women wore a veil or handkerchief instead of the cap. One of the ministers argued that the Scriptures called for a covering but not for a particular style. But some contended that the wearing of a special cap was a "Church ordinance [regulation]." The conference decided that the cap was to be worn as a "prayer head covering" but did not call it an ordinance. After Daniel Kauffman's *Manual of Bible Doctrines* was published in 1898, in which he referred to the practice as an ordinance, district conferences began to refer to the wearing of the prayer cap as an ordinance . . .[39]

It may be startling to realize that the cap or covering, one time the fashion of the world, was given hallowed meaning, that is, given biblical symbolism in a status with baptism and communion (and other ordinances).[40]

There are many styles of caps/coverings worn by Mennonite and Amish (and various Brethren and Dunkard) women over the years. The style is determined by the particular group of which one is a part. In Pennsylvania's Lancaster County in 1970 there were as many as seventeen distinct styles of caps, and at one time the plain clothes department of Hager and Brother Store in Lancaster had approximately 100 different styles.[41] Some caps have ribbons or strings and some do not. It is considered more

37. Jonas Smucker Hartzler (August 8, 1857–April 1, 1953) was ordained to the ministry on April 18, 1881, at Hawpatch near Topeka, Indiana. He attended Wooster College and Cook County Normal School and taught public school until he began as Bible teacher at the Elkhart Institute in 1895; taught and served in various capacities at Goshen College 1903–18; was the first pastor of College Mennonite Church, 1903–23, and pastor of Prairie Street Mennonite Church,1923–40.

38. Gingerich, *Mennonite Attire*, 127.

39. Ibid., 127–30.

40. In the MC in the twentieth century, largely through the influence of Daniel Kauffman, seven ordinances were taught. They were baptism, communion, footwashing, marriage, anointing with oil, the holy kiss, and the prayer covering. See chapter 3 for more on ordinances.

41. Gingerich, *Mennonite Attire*, 131. See the photo of the 1960s advertisement from the Hager Store in Lancaster, Pennsylvania, on page 2.

conservative to have strings/ribbons. Sometimes the strings hang lose; sometimes the strings are uncut and hang loose behind the head or beneath the chin. Some Russian Mennonite women wore bows on the tops of their heads in the place of caps.[42]

Over the years the styles of caps changed, generally getting smaller and, as we know from the Middlebury story, headgear without strings became common. To counteract this, conferences in the MC made rules. In 1925, the Indiana-Michigan Conference rules state, "The head dress of our sisters shall be plain, serviceable, consistent with the prayer head covering, and a shape and form that cannot be mistaken for any form of hat." In 1933 the conference amended that to clarify that the headwear ". . . shall be a bonnet or hood that is plain, serviceable . . ."[43] In 1937 the Lancaster Conference dictated that "round coverings are not allowed. Omitting ties on bonnets and coverings is a departure from this standard." In 1943 it was stated that the covering was to be of a "square pattern, including ties."[44] The concern was that if the covering had round corners rather than square corners at the ears, it would be easy to have no strings attached, and after the strings were gone, the coverings would get smaller and smaller until they disappeared! And to some extent, that is what happened.

This concern is cited in a 1913 editorial in the *Gospel Messenger* of the Church of the Brethren. The article was reprinted in the *Gospel Herald* on August 12, 1923, the year that the hat-wearing women were denied communion in Middlebury.

> The introduction of the hat means, ultimately, the elimination of the prayer-covering in our regular services. The hat and the prayer veil, as everybody knows, do not go together. They can not live together. At least they do not.[45]

In the same issue, Minerva Kauffman of Volant, Pennsylvania, makes a case for wearing the devotional covering at all times—as one should pray without ceasing. She also clarifies that the bonnet is not a substitute for the covering:

> . . . it should be remembered, there is a difference between the special veiling that Paul speaks of and the protection head gear. I have seen certain sisters who wore the bonnet as a covering, but that is not the special veiling; it is only the protection head gear.[46]

The general turn to authoritarianism in the early twentieth century for MCs included a codification of nonconformity practices. That is, dress and behavior requirements were arranged into systematic forms or codes that were spelled out in various pamphlets and books. For the relatively conservative groups, visibly distinctive apparel

---

42. Ibid., 132, 134–35.

43. Joe Springer, curator of the Mennonite Historical Library at Goshen College, in email to Hartzler, March 16, 2012.

44. Gingerich, *Mennonite Attire*, 136.

45. Author not given. *Gospel Herald*, August 12, 1923, 418.

46. Kauffman, "Devotional Covering," 429.

and hairstyles continued into the 1970s (and into the current era by many women in the Conservative Mennonite Conference).

Conservative dress was a new practice for some early twentieth-century Mennonite groups who in the nineteenth century had worn stylish clothing and even jewelry in some cases. Eugene Bontrager refers to jewelry that some Forks Mennonite women hid when they were no longer allowed to wear it.[47] Leota Leer (born 1919) from the Middlebury Mennonite Church remembers that her grandmother tore up photos of herself and her three daughters. Leota thinks the reason was because their clothes in the photos were too fancy and her grandmother felt ashamed. Or perhaps it was a sermon on humility that prompted her to destroy photos that would have been treasured by her offspring.[48]

Whether wearing conservative clothing or fashions of the day, whether displaying jewelry or not, the principle of nonconformity has remained important among most Mennonites even though physical manifestations are typically no longer obvious. In fact, the word "nonconformity" is probably seldom used in MC USA congregations today, but the idea of "a third way" is familiar to many, somewhere between extreme separation from the world and total involvement in worldly affairs. Harold S. Bender's "Anabaptist Vision," first articulated in 1943, included the concept of a third way.[49]

GENERAL CONFERENCE MENNONITE CHURCH

There was an undercurrent of change in the mid-nineteenth century affecting the church life of Mennonite folks in the eastern and middle United States. People in every age may be inclined to think that change is a new phenomenon. But no, in each era there are uncertainties and changes.

Mennonites in North America

The first period of Mennonite history in America roughly coincides with the colonial period (1683 to 1783). This was a time of immigration, settling into a new way of life, and setting of patterns. Mennonite immigrants had great appreciation for the new-found religious freedom in the new world, and there was also a deep awareness of separation from the surrounding world because of differences in religious convictions and practices, and to some extent in language and customs. Outside pressure urging political participation and military service during the Revolutionary War was a challenge for Mennonites.

---

47. Bontrager, *Forks Mennonite Church*, 22.

48. Leota Leer in telephone conversation with Hartzler, 2011.

49. Thirdway.com is an internet "café" that offers Mennonite reflections on current issues, a weekly column on family and values, and many links to Mennonite related sites.

Because of minimal European contacts and increasing isolation in America, patterns of life and thought, customs, and traditions among American Mennonites became somewhat set and authoritative after the Revolutionary War (1789) to the mid 1800s. During this second period of American Mennonite history, leaders tended to be older and untrained. Blood relationships, a cultural church, and separation on a social and religious basis, "tended to crowd out the personal, voluntary, glowing spiritual life of the 'new creature in Christ' which had been so real and vital in earlier days."[50]

John C. Wenger wrote the following about these early Mennonites in America:

> Their Christianity was not that of "radical" Christians; it had settled down to a comfortable, conventional, denominational type. There was no thought of evangelistic work, no need for any kind of mission work, no occasion to alter any of the set patterns of worship. The faith and practice of the immigrants was good and satisfying; why change? From 1683 to the ordination of John H. Oberholtzer almost 160 years later, no significant changes were made, and no one intended to make any. The Bible had not changed; why should anyone introduce any innovations? Only with great effort would it be possible to introduce Sunday schools, evangelistic services, Bible study and prayer meetings, evening services, and church boards of charities, publication, education, and missions.[51]

General Conference Beginnings

John H. Oberholtzer (1809–95) was a key leader in one of the groups that eventually formed the General Conference Mennonite Church. Starting at age sixteen he was a schoolteacher and he also became a locksmith to supplement his income. Between school teaching and his locksmith shop, Oberholtzer was in daily contact with a wider variety of people and ideas than other Mennonites in his area, who tended to associate only with other Mennonites.[52] At the age of thirty-three, Oberholtzer was called by lot to become the pastor of his congregation, Swamp Mennonite Church. He would have been expected to remain in that congregation the remainder of his life. However, he became a fluent and fascinating speaker and preached in neighboring churches of other denominations, an unheard-of innovation among Mennonites of that time.[53]

In October 1847 Oberholtzer took the lead in organizing a new Mennonite conference (which eventually became the Eastern District Conference of the General

50. Kaufman and Poettcker, "General Conference Mennonite Church (GCM)."

51. Ibid.

52. Born on a farm in Berks County, PA, John H. Oberholtzer (January 10, 1809–February 15, 1895) was the son of Abraham and Susanna (Hunsberger) Oberholtzer; his great-grandfather Jacob Oberholtzer had come from Switzerland to Philadelphia in 1732. Kaufman and Poettcker, "General Conference Mennonite Church (GCM)."

53. Fretz, "Oberholtzer, John H."

Conference Mennonite Church denomination) with other ministers and leaders who were also dissatisfied with the old ways of doing things. This division, perhaps the most far-reaching of all schisms in the American Mennonite Church, was not about changing the basic doctrines of the church. Instead it was the desire of Oberholtzer and his followers to introduce new ways of *spreading* the Gospel, such as Christian education, missionary work, and publication.[54]

Most historians view Oberholtzer as open-minded and "a man of considerable ability and initiative." His major contributions including writing of the *Ordnung,* the first known Mennonite church constitution (1847); beginning children's instruction classes consisting of singing, praying, and memorization of Scripture, which eventually led to one of the early Mennonite Sunday schools in America in 1857; and editing, printing and publishing (beginning in 1852) *Der Religiöser Botschafter* (*The Religious Messenger*), the first North American Mennonite church paper to last beyond one issue. This paper, and its successor (*The Christian People's Paper*), did much to establish the Mennonite General Conference denomination; to promote the founding of Wadsworth Institute, the first Mennonite school of higher education; to publicize mission work among Native American peoples in Oklahoma; and ultimately to bring large numbers of Russian Mennonite immigrants who arrived in the 1870s into the General Conference Mennonite Church.[55]

West Point, Iowa, was the location of a historic meeting in 1860. Two local congregations, West Point Mennonite Church (organized in 1849 and no longer existing) and Zion Mennonite Church of Donnellson (organized in 1851), had decided one year earlier to work for a union of all Mennonites in America. They agreed to invite other Mennonite churches to join their union and meet with them at West Point on the second day of Pentecost 1860. The goal was not to start a separate branch of Mennonites but to form a loose union of all Mennonites, to carry on certain activities that Mennonites had in common, such as missions, but not to exert centralized control over congregational discipline.[56] This was distinctly different from what would develop in the "old" Mennonite Church in the 1890s.

Oberholtzer joined the group in Iowa, and by the end of the meeting, the predecessor of the General Conference Mennonite Church had begun with Oberholtzer as the chairman of the new conference. From the very beginning, the goal was to reunite all Mennonites in America, and the emphasis was on "unity in essentials; liberty in nonessentials; and love in all things."[57]

---

54. See also John Ruth's *Maintaining the Right Fellowship: A Narrative Account of Life in the Oldest Mennonite Community in North America.*

55. Pannabecker, *Open Doors,* 16–39.

56. Pannabecker lists the agreed upon resolutions followed by a critique in *Open Doors,* 47–50.

57. Gingerich, "West Point Mennonite Church."

General Conference Polity

Joseph Stuckey[58] was a preacher and bishop in the Amish General Conference in Illinois whose story illustrates the congregational polity of the General Conference Mennonite Church. In 1872 his relationships with the other Amish bishops became strained because Stuckey refused to excommunicate a Joseph Joder (Yoder), a member of Stuckey's congregation who had written a poem about universalism, a belief that everyone will or may be saved. Joder was responding to his understanding of the love of God and reacting to the church's strong emphasis on the wrath of God and the eternal punishment of sinners. The Amish conference appointed a committee to work with Stuckey and the committee decided to disfellowship him—because he would not disfellowship Joder![59]

Stuckey and his congregation and numerous other Amish congregations in Illinois gradually drifted from the mainline Amish and were referred to as "Stuckey Amish." Some years later, younger ministers in these congregations, including Stuckey's grandson Aaron Augspurger, wanted to have ministers' meetings for instruction and support, but Stuckey hesitated to organize such a meeting. He did not want to risk a repeat of the kind of tensions that had occurred in 1872. He finally consented to a meeting of ministers, which continued as conferences from 1899 to 1907. Augspurger explained that Stuckey's "opposition to a conference was due not so much to benefit of united action as it was to wrangling over nonessentials."[60]

The conference meetings begun in 1899 included Bible study and a discussion of the doctrines of the church. The meetings were "inspirational and not legislative."[61] Eventually the leaders found it necessary to be more organized and in 1908 (after Stuckey's death in 1902) the Central Illinois Conference of Mennonites was formed from the "Stuckey" Amish. The conference dropped Illinois from its name, being called the Central Conference of Mennonites in 1914. In 1946 the conference united with the General Conference Mennonite Church, and in 1957 the Central Conference merged with the Middle District of the General Conference Mennonite Church to form the Central District Conference of the denomination.[62]

Stuckey's legacy is significant. He hesitated to embrace centralized church authority, promoting a congregational polity in which membership decisions rest with the local congregation. At the same time he affirmed the Bible as guide for faith and life.

58. Joseph Stuckey (sometimes spelled "Stucky"), was born in Alsace July 12, 1825. He became the recognized leader of the Amish Mennonites of Central Illinois. From 1872 to his death on February 5, 1902, he was pastor of the North Danvers congregation. As a preacher and bishop he officiated in many ordinations, weddings, communion services, etc., traveling widely among Amish and Mennonites in the central states. Weaver and Bender, "Joseph Stuckey."

59. W. Weaver, *Central Conference*, 96.

60. Quotation from Aaron Augspurger is in W. Weaver, *Central Conference*, 99.

61. Ibid.

62. Pannabecker, *Open Doors,* 78; W. Weaver, *Central Conference,* 248. Weaver says the Central Illinois Conference of Mennonites formed in 1908 and Pannabecker says it was in 1909.

The story of Joseph Stuckey, creatively written as a dramatic monologue by Richard Bucher (pastor of North Danvers Mennonite Church, 1994 to 2012) was presented at the Central District Conference annual meeting in June 2010. Stuckey's remarkable life story is encapsulated in this piece, a version of which is in appendix G.

AMISH MENNONITES AND OTHER MENNONITE GROUPS IN INDIANA

"We submit the following report for your prayerful consideration: (1) We are glad to note the fact that a kind and [brotherly/sisterly] feeling has been developed and maintained between the members of both conferences in a commendable way, . . . that there has been a gradual flowing together of our members in the church organizations and activities; (2) that fellowship and . . . privileges [will] be extended to all members of both . . . bodies; (3) we are sincerely hoping and prayerfully looking forward to the time when the two conferences may be completely merged into one body to the praise of His glory."

This quotation sounds as though it could have been a memo put out to two Mennonite denominations in the early twenty-first century or to the members of both Pleasant Oaks Mennonite Church and First Mennonite Church of Middlebury while they were in the process of re-uniting in 2009. It is not; rather, it was written a century earlier in a 1915 report of a committee of members from two Ohio conferences. The committee met to work on the feasibility of merging the Ohio Mennonite Conference (begun in 1834) and the Eastern *Amish* Mennonite Conference (organized in 1893), a merger completed in 1927 forming the "Ohio Mennonite and Eastern Amish Mennonite Joint Conference".[63]

The re-uniting of the Mennonite and Amish Mennonite conferences in Ohio was part of a trend that had begun earlier in Indiana. Begun in 1913 and completed in 1916, these two branches of the historic streams of Anabaptists in America were re-united to become the Indiana-Michigan Mennonite Conference. In Ohio, the occasion was one of "general rejoicing that after centuries of separation we are again made one in Christ Jesus." Grant Stoltzfus concluded in a history of the Ohio Conference: "Thus came to a climax a sixteen-year labor of love among Christian statesmen. It was an accomplishment in the direction of unity for which there was strong approval with sincere gratitude for God's guidance in the proceedings."[64]

The story of the Amish Mennonites in the United States is background for the account of growth and schisms in Mennonite groups in Indiana. Amish Mennonites developed from one of the three major divisions among the Amish Church in America in the last half of the 1800s. One group, the *Old Order Amish*, resisted change and has continued as unorganized but close-knit group settlements. Another group, the

63. In the 1950s the name was shortened to "Ohio and Eastern Mennonite Conference." Stoltzfus, *Ohio and Eastern Conference*, 198.

64. Ibid., 196, 202.

more progressive Amish organized three district conferences after 1882: Eastern Amish Mennonite, Indiana-Michigan Amish Mennonite, and Western District Amish Mennonite, all of which later merged with the "old" Mennonite Church.

In addition, an *in-between group* of congregations, which did not accept either the old order or the progressive position, organized the Conservative Amish Mennonite Conference (which later dropped the name Amish) in 1910.[65] Another historically related group, the Beachy Amish Mennonites (who formed in 1927 by Old Order Amish reformers), now use the name "Amish Mennonite," but not in continuity with earlier Amish Mennonites. There is a significant population of both Conservative Mennonites and Beachy Amish Mennonites (commonly called Beachys) in northern Indiana. Both groups subscribe to and use the Dordrecht Confession. The Beachys refer to their association of congregations as a "fellowship," deliberately avoiding the degree of centralization often associated with a conference. They are organized well enough to function, and yet at the same time, preserve the congregationalism that they highly value.[66]

Amish Mennonite Conferences

The *Diener-Versammlung* (Amish Mennonite ministers' meetings) existed from 1862 to 1878 as area associations. The Indiana-Michigan Amish Mennonite (AM) Conference (1888–1917) was the first of the three AM conferences to be organized after the *Diener-Versammlung* no longer met. The Indiana-Michigan AM Conference held its first meeting in the Maple Grove Church southwest of Topeka, Indiana, on April 7, 1888. Several of the members of this AM Conference participated in the discussions of the Indiana Mennonite Conference in October 1888, when that body passed a resolution favoring a Mennonite general conference for church-wide organization.[67]

Beneath the late nineteenth and early twentieth century urges toward union (or really re-union) was a wave of evangelism that spread through North America.

---

65. The Conservative Mennonite Conference (CMC) is a Christian Fellowship of evangelical Anabaptist churches in North America. In 2010 the CMC had 110 congregations with 11,557 members in twenty-four states, one each in Ontario and Mexico. CMC also maintains active contact with international affiliates in Costa Rica, Ecuador, Germany, Haiti, India, Kenya, and Nicaragua that represent about 450 congregations. The CMC school of higher education is Rosedale Bible Institute in Irwin, Ohio. http://www.cmcrosedale.org.

66. In 2010 there were 153 Beachy Amish congregations throughout the world with a total membership of 8,986. This included congregations in Ontario, in most states east of the Mississippi, and in a few states west of the Mississippi. Yoder and Beachy, "Beachy Amish Mennonite Fellowship."

67. Umble, "Indiana-Michigan Amish Mennonite Conference." Mennonite General Conference was the over-all representative body of the ["old"] Mennonite Church. It was formally organized in 1898 and was superseded in 1971. "The conference had an advisory and consultative role in relation to the district conferences and general boards. . . . In spite of its lack of authority, the pronouncements of the General Conference in matters of faith and life carried great weight, and the work of the committees which it created and directed had great value and influence for the church at large." Bender, "Mennonite Church General Conference."

Meetings among the Indiana Amish and Mennonites were promoted by bishop Daniel J. Johns. Congregations of both groups joined in the founding and support of charitable institutions.

From the beginning, ministers of the two Indiana conferences (Indiana-Michigan AM Conference and Indiana Mennonite Conference) were welcomed at the other conference meetings. In the years immediately preceding the merger in 1916, the Amish Mennonite conference was referred to as the "spring conference" and the Mennonite conference as the "fall conference." Before they merged, the two conferences cooperated in organizing a district mission board in 1911. Early leaders in the Indiana-Michigan Amish Mennonite Conference were bishop Jonathan Kurtz (1848–1940), bishop D. D. Miller (1864–1955), bishop D. J. Johns (1850–1942), and preacher Ira S. Johns (1879–1956).

Amish Mennonite Congregations in Elkhart and LaGrange Counties

The first known Anabaptist worship service in Indiana was on Easter Sunday, March 27, 1842, at the home of Amish preacher Joseph Miller (1808–77) in Clinton Township, Elkhart County. Miller had arrived in Elkhart County from Somerset County, Pennsylvania, nine months earlier, along with his family and three other Amish families. The first ministers of this Clinton congregation were Joseph Miller and Isaac Schmucker (1810–93), who was ordained bishop in 1843.

Preacher Jonas D. Troyer (1811–97) from Logan County, Ohio, arrived in the congregation in 1854, and was immediately ordained bishop by Isaac Schmucker. Considered one of the chief leaders in the formation of the Amish Mennonite movement of the 1850s, Troyer was a "very gifted speaker and a man of a firm will who maintained a milder discipline in the church than the more conservative members of the congregation. Troyer also brought the innovation of holding baptisms in streams (by pouring, not immersion) rather than in private homes which had been the usual practice."[68]

In 1854 there was "a noteworthy, lamentable, and complete division" in this Clinton township congregation, lamentable because it tore apart families. The more conservative folk stayed with Joseph Miller (minister 1842–46 and bishop 1846–77) and developed into the Old Order Amish that spread throughout the area. Isaac Schmucker and Jonas Troyer led the progressive group, which became a new congregation eventually known as the Clinton Frame congregation.[69] This group continued to meet in homes until a meetinghouse was constructed, most likely in 1863 near the location of the present-day *Clinton Frame Mennonite Church*, five miles east of Goshen and eight miles south of Middlebury. After having a church building they

68. Wenger, *Mennonites in Indiana and Michigan*, 165, 334. This became a prominent issue in the Old Order versus Amish Mennonite separation. Troyer was on the path that led to the more progressive Amish Mennonite side. Theron Schlabach in email correspondence with Hartzler, April 15, 2011.

69. Estes, *Heritage of Faith*, 4.

were sometimes called the "Church-House Amish" to distinguish them from the Old Order Amish, who still hold worship services in homes.

The tearing apart of families continued among the Amish of Indiana. In 1857 the Forks Church was established just across the line into LaGrange County "for the progressives living there."[70] The issues in the 1850s leading up to the beginning of the *Forks Mennonite Church* were differences in clothing regulations, method of baptism, accepting local political office, entering into business enterprises, education beyond eighth grade, adopting English over the German language, and offering Sunday school services.[71]

In LaGrange County to the east of Clinton Frame and Forks, another Amish Mennonite congregation began in 1854 when Isaac Schmucker, minister and bishop who was one of the early leaders at Clinton Frame, organized eighteen charter members to become *Maple Grove Mennonite Church* in rural Topeka. The congregation worshiped in homes until their first meeting house was built in 1856 southwest of Topeka.

A "bright new chapter" began at the Clinton Frame church in 1892 when Daniel (D. J.) Johns,[72] an able schoolteacher, was ordained a minister. "Alert and flexible mentally, with a deep desire for the welfare of the church, Johns was a progressive leader in the best sense of the word." Bishop Joseph Stuckey came from Illinois for the ordination of "Daniel Tschantz," as Stuckey pronounced his name. As a teenager Johns had come from Somerset County, Pennsylvania, to Elkhart County with his parents in 1865. After becoming minister at Clinton Frame, Johns wore a beard because of the strong belief of Clinton minister Jonas Troyer that "at least the ministers ought to wear beards."[73] "However, Johns held rather open attitudes on some subjects, tolerating the wearing of hats rather than bonnets by the women. But by 1890 Johns felt forced to become more strict through pressures put on him by other Amish Mennonite leaders."[74]

The increased strictness among some Mennonites in the late nineteenth century was related at least in part to concerns about keeping the young people in the church. The "plain dress" of Amish and Mennonite women, for example, was at one time the typical dress for women in the wider culture, in "the world." As changes in fashions occurred, just like in all the generations since then, young people (and some older ones) wanted to embrace the new trends. Church leaders thought it was

---

70. Ibid.

71. Bontrager, *Forks Mennonite Church*, 19. Forks Mennonite Church had their Sesquicentennial Anniversary Celebration in October 2007. In 2010 the group continues as the Forks Mennonite Church at the same location five miles southeast of Middlebury.

72. Daniel J. (D. J.) Johns (September 8, 1850–May 22, 1942) was a great-grandfather of Dale Schlabach, POMC member and lay leader from 1974 to 2009, and Lois Johns Kauffman, Central District Conference minister beginning in 2008. Johns had been ordained bishop in 1887 and served Clinton Frame and Forks Mennonite Churches and then Middlebury Mennonite beginning in 1904. Johns contributed to many church institutions. Wenger, "Johns, Daniel J."

73. Wenger, *Mennonites in Indiana and Michigan*, 334.

74. Estes, *Heritage of Faith*, 5.

their responsibility to keep young people from taking on the clothing and customs of the world, fearing that would lead to the young people leaving the church. They felt called to keep the church "separate" from the world, and one way to keep the church separate was to have a distinctive wardrobe. When one considers the motivation for the conservative requirements, it is easier to understand that the conference leaders had good intentions, even when their specific actions seem severe.[75]

Members and ministers of Clinton Frame continued to disagree on how strict the discipline of the church should be. Some favored open communion, more leniency in dress, especially for women, and shaving among the men, while others held to the traditional ways. In 1892, fifty of the more "progressive" Clinton Frame members were banned from communion. The older bishop, Benjamin Schrock (then age seventy-three), who was described as a faithful pastor and bishop of the Amish Mennonite Church of Clinton Township for many years, stood with these fifty members.[76]

That group of dissatisfied and banned members invited the liberal Amish bishop Joseph Stuckey from Illinois to come to help them. They met with Stuckey (and Peter Schantz who accompanied Stuckey) in the Clinton Frame meetinghouse on June 22, 1892, but the locks were then changed, and they were not allowed to have additional meetings in that space. Instead, from June 23 to June 27, this progressive group met in the Union Chapel located in the area of the present-day Union Cemetery, southwest of the Clinton Frame meetinghouse. On June 28, twenty-two new members joined the group by baptism and confession of faith, bringing the number to seventy-two. Following the receiving of the new members, bishop Schrock led the group in a communion service.[77]

The new congregation met in the Union Chapel temporarily, and by October 20, 1892, they had completed a new building on Silver Street, a mile north of the Clinton Frame meetinghouse and five miles east of Goshen. Benjamin Schrock was the first minister of the new congregation, which took the name *Silver Street Mennonite Church*. Joseph Stuckey and Peter Schantz returned from Illinois to help dedicate the new meetinghouse on October 23, 1892, and then led evangelistic services in the week following. By that time there were eighty-seven members who celebrated communion with Stuckey and Schantz. An early member later wrote, "The members of the Silver Street

75. An important criterion according to Theron Schlabach had been "whether dress and demeanor and attitude toward accepting the church's counsel exhibited humility or pride. By 1923, the marks of humility and pride had been codified" nearly to the point of legalism, and the humility versus pride criterion was practically lost. One can find "admonitions in conference resolutions in the nineteenth century calling people to more humble attire. With humility theology there was (and, at best, still is) a certain kind of spirituality behind plainness, not just the legalism that progressive Mennonites and Amish have railed against." Theron Schlabach in email correspondence with Hartzler, April 15, 2011.

76. Benjamin Schrock (1819–95) came to Clinton Township in 1872. He had earlier been ordained minister (1852) and bishop (about 1854) in the Howard-Miami Amish Church near Kokomo. Wenger, *Mennonites in Indiana and Michigan*, 323.

77. The names of these fifty plus twenty-two are listed in the history of Silver Street Mennonite Church written for the ninetieth anniversary celebration in 1982. Estes, *Heritage of Faith*, 6–7.

Church will ever owe a debt of gratitude to Reverend Stuckey and Reverend Schantz that these brethren sacrificed their own work and the comforts of home to assist the new church in every way possible in giving counsel and advice in the dark hours of trial."[78]

A heart-warming story that accompanies this schism is that D. J. Johns, bishop of the Clinton Frame congregation, loaned his congregation $1,000, which the congregation in turn gave to Silver Street for the share of the equity that the banned members had in the 1888 Clinton Frame meetinghouse.[79] This most likely helped to smooth the feathers that were ruffled when earlier, the locks on the church house door had been changed! This goodwill was matched by the wisdom of Brothers Stuckey and Schantz who emphasized that positive attitudes toward the Clinton Frame congregation would be very important for the success Silver Street as it ministered to the community. They encouraged the Silver Street folks to always be forgiving, kind, gentle and patient, manifesting a truly Christian spirit. The Silver Street congregation felt a need for fellowship with other church bodies so in 1898, they united with the Middle District of the General Conference Mennonite Church, and then joined the Central Illinois Conference of Mennonites in 1911.[80]

The Silver Street congregation helped begin two additional congregations in its early years. In 1893, just a year after the Silver Street meetinghouse was dedicated, Silver Street pastor John C. Mehl was asked to also provide services in the Topeka area to the east for the Silver Street members in that vicinity. Within a year, the *Topeka Mennonite Church* began. In 1913 a second offspring of Silver Street was born when Alvin K. Ropp, then pastor of the church, organized the *Eighth Street Mennonite Church* in Goshen.[81]

There was also Mennonite activity in the village of Middlebury as early as 1868 when the Brenneman brothers, Daniel from the Yellow Creek area south of Elkhart and Henry of Ohio, preached to a "large, attentive, and very orderly audience" in Middlebury.[82] However, there was apparently not an effort to begin a Mennonite church in Middlebury until 1902. The story of the first Mennonite church in Middlebury continues in chapter 4.

In 1915 the Indiana-Michigan Amish Mennonite Conference reported eleven congregations. In Indiana were Clinton Frame, Forks, Middlebury, Maple Grove, Nappanee, Leo, Howard-Miami, and Linn Grove.[83] The congregation on the campus

---

78. W. Weaver, *Central Conference*, 113–14.

79. Estes, *Heritage of Faith*, 6–7.

80. W. Weaver, *Central Conference*, 114, 249; D. Graber, "Silver Street." There seems to be a discrepancy in the number of members of Silver Street in 1924 and 1926. Daniel Graber (pastor from 1954 to 1959) reported in the *Mennonite Encyclopedia* in 1959 that there were 250 members in 1924; William Weaver reported in his 1926 book that there were 205 members in 1926. The Central Illinois Conference became known as the Central Conference of Mennonites in 1914 and joined the General Conference Mennonite Church in 1946.

81. Ibid. In 1984 the Silver Street congregation moved into Goshen and changed their name to Silverwood Mennonite Church.

82. Wenger, "First Mennonite Church."

83. Umble, "Indiana-Michigan Amish Mennonite Conference."

of Goshen College was a "union" church, a member of both the Indiana-Michigan Amish Mennonite Conference and the Indiana Mennonite Conference.[84]

"OLD" MENNONITES IN INDIANA

The Mennonite Church in North America began in 1683 when the first congregation of Mennonite immigrants started meeting. However, the group was not formally organized until 1898. This group has continuity with the early Anabaptists in Switzerland who eventually took their name from Menno Simons. As noted above, at times the group has divided, such as the Amish division in 1673 and the Oberholtzer split (beginning the General Conference Mennonite Church) in 1847. The group that continued with the name Mennonite is referred to in this book as the "old" Mennonite Church or MC.

Indiana Mennonite Conference

In its beginning in the 1850s, the Indiana Mennonite Conference was somewhat of an extension of the Ohio Conference. Typically the Ohio ministers met with the Indiana ministers in the fall, and the Indiana ministers met with the Ohio ministers in the spring. The first Indiana conference for which minutes have been preserved was held at the Yellow Creek meetinghouse in 1864.[85]

Concerns of the Indiana Mennonite Conference included primarily the problems that the bishops, preachers, and deacons faced, such as whether Mennonites should vote in political elections, how best to resist worldly attire, a biblical understanding of the ban, and how to respond to divorced and remarried people. Regarding divorce and remarriage, the 1887 conference considered the eligibility for membership of a divorced man who was planning to marry a woman in the church. John F. Funk of Elkhart and Henry Nice of Illinois gave "decisive addresses," and the conference decided that the man could be received as a member. That decision was in contrast to a similar situation a year later in 1888 in the Indiana-Michigan Amish Mennonite Conference in which the question of membership for a divorced person was brought to the conference. The majority of conference leaders were "in favor of taking such a one into the church, but [the decision] was given into the hands of the Nappanee ministers, it being their case." Thus, for the Amish Mennonite Conference, the authority to make this decision lay in the congregation.[86]

In the early decades of the Mennonite conference meetings, only ordained men (of course there were no ordained women) participated. The men typically came together quietly with no appointed moderator and no prepared program. They began

84. Ibid.

85. Wenger and Krabill, "Indiana-Michigan Mennonite Conference."

86. Wenger and Krabill, "Indiana-Michigan Mennonite Conference"; Minutes of the Indiana-Michigan Mennonite Conference, 1864–1929, 140.

with singing and a silent opening prayer. Then the older bishops gave messages of exhortation. After the devotional service, one or more bishops exhorted the ministers to maintain the historic and biblical principles of the brotherhood. Anyone was then free to make any further remarks or to bring questions before the group for counsel and decision. Especially in the 1870s, the Indiana Mennonite Conference struggled with problems related to the transition from old to new customs regarding practices and to the transition from German to English.[87]

Two schisms of note within the conference involved leaders from the Yellow Creek congregation. Bishop Jacob Wisler (1808–89) and his followers seceded from conference in 1871 because the conference supported the introduction of Sunday schools, and tolerated other changes from the "old order." This was the beginning of the Wisler or Old Order Mennonite branch.

Daniel Brenneman was a charismatic evangelist with a progressive mind. He was born and spent his early life in Ohio, joined the Mennonite Church in 1856, and soon afterward was called by lot to be a preacher. In 1864 he moved with his family to Elkhart County where he lived the remainder of his life. Brenneman was a "vigorous speaker and was considered one of the most able of Mennonite preachers." He was noted for his progressive views and early in his ministry began to preach in English. In 1872 in Masontown, Pennsylvania, Brenneman and John F. Funk conducted the first revival meetings in the Mennonite Church in the United States.[88]

Brenneman got involved in the controversy between the progressive and conservative elements of the church. He supported revival meetings, prayer meetings, women giving public testimonies, and singing in parts when such innovations were frowned upon by other leaders in the Indiana Mennonite Conference. All these practices were eventually accepted, but Brenneman was impatient, and sadly, he was excommunicated in 1874. Being unable to find another suitable denomination, he organized a congregation in Goshen in 1879, first called the Reformed Mennonite Church. A series of mergers with other splintered groups became the Reforming Mennonites, then the Mennonite Brethren in Christ, and eventually an element of the United Missionary Church.[89]

The Goshen congregation later was named Brenneman Memorial Missionary Church in memory of its first minister. In 1980 the congregation moved to State Road 15 north of Goshen. Brenneman also led in the organization of the Nappanee Missionary Church in 1897. The greatest differences between the Missionary Church and

---

87. Ibid.

88. Storms, "Brenneman, Daniel."

89. The story of Daniel Brenneman (June 8, 1834–September 10, 1919), including his colorful review of other denominations, is given in Wenger's *Mennonites in Indiana and Michigan*, 379–84. Wenger also gives details of the merging of splintered Mennonite groups that became the United Missionary Church in 1947.

the Mennonite Church are the loss of the traditional peace teaching in the Missionary Church and the Missionary requirement of baptism by immersion.

"Old" Mennonite Congregations in Elkhart and LaGrange Counties

Clinton Brick Mennonite Church traces its beginnings to 1850 when a Mennonite fellowship was organized in Clinton Township in eastern Elkhart County. Mennonites settlers had arrived in western Elkhart County around 1839 and began the Yellow Creek Mennonite Church in 1848. In 1846 Mennonites Jacob J. and Lucy Garber moved from the west to the east part of the county. During its first five years, the new fellowship was served by ministers from Yellow Creek, including Jacob Wisler, John Funk, Daniel Brenneman, and John S. Coffman.

As noted above, Amish folk had settled in Clinton Township in 1841, and eventually an Amish Mennonite group met about two miles west and one mile south of the Mennonite group. The Mennonite group built a log cabin in 1854, which they replaced in 1880 with a brick structure, using materials from a nearby brick yard. This congregation was eventually called Clinton *Brick* Mennonite Church to distinguish it from the Clinton *Frame* Amish Mennonite Church, which later dropped *Amish* from its name.[90]

The *Shore Mennonite Church* is located one mile south and one mile east of Shipshewana in LaGrange County, just off US 20 near Shore Lake. In the early 1860s church services were held in a barn or homes of Mennonites in that area. A few years later a schoolhouse was used for services. The members residing in this community held membership with the Clinton Brick Church, and for many years after the Shore Church was organized, the ministers served both congregations. In 1874 a meetinghouse was built on the west side of Shore Lake. In 1893 this building was moved across the road and enlarged. At that time the name "Shore" was given to the small village, the school, the church, and the lake.[91]

In 1901 members of the Shore Church and the Forks Church who lived in the village of Emma, five miles north of Topeka, wanted to worship closer to home. Reuben Yoder,[92] great grandfather of J. O. Yoder (of the WSMC/POMC congregation) had come from Pennsylvania to Indiana in a covered wagon in 1851. Twenty days before leaving Pennsylvania, he had married Harriet Riehl, a Lutheran woman of German descent. They now lived west of Emma, and Reuben had determined the distance between his home and the Forks Church by cleverly tying a ribbon on the rim of the buggy wheel. By watching the ribbon, he counted the revolutions of the wheel. (Meanwhile, the horse knew the way to go!) He had measured the distance around the wheel, and thereby calculated that it was about five miles between his home and the

90. Kauffman, *Brick by Brick*, 10.

91. Coffman, "Shore Mennonite Church."

92. Reuben Yoder, January 9, 1831–March 18, 1912. From family members and obituary: http://www.mcusa-archives.org/MennObits/12/apr1912.html.

church building, a challenging distance on unpaved roads during some seasons of the year. So the *Emma Mennonite Church* was begun.[93]

Existing Mennonite congregations in Elkhart County that were organized by 1901 include Yellow Creek (1848), Clinton Brick (1850), Holdeman (1851), Olive (1862), Shore (1860s), Prairie Street (1870), North Main Street in Nappanee (1880), and Emma (1901). The Goshen College congregation began in 1903. There is much available historical data about these congregations, including congregational histories and summaries in *The Mennonites in Indiana and Michigan* by Wenger.[94]

THE "MERGED" INDIANA-MICHIGAN MENNONITE CONFERENCE

Beginning in Indiana in 1916, two of the largest branches of the historic streams of Anabaptist groups in America ("old" Mennonites and Amish Mennonites) were re-united. In the Indiana-Michigan Mennonite Conference it was an occasion of "general rejoicing that after centuries of separation[95] we are again made one in Jesus Christ." In 1920–21 the same groups in Illinois, Iowa, Kansas, Nebraska, North Dakota, Missouri, and the Pacific Coast merged to form a body of 7,500 members. The Ohio groups completed their merger in 1927. Albert (A. J.) Steiner, a member of the feasibility committee for the merger in Ohio, considered the joining together of the two conferences as "crucial and necessary" for the future of the Ohio Mennonite Conference as it faced differences regarding doctrine and nonconformity.[96]

It must be noted that the re-union of these two branches of Anabaptists did not include all of the Amish or Mennonites in America. The re-uniting Amish were those who in the nineteenth century had made changes from German to English, had begun to worship in meetinghouses instead of homes, and in other ways had taken on new customs and practices in church life. Many Amish have continued in the traditional ways that resist innovations in transportation, dress, worship, and church life. In 2010 there were more than 200,000 Amish people who maintain the ways of their forebears with remarkable steadfastness. They are formally known as the Old Order Amish; the progressives who joined with the Mennonites have lost the name *Amish*.

In northern Indiana Mennonite congregations in the late 1800s and early 1900s, power gradually became concentrated in conference leaders, and individual congregations had less authority in decision-making. Congregations in the Amish Mennonite tradition before this time had enjoyed freedom in governing their individual churches as they felt led, whereas throughout the "old" Mennonite Church, decision-making

---

93. Bontrager, *Forks Mennonite Church*, 23.

94. The dates of beginnings of congregations are not always clear. Should the date be the first time folks met to worship and explore becoming a congregation, or when the congregation was finally organized with a minister?

95. This reference is to the Mennonite/Amish schism in Switzerland in 1693.

96. Stoltzfus, *Ohio and Eastern Conference*, 196, 203.

came to rest much more in the hierarchical system of conferences and bishops.[97] This dynamic was part of the social and religious turmoil of the time when some groups of Mennonites held to rigid doctrines and ethics implemented by central authority, while others operated with a congregational polity and became assimilated into secular culture in varying degrees. The struggle between these two different understandings of faithfulness was most passionately played out in northern Indiana.

Bishops who collaborated with other bishops and conferences became power houses of authority over congregations. From his perspective of having been deeply involved in both MC and GC institutions, Paul Whitmer wrote in 1952, "Such a program inevitably became . . . unresponsive to any elements in the church except those . . . who agreed with the leadership."[98]

Most denominations had the hierarchical power structure from the time of early Christendom. Anabaptists had been different from their earliest days. Two examples from the life of Michael Sattler illustrate this. In *The Legacy of Michael Sattler* John Howard Yoder notes that in 1526, Sattler referred to what "I together *with my brothers and sisters* have understood out of Scripture."[99] On February 24, 1527, Sattler gathered together a group of Anabaptists, essentially a ragtag group of radical thinkers, and led the group in coming to consensus, the outcome being the corporate document, the Schleitheim Confession.

Soon after Schleitheim, Sattler was captured and tried. At his trial, he asked the court to read the charges against him. Before responding, Sattler asked permission to "consult with his brothers and sisters; this was granted to him."[100] This illustrates "Sattler's understanding of process for a New Testament church as residing in interaction among gathered disciples; he thus needed counsel of fellow believers to make sure what he would be saying was in line with the sentiment of his gathered faith community—both women and men!"[101]

Whitmer described the original purpose of the General Conference of the "old" Mennonite Church (organized in 1898) to be "to give the church a better and more unified program." However, as Whitmer stated, there was also a change in the way the organization functioned.

> At first the General Conference was considered to be an advisory body and it was frequently so stated. But either by design or otherwise, it gradually assumed legislative functions and spoke in the name of and for all the (Old) Mennonite and Amish Mennonite churches that constituted the General Conference and the boards under the General Conference. The legislations

97. Whitmer, *Autobiography*, 93.

98. Ibid., 94.

99. Yoder, *Michael Sattler*, 20.

100. Ibid., 71.

101. Leonard Gross in email communication with Hartzler, December 1, 2010. Michael Sattler was burned at the stake on May 20, 1527, and his wife, Margareta, was drowned two days later.

became more specific and authoritative in tone and purpose until it was generally accepted as the highest authority in the church.[102]

This function of conference and its leaders directly affected the growing tension in congregations that eventually resulted in schisms.

Before the 1916 merger, both the Indiana Mennonite Conference and the Indiana-Michigan Amish Mennonite Conference had created executive committees that led away from congregational autonomy and toward centralized organization and authority. With the newly formed Indiana-Michigan Mennonite Conference, an active five-member executive committee assumed power that was apparently greater than that of any other area conference in the Mennonite Church. The person most responsible for this centralization of power was bishop Jacob K. Bixler,[103] whose actions affected the events in Middlebury in 1923. Bixler did not conserve Mennonite traditions. Leonard Gross described Bixler as promoting a "new 'progressive' Fundamentalist-tinted authoritarianism from above."[104]

There was a turning point in 1922 in what historians describe as the conference struggle between conservatives and progressives. A petition signed by 149 people from seven congregations in the Indiana-Michigan Conference expressed objection to what they considered to be Bixler's heavy-handed, authoritarian methods. The accusations against Bixler included "self-willed administration of the bishop's office," interfering in congregations for which he was not responsible, advocating against certain church institutions and individuals, and "for his manner of conducting excommunications."[105]

Rich Preheim details the response that an investigating committee made to the charges against Bixler. The bishop was largely defended, and furthermore, the investigating committee confirmed the authority of the executive committee, calling on it to bring Indiana-Michigan congregations "into harmonious relations with the doctrines of the church and the regulations of conference." In addition, anybody challenging the decision of the investigating committee would be reprimanded. Preheim concludes, "Now, despite precedent and the constitution's instructions, the executive committee was no longer just supervisor and coordinator of Indiana-Michigan affairs but final arbiter of faithfulness as well."[106]

---

102. Whitmer, *Autobiography*, 91.

103. Jacob K. Bixler (September 5, 1877–December 20, 1939), son of John and Barbara (Huber) Bixler, was born at Winesburg, Ohio, and died in Elkhart, Indiana; at age five moved with his family to near Wakarusa, Indiana, where he graduated from high school (one of the first "old" Mennonite graduates in the Midwest) and taught school for two years; married Susan Bailey and ordained as "old" Mennonite minister in 1904 and ordained bishop in 1907; became an influential leader in the Indiana-Michigan Mennonite Conference and Mission Board.

104. Wenger and Krabill, "Indiana-Michigan Mennonite Conference"; Leonard Gross in conversation with Hartzler, July 19, 2012.

105. Preheim, "Indiana-Michigan Mennonite Conference."

106. Ibid.

Paralleling the refusal to serve communion to certain women in Middlebury in 1923, was conference action at the College Mennonite Church on the campus of Goshen College. On February 21, 1923, the executive committee of conference met with the College congregation. Bishop D. D. Miller opened the meeting and said that he needed to work with the conference rules even though he did not agree with all of them. The conference officials then proceeded to ask members if they would stand by the regulations of Indiana-Michigan Conference. Records indicate that there were more than 200 members, but only fourteen responded, and some of them said, "No." When Miller officiated for communion two months later, only twelve people received the elements. Five days after that communion service, the executive committee decided to ask of all Indiana-Michigan members, as part of their pre-communion counsel, if they accepted the conference rules and regulations.[107] Whether the incident in Middlebury occurred before or after this decision may be a moot point. The pattern had been set and the fallout in Middlebury was a painful schism.

In June 1923 the conference appointed a committee of eleven persons to enforce the rules of conference. Suspect ministers and deacons were interviewed by the committee. Barker Street minister William (W. W.) Oesch[108] told the committee, "I am willing to try to apply recent decisions as best we can under conditions, reserving freedom of judgment and action when the integrity of the congregation is at stake."[109] In September the committee revoked the credentials of a number of ministers: W. W. Oesch, Irvin R. Detweiler,[110] Raymond L. Hartzler[111] of Maple Grove, Ezra S. Mullet of North Main in Nappanee, and Simon S. Yoder[112] of Middlebury. This, in effect, meant

107. T. Schlabach, "The Past in Perspective," 26; S. Miller, *Goshen College*, 85; Preheim, "Indiana-Michigan Mennonite Conference."

108. William W. Oesch (July 16, 1884–May 16, 1977) grew up in Missouri and graduated from Goshen College in 1910. He was ordained at Barker Street Amish Mennonite Church (eight miles northeast of Middlebury) in 1914 and served as pastor there until he and most of the congregation left the conference in 1923. He and his wife, Elva Alice Garber, became members of Warren Street in 1928.

109. Preheim, "Indiana-Michigan Mennonite Conference."

110. Irvin R. Detweiler (August 24, 1873–February 22, 1946) was Goshen College professor of Bible (beginning in 1909) and acting president (1920–22), and pastor of College Mennonite Church in 1908 and 1913–22. He had attended Elkhart Institute, Goshen College, Bethany Bible School, Garrett Biblical Institute, and Chicago University. Along with his first wife, Bertha (Zook), he served as a missionary to India, 1902–04. He was ordained to the ministry in 1904 and for one year was minister of Maple Grove Mennonite Church in Topeka, Indiana. He became a member of Eighth Street Mennonite Church in 1923 where he served as pastor 1923–31. In 2010 Rachel Kreider remembered the group standing in a semi-circle and being received into membership in 1923. As a teenager at the time, she became a member the same day. W. Weaver, *Central Conference*, 233; *100th Anniversary 1854-1954: Maple Grove Mennonite Church*, 8; Wenger, *Mennonites in Indiana and Michigan*, 274.

111. Pastor at Maple Grove in Topeka 1916–1923, Raymond L. Hartzler (November 28, 1893–June 27, 1988) was pastor at Carlock Mennonite Church 1928–41 and did much editing, board work, and conference work within the GCMC. Estes, "Hartzler, Raymond Livingston;" *100th Anniversary 1854-1954: Maple Grove Mennonite Church*, 8.

112. More information about S. S. Yoder, first pastor of Warren Street Mennonite Church, is in footnote 26 of chapter 4 (page 91).

that these men, who were not in sympathy with the Indiana-Michigan Conference requirement to enforce discipline, would no longer be allowed to preach in an Indiana-Michigan Conference congregation or officiate for communion or baptisms.[113]

Rachel Kreider noted that these were all educated men, men who had gone to college and developed a larger world view. Education invites questions and opens one to new ways of thinking. Education beyond grade school was discouraged in many Amish and Mennonite communities for this very reason. The boundaries were set to keep the young people out of the world, and regulations were the fences put in place to mark the boundaries. Education broke down some of the fences. In addition, colleges exposed people to the "ways of the world" and fostered a progressive mindset. In addition to losing many gifted, dedicated, and well-educated ministers, the actions of the Indiana-Michigan Conference in 1923 threw a wet blanket on passionate youth and put the brakes on the progressive movement within the "old" Mennonite Church.

It is interesting that, of the men whose ministerial credentials were removed by the Indiana-Michigan Conference in 1923–24, most had been ordained in Amish Mennonite congregations before the conferences merged, and then left for congregations that eventually became part of the General Conference Mennonite Church. And yet, some perceived the 1916 creation of Indiana-Michigan Mennonite Conference as a "momentous change, one heralded as an advancement of God's kingdom, a glorious example of unity in nonresistant faithfulness and mission and at least a partial healing of a regrettable centuries-old schism."[114] On the other hand, Grant Stoltzfus lamented in 1969, that "the Old World schism of 1693 is still not completely healed."[115] Celebrating the signs of hope while lamenting the losses is one way forward for a church who in each generation tries to be faithful in following Jesus.

---

113. Wenger, *Mennonites in Indiana and Michigan*, 42. Wilbur W. Miller, a minister at Forks and son of bishop D. D. Miller, was silenced in 1924.

114. Preheim, "Indiana-Michigan Mennonite Conference." As history shows, there were other negative repercussions of this union; e.g., the Amish Mennonites gave up some features of their congregational polity.

115. Stoltzfus, *Ohio and Eastern Conference*, 203.

3

Early Mennonite Institutions

Education and Publications

The earth, O Lord, is full of your steadfast love;
teach me your statutes.
Teach me good judgment and knowledge,
for I believe in your commandments.

PSALM 119:64, 66

VINORA WEAVER AND VESTA Zook waited until they were out in the middle of the Atlantic Ocean before they threw their Mennonite bonnets overboard. They were on board the *Regina de Italia* en route from New York City to Constantinople (now Istanbul), Turkey. One morning when there were only a few people on deck, Vinora and Vesta made their way to the railing and ceremoniously flung their bonnets into the deep.

It was 1921, and Vinora Weaver (later Salzman) and Vesta Zook (later Slagel) were the first female Mennonite Central Committee (MCC) workers to be sent abroad. They were going to assist refugees who were leaving Russia after their lives had become intolerable following the Great War and the Russian Revolution. Back in the Emma Church near Topeka, Indiana, Vinora and the other women had been expected to wear black bonnets whenever going out into public. Vinora and Vesta were careful to wear their bonnets and other mandatory garb when they stopped in Scottdale, Pennsylvania, on their way to New York City. Here they met some of the conservative "higher-ups" in the Mennonite Church and knew it was important to make a favorable impression. They also stopped in Akron, Pennsylvania, where they met Orie O. Miller (one of bishop D. D. Miller's sons), who, as the leader of MCC, coached them and accompanied them to their ship.[1]

Seniors and friends at Goshen College, 1918. Front row: Ruth Yoder, Vesta Zook (?), Maude Byler, Harold Bender; second row: Elizabeth Horsch, Vinora Weaver, Bernice Lehman, Alma Warye; back row: Raymond L. Hartzler, Fannie (Stoltzfus) Weaver, William B Weaver, Jesse Smucker. William B. Weaver was on the Goshen College faculty in 1918 and was married to Fannie (Stoltzfus) Weaver. Vesta Zook was also on the faculty in 1918.

Vinora and Vesta knew they wouldn't be wearing their bonnets in Constantinople, away from the leaders of the Indiana-Michigan Mennonite Conference where the regulations in 1921 were stiffer than when they had been students at Goshen College. They were photographed with classmates and friends in 1918 wearing stylish dresses and no coverings or bonnets. In the autumn of 1920, both Vinora and Vesta were employed by Goshen College, Vinora teaching in the business school and Vesta teaching

1. Vinora Salzman tells this story in her autobiography, *Day by Day, Year by Year*, 16–31. Vinora Weaver Salzman (August 10, 1895–January 8, 1990) grew up near Emma, Indiana, and was the youngest sister of William Weaver (author of *History of the Central Conference Mennonite Church*), and Samuel Weaver (preacher at Forks, 1904–16). Her traveling companion en route to Constantinople was Vesta Zook Slagel (1891–1973) from Topeka, Indiana.

home economics.[2] The "old Goshen" of 1922 and earlier did not demand conservative Mennonite attire. However, when Vinora and Vesta's classmates Elizabeth Horsch and Harold S. Bender returned to the newly reopened Goshen College as faculty in 1924, Elizabeth was required to wear the specified bonnet and Harold had to be willing to wear a plain coat.[3]

In many ways, Vinora and Vesta represented what was happening among Mennonites in North America in the early twentieth century. More men and women were attending high school and college, preparing to make a mark on the world that was opening to them. Education, publications, and mission programs offered boundless opportunities. Dozens of Mennonites left the farm for towns and cities, the American frontier, and even foreign fields.

During the Great Awakening (1890–1914), many North American Christians, including Mennonites, experienced spiritual renewal along with an increased fervor in revivalism, evangelism, and mission work. Theron Schlabach labels the Mennonite experience in the Great Awakening as a "Quickening." During these decades, Mennonites engaged in revivalism; church-wide programs and institutions developed and flourished; and there was a general spirit of activism expressed as "vigorous Christian service" and "aggressive work." Quickened Mennonites became less "quiet in the land" and with accelerated tempo, turned to outward-looking evangelism and service to others.[4] The passion and zeal of this quickening was behind the rise of Mennonite evangelism and mission work as well as Mennonite education and publications.

Equipped and quickened, young Mennonites developed a missionary fervor and, particularly after World War I, the call to offer relief to those devastated by war took many overseas. The quaint clothing restrictions of the "old" and Amish Mennonites became almost irrelevant, a trivial pursuit, to those involved in the huge challenges that came with responding to Jesus' great commission to go into all the world. Who cared about what style coat a man wore or what a woman had on her head as they were distributing blankets to shivering refugees in war-torn Europe?

Along with the positive outcomes of early Mennonite publications, educational institutions, and missions, one might wonder if some important values were lost in the frenzy of aggressive work. Schlabach makes a case for the loss of humility in the theology and rhetoric of quickened Mennonites. In 1898 Abram Kolb, associate editor for the *Herald of Truth,* complained about the nervous activism that made Christianity "all work—one continued earnest, active, hurrying, rushing, hustling, pushing whirl of active work." He called instead for holding communion with God in one's closet, a spiritual discipline that continues to be beneficial for a balanced life in an overly-busy world.[5]

2. Salzman, *Day by Day*, 15.

3. Keim, *Bender*, 161–2.

4. T. Schlabach, *Gospel Versus Gospel*, 48.

5. T. Schlabach, "Nineteenth-century Humility: A Vital Message for Today?" edited transcript of Schlabach's address given at the annual meeting of the Mennonite Historical Association of the

WADSWORTH INSTITUTE

Goshen College was one of the first North American Mennonite institutions of higher education, but not *the* first. The Wadsworth Mennonite School, or simply the Wadsworth Institute, operated in Wadsworth, Ohio, from January 1868 until December 1878. The institute grew out of the 1860 initiative in Iowa for union of Mennonite groups, particularly in missions, publications, and theological education.[6]

The school at Wadsworth was to provide three years of instruction primarily in Biblical subjects and largely in the German language. Carl Justus van der Smissen, a university-trained Mennonite pastor from Germany, came as the primary teacher. Teacher van der Smissen and his wife and two daughters brought a European culture with a background of books, music, and wealth and also a deep spirituality and keen interest in mission work, evangelism, and young people. They had a great influence on the young people from the rougher American communities. Yet, because of conditions inherent in the situation, difficulties arose early in the life of the school. Friction developed within the faculty between van der Smissen and Christian Schowalter, the principal from Iowa.

Wadsworth Institute lasted only a decade. The goal of bringing together Mennonites from the various streams was largely unmet. Historians offer theories about why MCs ("old" Mennonites) did not join the endeavor, one being a perceived lack of humility on the part of planners and leaders of the school. Largely unspoken, "barely articulable," the MC definition of faith had substituted humility for an earlier Anabaptist emphasis on suffering, and the progressives of the GC branch of Mennonites showed subtle signs of lacking humility.[7]

And yet, the school was not a failure. Some 209 students attended the school, at least 130 of them from Mennonite families. Ministers were trained, marking the beginning of the change from lay ministry to trained ministry, and the cause of missions was deeply woven into the Wadsworth program. One of the graduates who went on to make significant contributions to the GC Mennonite Church was Samuel F. Sprunger of Berne, Indiana. In some ways, Wadsworth Institute paved the way for future Mennonite schools of higher education.[8] Mennonite youth were being educated; the only question seemed to be when a *lasting* Mennonite school would begin to educate its youth.

Cumberland Valley, November 19, 1996. http://www.mcusa-archives.org/mhb/Schlabach-humility.html; T. Schlabach, *Gospel Versus Gospel*, 48.

6. Pannabecker, *Open Doors*, 54, 59. Earlier, a Mennonite seminary in Amsterdam was started in 1735 and Mennonites in Russia had operated teacher-training schools. In addition, the Emmetal School, a forerunner of Bethel College in Newton, Kansas, operated in 1882–83, the Mennonite Seminary in Halstead, Kansas, followed, and Bethel College began in 1893.

7. T. Schlabach, *Peace, Faith, Nation*, 130; Ruth, *Maintaining the Right Fellowship*, 239. To many nineteenth century "old" Mennonites, education in general showed pride.

8. Pannabecker, "Wadsworth Mennonite School."

The 1866 Wadsworth bell in its original location—barely visible in the cupola—at Wadsworth Institute (1868–1878), the first Mennonite school of higher education in North America (above), and in its present location at Anabaptist Mennonite Biblical Seminary (Elkhart, Indiana), where it was installed in 2004. The bell again calls students, faculty, and staff to worship.
AMBS photo by Steve Echols.

EARLY MENNONITE EVANGELISTS AND PUBLISHERS

Stories from the sixteenth century clearly illustrate how the invention of the printing press had an indisputable effect on the Protestant Reformation. Perhaps equally influential near the end of the second millennium have been computers and access to the World Wide Web. In the western world, and increasingly throughout the east and global south, people of all ages have access to more information and ideas than was imaginable one hundred years ago. Handheld technology has changed communication throughout the world. Changes in the second half of the nineteenth century did not seem as dramatic, but the circulation of newspapers and magazines and the establishment of institutions of higher education had a profound effect on Mennonites in North America.

John Fretz Funk

During the years 1903 to 1906 the first Mennonite Church in Middlebury purchased materials from the Mennonite Publishing Company in Elkhart. This publishing venture, beginning operation in Elkhart in 1867, had begun in Chicago by John F. Funk in 1864.[9] Funk was born in 1835 into a Mennonite family in Bucks County, Pennsylvania, and lived there until he was twenty-two years old. He received his education in public schools, at a private school conducted by the Baptist denomination, and at Freeland Seminary.[10] He was trained as a school teacher and taught in his home community before moving to Chicago in 1857 to work in the lumber business with his brother-in-law, Jacob Beidler.

Funk attended a Presbyterian church in Chicago with the Beidlers, and during a Presbyterian revival in 1858 he made a Christian commitment. He considered membership in that denomination, but after his study of baptism (guided largely by a booklet written by his great-grandfather Heinrich Funck who had migrated from Holland), Funk returned to Bucks County, Pennsylvania, to be baptized and received into the Mennonite Church in 1860. To his knowledge, he was then the only Mennonite in Chicago.

---

9. John Fretz Funk (April 6, 1835–January 8, 1930) was born to Jacob Funk and Salome Fretz. Numerous summaries and biographies of Funk's colorful life are readily available. Two sources are the *Mennonite Encyclopedia*, Bender, "Funk, John Fretz," and his obituary at http://www.mcusa-archives.org/mennobits/30/jan30.html.

10. Freeland Seminary, now Ursinus College located northwest of Philadelphia, was established in 1848 by Abraham Hunsicker (1793–1872), who had been ordained as a minister of the Skippack Mennonite Church in early 1847. Later that year, Hunsicker and John Oberholtzer left the "old" Mennonite Church and organized the Eastern Conference of Mennonites that later helped to form the General Conference Mennonite Church. When Hunsicker was elected as minister "he felt more than ever before the need of a provision for more and better knowledge and resolved before God to found a school that should afford to others means of obtaining that of which he was deprived." By the time Funk attended the school, Hunsicker had been expelled from the Eastern Conference because of his liberal beliefs. Krahn, "Freeland Seminary"; Preheim, "Indiana-Michigan Mennonite Conference."

In the early 1860s Funk worked with Dwight L. Moody[11] in mission Sunday school work. During the Civil War of 1861–65, Funk saw that many Mennonite and Amish young men joined the military effort. This troubled him, so he wrote and published a booklet on nonresistance, "Warfare: Its Evils, Our Duty," in July 1863. With a passion to support the traditional Mennonite peace position and encouragement from other Mennonites, Funk began two religious monthly papers, the *Herald of Truth*, and its German counterpart, *Herold der Wahrheit*, the first issues appearing on January 1, 1864. When the first issues were out, Funk traveled back to Pennsylvania where on January 19, 1864, he married Salome Kratz, a neighbor of the Funk family who as a girl had been one of Funk's pupils. Upon returning to Chicago with Salome, Funk threw himself into publishing and church work. The two versions of the *Herald* were distributed widely, reaching a circulation of more than 1,000 by the end of the first year. Several Mennonite periodicals had been published earlier, but none had seen long-lasting or wide-spread success.[12]

In May 1865 Funk was ordained as a minister for the Cullom Mennonite Church, some fifty miles south of Chicago. Within two years Funk decided to give his full attention to his publications and other church work. So he sold his share of the successful lumber business in 1867 and moved his publishing business to Elkhart, Indiana, then a city of 3,000 people. John and Salome were the first Mennonites in Elkhart, although there were numerous Mennonites in the surrounding area.

As a publisher and minister, Funk was considered the most influential leader in shaping the course of the Mennonite Church from 1870 to 1900. H. S. Bender said, "One of Funk's great contributions was his creative combination of conservatism and progress. He had a deep historical sense and anchored the church in its great historic heritage." Funk was a progressive, and at the same time understood that it takes time for people to accept innovations. He valued the community of believers as the place of discernment and waited for the time when new ideas would be more acceptable. In 1872 he and Daniel Brenneman held the first revival meetings in the Mennonite Church in Fayette County, Pennsylvania, but revival meetings were not accepted in Elkhart County until later.[13]

John Funk's great influence came through writing, editing, and publishing, wide traveling and speaking, pastoral work, and conference work. He was instrumental in building the first Prairie Street Mennonite meetinghouse and served as its first pastor from 1871 to 1902. He was an organizer and supporter of the Mennonite Board of Guardians, an agency to assist Mennonites to emigrate from Russia to America in the

11. Dwight L. Moody (1837–99) was a well-known North American Sunday school organizer and evangelist and founder of Moody Bible Institute.

12. Preheim, "Indiana-Michigan Mennonite Conference."

13. Bender, "Funk, John Fretz."

1870s. Many Russian Mennonites met and were assisted by Funk as they passed through Elkhart on their way to new homes in Minnesota, Dakota, Nebraska and Kansas.[14]

Two of the most notable achievements of the Mennonite Publishing Company were the translation of the *Martyr's Mirror* and the *Complete Works of Menno Simon* and their publication in English. In addition, Funk published many historical articles on Anabaptism and built up an excellent Mennonite historical library, the core of the Mennonite Historical Library at Goshen College. By 1900, Funk had published more than 100 titles in English and German, including doctrinal and theological works, hymnals, Sunday school curricula, and history books. Funk also published *Die Mennonitische Rundschau* from 1880 to 1908 to serve the newly established Russian Mennonite communities in the prairie states and Manitoba. For a number of years he also published a "European edition" of the *Rundschau* to keep the Mennonites in Russia in contact with American Mennonites.[15]

Although Funk's newspapers were read by Mennonites from various branches, he was an "old" Mennonite. Elkhart became the strong center of church leadership for MCs as Funk gathered a group of progressive younger men around him to assist in the publishing business: John S. Coffman, the noted evangelist, as an editor in 1879; John Horsch, writer and historian, in 1887; and George L. Bender, mission leader, in 1890. As Funk's periodicals linked Mennonites across the continent, the MC mission headquarters began in Elkhart in 1892, and the first MC foreign missionaries were sent out to India in 1899 from a meeting in Elkhart over which Funk presided.[16]

Funk was ordained bishop in 1892, but he fell from favor with other Mennonite leaders, and his bishop credential was withdrawn in 1902. In addition, he suffered personal financial loss due to a bank failure in 1903, and a fire in 1906 caused the publishing company bankruptcy. Even though he served the Mennonite Church, Funk's publishing company had remained a private business. In 1908 the printing business was sold to the James A. Bell Company and the publications to the Mennonite Publishing Board, which had just purchased the printing plant of the Gospel Witness Company at Scottdale, Pennsylvania.[17] After living in poverty and paying back his loans, John Funk was again widely respected later in life.

Beginning in 2010, Prairie Street Mennonite Church has had an annual "Funk Fest" to explore and celebrate their founding pastor and his leadership in church renewal. Each year the church chooses a theme centered on one of five theme's from John F. Funk's extensive work: music, mission, mentoring, media, and migration.

---

14. Ibid.

15. Hostetler, *God Uses Ink*, 220–28; Bender and Thiessen, "Mennonitische Rundschau."

16. Bender, "Funk, John Fretz." Two of the first three missionaries sent were William and Alice Page who would later help to start the Mennonite Church in Middlebury as described in chapter 4.

17. http://www.mcusa-archives.org/mennobits/30/jan30.html.

John S. Coffman

As noted above, the first MC revival meetings were held by John F. Funk and Daniel Brenneman in 1872. However, revivalism was not established among MCs until 1881, with the "able and eloquent" evangelist John S. Coffman becoming the premiere Mennonite revival preacher through 1899. John S. Coffman[18] was born in Rockingham County, Virginia, twelve years before the Civil War began. After being baptized at age sixteen, Coffman escaped into Cumberland County, Pennsylvania, to avoid being drafted into the Southern army. After the war he taught school, conducted singing schools, and ministered in Virginia and West Virginia. In 1879 Coffman accepted the invitation of John Funk to come to Elkhart to be the assistant editor of the *Herald of Truth*. Over the next twenty years he wrote many Sunday school materials, edited the *Words of Cheer*, and helped compile *Hymns and Tunes*, published in 1890.[19]

Coffman was a strong promoter of Sunday schools and young people's meetings. However, it was as an evangelist that he probably made his greatest contribution to the Mennonite Church. "Protracted" or evangelistic services (revival meetings) were in general disfavor at that time, but Coffman's natural tact and winning personality broke down barriers and paved the way for evangelism in the Mennonite Church. Coffman was concerned about the large number of young people from Mennonite families who didn't join the church because of lack of spiritual encouragement and guidance. By 1900, revivalism was generally accepted among MCs, although its use was relatively conservative, without the emotional emphasis of some other denominations.[20]

Looking back in 1957, H. S. Bender said, "The spirit of evangelism and revival was spread by J. S. Coffman's widespread itinerant work, followed by others who imitated him . . . . New life was awakened, and thousands of young people were gathered in who otherwise would have been lost to the Mennonite Church."[21] Retaining the youth in the church where membership is voluntary has always been a concern of church leaders.

A minister in the Prairie Street congregation from 1879 to1899, Coffman collaborated with Funk on the *Minister's Manual* and *Confession of Faith*, 1891. As he traveled to Amish Mennonite and MC communities throughout the United States and Ontario, Coffman observed the need for and interest in higher education. He became convinced that Mennonite schools were necessary to keep young people in the Mennonite Church. He stood out among those who supported the Elkhart Institute, devoting much of his energy to this cause in the final years of his life. Although Coffman's life was cut short when he died from cancer at age fifty-one in 1899, his

18. John S. Coffman (October 16, 1848–July 22, 1899) was born to bishop Samuel and Frances Weaver Coffman. He married Elizabeth J. Heatwole and they had seven children. Their second son Samuel F. was also a Mennonite leader. John was ordained to the ministry in 1875. He was also gifted in music and led singing schools.

19. Barbara Coffman, "Coffman, John S."

20. T. Schlabach, *Gospel Versus Gospel*, 33.

21. Bender and Hostetler, "Mennonite Church (MC)."

"spirit of progress" lived on for many generations in memories and in the profound and prophetic words of his energetic and inspiring address, "The Spirit of Progress," given in 1896 at the opening ceremonies of the new building of the Elkhart Institute.[22]

Daniel Kauffman

There is no question that the MC leader in the first three decades of the twentieth century was Daniel Kauffman.[23] He grew up in a Mennonite community in rural Missouri and found early success as a public school teacher and administrator. He did not make a Christian commitment until age twenty-five, when during a three-week series of meetings led by Evangelist John S. Coffman, Daniel responded on the last night during the final song of invitation. Kauffman was ordained minister in 1892 after a unanimous vote in his "home" Mt. Zion congregation. Although he exchanged correspondence with John S. Coffman about moving to Elkhart, he remained in Missouri (but taught in the six-week Bible School at the Elkhart Institute) and was ordained bishop in 1896. He gave up his public school position the following year and served in the Mennonite Church the remainder of his life.[24]

Already in 1893 Kauffman was thinking about an MC umbrella organization that would bring some unity in the doctrines promoted by the church. He wrote an article about a "general conference" that was published in the *Herald of Truth* in early 1894. A gifted speaker and writer and natural organizer, Kauffman was a primary planner and the first moderator of the general conference of the Mennonite Church when it was formed as a joint venture of the "old" and Amish Mennonite churches in 1898.[25] This organizational body was a new approach to denominational structures for MCs; it created a central authority that, in practice, very often transcended the authority of the area conferences that had existed. This was a significant departure

---

22. Coffman Hall, a building on the Goshen College campus, was named in honor of John S. Coffman.

23. Daniel Kauffman (20 June 20, 1865–January 6, 1944), the son of bishop David D. and Elizabeth Winey Kauffman lived in Missouri 1869–1909. He earned the degree of Principal of Pedagogics at the Missouri State University, taught school in Missouri 1883–97, and served as county commissioner (superintendent) 1887–90. He was married in 1887 to Ota Bowlin, who died in 1890. They had two children, one of whom died in infancy. In 1902 he married Mary "Molly" C. Shank. They had six children together, only three of whom grew to adulthood.

24. Ibid., 24–25. A. Gingerich, *Daniel Kauffman*, 17–18, 24–25. This biography was commissioned by the Historical Committee of the Mennonite General Conference.

25. Although easily confused, the general conference of the "old" Mennonite Church is not the same as the General Conference Mennonite Church. The first is a structure within the "old" Mennonite Church and the second is a denomination. Even more confusing, the official name of the denomination that began in 1860 was General Conference of the Mennonite Church of North America; in 1950 the name was simplified to General Conference (GC) Mennonite Church. When the "old" Mennonite Church organized a general conference in 1898, GC Mennonites referred to it as General Conference Two.

from the congregational polity already in effect among Amish groups and in the General Conference Mennonite Church.

Daniel Kauffman's first of three editions of *Bible Doctrines* was published in 1898, making him the "doctrinal father" of the MCs. These three volumes and many additional pamphlets laid out a codified set of beliefs to which Mennonites were expected to adhere. The defining significance given to specific rules was a reconfiguration of faithfulness, a new, less historical approach to defining faith and life for the Mennonite Church.[26] The 1898 edition of 272 pages was titled *Manual of Bible Doctrines: Setting Forth the General Principles of the Plan of Salvation, Explaining the Symbolical Meaning and Practical Use of the Ordinances Instituted by Christ and His Apostles, and Pointing Out Specifically some of the Restrictions which the New Testament Scriptures Enjoin upon Believers.* The important principle of nonresistance, living a peaceful life and refusing violence, was listed as a restriction. Later Anabaptist theologians acknowledged peace as the heart of the gospel, but Kauffman categorized important Anabaptist principles as restrictions, giving a negative impression that was likely not intended.[27]

The 1914 edition of 701 pages, titled *Bible Doctrine: A Treatise on the Great Doctrines of the Bible pertaining to God, Angels, Satan, the Church and the Salvation, Duties and Destiny of Man*, was compiled by a committee appointed by the Mennonite General Conference with Daniel Kauffman as editor. The title of the 1928 edition was not so lofty (*Doctrines of the Bible: A Brief Discussion of the Teachings of God's Word*), but it still contained 639 pages! The 1928 edition, "assisted by a committee of twenty-one brethren," omitted J. E. Hartzler's chapter on salvation that was part of the 1914 edition.[28]

In some places Kauffman's 1928 edition of *Doctrines of the Bible* is still in use.[29] For many years it was a primary textbook for Bible classes in some Mennonite schools. It was in the 1898 version that Kauffman first named the status of the devotional covering to be an ordinance, putting it in the same category as baptism and communion.[30] Kauffman's elevation of ordinances challenged individualism and emphasized the church, but the ordinances tended to be signs of ethical achievements instead of evidence of God's grace. There was a separation between doctrines and ethics, that is, what one believed and how one lived. These ordinances, especially the covering,

26. Erb and Gross, "Kauffman, Daniel." Doctrine is a codified set of beliefs that must be adhered to, rules to be followed. The term "doctrine" was hardly known within Mennonite circles before 1894 when Kauffman introduced the idea into the pages of the *Herald of Truth*.

27. T. Schlabach, "Reveille for *Die Stillen im Lande*," 225.

28. This was not surprising since Hartzler joined the "progressives" at Bluffton in 1921.

29. The Mennonite Historical Library holds a copy of the hardcover 2000 twenty-sixth printing of the 1928 version as well as an undated Spanish version with a 1986 binding.

30. Krahn and Rempel, "Ordinances." Kauffman also elevated the "kiss of peace" or "holy kiss" to the level of an ordinance. The seven ordinances taught to generations of MCs were baptism, communion, footwashing, marriage, anointing with oil, the holy kiss, and the prayer covering. In Mennonite tradition, most descriptions of ordinances focus on baptism and communion. However, the sixteenth century leader Dirk Philips (1504–68) also described seven ordinances, but his list did not include the devotional covering and the holy kiss.

helped to solidify boundaries between "old" Mennonites and other Protestants, including some other Mennonites.[31]

Daniel Kauffman was a churchman with strong intellect and personality and was very influential as a moderator of the MC general conference and member of numerous denominational committees. However, his greatest contribution to the Mennonite Church was probably through his editorial work. In 1905 he became editor of the *Gospel Witness* and in 1908 editor of its successor, the *Gospel Herald*, the official MC paper, remaining in this position through 1943. For these decades he had great influence on MCs where the pen was certainly "mightier than the sword." Although a theological conservative, Kauffman was often a reconciler of different views. Some Mennonite "crusaders" were even more conservative than Kauffman and accused him of a "liberal taint," especially in his 1914 edition of *Bible Doctrine*.[32]

Although by most standards Daniel Kauffman's professional life was marked by outstanding achievements, his personal life was one of multiple losses. On August 17, 1887, Kauffman married Ota J. Bowlin. After the birth of two children, one of whom died in infancy, Ota died in 1890. Twelve years later (February 6, 1902), he married Mary C. Shank, who survived him. However, of the six children born to them, one died at age three months, one died at age eight months, and one drowned when a teenager. The year was 1922 and Kauffman was serving as president of Goshen College. It was not a position to which Kauffman had aspired, but the Board of Education determined that he was the "man to stand in the gap" created by the tumultuous tensions surrounding the school. Kauffman moved his family from Scottdale, Pennsylvania, to Goshen for the school year and it was during Christmas vacation that "splendid and promising" sixteen-year-old Paul Kauffman, while skating with Goshen Academy classmates on the Elkhart River above the dam, broke through the ice and drowned.[33]

In spite of this great loss, there was little support for the conservative Kauffman among Goshen students and townspeople, who at least imagined running Kauffman out of town. Even though he was the "unmatched arbiter of mainstream Mennonite thought," he was fifty-seven years old and had been out of academia for many years.[34] It was for appropriate reasons that Kauffman's daughter described that academic year as a walk through the "Valley of Humiliation." If a leader such as Daniel Kauffman couldn't keep Goshen College open in 1923, its closing was likely inevitable. Kauffman went back to Scottdale and edited the *Gospel Herald* for twenty more years and Goshen College closed for the academic year 1923–24. When it re-opened it was quite a changed institution, and history would not forget the painful experiences of 1923–24.

31. Ibid. Published in 1954, J. C. Wenger's *Introduction to Theology* returned to a focus on two ordinances, baptism and communion, although footwashing and anointing with oil have also been essential Mennonite practices.

32. T. Schlabach, *Gospel Versus Gospel*, 115.

33. A. Gingerich, *Daniel Kauffman*, 80.

34. S. Miller, *Goshen College*, 81, 84.

Schlabach states that "the great failure of Daniel Kauffman was that he never marked out a third ground for Mennonites other than Protestant Fundamentalism and Protestant liberalism." A glimpse into the next era of Mennonite life shows that the influence of Daniel Kauffman gave way to the growing influence of Harold S. Bender and the "Anabaptist Vision" that he articulated. This relatively moderate way, somewhere between conservative fundamentalism and liberalism, attempted to understand scripture and life in light of Mennonite history and Mennonite understandings. Faithfulness and discipleship were emphasized over doctrine, right living over right beliefs.[35] Goshen College, an institution in which John Coffman, Daniel Kauffman, and H. S. Bender were all intimately involved, is one place to observe changes in the Mennonite church.

ELKHART INSTITUTE AND GOSHEN COLLEGE

The Goshen College motto, "culture for service," illustrates the tension between the church and academic arms of Mennonitism. From the beginning of the Elkhart Institute when there was a temporary split in the Prairie Street congregation[36] through 2012 when Mennonite Church members lament that Goshen College seniors are more unsettled in their faith than first year students, the tension has been alive. The tension was perhaps greatest in 1923 when the college closed for one year.

The Early Years

The Elkhart Institute, the forerunner of Goshen College, began in 1894 as a secondary school, first owned and operated by Dr. H. A. Mumaw, a Mennonite physician with a strong interest in education. In 1895 the school was transferred to corporate ownership and was run by an unofficial group of laymen and ministers in Elkhart until 1903, and then in Goshen (as Goshen College) until November 1905. In 1905 the school was turned over to the newly organized official church agency, the Mennonite Board of Education (MBE). Board members were selected from the regional conferences of the Mennonite and Amish Mennonite Churches. This put the management of the college into the hands of people from church conferences, some of whom didn't value the liberal arts education that the school was developing.

The school faced opposition and misunderstanding from the beginning. Many Mennonites were opposed to higher education; the fear was that education might lead to pride or people might give up nonconformity and/or leave the church. Indeed,

---

35. T. Schlabach, *Gospel Versus Gospel*, 116.

36. Although this could be an example of a congregation that split and then came back together, it lasted only a few years and is therefore considered significantly different from the eighty-six-year split in Middlebury.

C. Henry Smith confirmed that "humility was not one of our outstanding virtues as pioneer teachers at the institute. . ."[37]

As an evangelist, John S. Coffman was highly influential among Mennonites and Amish Mennonites and his sensitive advocating for Mennonite education persuaded many to become supportive of the Elkhart Institute. Numbers of students and support increased among both Mennonite and Amish Mennonites and in 1899 the Indiana-Michigan Amish Mennonite Conference officially endorsed the school.[38]

Jonas S. Hartzler (1857–1953), who had been pastor of Maple Grove Amish Mennonite Church and joined the faculty in 1895, was a key person in the early life of the Elkhart Institute and Goshen College. An early promoter of Mennonite education, Hartzler lamented that previously Mennonite young people had gone to schools of other denominations, saying, "The boys had the education, but other denominations had the boys." Later J. S. Hartzler served at Goshen as instructor in Bible and education, business manager, and first pastor of the congregation that met on the college campus.[39]

By 1896 the Elkhart Institute had enough students, faculty, and supporters to erect its own building on Elkhart's Prairie Street, opposite Prairie Street Mennonite Church. In 1898 Noah E. Byers, a Mennonite from Sterling, Illinois, was hired as principal.[40] Byers was a new graduate of Northwestern University with a large vision for Mennonite intellectual life and the ambition to raise Elkhart Institute's academic standards. The student body grew more rapidly beginning about 1900, reaching a peak of 245 in 1902–3, including the Summer Session and Special Bible Term. At that time the school had no campus other than the lot on which the building stood. The need for space for expansion led to the search for a new location that culminated in the move

37. Smith, *Mennonite Country Boy*, 190. C. Henry Smith (June 8, 1875–October 18, 1948) was born in Metamora, Illinois to bishop John and Magdalene Schertz Smith. Both of his grandfathers immigrated from Alsace-Lorraine about 1829. Smith was the first known American Mennonite to earn a PhD, doing so at the University of Chicago in 1907. He was dean and professor of history at Goshen College 1906–13 before going to teach at Bluffton College. Smith's doctoral dissertation was published as *The Mennonites in America* in 1909 and remained the only comprehensive Mennonite history of American Mennonites into the 1950s. Smith's legacy includes the C. Henry Smith Trust that sponsors an annual Peace Lecture given by a faculty member of a Mennonite-affiliated college or university, as well as oratorical contests at Mennonite-affiliated colleges and universities.

38. Preheim, "Indiana-Michigan Mennonite Conference."

39. S. Miller, *Goshen College*, 15. See footnote 37 in chapter 2 (page 39) for more biographical information on J. S. Hartzler.

40. Noah E. Byers (July 26, 1873–June 15, 1962) was a pioneer in Mennonite higher education, spending his active life as a teacher and administrator. He was one of the first members of the "old" Mennonite Church to attend high school and college, receiving a BS degree from Northwestern University (1898), an MA degree from Harvard (1903), and took additional graduate work at other universities. He served as principal of Elkhart Institute, (1898–1903), president of Goshen College (1903–13), and dean and professor of Bluffton College (1913–38). Byers also gave leadership to the movement for inter-Mennonite cooperation and unity. Willard Smith, "Byers, Noah E."

to Goshen in 1903 as the result of an attractive financial offer, with the condition that the name become Goshen College.[41]

Byers reorganized the school, established it on a sound academic basis, and then led its development into a junior college (1903) and finally a senior college (1908). Byers gathered a faculty who had studied at highly respected institutions. C. Henry Smith taught from 1898 to 1900 and then again joined the faculty in 1903 with a master's degree from the University of Chicago. He earned his PhD from the same school in 1907, served for a time as Goshen's academic dean. He later declared that faculty members were not

> . . . superannuated ministers nor outworn church workers. These young men were all fresh from college themselves, from such schools as Harvard, Northwestern, Chicago, Oberlin, and the University of Illinois. They had not yet outgrown their youthful enthusiasms. They were still eager students themselves and, consequently, inspiring teachers all of which had its influence on student ideals and purposes.[42]

The momentum begun at the Elkhart Institute continued in Goshen with seventy-seven students beginning the 1903 school year and fifty-eight new students enrolling in January 1904. Twelve faculty members, almost all under age thirty, taught with keen intellectual inquiry and a passion for expanding students' horizons. Although most faculty members were Mennonites, students' studies and experiences opened up the world far beyond Mennonite circles. The Young People's Christian Association (YPCA) was introduced by Byers at the Elkhart Institute and continued to thrive in Goshen. Soon the college sent delegates from its YMCA and YWCA to annual national conferences at Lake Geneva, Wisconsin, and Lakeside, Ohio, where they were exposed to Protestantism with a devotional flavor.

In keeping with the collegiate spirit of the time, school loyalty developed early at Goshen. The college song ("Goshen College, ever singing . . .") was composed in 1911 and students entered into friendly competition with other denominational colleges in oratory, debate, and athletics. J. S. Coffman's 1896 "spirit of progress" continued into the twentieth century along with a zeal for service informed by culture. From the time President Byers articulated the motto "culture for service" in his inaugural address in 1903 through the decades of seeking a balance between culture and service and Christian faith, the liberal arts foundation of the college has prevailed.

However, threats to the balance also occurred from the beginning. As noted above, control of the college changed from the unofficial group of ministers and interested people who were led by the progressive and independent-thinking Byers. The "take-over" of control of the college by the Mennonite Board of Education (MBE) in 1905 was part of the bigger movement in the "old" Mennonite Church to align all

41. Bender, "Elkhart Institute."
42. Smith, *Mennonite Country Boy*, 202.

the developing church agencies and institutions under one organized body, the General Conference of the "old" Mennonite Church. The advantage of having a system of checks and balances is clear. But the strain of being managed by a diverse group of people caught up in the cultural and religious tensions of fundamentalism and progressivism was great indeed.[43]

Because the college was located within the territories of Indiana Mennonite Conference and the Indiana-Michigan Amish Mennonite Conference, the ministers in those conferences put additional pressure on the college leadership and students to conform to conference guidelines. President Byers began wearing the plain coat in 1910, but in 1913 he resigned his Goshen position and accepted a position at Bluffton College, the progressive Mennonite school 130 miles east of Goshen. Goshen Dean C. Henry Smith as well as Professor Boyd D. Smucker followed Byers to Bluffton, and while Professor Paul Whitmer considered doing the same, he was persuaded to become the new Goshen dean. Moving into the Goshen presidency was the rather flamboyant, well-educated, evangelical preacher John Ellsworth Hartzler, thirty-four-year-old 1910 Goshen alumnus. Hartzler had been pastor of Prairie Street Mennonite Church since 1910 and professor and dean of Goshen's Bible department since 1911.[44]

In contrast to an early emphasis on opening the world to students, by 1914 the MBE began expressing concern about "safeguarding" students. A textbook committee was appointed to cull from both Goshen and Hesston College (begun in Kansas in 1909) any objectionable material that might sway students away from Mennonite conservative doctrine. Fear of the highly suspect and not clearly defined "modernism" prompted much concern for the MBE.[45]

Complaints from Mennonites, especially from three church leaders in the eastern states, George R. Brunk (senior) from Virginia, John H. Mosemann (senior) from Lancaster, and John Horsch from Scottdale, escalated to

> wholesale attacks on the character of the college. The young school's failures to
> meet church expectations formerly treated by critics as blemishes on a basical-
> ly healthy frame, were increasingly attributed to an unsound Goshen College

43. Theron Schlabach's *Gospel versus Gospel* includes an extensive review of Protestant Fundamentalism and fundamentalism among Mennonites. Paul Toews offers the following in "Fundamentalism": "Fundamentalism among Mennonites was as much an effort to redefine the relationship between culture and Christianity as a crusade to root out theological modernism. It was significantly a cultural movement because the theological modernism in the Mennonite world was only incipient and marginal. Cultural Fundamentalism was a way to codify doctrine, reassert churchly authority and redefine cultural boundaries. More rigid forms of authority and order are antidotes to rapid social change."

44. See footnote 13 in chapter 1 (page 8) for more biographical information on J. E. Hartzler.

45. S. Miller, *Goshen College*, 58–60. Modernism was a movement within Protestant Christianity originating in the latter half of the nineteenth century that sought to establish the meaning and validity of Christian faith in relation to human experience and to reconcile and unify traditional theological concepts with the requirements of modern knowledge. Modernism generally implied an acceptance of biblical criticism, openness to Darwin's theory of evolution, and belief in the human potential of solving all social problems.

as such, as if the institution itself were diseased . . . . An engagement by a range of Mennonite thinkers with the difficult questions posed by bringing the liberal arts into a sectarian Christian setting undoubtedly would have served the institution and its constituents well. But most Goshen College critics after 1913 gave themselves more readily to anxiety over the vaguely-defined threat of modernism—an all-purpose bogeyman brought to Mennonites' attention mainly by the literature of Protestant Fundamentalism—than they did to more particular, pertinent questions about Mennonite acculturation that might profitably been raised at this time. Such questions about Mennonite acculturation were actually as much church as college issues. But they were being lost in a general, often sloppily-conducted national debate about modernism, fundamentalism, liberalism, and so forth . . .[46]

Illustrative of the difference in "liberal" and "conservative" thinking is an exchange between J. E. Hartzler and John Horsch.[47] President Hartzler supported a progressive, liberal arts education that prepares students to contribute to and improve the modern world. The idea of active participation in the world was inconsistent with the traditional Mennonite interpretation of nonconformity and separation from the world. John Horsch, the former Mennonite Publishing Company employee in Elkhart, was a fervent conservative defender living in Scottdale, Pennsylvania, in 1913. He sent the new Goshen president a letter criticizing Hartzler for his liberal agenda that he understood to be in conflict with solid, biblical fundamentals. "I believe religion must be founded on an unchanging body of dogma," Horsch wrote. Hartzler responded by referring to the Sunday schools, publications, and mission advancements initiated by Horsch's peers. "Christianity never changes; Christianity never disintegrates; the Gospel of Christ is always the same," Hartzler wrote. "But men do change their interpretations of the Gospel and change their methods of application of the same."[48]

The ingenuity, dedication, and perseverance of President J. E. Hartzler and the loyal J. S. Hartzler (Bible professor and business manager of the college and treasurer of the MBE) kept Goshen College moving forward with a new science hall and experimental farm for the new agricultural program. However, in spite of admirable fundraising efforts on the part of both Hartzlers, donations did not keep up with expenses. In addition to financial strain, other tensions that had been brewing at the college erupted in 1916–17 with the joining of the Indiana Mennonite Conference and Indiana-Michigan Amish Mennonite Conference.

Many observed that in this merger greater power was given to the conference and its bishops. Authority in the leadership was the Mennonite model as compared

---

46. Ibid., 60.

47. In 1913 John Horsch (December 18, 1867–October 7, 1941) was German editor at the Mennonite Publishing House in Scottdale, Pennsylvania, and researcher and writer of Mennonite history and theology.

48. Preheim, "Indiana-Michigan Mennonite Conference."

with the Amish Mennonite polity of more congregational autonomy. Regulation dress was the big issue. All members were expected to "refrain from conforming to the world: the brethren in wearing gaudy dress, fashionable hats . . . etc.; the sisters in wearing insufficient, transparent, or superfluous attire." Women were expected to wear only plain bonnets.[49]

The "irregularities" of Hartzler and Hartzler in the financial management of the college came to the attention of the Board of Education in 1917, resulting in the resignations of both J. S. Hartzler and J. E. Hartzler during the 1917–18 school year. Along with numerous other church responsibilities, J. S. remained pastor of the College Church congregation until 1923 and was then pastor of Prairie Street Mennonite Church from 1923 until 1940. In 1918 J. E. left for Bethel, the GC school in Kansas, where he was professor of Bible and then president in 1920–21. In 1921 he became president of Witmarsum Theological Seminary at Bluffton, Ohio.

One man who loved Goshen College and would have preferred to remain there was Paul E. Whitmer, professor of English and Bible from 1908 to 1916. Whitmer was also pastor of College Mennonite Church periodically during those years (1905–6, 1910–13, and 1916–17).[50] In his unpublished autobiography he tells about the great dilemma he and his wife (Fannie Yoder) faced when in 1916 he was told directly that remaining at Goshen for all faculty members would depend on adherence to the demands on dress. The local conference was putting on the pressure to "conform or get out." He described it as a struggle between personal and denominational nonconformity.[51] Whitmer joined Byers and Smith at Bluffton in 1917.

The newly-merged conference also objected to Goshen's intercollegiate athletics and choir concerts in non-Mennonite churches and held a special session in 1920 to address the concerns, particularly dress. The conference urged the MBE to do its utmost to police the school. (Interestingly, some of the same men served on both the MBE and conference executive committee.) Four presidents followed in the five years following Hartzler's departure: missionary George J. Lapp, MBE president H. Frank Reist, minister Irvin R. Detweiler, and publisher Daniel Kauffman. Finally at its annual meeting on June 18, 1923, the MBE decided to shut down Goshen College for a year, providing time for a conservative shift in policy and procedures and for nonconforming faculty members to be replaced with people who agreed to tow the line. This action underscored the effect that Fundamentalism was having on church leaders and the power in the hierarchical structure that had come into the "old" Mennonite Church.

When Goshen College reopened in September of 1924, a somewhat somber faculty was under the leadership of Sanford C. Yoder, a minister and bishop from Iowa who had served on the MBE and was secretary of the Board of Missions and Charities. An illustration of the change in Goshen College is in the story of Harold S. Bender,

49. Springer, *Centennial Chronicles*, 18.

50. See footnote 23 in chapter 2 (page 34) for more biographical information on Whitmer.

51. Whitmer, *Autobiography*.

graduate of the class of 1918. Harold had taught two years at Hesston College, studied theology at both Garrett Institute and Princeton Seminary, married Elizabeth Horsch, and was studying in Europe during the year Goshen College was closed. S. C. Yoder invited Harold to join the faculty in 1924, but much negotiating took place before the deal was sealed, and plain attire was only a small part issue. Harold had been part of a progressive Goshen College and maintained friendships and academic ties with many progressives. He was theologically orthodox and conservative and yet he was progressive in his tolerance for opposing viewpoints—and in Europe Harold had worn a mustache and Elizabeth a hat! Consequently, Yoder assigned him to teach history instead of Bible and theology, even though he had as much or more theological education than any other MC Mennonite. He would have to win the confidence of the people of northern Indiana (that is, a committee of the Indiana-Michigan Conference) before he could teach Bible and theology.[52]

Congregations in Goshen and Middlebury

The early life of Goshen College parallels in time the beginning of the Mennonite congregations in Middlebury. Mennonite churches began in both Middlebury and Goshen in 1903. On the Goshen College campus, a unique congregation came into being that reflected the two main strands of the college's constituency, Mennonite and Amish Mennonite. The congregation chose to affiliate with both conferences, an unprecedented undertaking that was complicated but manageable. In 1904 fifteen college students made Christian confessions and were baptized. The Mennonite students received baptism indoors in February, while the Amish Mennonite candidates waited until April when the temperature of a nearby stream was warm enough for their bishop to perform the ceremony by "pouring" while standing in the stream.[53]

The issues at College Mennonite Church in the early 1920s were similar to those in Middlebury and some of the players were the very same people. As bishop for both the Middlebury Church and the Goshen College Church, D. D. Miller was the link to the conference for both congregations. It was his responsibility to keep people in the congregations in line with conference expectations. Joe Springer explains that "having survived recent threats to its power, the Indiana-Michigan Conference executive committee had begun re-exerting its authority over congregations, using issues like bonnets and life insurance as tests." Trying to maintain normalcy, College Mennonite Church met to select Sunday school officers on August 27, 1924. Bishop D. D. Miller and fellow bishop Dan Troyer arrived at the meeting and announced that it would be useless "to reorganize as [this] would not be recognized by conference or school board." What

52. Keim, *Bender*, 161–6.
53. S. Miller, "One remarkable year."

Miller offered instead was a plan that required that "members who wished to remain in good standing" would sign a statement saying they would be loyal to the conference.[54]

Somewhat different but corresponding events occurred in Middlebury in 1923. Though not as well documented as the interactions in Goshen, the Middlebury story through the beginning of the Warren Street Mennonite Church is told in chapter 4.

BLUFFTON COLLEGE/UNIVERSITY[55]
AND WITMARSUM THEOLOGICAL SEMINARY

From its beginning, Warren Street Mennonite Church had associations with Bluffton College and Witmarsum Theological Seminary. The preacher at the Warren Street dedication service on May 24, 1924, was Paul Whitmer, then dean of the seminary at Bluffton. J. E. Hartzler preached at Warren Street on August 10, 1924, the first of numerous visits to the congregation. At that time Hartzler was president of the Witmarsum Seminary.

The closing of the Wadsworth School in 1878 left central Ohio without a Mennonite institution of higher learning, but interest in a church school did not disappear. Before continuing the pursuit of a General Conference college, S. F. Sprunger from Berne insisted that the promoters *consider* uniting efforts with the MC school already begun in Elkhart. Consequently, in 1897 Sprunger, Noah Hirschy, and J. F. Lehman went to Elkhart to visit with John F. Funk and have dinner with John S. Coffman. Theological and cultural differences between GCs and MCs were too great to collaborate at that time, so plans for a GC school continued.[56]

Bluffton College began in Bluffton, Ohio, in 1899 as Central Mennonite College, a school of the Middle District of the General Conference Mennonite Church. Having a relatively small group of constituents, this GC school sought other than Mennonite students, becoming more of a community college than Goshen. The school struggled, but a significant boost came to Bluffton in 1913 when twenty-four educational leaders determined that it was time for a Mennonite theological seminary that would serve all Mennonites and that the institution should be established in connection with one of the schools already controlled by the Mennonite people. Goshen and Bethel (in Kansas) were the only Mennonite colleges offering a full four-year college course at that time, yet neither chose to house the seminary. So Central Mennonite in Bluffton, though but a small junior college with an uncertain future, was the chosen location, and the school became Bluffton College and Mennonite Seminary in 1914.

In 1921 the seminary became a separate institution with the name Witmarsum Mennonite Seminary (named after Menno Simons' birthplace). Designed to be a unifying agency among Mennonites, the board of trustees of the seminary included

54. Springer, *Centennial Chronicles*, 26.

55. Bluffton College became Bluffton University in 2004.

56. Bush, *Kobzar*, 34.

representatives from six different Mennonite branches in North America: General Conference Mennonite, Central Conference, Mennonite Brethren, "old" Mennonite, Evangelical Mennonite, and Mennonite Brethren in Christ. Although the seminary had students from all six Mennonite groups, the support was limited largely to the General Conference and Central Conference groups. Leading the Witmarsum Seminary were J. E. Hartzler as president and Paul Whitmer as dean. Both had served as MC pastors and college professors and Hartzler had been president of two colleges, Goshen and Bethel. Witmarsum students came mostly from Bluffton and Bethel Colleges, with a few from Goshen. The Seminary graduated a total of twenty-six men and three women in its eleven-year history before closing in May 1931.[57]

Noah Calvin Hirschy was the first president of Central Mennonite College. Samuel K. Mosiman joined the faculty in 1908 and became president of Central Mennonite/Bluffton College in 1910, a position he maintained until 1935.[58] Mosiman was known for his skills of tact and church diplomacy.[59] Along with Noah Byers and C. Henry Smith, who left Goshen College in 1913 and joined the faculty at Bluffton, Mosiman led the school in not only Biblical and theological progressivism, but also promoted political progressivism. At one point Mosiman dabbled in Democratic Party politics in Ohio and later Bluffton leaders supported Republican Party members and embraced national political progressivism. In addition, American nationalism found some acceptance among Bluffton leaders, with Mosiman describing a new men's dormitory (Lincoln Hall) as an "incentive to the development of patriotism and as a stimulus to the study of good Government," and Smith writing a series of articles in 1914 for the *Christian Evangel* titled "The Hand of God in American History."[60]

Historian Perry Bush describes Bluffton as creatively utilizing "a progressive Anabaptist approach to Mennonite higher education." While that summarizes more than a century of an institution's engagement with academia, faith, and culture, "joining

57. Whitmer, "Witmarsum Theological Seminary." After 14 years the seminary reopened in Chicago under a new name (Mennonite Biblical Seminary) and organization but with the help of $11,000 in liquid assets and the library and equipment of Witmarsum Seminary. In 1958 Mennonite Biblical Seminary joined with Goshen Biblical ("old" Mennonite) Seminary to become Associated Mennonite Biblical Seminaries. In 2012 the name was changed to Anabaptist Mennonite Biblical Seminary.

58. Samuel K. Mosiman (December 17, 1867–January 24, 1940), son of Christian and Anna Kinsinger Mosiman, grew up near Trenton, Ohio; studied at Wittenberg Academy and College, Springfield, Ohio, where he received his BA in 1897; served as superintendent of the Mennonite Indian Mission school in Oklahoma 1897–1903; BD from McCormick Theological Seminary, Chicago, in 1905; PhD from Halle-Wittenburg University, Germany, in 1907; married Amalia Krehbiel in 1902; she died on the ship en route to Germany with Mosiman in 1905; married Emilie Hamm in 1909; they had no children. Although Bluffton had many long-term faculty members, only one person served as Bluffton's president longer than Mosiman's twenty-five years. Lloyd L. Ramseyer (married to Ferne Yoder from Middlebury) was president for twenty-seven years, 1938–65.

59. Bush, *Kobzar*, 60–62. Mosiman's wife, Emilie Hamm, remembered for her big floral hats and flowing skirts, became known as Bluffton's First Lady. At age twelve she had migrated from Prussia to Nebraska with a prominent Mennonite family and she and Mosiman married in 1909.

60. Bush, *Kobzar*, 67–68.

Mennonite culture and consciousness with that of a progressive, democratic American society" was difficult at times and perhaps impossible at other times. President Mosiman gave contradictory messages during the First World War. While giving a nod to Mennonite pacifist principles, he also spoke forthrightly in support of the war. When the United States entered the conflict, Mosiman wrote to his friend James Cox, then governor of Ohio, saying, "Believing it to be the duty of each citizen to bear his part of the burden of war and his share of the perils . . . assign me to any work that I can do." He also offered that Bluffton students would "do all that lies in their power to alleviate the sufferings of our soldiers . . . or do any work that they can do and to which you may call them." He explicitly encouraged young men to enter noncombatant service (the only form of alternative service that was legal in World War I), urging them to be patriotic.[61]

Meanwhile at Goshen and in many other Mennonite communities, the First World War brought Mennonite church leaders, members, and scholars face to face with their core beliefs regarding the teachings of Jesus. While Mosiman was president at Bluffton, H. S. Bender and Guy Hershberger joined the Goshen College faculty and would lead the Mennonite world in understanding peace to be at the heart of the gospel. In the "old" Mennonite Church there were numerous incidents of angry reactions on the part of both government and neighbors against Mennonites. In August 1918, US federal agents raided the Mennonite Publishing House in Scottdale, Pennsylvania, and confiscated its supply of brochures explaining nonresistance. While many Amish and MC young men suffered torture and imprisonment for being conscientious objectors, Mosiman considered the advice of MC and Amish leaders who encouraged noncooperation with military orders to be "wicked and foolish."[62]

Numerous stories illustrate how war bonds were viewed from polar opposite extremes among Mennonite folk during World War I. On one hand, strong pacifists and war resisters were forced to purchase war bonds. A series of stories is told by James Juhnke about incidents in Kansas in which numerous Mennonites were persecuted for refusing to buy war bonds.[63] Although not necessarily representing the majority of Bluffton faculty during the years of World War I, Mosiman promoted the purchase of war bonds. One might wonder if his time of study in Europe was a factor in his patriotic leanings.

President Mosiman estimated that by 1919 about 150 Bluffton students had served in the military in some capacity in addition to five faculty members. And yet peace rhetoric continued and in 1922 Bluffton hosted a major conference of the three

61. Bush, *Kobzar*, 19, 36, 67, 85. James Cox had been a guest in the Mosiman home and gave a speech on campus on at least one occasion in 1913. It is important to acknowledge that not all leaders at Bluffton College were ambivalent about the traditional Mennonite peace position. Lloyd Ramseyer (president 1938–65) "was a valiant proponent of truth, forthrightness and practicality in all phases of life and a strong supporter of the Mennonite peace position at a time when such a firm stand was not popular." Gratz, Delbert. "Ramseyer."

62. Loewen and Nolt, *Through Fire and Water*, 168; Bush, *Kobzar*, 84–85.

63. Juhnke, "Mob Violence and Kansas Mennonites."

historic peace churches. Still, there was a growing distance between the college and some of the Mennonite groups that had supported Bluffton in 1913. Central Conference leader Aaron Augsburger accused the college of not upholding Mennonite peace principles and the Mennonite Brethren in Christ and the Defenseless Mennonites withdrew their support in the early 1920s.[64]

Mosiman and some faculty members were distracted by numerous accusations of modernism, which were for the most part false claims. Blufftonites were progressive, not modernists. Mosiman claimed he and the school held to a "conservative evangelical theology," but they were clearly not into Fundamentalism, a movement that engaged many Mennonites. Nevertheless, Bluffton's student population grew, reaching 300 in the 1923–24 school year with an influx of students from Goshen during its year of closing. In 1925 Bluffton's total enrollment was 395 with 70 percent of the students from Mennonite homes and six branches of Mennonites represented. Twelve other denominations were also represented and students came from eleven different states with Ohio, Indiana, Illinois, and Pennsylvania leading in the order named. The effects of the depressing US economy in addition to criticisms of liberalism (if not modernism), even from former supporters in GC congregations, was a smaller student body with fewer Mennonites—less than 50 percent in 1929.[65]

It is not known if President Mosiman or C. Henry Smith ever visited Warren Street in Middlebury, but as noted above, J. E. Hartzler was a regular guest. This suggests that the progressive themes that were prevalent at Bluffton were well received at Warren Street. Did the Mosiman ambivalence about participating in and supporting war seep into the minds of Warren Street members? How did connections with various progressive Mennonites affect the thoughts and practices of Mennonites in Middlebury? Did the vibes of individualism promoted by J. E. Hartzler find a home at Warren Street as the congregation wrestled with questions of authority?[66]

Susan Fisher Miller, author of Goshen College's centennial history, points out that three men, all living in 1923, symbolize several generations who had vied for authority in the Mennonite Church. J. E. Hartzler remained a liberal-leaning progressive throughout his life, serving first as a minister in the "old" church, then professor and president of both Goshen College and Bethel College (Kansas), president of Witmarsum Seminary, and professor at Hartford Seminary. In some ways Hartzler took a circuitous path, returning to Goshen for the last years of his life. Daniel Kauffman, who as a young man in Missouri was considered progressive, later came to represent and speak for the conservative element of the church as publisher, writer of doctrine, member of the Mennonite Board of Education, and Goshen College president for one year. The octogenarian John F. Funk had led the church with progressive ideas from 1870 to 1900 as a publisher and minister. "Each of these figures, in their turn

---

64. Bush, *Kobzar*, 86–87, 98.

65. Bush, *Kobzar*, 86; Smith, C. Henry, "Bluffton"; Bush, *Kobzar*, 95, 113.

66. Individualism is discussed further in chapter 10.

and in varying degrees, had felt their base of authority shift underfoot in response to counter-currents in the church."[67]

The stories of three Weaver siblings from LaGrange County, Indiana, is illustrative of how some people coped with the currents and counter-currents of the "old" Mennonite Church in the early twentieth century. In a highly unusual move, Sam Weaver (1880–1935) resigned from his position as minister at Forks Amish Mennonite Church and joined a Central Conference church (Eighth Street) in 1923. William B. Weaver (1887–1963) was ordained in the "old" Mennonite Church, was pastor of Prairie Street for six years, taught at Goshen College for eight years, and then became pastor of a Central Conference church (North Danvers) in 1922. A sister, Vinora Weaver Salzman (1885–1990), attended Goshen College and briefly taught there. After serving with MCC in Constantinople, she joined a Central Conference congregation in Illinois and remained with General Conference congregations for the remainder of her life. She was very involved in the life of the church, often preaching and even being invited to pastoral positions. Instead, she kept lower profile jobs, her final one being in the library at the Mennonite seminary in Elkhart (1961–72). During her time there, the MC and GC seminaries merged, a significant step toward the eventual merger of these two Mennonite denominations.

67. S. Miller, *Goshen College*, 93.

4

The "First" Mennonite Congregation in Middlebury

I was glad when they said to me,
"Let us go to the house of the Lord!"

PSALM 122:1

Where did you get that hat? Where did you get that tile?
Isn't it a nobby one, and just the proper style?
I should like to have one just the same as that.
Where'er I go they shout "Hello! Where did you get that hat?"

JOSEPH J. SULLIVAN, 1888

IT'S LIKELY THAT "WHERE did you get that hat" was sung in Middlebury during the early years of the twentieth century. The town band may have played this catchy tune at a concert. "A new bandstand is being built in the town park," reported the *Middlebury Independent* on Friday, July 21, 1922, and it was hoped that it would be finished in time for the concert the following Thursday evening. Harry Bloom reported that the town had several bands that gave weekly concerts on "balmy summer evenings, with now and then an ice cream social to top off the event."[1]

If the song "Where did you get that hat" was being played and sung around Middlebury in 1922, it is easy to imagine that young women, including Mennonite young women, would want to wear a *nobby* (first quality or finest design) hat—not an old-fashioned bonnet!

At least a few Middlebury Mennonites participated in school and town music groups in the 1920s and 1930s. Lowell Troyer was in the 1925–26 Middlebury School

---

1. Middlebury History Committee, *Town Beautiful*, 165.

Orchestra and a few years later, both Lowell and his brother Lotus were in the Middlebury German Band, not only playing horns but also sporting mustaches. In 1941 Doneta Hershberger (later Burkhardt) modeled the high school band uniform.[2] Doneta's parents (Freed and Nina Hershberger) as well as Lotus and Lowell's parents (Ellsworth and Edna Troyer) were charter members of the Warren Street congregation in 1923. Would these young people have been playing band instruments if their parents had remained in the Amish Mennonite Church?

At the turn of the twentieth century Middlebury did not have a Mennonite church. However, by 1902 about forty Mennonites and Amish Mennonites had moved into Middlebury and the near vicinity. A group of twelve people from the Forks, Shore, and Clinton churches met together in August 1902 in the home of Dr. and Mrs. William B. Page.[3] Dr. Page and his wife, Alice Thut Page, had recently returned from the mission field. They had been two of the first three "old" Mennonite missionaries to go to India, William being the first medical missionary. While William (who had connections with the Forks congregation) was in medical school in Chicago, he and Alice were among the founders of the Chicago Home Mission. After a farewell service at Prairie Street Mennonite Church in Elkhart on February 15, 1899, they set sail for India one week later with their infant son.[4]

Of course there was not a lot of international travel in those days, but George Lambert, an Elkhart Mennonite, had traveled the world. There was a severe famine in India beginning in 1897, and in *India, the Horror-Stricken Empire,* Lambert reported and illustrated the desperate famine conditions that he had witnessed firsthand. Upon arriving in India, Dr. Page wrote, "We at once find everything very much different from anything that we have ever seen before." Students and faculty of the Elkhart Institute followed with interest what was happening in this missionary effort. In an October 1899 issue of the *Institute Monthly* (the Elkhart Institute's newspaper) was a front page photograph of Jacob A. Ressler (the third missionary who had gone with the Page family) with Dr. and Mrs. Page, all wearing white cork helmets, standing in front of a grove of palm trees.[5]

Foreign mission experiences gave inquiring Mennonites significant openings into a world much larger than most folks in Middlebury could imagine in the early

2. Middlebury History Committee, *Town Beautiful,* 167–68. Lowell and Lotus Troyer were both baptized at Warren Street Mennonite Church and later were both ordained as Mennonite ministers.

3. William B. Page (January 5, 1871–June 14, 1945) was born in Pennsylvania to Tobias and Anna Brubaker Page who moved to northern Indiana in 1889. William graduated from Valparaiso University in 1887, Ada College (Ohio) in 1890, and Chicago Medical College in 1896; He married Alice Thut July 3, 1895. Alice (February 1872– September 22, 1951) was the daughter of Peter B. and Mary Steiner Thut who moved to Middlebury in 1901.

4. William B. Weaver, *History of the Central Conference,* 127. Weaver was a fifteen-year-old living in LaGrange County in 1902; Sam Troyer in a historical information report in the Mennonite Archives, First Mennonite Church, Middlebury, Indiana, III–14–31, box 1/3; Bontrager, *Forks Mennonite Church,* 24.

5. Susan Fisher Miller, *Culture for Service,* 26–30.

1900s. Middlebury Mennonites were likely fascinated with the opportunity to visit with people who had lived in Chicago and India—though only briefly in India, as the Page family returned to Indiana in 1900 due to illness.

The Pages and Ressler located in Dhamtari (a town in east central India) in November 1899 just as another famine was reaching its worst point. They initially built bamboo huts in which to live but soon built bungalows, a hospital, and an orphanage. The Indian government was doing relief work at Dhamtari, and officials were grateful for the help of the missionaries, but alas! Dr. Page overworked.

> Dr. Page was given charge of the government poor house and kitchen and he undertook the construction of numerous wells in Dhamtari. He at one time had seventeen wells in operation. In March 1900, cholera broke out which raged for four months. He attended every call that came to him from those stricken with the dread disease besides keeping his hospital and dispensary going. Poor-house patients numbered between thirty and fifty each day. Fifteen hundred men, women, and children were fed in the kitchen.[6]

Due to overwork, Dr. Page himself became ill with cholera, and because he had not recovered by July 1900, he was taken to Calcutta where he was hospitalized for severe dysentery. When he was finally released more than a month later, he weighed only 110 pounds and was "told to remember that one foot was still deep down in the grave" and that he should not return to work for at least six months. Reluctantly, the Page family returned to America in October 1900. They settled in Middlebury in 1902 where Dr. Page practiced medicine. In 1910 they moved to Goshen and were founding members of the Eighth Street Mennonite Church.[7]

THE EARLY YEARS

During the winter of 1902–1903 a group began to meet in Middlebury weekly for a song and prayer service and to study the Sunday school lesson for the following Sunday. The group met in the Ben A. and Clara (Hochstetler) Bontrager home on East Warren Street and increased in number to about forty. Although preaching services didn't begin until 1904, a Sunday school was formally organized on May 10, 1903. The May 8, 1903, issue of the *Middlebury Independent* reported that "the Mennonites have made arrangements to hold services in Prescott's Hall and will meet there Sunday at 5:00 p.m. to organize Sunday school. They will arrange for regular preaching services later." At that time Prescott Hall was apparently one block west of the post office. The building had first been the Middlebury Baptist Church, erected in 1843 on the north

6. "Doctor, Missionary, Called Away in Death," *Mennonite Weekly Review*, June 28, 1945, 1.

7. Jacob A. Ressler, "The Hospital" in a Report Booklet from the Mission Committee. Mennonite Archives, William B. and Alice Thut Page Papers, 1898–1951. Box 1, Folder 12. HM1–371; "Doctor, Missionary, Called Away in Death," *Mennonite Weekly Review*, June 28, 1945, 1.

edge of the city park. In 1877 O. O. Prescott purchased the building and moved it several blocks. Prescott remodeled the building and made it into a playhouse and dance hall. The town history book reports that many were "the parties that have held forth within its walls"! The Middlebury Mennonites rented this hall in 1903 and later purchased it and used it until 1911.[8]

Leaders of the Middlebury Sunday school kept records from June 7, 1903, through at least July 22, 1906. Attendance was sixty-one on that first Sunday in June with fifty pupils, seven teachers, and four officers. The "collection" totaled $.91 that day. The teachers were Brother Stalter, Sister Balyeat, Mrs. Karch, Sister Page, Brother Blough, Brother Bontrager, and Brother Hostetler. Additional teachers during the next months included Brother Honburger, Brother Honerich, and Sister Thut (perhaps the mother or a sister of Mrs. Page).[9]

Along with the attendance and collection totals, the minutes include the number of the opening song for each Sunday, the scripture passage read, the name of the lesson for the day, and often the name of the person (always a man) who prayed—one of the male Sunday School teachers or Brother Stauffer, Brother Hooley, Brother Thut, or Brother Yoder. The song leader is not named in the minutes nor is the name of the songbook given. It may have been the *Church and Sunday School Hymnal with Supplement* printed in 1902 by J. S. Shoemaker in Freeport, Illinois, or *A Collection of Psalms and Hymns Suited to the Various Occasions of Public Worship and Private Devotion*.[10]

The leaders must have been pleased when an additional eighteen people came on the second Sunday (June 14, 1903). There were seventy-nine people present and $1.07 was collected. For the next three years the attendance varied from twenty-two to one hundred seventeen. The record does not indicate whether these are children or adults or some of each. It can be assumed that at least some of the classes were for children as there were female teachers. On at least one Sunday there were four female teachers.[11]

The October 9, 1904, minutes begin including the number of visitors at the Sunday school. These numbers vary from zero to thirty-three. Sometimes the number of visitors is a high percentage of the number of attendees. For example, on November

8. Middlebury History Committee, *Town Beautiful*, 43, 193. The *Middlebury Independent* gives the rental fee as $20 per annum and Sam Troyer gives the fee as $40 per year. Sam reported that the congregation later bought the building and equipment, lights, chairs, stoves, etc. for $500.

9. Ben A. Bontrager (1858–1943), "Sunday School Records, 1903–1906," Mennonite Archives, First Mennonite Church, Middlebury, Indiana, III–14–31, box 1, folder 2. Although the script used in this record varies, inside the front cover is written: "Records Kept by Ben A. Bontrager, 1858–1943, Charter Member of the Middlebury Congregation." Only two signatures of the Sunday school minutes are noted, that of Inez Bernice Schrock on July 10, 1904, and July 2, 1905, and periodically thereafter and Nellie Bontrager on May 27, 1906. The record book does not include the names of teachers after October 4, 1903, nor are the first names of teachers given. Neither are the classes described other than by numbers one through seven.

10. Ibid. *A Collection of Psalms* had been compiled by a committee of Mennonites in Virginia and had been printed by John Funk in Elkhart.

11. Bontrager, "Sunday School Records."

13, 1904, there were thirty visitors out of ninety people present; on December 4, 1904, there were thirty-three visitors out of seventy-four people present; and on May 6, 1906, there were fifty-four visitors out of one hundred one people present.[12]

The "collection" during 1903 to 1906 varied from $.39 to $1.91, averaging about one and one-half cents per person per Sunday. The record indicates that money was paid to the Mennonite Publishing Company in Elkhart and to David Cook Publishers for Sunday school materials. On the back page and inside the back cover is the following: Dr. Page, Superintendent; Henry Karch, Assistant Superintendent; Madie Bontrager, Secretary; David Blough, Chorister; Charlotte Thut (sister of Alice Page), Assistant Chorister. Other names listed are Elmer Walters, Mrs. Walters, and Mary Thut (mother of Alice Page).[13]

The Middlebury Mennonite Church was organized in 1904 after a petition with thirty-four signatures had been presented to both the Mennonite and the Amish Mennonite conferences. Records indicate there were thirty-two charter members, and it is thought that preaching services began on Sunday, July 31, 1904, with Daniel D. Miller of Forks Amish Mennonite Church preaching the first sermon.[14]

Dr. William Page was elected moderator of the group, and a business committee was selected that included Henry Karch (later a charter member of Warren Street), B. A. Bontrager, and P. B. Thut.[15] Andrew J. (A. J.) Hostetler, who had been ordained deacon at Forks in 1896 and preacher in 1898, became the first pastor of the Middlebury congregation,[16] and D. J. Johns served as bishop. The first communion services were held on November 13, 1904, with D. J. Johns officiating, assisted by Simon S. Yoder, at that time a deacon in the Forks congregation.[17]

The Middlebury congregation purchased three lots on Lawrence Street, and "with the aid of the town people and the surrounding congregations a substantial

12. Ibid.

13. Ibid. The record shows that $10.71 was paid to Mennonite Publishing Company and $11.59 was paid to David Cook during those three years. On the last page is a list of papers that include: "little learners paper, junior quarterlies, and cooks comprehensive quarterly scholars addition [*sic*] with text."

14. "Churches Have Important Place," *Middlebury Independent*, June 18, 1936; Wenger, "First Mennonite." Daniel D. Miller would become a bishop in 1906. In 1904 he was a preacher. He was the bishop who denied communion to the young women at Middlebury Mennonite in 1923. The records about the date of the first preaching service are not consistent.

15. P. B. Thut was likely Peter B. Thut, the father of Alice Page.

16. Andrew J. Hostetler (August 18, 1858–November 24, 1925) was born in Holmes County, Ohio, moved with his family to Emma, Indiana, at age six, and to Middlebury in 1890. His first wife, Anna A. Schrock, died February 20, 1891, leaving Hostetler with two young children, Cora (January 27, 1886–July 17, 1911) and Charles (November 1, 1888–April 25, 1950). He married Rebecca Hostetler (August 31, 1870–1965) on December 27, 1891 and they had one child who lived to adulthood—Leroy (Roy), who according to Joni Hochstetler (reported to J. O. Yoder in 2011) married Pearl Mast and died as a young man.

17. "Churches Have Important Place," *Middlebury Independent*, June 18, 1936, 4. In about 1913, D. J. Johns was relieved from the work of bishop in Middlebury and the congregation was assigned to D. D. Miller of the Forks congregation.

brick building was erected" in 1911. The building was constructed by Jacob C. Hershberger for $6000 on East Lawrence Street, just east of South Main Street in downtown Middlebury at the location where it has remained for more than 100 years. When the building was dedicated on August 20, 1911, there were 126 members.[18]

The Mennonite Church of Middlebury on Lawrence Street built in 1911.

Simon S. Yoder transferred his membership from the Forks congregation to the Middlebury congregation, and in 1907 he was ordained into the preaching ministry. In the absence of a deacon, the congregation appointed members to act as "visiting brethren" until November 11, 1911, when deacon Jacob C. Hershberger transferred his membership from the Clinton Brick congregation.[19] On October 14, 1920, the membership had reached 228, but "lost out again," so that in November 1923 the membership was 110.[20]

S. S. Yoder focused on the positive contributions of people and did not like to dwell on negativism and nonessentials. He was first a farmer and school teacher and then a minister—because he had been chosen by lot. So he was naturally interested in Christian education. Yoder was remembered as a progressive leader for the time that he served. Ernest Litwiller, who was a young person in the Middlebury church in the early 1900s, remembers that Yoder organized a literary club called Orion. This club was for high school and young married people. The purpose was to have a positive atmosphere in which young people could meet and learn about literature. These were

18. "Churches Have Important Place"; Sam Troyer report, Mennonite Archives, First Mennonite Church, Middlebury, Indiana, III–14–31, box 1/3.

19. Jacob C. Hershberger was the father of Freed Hershberger and grandfather of Don Hershberger and numerous other people in WSMC/POMC. According to Ken Pletcher, another descendent, this was the same Jacob C. Hershberger who built the 1911 meetinghouse.

20. "Churches Have Important Place." Likely 'lost out again' refers to the departure of the families who began the Warren Street congregation.

wholesome activities—alternatives to going to movies or other "worldly" activities. Literary societies became common in Mennonite Churches, with two of the earliest of these at the Forks church (1910) and Middlebury (1912).[21]

Conflict existed in the congregation related to the pre-communion sessions, held a week or two before each communion service. (Communion was typically observed once or twice each year in those days.) All members were expected to attend this meeting, and if necessary, meet individually with the deacons to confess any notable sins they had committed. If the deacons decided that the sin was serious enough, the member had to confess before the congregation in order to receive communion. Prominent among such sins were: owning life insurance policies, fornication, and unacceptable hats, hair styles, and clothing. It seemed that the women and girls were particular targets for these public confessions. There was much pressure for them to conform to wearing only bonnets or hoods[22] that had strings. Deacon Earl Miller is remembered as being particularly observant as to which girls failed to conform. If he saw a girl not wearing the prescribed headgear, then a visit to her home and a personal confrontation about the matter was in order.[23] The boys and men were not required to dress differently. They could wear regular suits and neckties.

The controversy about attire came to a head in the spring of 1923 when church leaders called a number of people before the church council. Bishop D. D. Miller came to Middlebury to preside over the communion service. (At that time, only bishops presided over baptisms and communion.) Before the communion service, Miller stood up and announced that twelve girls were not conforming to the dress code of the Indiana-Michigan Conference, and would not be allowed to receive communion. As names of the girls (ages sixteen to twenty-three) were read, they were asked to stand. If they would confess their sin and promise to conform, they could partake.

The girls did not respond and were automatically excommunicated.[24] The communion service proceeded without them. The parents of these girls were not excommunicated nor were any young men. Lillian Litweiler Yoder, one of the girls excommunicated, spoke about this event in an interview:

21. Bender and Krahn, "Literary Societies."

22. A hood was typically a bonnet with fabric draping down over the neck and sometimes onto the shoulders.

23. Charles and Lois (Buchtel) Tyson personal interview with VonGunten, February 15, 1984; Lillian (Litwiller) Yoder personal interview with VonGunten, March 7, 1984. According to the *Middlebury Independent* article, Earl was ordained as deacon on November 16, 1924, so he was not the deacon who personally visited the young women who were denied communion in 1923. Nevertheless, the reputation of being strict seems to have followed him.

24. In 2010 the question arose as to whether the Middlebury girls were actually excommunicated or just restricted from taking communion. The question came up for discussion when Hartzler was told the story about a "progressive" woman from the Forks congregation who stopped wearing the bonnet with strings about 1918. The woman continued to attend services after her visit from the bishop, but she remained seated on communion Sundays because she was not served.

We twelve girls were excommunicated on the basis of our refusal to conform to the bishop's decree. There was no consideration given to good character or spiritual dedication. I knew of those whose moral conduct was bad, but they wore the "*hat with strings*"! The bishop's answer to our argument was "a *real* Christian would be willing to wear the hat [with strings]!"[25]

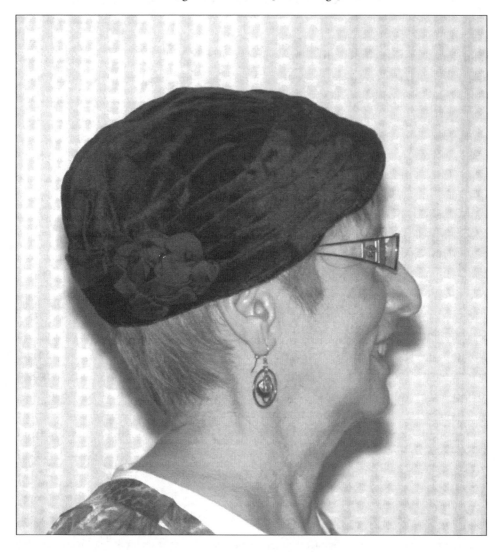

Sara VonGunten models the hat that belonged to her mother, Lillian Litweiler, the "hat that caused the trouble" in 1923. It is not totally clear whether this is the hat that Lillian wore instead of a more conservative bonnet, or if this is the hat that was the prescribed headwear of the Mennonite Church and Lillian had removed the strings, but most likely it was the former.

There are a few scant financial records from 1904 to 1923 in the archival collection of the first Middlebury Mennonite church on Lawrence Street but little other

25. Lillian (Litwiller) Yoder personal interview with VonGunten, March 7, 1984. What Lillian called the "hat with strings" was usually referred to as a bonnet.

information. Annual reports are recorded beginning in 1924, but no mention was made of the large number of people who left in 1923, or of the existence of the Warren Street Mennonite Church. However, there are notes reporting on a special meeting held March 11, 1923. The meeting was opened with prayer by D. D. Miller. "After a brief exhortation by Brother D. D. Miller relative to accepting the resignation of the board of trustees Sam C. Eash, David E. Yoder, and Rollin Mishler, it was decided to accept the same and elect an entire new board resulting in the election of John Mecum for three years, Albert Beck two years, and Albert Cripe one year . . . and the board to decide as to their respective territories." One might surmise that there was a significant dispute when all the members of the board of trustees resign at the same time!

Brief notes of the annual business meeting on November 23, 1923, are also available. The meeting opened with song and prayer and D. D. Miller was the moderator. Notes include Sunday school officers, young people's meeting, money from the library fund to pay the Sunday school supplies, and church officers. Again, no mention was made of the number leaving the church earlier in the year.

In the 1923 division in Middlebury, pastor A. J. Hostetler remained with the congregation on Lawrence Street and the Indiana-Michigan Mennonite Conference along with about 110 members. Pastor Simon S. Yoder[26] and about 100 members withdrew—approximately eighty of whom became the Warren Street congregation and joined the Central Conference of Mennonites in 1926. The "first" Mennonite church continued to grow with Hostetler as pastor.[27]

26. Simon S. Yoder (May 5, 1878–September 3, 1943), first pastor of Warren Street Mennonite Church, was the son of Simon Yoder and Fannie Miller Yoder from LaGrange County. He was a first cousin of William B. Weaver (minister and author) and Samuel E. Weaver, minister at Forks 1904–1916; attended normal school to prepare to teach school which he did for thirty years; was baptized in the Forks congregation in 1893; was ordained deacon at Forks Amish in 1904 and preacher at Middlebury in 1907; served as a member of the Sunday school program committee of Indiana-Michigan Conference from 1904 to 1916; was chairman of the Executive Sunday School Committee from 1916 to 1923. Simon married Sarah Troyer May 14, 1899, and they had five children: Ferne (married Lloyd Ramseyer, later president of Bluffton College); Ruby (married Paul E. Mishler and lived in Ohio); Mabel (married Walter R. Hershberger from Ohio); Grace (married Charles Rae, lived in Arizona for many years, died May 5, 2010); and Samuel T. (married Mildred Berry) who owned a grocery store in Middlebury. At least two grandchildren, Robert Ramseyer of Bluffton and Tom Yoder of Goshen, visited POMC on June 24, 2007.

27. The number of charter members reported in various sources varies between seventy and one hundred. In Wenger's 1957 description of First Mennonite Church, he notes that "In this [1923] division Hostetler remained with the Indiana-Michigan Conference, together with 110 members, while Yoder and about 100 members withdrew . . ." In 2009 a list titled "Charter Members of Warren Street Mennonite Church 1923" was found in a file in a locked drawer in the POMC pastor's office. This list has eighty-three people and includes older children of numerous married couples, presumably baptized members, but not younger children of these same couples. This list is in appendix I. It is thought that the number one hundred came from the information in the *Middlebury Independent* in 1936 that states that one hundred people left the established congregation. There is some evidence that not all who left joined the new congregation; some went elsewhere, so eighty-three is likely the accurate number.

TWO MENNONITE CHURCHES IN MIDDLEBURY, 1923-2009

For reasons that only can be speculated, pastor Hostetler's second wife, Rebecca, and granddaughter, Treva Schrock, became charter members of the new congregation. Perhaps Treva was one who stopped wearing the bonnet with strings. Treva was the daughter of Hostetler's daughter, Cora, who had married Melvin D. Schrock and died July 17, 1911, three days after giving birth to their fourth child.[28] Cora had been five years old (and her brother Charles was two) when her mother (Anna, Hostetler's first wife) died, and she herself died when her oldest child, Leland, was "not yet six" and Treva was four. Treva (April 15, 1907–February 13, 1996) and Leland were born in Idaho and were living in Maymount, Saskatchewan, at the time of their mother's death. By 1920 Treva was living with her grandfather (Andrew J. Hostetler) and step-grandmother (Rebecca).[29] Treva was sixteen in 1923, and perhaps this family who had known tragic deaths was very willing to give in to a motherless sixteen-year-old girl's preference for fashion.[30]

A. J. Hostetler, the minister of the Mennonite Church on Lawrence Street, died in 1925. His widow, Rebecca, remained at the Warren Street Mennonite Church until her death in 1964. She is remembered by the grandchildren of her stepson, Charles, as a "plucky" woman whose neighbor called Charles' daughter to report that the old woman was "up on the roof again, trying to nail down some shingles!"[31]

Whether the Middlebury congregation split over discipline in the church, the authority of conference, or "liberalism" as deacon Earl Miller stated, it seems that a conservative element confused a static, non-changing culture with nonconformity, and strings on bonnets were the straws that broke the camel's back.[32]

What was happening in northern Indiana in the early 1920s that set the stage for conflict that led to schisms? The earlier Amish type of congregational polity had given way to a strong hierarchical system of leadership where bishops and boards dictated doctrine and behavior. This episcopal type of polity was stronger in the "old" Mennonite church during the early 1900s than any time before or since, and the tension that occurred throughout "old" Mennonite congregations in North America was most vividly played out in northern Indiana. A hierarchical polity is in contrast to the congregational polity that was common in the Amish, Central Conference of

---

28. From Cora's obituary in *Gospel Herald*. By 1920 Melvin Schrock, Treva's father, had moved to Elkhart County and his household included himself, two sons (Leland and Moody), and his widowed mother.

29. Information from Joe Springer, Curator of Mennonite Historical Library at Goshen College, in an email to Hartzler, March 26, 2012.

30. Treva Schrock married John W. Steele (whose family had lived next door to Andrew and Rebecca Hostetler) on September 13, 1925 and moved to Goshen where she was a member of the Goshen City Church of the Brethren and died in 1996.

31. Ned, Ann, and Kathy Kauffman in phone conversations with Hartzler March 23, 2012.

32. Notes from Earl Miller found in the membership book at First Mennonite Church.

Mennonites, and the General Conference Mennonite Church. The congregationally-focused polity of the GCMC was so strong that, although there was some structure that included regular conferences, the denomination did not establish central offices until 1950, whereas the "old" Mennonite Church had organized in 1898.[33]

When A. J. Hostetler died in 1925, the congregation on Lawrence Street was left without a resident minister. No minister is listed in the *Mennonite Yearbooks* from 1926 through 1929 although Earl Miller is listed as deacon beginning in 1925.[34] Silas Yoder is listed as minister in 1930 through 1943.[35] Wilbur Yoder was chosen by lot and ordained preacher at Lawrence Street by D. D. Miller on December 20, 1936.[36] For a brief time beginning in 1941 there were three ministers named Yoder at Lawrence Street: Silas Yoder, Wilbur Yoder, and Simon S. Yoder—after Simon's credentials were restored by the conference in 1941. Both Silas and Simon died in 1943.[37]

The Mennonite Yearbook lists the following numbers of members at Lawrence Street: 163 in 1928, 187 in 1930, 230 in 1936, 262 in 1940, 400 in 1956, and 433 in 1960. In 1947 the congregation established an outpost in Three Rivers, Michigan, first a Sunday school and then later, Moorepark Mennonite Church. The Lawrence Street church building was enlarged in 1950–51. Harold A. Yoder assisted Wilbur Yoder from 1946 to 1959. Wilbur Yoder was chosen by congregational vote to be ordained bishop on August 30, 1959.[38]

With the membership being greater than 430 in 1960, the sanctuary was overflowing, and consideration was given to dividing into two congregations. On January 23, 1961, 80 percent of the members voted favorably to divide and build a second meeting-house, but finances were not favorable for that action at that time. Tensions described as a "fermentation of unity" in the congregation had begun in the late 1950s, and in 1961 the problems erupted. By 1961 Wilbur Yoder had been pastor of the Lawrence Street church for nearly twenty-six years and had "accumulated a sizeable amount of power over the congregation." At times Wilbur's wife, Suzanne, played "a determinative role. Throughout the period of trouble she assumed a highly defensive position and from

33. Episcopal polity is a form of church governance that is hierarchical in structure with the chief authority over a local congregation resting in a bishop. Church polity is further addressed in chapter 10.

34. No minister is listed in the Mennonite Yearbooks from 1926 through 1929. Earl Miller (Oct. 16, 1880–May 21, 1969) is listed as deacon beginning in 1925; he served as deacon through 1957 when he retired. He was a charter member of Bonneyville.

35. Little mention is made of Silas Yoder (May 7, 1868–March 1, 1943) in the Lawrence Street records but he is named in the Mennonite Yearbooks as minister 1930–1943. According to his obituary, he was ordained a minister on April 9, 1905 at Clinton Frame and was active in the ministry for about 35 years, beginning in Middlebury about 1925.

36. Wilbur Yoder (October 8, 1909–January 23, 1974), the son of Samuel T. and Mattie (Hostetler) Miller, was born in Middlebury and died there from a heart attack; was married to Suzanne Troyer (d. July 28, 1999), daughter of Levi and Savilla Miller Troyer, on November 23, 1929; was survived by three children, Barbara, Floyd, and Forrest.

37. More information about Simon S. Yoder is in chapter 5.

38. Wenger, *Mennonites in Indiana and Michigan*, 182–83.

time to time lashed out at an unsuspecting individual. . . . In this kind of atmosphere, with its frequency of inflammatory remarks, the crisis mushroomed rapidly."[39]

Galen Hershberger, in a 1974 paper written while he was a Goshen College student in John A. Lapp's History Seminar, said that "sociological factors rather than theological issues played a major role in dividing the [congregation] in 1962." He describes the tensions as a "personality clash between some people and Wilbur rather than a conflict between two groups of people," stating that there were no real doctrinal issues. J. C. Wenger (moderator of the Indiana-Michigan Mennonite Conference 1954–1964) described the conflict as "differing attitudes in the congregation toward Wilbur Yoder."[40]

Wilbur Yoder had limited formal education, and it seemed that he felt somewhat defensive about this. At the same time, Wilbur was considered an outstanding evangelistic preacher and was highly regarded in some circles. He traveled to various places in North America to hold evangelistic meetings. His preaching was a factor in many former Amish people joining the Mennonite church. However, some specific members were upset when other new members didn't change their habits of drinking and smoking, and Wilbur seemed to ignore this. There was a specific "drinking party" in December 1959 after which Sunday school superintendent LeRoy Hostetler expected Wilbur to enforce discipline. Apparently Wilbur did not. Long-time deacon Earl Miller, a conservative traditionalist and a strong disciplinarian, thought that Wilbur's "progressiveness hindered the work of the church and a certain amount of tension existed between them."[41]

In February 1961 some Lawrence Street members went to J. C. Wenger with a list of thirty-six grievances which included some inflammatory remarks, some judgmental statements, and some valid concerns. Two weeks after Easter, on April 16, 1961, Wilbur Yoder read his resignation before the congregation.[42] The congregation was without a pastor for several months until in September 1961, the conference executive committee appointed Samuel J. Miller as acting pastor.[43]

The executive committee of conference interviewed members in July 1961 and learned that one group had ready a petition to circulate which asked for Wilbur to be restored as pastor if he would get a 51 percent vote. The petition included the requirement of confessions from the "grumblers," or they would forfeit their

---

39. Eash, "Bonneyville," 1–4; Galen Hershberger, "First Mennonite," 1, 6–7.

40. Galen Hershberger, "First Mennonite," 1; Wenger, *A Life Sketch*, 68.

41. Galen Hershberger, "First Mennonite," 7.

42. Ibid., 8–9. The thirty-six grievances are included in Hershberger's paper as appendix I. Wilbur's credentials as minister and bishop in the conference were not withdrawn; he simply withdrew from responsibility at Middlebury Mennonite.

43. Harold A. Yoder ended his pastoral term in 1959. Samuel J. Miller was a bishop who had served as pastor of the Leo Mennonite Church 1944–60. He was the father of LeAnna (Mrs. Earl) Stalter, long-time member of Lawrence Street.

membership. What has been described as a personality clash developed into sub-groups, secret meetings, and escalating tensions.[44]

On April 8, 1962, less than a year after Wilbur Yoder had resigned, J. C. Wenger was back at Lawrence Street where he read a statement and then had the congregation vote to determine whether Wilbur should be the pastor again. Approximately 70 percent of those present wanted Wilbur to come back. That very evening J. C. officiated at a communion service, the first in more than a year. The meetinghouse was packed with what seemed to be happy people. Two weeks later on Easter Sunday, April 22, a second vote was taken in which 82 percent favored Wilbur being restored and 18 percent were opposed. On that very day, Wilbur was re-installed. During the service J. C. Wenger said, "We hope that the church may grow so well that it will soon be necessary to swarm and form two sister congregations."[45]

It was a lovely idea that the congregation might happily swarm like bees and joyfully begin another congregation, but that is not the way things developed. It was an unpleasant division in the church that led to the formation of Bonneyville Mennonite Church, not dissimilar to the beginning of Warren Street, in that a group left Lawrence Street because they were dissatisfied. But in one sense, the situation was exactly opposite: the group that departed in 1962 thought that the minister was too lax in his discipline.

One report is that Bonneyville Mennonite Church was started in 1962 by a group of local Mennonites who wanted to start a witness for Christ in the Bonneyville area. But the fact is that there were significant conflicts between the two groups at Lawrence Street. At one point the Lawrence Street church council "definitely declined" the request of the departing group to use the church cabin as a meeting place until finding a new location. The council gave the basis of their decision in some rather judgmental statements. They could not reconcile the "minority" group's manner of leaving with "the Spirit of Christ and their own testimony." This was based on the fact that soon after the communion service on April 22, some of the group resigned their offices in the church. The council added, ". . . we don't want to create a situation with the risk of further conflict and disagreement; therefore we decline their request."[46]

On May 7, fifteen days after Wilbur Yoder was re-installed as pastor, a group met with the executive committee of the conference (including J. C. Wenger and Galen Johns, conference secretary) for the purpose of finding "the will of God and the conference." The group decided to "swarm" and form a new congregation. After interviewing people for a college history paper, Brent Eash said the "major stimulus of friction was apparently the leadership of" Wilbur Yoder; also "the somewhat differing views in the congregation over the need to expand and even form two smaller congregations

44. Galen Hershberger, "First Mennonite," 11–12.

45. Ibid., 14–15.

46. Ibid., 16–17; a letter from J. C. Wenger to the Middlebury church council in the archival material at First Mennonite Church; Hershberger includes in his appendix VI the outlined reasons for refusing the use of the cabin.

to handle the needs of a growing membership." Sixty-two members gathered for their first worship service on May 20, 1962, held in the Clinton Christian Day School south of Middlebury. The group built a new meetinghouse three miles east of Bristol and five miles northwest of Middlebury and chose the name Bonneyville. Galen Johns began as pastor on December 1, 1962.[47]

On October 10, 1962, the group in Middlebury changed their name from Lawrence Street Mennonite Church to First Mennonite Church of Middlebury. Former FMC pastor Sam Troyer said that the reason for the change was because the other Mennonite church in Middlebury was "Warren Street" and there was often confusion between the names.[48] If they had waited two years, the confusion over names would have passed, because by the end of 1964 the other group was planning their move to their new location, already named Pleasant Oaks. How interesting that the name "First Mennonite" was chosen for a congregation that had just suffered a second schism earlier in 1962.

Wilbur Yoder ended his formal ministry at First Mennonite in 1966. Sam Troyer came from a pastoral position in the Upper Peninsula of Michigan and was installed as pastor at First Mennonite on February 5, 1967. Sam and his wife, Betsy, and their three school-age children moved into the parsonage next to the church building on Lawrence Street. Sam had an eighth grade education, a GED diploma, and only a few years of pastoral experience. However, with the support of the congregation, he completed degrees at Goshen College and AMBS during his years in Middlebury (1967–1982). During Sam Troyer's time at First Mennonite, a trusted elder team was established. Sam also remembered a strong bond in the Middlebury Ministerium Association during those years.[49]

When the Troyers moved to Pennsylvania in 1982, David Helmuth became the next pastor. David and his wife, Naomi, had earlier been missionaries in Puerto Rico. Before coming to Middlebury in 1983 David had worked on the Board of Congregational Ministries. He came with a passion for the equipping the saints for ministry and took initiative to begin the First Mennonite Stephen Ministry program, a program to train and support lay pastoral care visitors in the congregation. During David's years at First Mennonite, one hundred lay people were trained to be Stephen Ministers. David retired in 1995.

Linford Martin became the lead pastor of First Mennonite in 1996 and, continuing the pattern of long-term lead pastors, remained until 2011. The pastoral team grew in numbers during those years. There had often been a second pastor, with numerous men serving as youth pastor. The first female pastor, Pamela Yoder, was hired in 2002 as pastoral care coordinator, and within the first year her title became associate pastor of pastoral care. When First Mennonite celebrated their centennial in 2004, there were four ministers on the pastoral team: Linford Martin, lead pastor; Pamela Yoder, pastor

47. Eash, *Bonneyville*, 1–4.

48. Sam Troyer in phone conversation with Hartzler, October 27, 2010.

49. Ibid.

of pastoral care, 2002–2011; Paul Leichty, minister of music, 2004–2006; and Daniel Yoder, pastor for youth and young adults, 2004–2008. In 2012 two interim ministers served the congregation: Gary Martin and Steve Thomas.[50]

During the first forty or fifty years of two Mennonite congregations existing side by side in Middlebury, there was little interaction. Even though Warren Street pastor Simon S. Yoder and his wife returned to the church on Lawrence Street in the last years of his life and Yoder was received back into the fellowship of the Indiana-Michigan Conference in 1941, the pain of the 1923 Middlebury schism was not quickly forgotten.[51] In 2010 Leota Pletcher Miller Leer, long time member of First Mennonite Church, reflected on her home congregation. Leota's maternal grandparents (Clara and Ben Bontrager) were charter members in 1904. In fact, the first Sunday school was in their home at 308 East Warren Street, the home where Leota lived in 2012. Leota was four years old in 1923, at the time of "the squabble," and remembers that friends and relatives were divided between the two congregations. Leota's family left Middlebury, at least in part because of the conflict. They moved to Elkhart where they attended the Prairie Street Mennonite Church. Leota remembers one man who left the church at that time, and because of his bitterness, he never went to church again—anywhere. Were there others who were lost to the church over this squabble?

After marrying Vernon Miller from the Forks church and moving back to the Middlebury area, Leota returned to Middlebury Mennonite with her husband in 1936. She observed that during those years there was very little interaction between the members of the two congregations, and she thought that was strange. She remembers people speaking in a critical way of those who had left and were now going to Warren Street.

In a paper written for a Goshen College class taught by J. C. Wenger in the early 1950s, Charles Yoder wrote about the history of the Middlebury Mennonite congregation through 1923. He described the aftermath of the Lawrence Street/Warren Street division in this way: "After the schism both sides began to think about what had just happened. Both sides realized that they were too radical and didn't ever try to reason with one another, but nothing could be done . . . ."[52] In a conversation in 2009, Yoder stated that his conclusion was based on his observations as a youth and interviews with five people. He said that during his growing up years in the 1940s, there was very little if any interaction between the two congregations. The only time members of the congregations got together was for the community Lenten services. He remembered references to Warren Street members as "those people." It was like they were from a

50. The lead ministers at the church on Lawrence Street have all served relatively long terms: Andrew Hostetler, 21 years, 1904–1925; Silas Yoder, 10 years, 1926–1936; Wilbur Yoder, 29 years, 1936–1966 (minus one year); Sam Troyer, 15 years, 1967–1982; David Helmuth, 12 years, 1983–1995; and Linford Martin, 15 years, 1996–2011.

51. Wenger, "First Mennonite Church."

52. Charles Yoder, "History of Middlebury Congregation." This quote is also given in Ken Gingerich, ed., *First News and Views, Centennial Edition*, 5.

totally different denomination. In fact, Yoder didn't learn of the similarities among the various Mennonites until he served in PAX.[53]

The language deacon Earl Miller used to describe the "split or division" in the church, helps to explain why Warren Street seemed like a different denomination. He said those at Lawrence Street "remained true to the Mennonite faith and continued to worship under the rulings and discipline of the Mennonite Conference."[54] Surely he knew about the General Conference Mennonite Church and the Central Conference of Mennonites who also held to "a Mennonite faith." Comments such as these likely drove a wedge deeper into the schism.

In 2012 Margaret Kauffman Sutter talked about growing up in the Warren Street congregation. She was very involved in the church and, as a teenager in 1943, she initiated fund-raising for the first organ which arrived in 1946. She remembers feeling "irked" that the Lawrence Street and Warren Street churches were separate. She had friends at Lawrence Street and longed to go to church with them. However, she stayed at Warren Street and faithfully played the organ, even returning home to Middlebury regularly while a student at Goshen College. She is "absolutely pleased" that the two congregations re-united in 2009, describing it as an answer to prayer.[55]

OTHER AREA MENNONITE CONFLICTS AND SCHISMS

Middlebury was not the only congregation where dress regulations caused tensions in the early 1900s. In 1912 a Goshen College YMCA gospel team was sent to Barker Street Mennonite Church.[56] William B. Weaver was a part of the team and reported on revival meetings at Barker Street. At the close of a series of meetings, forty-three people made a confession of faith. These were mostly young people and parents. Weaver reported that "all but two [of the forty-three converts] expressed their desire to unite with the church at Barker Street, but when the dress regulations of the Conference were presented as a qualification for membership, only eleven of the converts decided to join the congregation."[57]

In 1916 at Prairie Street Mennonite Church in Elkhart, bishop Jacob K. Bixler announced that six young women would be dropped from membership because of refusing to conform to "the order of the church." Regarding this incident, Elsie Kolb

---

53. Charles Yoder in phone conversation with Hartzler, November 5, 2009. The five people were Mrs. Ben Bontrager, Mr. and Mrs. Merle Pletcher, and Mr. and Mrs. Harvey Yoder.

54. Undated notes from Earl Miller found in the membership book at First Mennonite Church.

55. Margaret Kauffman Sutter in phone conversation with Hartzler, May 29, 2012. See chapter 7 for more about the acquisition of the organ.

56. Wenger, *Mennonites in Indiana and Michigan*, 199–202. The Barker Street Amish Mennonite Church had been established in 1863 and the first meetinghouse was built in 1893. It was on Barker Street Road about one-half mile north of the Indiana-Michigan state line, five miles northeast of Bristol and 8 miles northwest of Middlebury, about halfway between Vistula, Indiana, and Mottville, Michigan.

57. W. Weaver, *Central Conference*, 130.

Bender (mother of Harold S. Bender[58]) lamented to her son that it was "too bad that the girls have these things to contend with. In this case boys have less to fight against." The concern was likely attire and/or headwear, as at that time the Prairie Street congregation "had not yet become conservative in attire." J. E. Hartzler (the same one who later preached repeatedly at Warren Street), as pastor of Prairie Street in 1913, had helped to create a young people's social and literary association. In a 1914 photo of twenty-five young women at an association Fourth of July picnic, there was not one head covering or plain dress, but there were at least seven hats![59]

Back at Barker Street in Michigan the tension was such that, on August 5, 1923, the congregation made a deliberate decision to automatically sever its connection with the Indiana-Michigan Mennonite Conference if any member were dismissed or any minister silenced without the consent of the congregation. As noted in chapter 2, W. W. Oesch from Barker Street was one of five ministers whose credentials were removed by conference thirty days later on September 4. Two months later Oesch and all the members of the church (except for Harvey Friesner) withdrew from the conference and for the next five years, met in a former Methodist meetinghouse three miles north in Mottville.[60]

The above three conflicts did not lead to schisms *within* a congregation. As noted in chapter 3, College Mennonite Church dealt with the issue of authority, and a significant number of people left the congregation in the early 1920s, objecting to control by the conference. Many who left went to Eighth Street Mennonite Church and other GC congregations. There *were* schisms *within* Mennonite congregations in Middlebury and two other small towns in northern Indiana in 1923–24 (Topeka and Nappanee[61]) and a second schism in Middlebury in 1962.

Some question whether these separations must be labeled with the severe term "schisms." How much nicer it would be to think of new congregations as church plants. Nevertheless, Mennonite sociologist Cal Redekop defined schism as the "process of the weakening or destruction of social interaction and spiritual fellowship," and that indeed did occur.[62] It is difficult to acknowledge divisions as schisms and talk about them. Nearly forty years after interviewing Middlebury's First Mennonite members,

---

58. Harold Bender would later become a significant leader in the "old" Mennonite Church, the person who first articulated "The Anabaptist Vision."

59. Keim, *Harold S. Bender*, 34–35.

60. Wenger, *Mennonites in Indiana and Michigan*, 199–202. Mennonite Yearbooks list two men as ministers of the Barker Street Church: Oesch and Harvey Friesner (August 12, 1849–February 26, 1925). Friesner is listed as the only minister of Barker Street in 1924 and included as a minister of Lawrence Street in 1925. The group in Mottville apparently dissolved eventually. Fifteen people from that group (including Oesch) joined Warren Street in 1928.

61. Actually, Nappanee was significantly larger with census populations of 2,678 in 1920 and 2,957 in 1930; compared with Middlebury populations of 599 in 1920 and 656 in 1930; and Topeka populations of 512 in 1920 and 489 in 1930. Goshen's population was 9,525 in 1920 and 10,397 in 1930. http://www.stats.indiana.edu/population/PopTotals/historic_counts_cities.asp.

62. Redekop, *Brotherhood and Schism*, 4.

PART I: A Summary of Growth and Schisms among Mennonites

Galen Hershberger remembers the hesitancy people had in discussing the painful stories about Bonneyville's beginnings.[63]

The early 1920s Indiana Mennonite disaster, caused by differences in biblical interpretation and ideas about authority in the church, was played out slightly differently in Middlebury, Nappanee, and Topeka, Indiana. In Middlebury one "old" Mennonite congregation became two—an "old" Mennonite group and the other eventually GC—and the "progressives" found a new meeting place.

In Nappanee, fifteen miles southwest of Goshen, there had been two Mennonite congregations for many years. One group was organized in 1875 after groups of settlers had met for worship in homes and schoolhouses beginning in 1853. It was first known as the Amish Mennonite Church. In 1917 the group took the name West Market Street Mennonite Church. The first meetinghouse was erected in 1878, rebuilt in 1910, and remodeled in 1926 and 1955 into a frame structure with a seating capacity of about 250.[64]

While the West Market Street congregation had been an Amish Mennonite Church, the other Mennonite congregation in Nappanee was part of the Indiana Mennonite Conference. That group, which became North Main Street Mennonite Church, had been organized in 1880. The forty-two members of the congregation built a new brick meetinghouse in 1893. This was enlarged in 1912, 1921, and 1952 until it had a seating capacity of 450.[65]

The spiritual tornado in 1923–24 resulted in an upset-the-fruit-basket type of rearranging among the Mennonite churches in the Nappanee area. Fifty members of the West Market Street Church moved to the North Main Street congregation which remained in the Indiana-Michigan Conference. An additional fifteen West Market members left for other congregations. On the other hand, the pastor of the North Main Street congregation, Ezra S. Mullet, was silenced by the conference[66]; he withdrew with a group of thirty-five and joined the more progressive West Market Street Church. Adding to the upheaval, fifty-six members from *other* Indiana-Michigan Conference congregations transferred to West Market Street in 1923 and an additional twenty-five people came in 1924. The West Market Street congregation united with the Middle District of the General Conference Mennonite Church in 1926 and became First Mennonite Church of Nappanee.[67]

In the small town of Topeka, thirty miles northeast of Nappanee and sixteen miles east of Goshen, the disruptive and devastating winds severed a group of Mennonites in 1924. For a long time there had also been two Mennonite congregations in Topeka,

63. Galen Hershberger in phone conversation with Hartzler, September 17, 2012.

64. Wenger, *Mennonites in Indiana and Michigan*, 360–61.

65. Wenger, *Mennonites in Indiana and Michigan*, 86–87.

66. Mullet was one of five progressive ministers silenced by the Indiana-Michigan Conference in 1923. See page 57-58.

67. Wenger, *Mennonites in Indiana and Michigan*, 181, 360–61; Elden Schrock, *First Mennonite Church, Nappanee*, 10–11; Elva Mae Schrock, *75th Anniversary*, 4.

the village that was first known as Haw Patch. The Maple Grove congregation formed as an Amish Mennonite congregation in 1854, and in 1856, west of Haw Patch, they built the first Amish Mennonite meetinghouse in Indiana. In 1879 the congregation built a brick structure at the same location. In 1924, amid unrest concerning authority in the congregation versus authority of conference, about half of the 150 members withdrew from the Indiana-Michigan Mennonite Conference and took charge of the 1879 meetinghouse. The other members apparently departed quietly, met in homes temporarily, and then built a new meetinghouse with a seating capacity of 300 on South Main Street in Topeka. They dedicated their building in 1925 and maintained the name Maple Grove Mennonite Church.[68]

In 2012, Gladys Yoder Johns, who was born in 1919, reminisced about these events. She had a vivid memory of when she, as a five-year-old child, was playing in the yard while her father, Edwin J. Yoder, and grandfather, Daniel J. Yoder, were standing and talking a short distance away. At one point, Gladys ran over to them and was startled to see that her grandfather was crying. She didn't understand what was happening, but later learned that the schism of Maple Grove had split the family apart. Her grandparents and parents stayed with the Indiana-Michigan Conference, but one of her grandfather's brothers went with the progressive Mennonite group, and another left the Mennonite Church altogether.[69]

In 1893, the same year the name of the town was changed from Haw Patch to Topeka, John C. Mehl, pastor of the Silver Street Mennonite Church, began coming to Topeka to hold services every four weeks. In 1898 this group of relatively progressive Mennonites purchased the old Eden Chapel building from the Methodists and moved it to the west edge of town. It became known as "the church across the lake" and became a charter member of the Central Conference of Mennonites in 1908. Even though this group numbered around 100 in 1926, they built a 250-capacity brick meetinghouse on East Lake Street, one block east of Topeka's Main Street. Naming themselves the Topeka Mennonite Church, they began worshiping in their new location in 1927. The membership of the congregation nearly doubled in 1930 when ninety additional Mennonites joined them—the segment of the Maple Grove congregation who had remained in the 1879 meetinghouse and had joined the Central Conference of Mennonites in 1927.[70]

In some ways, the center of the 1920s whirlwind of destruction was in Goshen, where the tension was so great that Goshen College was closed for an academic year, and the congregation on campus held its breath. Tentacles of devastation reached out in various directions, influencing the disruptions in surrounding Mennonite

68. *100th Anniversary 1854–1954: Maple Grove Mennonite Church*, 3. Under the leadership of David Eugene Troyer, Maple Grove left the Indiana-Michigan Mennonite Conference in 1995. In 2007 Troyer was relieved of pastoral duties after it was discovered he had misappropriated large amounts of church funds. He was arrested in 2008. In 2012 Maple Grove Church remains an independent congregation.

69. Gladys Yoder Johns in conversation with Hartzler, 2012. Her father, Edwin J. Yoder (December 2, 1889–December 17, 1972), was ordained preacher at Maple Grove in 1925 and bishop in 1935.

70. Maggie Glick, *Looking Back*, 7–9.

communities. Another image, perhaps more accurate, would be that the cause of the schisms was dis-ease inside the congregations. Groups of people were not at ease with the different understandings and perspectives of other members. For some, believing and behaving in specific ways was required for belonging. Part 2 continues the story of the "progressive" congregation that began in Middlebury in 1923, a group that was sometimes called a "do as you please" church.

PART II

History of Warren Street and Pleasant Oaks Mennonite Church

Pleasant Oaks Mennonite Church,
by the power of the Holy Spirit,
exists to continue Jesus' work as we fully learn, live and proclaim
God's Good News of healing and hope.

A collage by Doris Hershberger of the Pleasant Oaks Family in 1979–80.

5

God's Faithfulness to All Generations, 1923 to 1984

Your steadfast love, O Lord, extends to the heavens,
your faithfulness to the clouds.

PSALM 36:5

WORLD WAR I ENDED in 1918, but conflicts within the Mennonite Church continued to increase. The leadership in the Indiana-Michigan Mennonite Conference made decisions about things that many thought were nonessentials, influenced the Mennonite Board of Education, and tried to exercise great authority over Goshen College. Goshen College was closed for the 1923–24 school year, and the congregation on the campus of Goshen College hung on by only a thread.

Apparently the young women in Middlebury who were denied communion in early 1923 continued to attend Middlebury Mennonite church services with their families. The two ministers at that time were Andrew J. Hostetler and Simon S. Yoder.[1] However, in September 1923 the controversy surrounding Simon S. Yoder's liberal leadership came to a head. Yoder and four other Indiana-Michigan Conference ministers were silenced by the conference leaders. He could not continue his pastoral duties in the Middlebury Church.

The twelve girls and their families began to meet on an informal basis with Simon Yoder. Lillian Yoder relates that she would have been interested in leaving the Mennonite Church altogether "and join with a completely different Protestant denomination." But Simon Yoder was tolerant of the problems and encouraged the group to stay together and form another church.

---

1. An extensive note about Simon S. Yoder (May 5, 1878–September 3, 1943) is on page 91.

The tradition in the "old" Mennonite Church had been that the devotional covering was a "prayer veil" as prescribed by the Apostle Paul to the Corinthians, and that women should always wear a covering when praying. The practice of wearing the covering has varied from time to time and place to place.[2]

Rachel Weaver Kreider (born in 1909) remembers that when she was a young girl, the women of her grandmothers' and mother's generations wore their coverings under their bonnets to the Forks Mennonite Church and took off their bonnets when they arrived. The younger women put on their coverings when they got to church, and didn't wear them at home. Rachel's generation did the same. She remembered a conversation in which an older relative confessed that she didn't wear her covering when praying in bed. She just used the bed covers!

Rachel was baptized at College Mennonite Church in 1922 and began wearing a covering. However, her membership there was short-lived. Along with numerous other people, her family left the college church during the "trouble at the college" in 1922 and 1923. They went to the Eighth Street Mennonite Church, less than one mile north of the college campus. At Eighth Street the young women wore modern hats.

From the beginning of the church on Warren Street, the Eighth Street congregation was a nearby sister church. In the early 1900s, there were two Mennonite churches in Goshen, one on the campus of Goshen College and the Mennonite Brethren in Christ congregation on Ninth Street.[3] On February 28, 1913, twenty people met to discuss the possibility of another Mennonite Church in Goshen. These twenty people were mostly members of Silver Street Mennonite Church who wanted a meeting place closer to where they lived.[4]

The February meeting in Goshen was chaired by Dr. William B. Page, the same man in whose home the group met to form the first Mennonite Church in Middlebury in 1903. In 1913 Dr. Page was a practicing physician in Goshen. His wife, Alice Thut Page, was appointed secretary for the group that became Fifth Street Mennonite Church (located at 616 South Fifth Street) and then Eighth Street Mennonite Church after moving to 602 South Eighth Street in 1920.[5] The new congregation became a member of the Central Illinois Conference of Mennonites in 1913.[6]

2. See chapter 2 for more on bonnets and coverings.

3 This group moved to the corner of Eighth and Jefferson Streets in 1925 and became the Brenneman Memorial Missionary Church. In 1980 they moved to a new location on State Road 15 on the north side of Goshen.

4. Kreider, *Eighth Street Mennonite Church*, 1.

5. Ibid.

6. Ibid., 3–6. The Central Illinois Conference of Mennonites was organized in 1908. Beginning in 1914 the group was called Central Conference of Mennonites. It was this conference that Warren Street joined in 1926. W. Weaver, *Central Conference*, 248–49.

EARLY YEARS OF WARREN STREET MENNONITE CHURCH (1923–1940)

Under the efficient leadership of Simon S. Yoder, a group of approximately eighty members from the Middlebury Mennonite Church "began to hold services" in a building on Warren Street in Middlebury.[7] They called themselves the West Side Church, and became Warren Street Mennonite Church on May 24, 1924, which was dedication Sunday for the new church building.[8]

Warren Street Mennonite Church building, 1923 to 1965.

The building was the old opera house behind the present-day Varns and Hoover Hardware Store on the corner of Main Street and Warren Street. Some people may have had theological reservations about starting a church in such a building. However, as noted in chapter 4, the first building used by the Middlebury Mennonite Church in 1904 had also been a play house, dance hall, and party center! In 1906, the Middlebury Improvement Association had formed and purchased a former harness shop building that a Mr. M. A. Page had purchased and moved to a lot on West Warren Street, one-half block west of Main. The old frame building had been overhauled and equipped

7. The number of charter members reported in various sources varies between seventy and one hundred. See footnote 27 in chapter 4 (page 91) for the explanation as to why eighty-three is likely the accurate number.

8. Olen Yoder (senior) diary.

with a "stage and all modern arrangement for an opera house." On April 6, 1906, the *Middlebury Independent* reported regarding the opera house that "everything seems to be coming our way." The opera house flourished as an entertainment center for the community and the school until 1923 when the school built a "grand gymnasium."[9]

Helen Plank remembers the first service in the former opera house. It was a happy occasion because the tensions and hassles were over, and the people could determine their own destiny. It was also a sad occasion. The opera building was old. As Helen remembers back, she commented:

> There were still tobacco and Ivory soap advertisement signs hanging on the walls. The tattered theater seats comprised the sanctuary "pews"—all vivid reminders of the comfortable building that we had been forced to leave![10]

Jonathan Miller, son of charter members D. Walter and Mabel Miller, sent a letter to WSMC pastor Floyd Quenzer in 1973 (on the occasion of the fiftieth anniversary celebration), in which he remembered the pulleys that were taken off the old stage equipment in the meeting space.

People came to this little church for a variety of reasons. Andrew (A. J.) Hostetler, co-pastor at Middlebury Mennonite with Simon Yoder, stayed with that congregation, but his wife, Rebecca, and granddaughter Treva Schrock joined the new congregation.[11] Olen Yoder (senior) stated that he and his wife, Barbara, came because they had four daughters. Their oldest daughter (Vera) was twelve, and Olen and Barbara did not want to have the difficulty with hairdos and hats that the other young girls had just been through.[12]

Thomas A. (Tom) Yoder, one of Olen's grandsons, reported that his grandfather had given a similar answer in a letter to him. Responding to the question about why his family left the Middlebury Mennonite Church, Olen wrote to his grandson, "My daughters wanted to bob their hair, and I didn't want the fight at church or at home!"[13]

The congregation worked together and redecorated the opera house. By Christmas time the "West Side" Church had Lester Hostetler of Smithville, Ohio, conduct a series of meetings.[14] Dedication Sunday was May 24, 1924. Paul Whitmer, dean of the

9. Middlebury History Committee, *Town Beautiful*, 150.

10. Helen (Litwiller) Plank personal interview with VonGunten, March 7, 1984.

11. More information about Treva Schrock Steele is in chapter 4.

12. Olen Yoder (senior) personal interview with VonGunten, March 7, 1984.

13. Tom Yoder conversation with Hartzler, August 30, 2009.

14. Lester Hostetler became the first pastor of the First Mennonite Church of Sugarcreek (Ohio) in 1926 when a group of eighty-four members withdrew from the Walnut Creek Mennonite Church. This division was similar to the 1923 division in Middlebury in that Walnut Creek was a congregation of the Ohio and Eastern Amish Mennonite Conference and eventually, the new congregation in Sugarcreek joined the GCMC.

Witmarsum Seminary in Ohio, led the service of dedication. The name of this congregation was now considered Warren Street Church, not West Side as it was first called.[15]

Olen Yoder (senior) included a few more items in his diary from 1924: On August 10, 1924, J. E. Hartzler preached,[16] on August 31, N. O. Blosser filled the pulpit, and on November 9, "W. W. Oesch preached for us." Olen notes that he worked at the church house on October 22, 24, and 25, but he doesn't mention what work he did.[17] Olen is remembered as a man who never preached but was very involved in the life of the church. He and his family attended church every Sunday morning and Sunday evening.[18]

Series of meetings, sometimes called protracted, evangelistic, or revival meetings, seem to have been held almost annually at Warren Street Mennonite Church. On January 22, 1925, a ten-day series of meetings began with Emanuel Troyer (of Carlock, Illinois), an outstanding leader in the Central Conference of Mennonites. As a result, eight young people were taken into the church that year. And on May 10 of that year, approximately eighty-five members of the church and visitors received communion.[19]

In May 1925 there were Evangelistic Union[20] meetings held in a gymnasium with a different speaker each evening.[21] J. E. Hartzler spoke on May 18, and after the evening service, Ora S. Kauffman took Hartzler to LaGrange. Olen Yoder noted that he rode along. It must have been a special treat for him to spend time with Hartzler who was highly educated, well-traveled, and respected by progressives in the Mennonite Church. Pastor S. S. Yoder's brother, Albert Yoder, from Cali, Colombia, was at the meeting on Sunday, August 23. Olen wrote that Brother Albert believed in divine healing, which must have been unusual in that it was noted.

Olen Yoder wrote in his diary that in January 1926 he started as teacher of the men's class, and on April 20 he and Ora Kauffman, Dan Friesner, Edwin Miller, Ira Schrock, Elmer Hostetler plowed oats ground for pastor S. S. Yoder.[22] If there were access to more diaries like Olen kept, we would be the recipients of many more details of how members of the new congregation participated in the life of the community. We do know that mutual aid was practiced, and the minister was given special help.

15. Olen Yoder (senior) handwritten memoirs, date unknown; Olen Yoder (senior) diary.

16. In 1924, John Ellsworth Hartzler (February 2, 1879–May 24, 1963) was the president of Witmarsum Theological Seminary at Bluffton College. He had formerly been president of Goshen College, 1913–1918. See footnote 13 in chapter 1 (page 8) for more information on J. E. Hartzler..

17. Olen Yoder (senior) diary.

18. J. O. Yoder conversation with Hartzler, September 7, 2010.

19. From information from the handwritten notes prepared by Olen Yoder for the dedication service of Pleasant Oaks Mennonite Church in 1965. It is information he gleaned from his personal diaries.

20. "Union" implies that other congregations were involved, perhaps outside the denomination, but certainly outside the Indiana-Michigan Conference.

21. A different speaker each evening was likely a way to get around the prohibition against "protracted" meetings.

22. These men are all included on the list of charter members of WSMC in appendix I.

By 1926 this group of people, now numbering eighty-one, applied for membership in the Central Conference of Mennonites.[23] With their application accepted, the members were once again connected with a larger Mennonite body and not just an independent church. Other northern Indiana congregations who were part of the Central Conference in 1926 were Topeka Mennonite, Silver Street, and Eighth Street.[24] New people continued to come to the Warren Street Church. In 1928 fifteen people came from the group that had been Barker Street Mennonite Church and had met in Mottville beginning in 1923. The group included the former Barker Street pastor and his wife, William W. and Elva Alice (Garber) Oesch.[25]

There are few written records found about the early years of Warren Street Church, and even in 1984, memories were vague. One humorous memory of the church came from the descendents of Silas Litwiller. He was the church janitor, and every Sunday at 4:00 a.m. he went to the church to fire up the old, old furnace. It never wanted to draw correctly, and more often than not it gave out much soot and little heat. By the time church was ready to begin, the church temperature was comfortable, but Silas was always black from head to toe after repairing and coaxing the old furnace into one more Sunday of service. Eventually, there was a new furnace!

The congregation experienced several "untimely" deaths during the early years. On February 7, 1927, Velma Grace Yoder, nine-year-old daughter of founding members Barbara and Olen Yoder, died following a ruptured appendix. The following year on March 16, 1928, her first cousin, Rubye Ruth Yoder, eighteen-year-old daughter (born August 13, 1909) of Wilma and Levi Yoder, also died. Her death certificate says she died of ulcerative colitis. Eight years later, twelve-year-old Mary Ellen Plank, daughter of Elsie and Melvin Plank, died on August 16, 1936. It is easy to imagine that the stress of grief fell on these people like a cold wet blanket in winter. It was a time when many things were not talked about, but one would hope that the mourners somehow felt the loving presence and comfort of God, directly and through the church community.

Ministers during this beginning era of Warren Street were Simon S. Yoder, Lee Lantz, and E. A. Sommer.[26] Simon Yoder and his family continued to attend Warren Street after he was no longer the pastor. For five years, from about 1934 to 1939, he regularly commuted from Middlebury to Kouts, Indiana, to minister to a Central

23. W. Weaver, *Central Conference*, 128. In addition to names of charter members in appendix I, a 1927 list in Olen (senior) Yoder's diary includes Kathryn McCreary, Mary Thut, Alice Gerig, Roy Zimmerman, Mrs. Edna Freye, and Mr. and Mrs. Perry Prough.

24. W. Weaver, *Central Conference*, 249. The Central Conference of Mennonites became part of the General Conference Mennonite Church in 1946. In 1957 the Middle District and the Central Conference joined to become the Central District Conference of the General Conference Mennonite Church.

25. Olen Yoder (senior) handwritten memoirs, date unknown, 3; W. Weaver, *Central Conference*, 128–29; 237–38.

26. The names of WSMC/POMC pastors, their dates of service, and personal notes are included in appendix H.

Conference congregation there.[27] His ministerial credentials remained with the Central Conference of Mennonites until 1941, when he was finally "received back into the fellowship of the Indiana-Michigan Conference." One of Simon's grandsons confirmed that near the end of his life, Simon desired restored relationships with the "old" church, so he and his wife returned to Lawrence Street.[28] As was true for most Mennonite ministers in the early twentieth century, Simon Yoder was not paid a salary for his pastoral work. However, Olen Yoder (senior) stated, "We men did a lot of farm work for him." In addition, Simon Yoder taught public school in Elkhart and LaGrange Counties for thirty years.[29]

Lee Lantz began as pastor in 1930 and is remembered for his emotional enthusiasm. He spoke loudly and excitedly and had lots of energy. It is believed by several persons who were members at that time that pastor Lantz was paid a salary, probably very small, but it was the beginning of a paid clergyperson at Warren Street.[30] Lee Lantz had been born in Illinois in 1873 and was baptized at North Danvers by Joseph Stuckey in 1891. He attended Eureka College and graduated from Moody Bible Institute. He was ordained at Congerville Mennonite Church in 1899 where he had served as pastor. He also was pastor at First Mennonite Church in Normal (during which time he was ordained as bishop in 1907), and Nampa Mennonite Church in Nampa, Idaho, from 1908 to 1911 and again from 1918 and following, before coming to Middlebury.[31]

In the early years there was also an emphasis on activities for youth. Lotus Troyer remembers Mrs. Lantz, the pastor's wife, as an enthusiastic youth leader even though the youth group was small in numbers. The Lantz family left Middlebury in 1934 to accept a calling at the Sixty-second Street mission in Chicago. As the Lantz family was leaving Middlebury, the following was in a local newspaper:

> Rev. Lee Lantz, who has served as pastor of the Warren Street Mennonite Church here, was notified Saturday of his transfer to a position as superintendent of mission work in Chicago. Rev. Lantz's successor has not yet been chosen.
>
> Rev. and Mrs. Lantz and family came to Middlebury from Nampa, Idaho, four years ago, and during their residence here have won the friendship of the entire community. Their departure is a surprise to local people, who regret to learn of the transfer.

---

27. Pannabecker, *Faith in Ferment*, 270–71; Robert Ramseyer (grandson of S. S. Yoder) in conversation with Hartzler, September 30, 2012. Kouts Mennonite Church existed from 1918 until 1947.

28. Wenger, "First Mennonite Church." Robert Ramseyer in conversation with Hartzler, September 30, 2012. Simon's funeral was "conducted in the Mennonite Church at Middlebury where Ernest E. Miller of Goshen College preached an impressive sermon to a large audience assisted by D. D. Miller and the pastor, Wilbur Yoder." *Gospel Herald*, October 14, 1943.

29. In some groups, the practice of not paying ministers continued for a long time. Some congregations regularly collected "love offerings" for the ministers.

30. Olen Yoder (senior) personal interview with VonGunten, March 7, 1984.

31. W. Weaver, *Central Conference*, 219.

> Rev. Lantz has submitted the following and requests that it be published: "We wish to acknowledge publicly the pleasant fellowship and kindness shown us by the Christian people of Middlebury and community while living here. We are grateful for these pleasant associations, irrespective of denominational lines, which associations have greatly enriched our lives. Our ministerial fellowship has been very pleasant with never a discord. Every possible courtesy has been shown the church by our local newspaper, which is a great advantage to the churches. We shall greatly appreciate having any of our friends call on us at 6201 S. Carpenter St., Chicago . . . . We assume the duties beginning next Sunday, August 5." Rev. and Mrs. Lee Lantz, Mary Elizabeth Lantz.[32]

The church suffered from the difficult economic times of the Great Depression (1929 to 1939). In order to earn money, the ladies of the church served meals in the town sale barn. The emphasis was on missionary work, as much of the women's sale barn money went to missions. There are a few notes in the Warren Street papers about sending canned fruits and vegetables to the Sixty-second Street Mission in Chicago. On at least one occasion, the Lantz couple returned from Chicago to collect the fruit and vegetables.

In 1934 Emil (E. A.) Sommer, originally from Flanagan, Illinois, began an eight year pastoral assignment at Warren Street. E. A. Sommer, who had attended Moody Bible Institute, and his wife, Lydia May (Augspurger), had been the first representatives from the Central Conference of Mennonites to go to the Congo mission field in 1917, where he was in charge of a Bible School for training native teachers. They served until 1926 and then returned to the United States due to ill health. After Lydia's death in 1930, E. A. Sommer returned to the Congo alone for two more years before coming to Middlebury.

WSMC members wondered if this was Sommer's first experience in pastoring a church in North America because he is remembered to have remarked to a prospective bride and groom: "You will be the first white couple I ever married!" E. A. Sommer was a good storyteller and was considered to be a good man by all who knew him, but some thought he was not a dynamic leader.[33]

The Warren Street church grew in numbers in the first several years to 115 members in 1932 with an average attendance of ninety-three. However, following 1936 the numbers diminished slowly to a low of fifty-eight members in 1964, with only thirty-eight *active* members.

Helen Plank attributed the diminishing numbers to a defeated people. Helen observed that they had come out of negativism and quarreling and they did not know how to express their faith in positive terms. She observed that church seemed to have no goals, and the community did not really understand the turmoil that had caused the break with the more prominent and affluent Middlebury Mennonite Church. Many of

---

32. Yoder (senior) personal notes; *Middlebury Independent,* August 2, 1934.

33. Ernest Litwiller personal interview with VonGunten, March 21, 1984.

the wounds did not heal with the first generation. It seemed that it was not until that generation died that the feelings of a poor self-image slowly began to disappear.

Another factor in the lack of growth at Warren Street was that the young people did not return to Middlebury because there were few jobs in this small town. However, this small congregation produced two ordained ministers during this time: Lotus[34] and Lowell[35] Troyer. They are remembered as good speakers who, after leaving Middlebury, were brought back for missionary emphasis, for special services, Wednesday night prayer meetings, and Sunday evening services.

Other special guest preachers included William B. Weaver and J. E. Hartzler. Weaver held revival meetings at WSMC in 1938 while he was minister of North Danvers Mennonite Church in Illinois. J. E. Hartzler was a noteworthy evangelist, teacher, and preacher, first in the "old" Mennonite Church and then in the GC denomination. He held meetings at WSMC in 1940–41 and in October 1954; in addition, he preached on several special occasions.

WORLD WAR II (1941–1945)

As the decade of the 1930s drew to a close, the Great Depression was ending, but a war was beginning. Even though Warren Street was part of the Anabaptist heritage of nonresistance, this was not a teaching that had been strongly emphasized in the congregation. The reaction to the war at Warren Street, as well as among Mennonites in general, ran the gamut of alternatives. Many served as sailors, soldiers, or noncombatants in the military. Others, when drafted, took the traditional Anabaptist stance of alternative service, which in World War II was serving in Civilian Public Service (CPS). Some Mennonite congregations excommunicated their young men who participated in military service or required a public confession after returning, but Warren Street left the decision up to the individual.

Some twenty-first century observers are concerned that "letting up to the individual" implies that there was inadequate teaching about Jesus' teaching on love of enemies and the traditional Mennonite position on nonresistance. It may be that Mennonites in Middlebury had a vivid memory, conscious or unconscious, of the blasting of conscientious objectors during World War I. An editor in the *Middlebury Independent* in 1918 said that COs were "not fit to mingle with the vermin of the earth" and that they "will avail not, and there will be no other country in the universe

---

34. Lotus Troyer (July 17, 1915–December 19, 1994) served as pastor in Summerfield, Carlock, Flanagan, and Meadows Churches in Illinois and Oak Grove in Ohio; he also served as president of the Central District Conference.

35. Lowell Troyer (March 17, 1912–September 14, 2004) became pastor of the McKinley Mennonite Church in McKinley, Michigan, in 1951 when a chapel was built to strengthen the work that had been started a few years previously by the Comins church. Lowell and his wife, Mary, later returned to Pleasant Oaks where they remained until their deaths. Melvin Gingerich, "McKinley Mennonite Church."

to which they can flee in order to escape their galling chains."[36] Indeed, it would take a very strong teaching on nonresistance and pacifism to remain steadfast in the face of this kind of sentiment in the community. What was the teaching at WSMC/POMC?

J. O. Yoder was a college senior in 1941 when draft numbers were drawn. Although he had grown up at Warren Street (son of Olen and Barbara), he said he knew very little about the theology of nonresistance. He registered as a conscientious objector, but he received a deferment because of a physical problem related to having had rheumatic fever as a child.[37]

In 2009, Don Hershberger, son of founding members Freed and Nina Hershberger, said he does not remember any teaching against participating in military service during his youth at Warren Street. His only memory was of one conversation when the pastor (likely E. A. Sommer, although Don did not remember) called him into the little back room.[38] "He said I would have to decide what to do about the draft. I could be a CO or join the army. The decision was up to me. I told him that I couldn't be a CO. I thought freedom was worth fighting for and I also remembered the criticism town people gave of COs who were afraid to go overseas and risk their lives; they were sometimes called 'chicken.'"[39] Don may have been affected by stories similar to the following:[40]

Lotus Troyer, who had grown up at Warren Street, had a frightening experience connected with his position on military service. He wrote his own story:

> I came from a Christian family and a church which has played a most important role in my life. In our family there were six boys—four of them served in the armed forces, but my brother Lowell and I chose to enter CPS with a 4–E classification. I had taught school in my hometown after college before being drafted. In CPS I served three years at Medaryville, Indiana, and another eight months at the mental hospital in Ypsilanti, Michigan.
>
> After my alternative service, I had not planned to teach school again, but the Middlebury School offered me a contract so I signed to start teaching the coming fall. One evening before school started a knock came on the door. "Come out here, Cork (my nickname for many, many years); some people want to see you." As I walked out, six or eight people proceeded to tell me that I had disqualified myself as a teacher because I had been a conscientious objector. I tried to explain that I had broken no law but had served my country in the way that my conscience had dictated. My wife, coming to investigate, turned on the porch light. People suddenly drifted into the shadows not

36. "Middlebury Should Be 100 Percent Patriotic," *Middlebury Independent*, April 5, 1918.

37. J. O. and Leona Yoder personal interview by VonGunten in 1984 and Hartzler in 2011.

38. Don Hershberger was born January 13, 1924. His age was ten through eighteen during the years that E. A. Sommer was pastor. Don entered the military service as a noncombatant in February 1943, at age nineteen.

39. Don Hershberger conversation with Hartzler, May 2009 and March 8, 2011.

40. Lotus Troyer completed CPS in 1945 or 46, after Don Hershberger joined the service, so this specific story would not have influenced Don's decision. However, there were other stories similar to this.

wishing to be identified. One disappointment was to see Paul Kauffman in the crowd. We were both members of the same church and our families had been close friends for years.

The aftermath of the encounter was interesting for a small Midwestern town. People took sides and it contained surprises as people either sided with me or the protesters. [The school] did not want to accept my resignation. After some deep soul searching and deliberation, I decided that if they were out to get me, these townspeople would do it sooner or later. I broke my teaching contract.

In retrospect, I think, the townspeople in the yard that night in Middle-bury did me a favor by moving me off center toward a career in the pastorate and not staying in teaching. God moves in mysterious ways to close and open doors. [41]

During World War I, Mennonites had felt tremendous pressure to buy war bonds as is described in chapter 3. Many Mennonite conscientious objectors (COs) were taken to army camps where they received harsh treatment including beatings and inadequate nutrition. Affected by the intense pressure on COs, Mennonites began to combine their refusal to fight with more positive work for peace. In the 1920s, Mennonite Central Committee (MCC) was formed by seven North American Mennonite groups to assist the hurting people around the world "in the name of Christ."

By the beginning of World War II, Historic Peace Churches in the United States (including Mennonites, Amish, Hutterites, Quakers, Brethren in Christ, and Church of the Brethren members) had options for alternate service. CPS allowed COs to work in forestry service, state psychiatric hospitals, and regional health projects, and nearly 4,700 people from the above groups participated. However, the records show that only two members of Warren Street chose this option. Twice during World War II, Warren Street published a list of "Boys in Camp" (on December 13, 1942) and "Names and Addresses of Boys gone from Our Church" (printed without a date, but clearly in 1943 or later).[42]

Of the eleven "Boys in Camp" in 1942, only two were registered conscientious objectors. Of those who were in the US military service, Calvin Hershberger was the only man known to be a noncombatant. Twenty names are on the later list, again with only two in CPS (the same two as on the first list, Lotus and Lowell Troyer). Fourteen men on the list were members of Warren Street or sons of members. Another six men were husbands of women who were members of Warren Street. Of these, at least two were in noncombatant service: Donald and Calvin Hershberger.[43]

This high percentage of young men in military service (80 percent plus on Warren Street's first list and 90 percent on the second list), as compared with those in

41. Lotus Troyer letter to VonGunten, received March 5, 1984.

42. These lists are available in appendix J.

43. Junior Olen Yoder was not on this list, even though he was twenty-three years old in 1942, as he had a farm deferment.

alternate service, is not inconsistent with later trends in GC congregations as shown by Kauffman and Harder in 1975. Of the 507 respondents from the GC denomination, 66 percent agreed that "The Christian should take no part in war or any war-promoting activities." Of the 1084 "old" Mennonite respondents, 87 percent agreed that participation in war and war activities was wrong for Christians.[44]

Other GC congregations have records similar to WSMC. For example, at Meadows Mennonite Church in Illinois during World War II, there were five men in CPS, two in noncombatant service, and twenty-three in combatant service. Guy Hershberger reported that of the GC men who served during the Second World War, 57.7 percent were in combatant service, 15.6 percent in noncombatant service, and 26.6 percent served in CPS. In the Eastern District of the GC denomination, 94 percent served with the military and "only 6 percent adhered to the principle of Biblical nonresistance."[45]

The Statement of Doctrine, which had been presented to the General Conference Mennonite Church at its 1941 delegate session at Souderton, Pennsylvania, includes in point six a clear position against participation in war:

> We believe that Christ lived and taught the way of life as recorded in the Scriptures, which is God's plan for individuals and the race; and that it becomes disciples of Christ to live in this way, thus manifesting in their personal and social life and relationship the love and holiness of God. And we believe that this way of life also implies nonresistance to evil by carnal means, the fullest exercise of love, and the resolute abandonment of the use of violence, including warfare . . .[46]

However, the Warren Street and Meadows congregations were not part of the General Conference in 1941. They were members of the Central Conference of Mennonites, which didn't join the General Conference Mennonite Church until 1946. So in a sense, this was the position of the Warren Street congregation beginning in 1946. However, the practice was that neither the denomination nor the conference dictated behavior for members of congregations.

Most of the early Anabaptists in Europe had refused to participate in military service and many Amish and Mennonite folk who immigrated to the Americas left Europe for religious freedom and specifically, for freedom to *not* participate in wars. How had the tolerance for participation in military service crept into the Mennonite Church? This will be further explored in chapter 10.

Don Hershberger joined the army but refused to carry a gun. He was consequently assigned to the medics. His brothers who had also grown up at Warren

44. Kauffman and Harder, *Anabaptists*, 133.

45. Estes, *From Mountains to Meadows*, 21–23; Guy Hershberger, *Second World War*, 39; J. Winfield Fretz, "Reflections at the End," 33–34.

46. General Conference Mennonite Church, "Statement of Doctrine (1941)." The statement is included in its entirety in appendix C.

Street also served: Junior Raymond[47] (J. R.) in the infantry and Calvin as a noncombatant medic. Calvin was stationed at Sheppard Field, Texas, and never left US soil. J. R. was deployed to Europe and was on the ground. It was with great emotion that Don told part of J. R.'s story.

On one occasion J. R. came upon a machine gun nest. He knew he had to shoot the enemy, or the enemy would shoot him. J. R. shot and killed the German. That haunted J. R. for the remainder of his life, causing him to awaken at night, screaming with terror. Don remembered that one time when J. R. began to share about this in Sunday school class, he was shamed by a class member. This was at the Middlebury Church of the Brethren where J. R. attended after marrying Donnabel Kindy. After the Sunday school incident, J. R. stopped going to church. He became alcoholic and died from cancer in 2003. J. R. survived the machine gun nest, but that day he became a victim of the war.

Don himself had a dramatic spiritual conversion experience while serving in the army. He was on a ship en route to England to care for wounded soldiers. It was around midnight when the captain came over the loud speaker telling everyone to get out on deck and to be *sure* to bring their life jackets. They were being chased by a German submarine.

In 2010 Don still vividly remembered the fear he felt. He was sure they were going to be torpedoed to kingdom come! He remembers shaking as he went to the back of the ship. "I just knew there would be no tomorrow. And then I heard a voice." It was loud and unmistakable. "*Now*, will you listen to me?" Don responded, "Yes, Lord." Soon after this, the "all clear" call came. The sub was no longer chasing them. This was a spiritual experience for Don and was a turning point in his life.

Another experience that Don will likely always remember is creeping along while lying flat on the ground to get to a wounded soldier to put a tourniquet on his leg, as bullets flew overhead. "He lost his leg, but I saved his life," Don reminisced. Don continued to support the military branch of the US government and often in prayers, thanked God for those men and women who "made the supreme sacrifice" by dying for their country. Don confessed that it was in part his brother's experience, as well as the vivid memory of wounded men dying in his arms, that prompted him to pray as he did.

When J. O. Yoder was pressed in 2010 for an explanation as to why he had decided to be a conscientious objector while many in the same congregation with the same ministers and Sunday school teachers entered the military service, he said he had learned the Golden Rule at age five or six. He does not remember his parents discussing the implications of this. His parents didn't *need* to talk about loving the enemy. He knew from Sunday school that that was the teaching of Jesus.

However, J. O. did confess to taking up a weapon on at least one occasion. His elderly Uncle Levi, who was self-reliant and living alone, reported that money was

47. In the early 1900s, a baby who was thought to perhaps be the youngest son was sometimes named Junior. It was not necessarily related to having the same name as the father.

disappearing from his billfold. His nephews, J. O. and Ralph Yoder, went on the alert; footprints in fresh snow helped with the investigation. One night J. O. and his brother took watch. With a kitchen broom, Ralph hid himself in a far corner in the kitchen and J. O. took a position at the far end of the dining room beyond the door to Levi's bedroom, livestock cane in hand. A period of silence followed. In due time, a car came into the driveway and stopped by the kitchen door. Uncle Levi was asleep in bed, his trousers with his billfold hung over the back of a chair. There was only a trickle of noise as the intruder entered. And then the clink of the belt buckle against the chair was the signal.

Bright kitchen lights brought a loud silence throughout the entire house. It continued and finally a voice, strengthened by the sturdy livestock cane, asked, "Are you coming out, or are we coming in after you?" A voice from the bedroom said in reply, "I'm coming out." A rather neat, tall, slim young man exited the bedroom. He came face-to-face with the brothers standing in the living room, armed with a kitchen broom and wooden livestock cane.

But these defense weapons were not needed. The intruder was given the choice to talk about what was happening, or for the county police to be called. He opted to talk it over. Sitting together at the kitchen table, he agreed to give back the money. Before parting, the midnight visitor was invited to an evening meal, along with his wife. He didn't accept the invitation and later reported that he didn't want his wife to know about the incident.

The war years were maintaining years at Warren Street. They were not years of innovation. It was also a time of disruption. One wife, left behind with a child while her husband served in the Philippines, tells of this period of time. This is Helen Plank's story:

> In two weeks time after the notice came to serve in the military, my husband, Alden, and son, David, and I had to move all our furniture back to Middlebury. David and I moved into an apartment above my parent's home. Only persons who have endured such separations know the terrible wrench that it is. Church people immediately assumed that being alone I was ready and willing to pick up the church jobs that were just waiting for helpless people like me. I tried to explain that only half of me was in Middlebury and that I needed time and understanding, but it didn't work. After all, "you have your mother to look after the baby . . ." Poor mother! My parents' lives were also disrupted.
>
> It was indeed a help to have other Warren Street people who were in similar circumstances to share my life. Doneta Hershberger Burkhardt, Arlene Yoder Holdread, Betty Kurtz Stump were all women who had moved back to Middlebury for the same reasons I had.
>
> We shared letters, problems and anxiety. Some of us did not know where our men were because of censored messages. However, all was not bad. We had good times too, and I will say that we never felt discriminated against by the church people who might have felt that the men should have been conscientious objectors.

Finally the war was over. My husband called from San Francisco to say he would be home in a week. It dawned on me that I had learned to live alone. It was a meeting of two different worlds. We were lucky. We became a real family again—not everyone did. In this respect our church and praying families at Warren Street were a wonderful support and gradually we were all able to find our places within the congregation. We felt whole again. Time does heal great wounds, but let's not forget. War is hell! [48]

While some families in the church were dealing with the questions and uncertainties and transitions related to World War II, there was a series of leadership changes at WSMC. E. A. Sommer had served the congregation for eight years and then five different pastors followed over the next six years, two of whom were seminary students who served for a summer.[49]

J. Herbert Fretz came from Bluffton College for the summer of 1942. He attended Westminster Seminary following his years at Bluffton, and then was invited to pastor his home congregation, Deep Run West Mennonite Church near Perkasie, Pennsylvania. This student pastoral experience seemed to endear the WSMC/POMC congregation to Herb for the remainder of his life. In the last years of POMC Herb and his wife, Helen, came for several special occasions.

A note in a WSMC church bulletin states that Robert W. Hartzler, pastor of Silver Street Mennonite Church, "is happy to serve as acting pastor (April 18 to August 15, 1943) until Rev. Bohn arrives." Robert Hartzler was active in the General Conference Mennonite Church as pastor, editor, and developer of church institutions.[50]

Ernest J. Bohn began as pastor in October 1943. Ernest had grown up in Woodford County, Illinois.[51] Interestingly, Ernest's wife, Nora Lantz, was from Topeka, and when they married in 1924, S. S. Yoder was the officiating minister. Ernest had been ordained in 1926 in Tiskilwa, Illinois where he pastored from 1925 to 1931. Before coming to WSMC, Ernest had served as pastor at Zion Mennonite Church in Souderton, Pennsylvania, from 1931 to 1943.[52]

Even though only two members were in CPS, while Ernest Bohn was pastor, the following CPS information was given:

48. Helen (Litwiller) Plank letter to VonGunten, received January 26, 1984.

49. The names of WSMC/POMC pastors, their dates of service, and personal notes are included in appendix H.

50. Robert Hartzler was one of the first people to graduate from Mennonite Biblical Seminary; he pastored Silver Street (March 1942–July 1946) and Eighth Street (1945–1962); he was the first editor of *Central District Reporter*. Robert was the chairperson of the committee commissioned to develop and administer Camp Friedenswald where construction began in 1950. Later he was instrumental in beginning the Oaklawn Psychiatric Center and was chairperson of the first board of directors of Greencroft, Inc.

51. Ernest's Bohn grandparents came from Alsace-Lorraine and his mother's parents from Switzerland. Ernest graduated from Goshen College, studied at Princeton Theological Seminary and graduated from Garrett Biblical Institute in 1926. W. Weaver, *Central Conference*, 235–36.

52. Ellis Graber, "Zion Mennonite Church."

As of November 15, 1944, the population of Mennonite Central Committee controlled CPS Camps and the breakdown into the various forms of service stood as follows: Total number in MCC camps, 3,514. The increase for the past six months has been a bit over 300 men. Of this number 1,407 are on special projects leaving 2,107 in the base camps. A break-down of the men on maintenance projects shows that 794 are serving in mental hospitals and training schools; 285 on dairy farms; 120 dairy testers; and 76 in agricultural stations.[53]

Pastor Bohn's last worship service at Warren Street before going to Grace Mennonite in Pandora, Ohio, was on February 25, 1945. The following message to the congregation was in the bulletin:

It has indeed been a pleasure to have become acquainted with the people of the Warren Street church. We have appreciated your friendly spirit and the many kindnesses which you have shown to us. It was therefore difficult to decide to accept another opportunity for service in another field which also offered to us the additional opportunity of educating our children in the institution which we will serve, and also to live in close proximity to our work. We shall always remember our Christians friends at Middlebury in prayer as you continue your efforts in the service of the Kingdom. May the Lord bless you as you call another pastor to lead you in your work here and as you strive to do God's will in bringing the gospel of Christ to needy souls in this community.

Very sincerely,
Ernest J. Bohn and Family

In addition to providing the names and addresses of service men in the bulletin, there are numerous other indications of WSMC members supporting people whose lives were disrupted by World War II. In November 1943 it was announced in the church bulletin that the Ladies Aid had received a letter from Lowell Troyer in Downey, Idaho, in which he thanked the ladies for cookies that had been sent. Lowell was doing forestry work at a CPS camp. In August 1944 it was announced that empty jars were available to do canning for CPS camps. One can imagine rows of jars of garden produce preserved for those men and women serving away from home.

Another indication that there was support for COs at Warren Street is in a church bulletin announcement on June 1, 1944:

At the Ministerial Association meeting in April one of the most important problems discussed was the CPS dependency problem.[54] It was pointed out at this meeting that such was not a matter of charity, but of mutual Christian helpfulness which is a fulfillment of Galatians 6:2. "Bear ye one another's burdens and so fulfill the law of Christ." In order to take care of this need

53. From the December 31, 1944 Warren Street bulletin.
54. The "dependency problem" refers to the dependent children and wives of CPS men. CPSers did not receive a stipend as did the men in military service.

each church will need to work out some method by which offerings can be directed for this purpose.

While church life went on at Warren Street, there was significant activity at the district and denominational level. Warren Street had joined the Central Conference of Mennonites in 1926. The Central Conference had been a denominational group (begun in Illinois by followers of Joseph Stuckey) that included Warren Street, Topeka, Silver Street, Eighth Street, Nappanee, and nine more congregations in Illinois. This conference officially became part of the General Conference Mennonite Church denomination on February 19, 1947.[55]

THE END OF AN ERA (1946-1959)

In April 1947 the young people presented the church with new offering plates. The bulletin announcement said, "These plates are made of myrtle wood, which is very rare. Myrtle wood grows in a small area on the Pacific Coast and in the Holy Land. The tree is mentioned in the Bible in several instances. Each tree is centuries old by the time it is big enough to use for wood. It takes a very fine polish as it is one of the hardest woods known." The young people also purchased a few library books, and after having read them, brought them to the church for others to read and enjoy. "They are on the back table. We hope to have a bookcase soon." Joanne Plank was the librarian.[56]

Alvin Regier, formerly a member of the Evangelical Mennonite Brethren Church of Henderson, Nebraska, had begun a term as pastor in 1945 and resigned his position, effective June 1, 1947. According to the church board minutes, pastor Regier had been paid $30 per week.[57]

As people were resettling after World War II, the membership in the church declined, in part because jobs were not plentiful in Middlebury. The financial strain became acute. Harold Thiessen, the pastor, was paid $15 per week and given the use of the parsonage. In May 1950 pastor Thiessen was given permission to teach in the public schools the following September to ease his financial burden.[58]

Every church board meeting recorded discussion of financial trouble. For example, in June 1951 the treasurer's report showed the church was behind in payments. Offerings

---

55. W. Weaver, "Central Conference Mennonite Church."

56. These offering plates are thought to be the same ones used through 2009. WSMC bulletin, April 27, 1947. Joanne was the daughter of Melvin and Elsie Plank. Her brother Keith was the architect for the 1965 building. When Melvin died in 1952, memorial monies to POMC (WSMC) bought a lectern in memory of Melvin. In 2009, this was gifted to Menno-Hof, the Anabaptist interpretive center in Shipshewana.

57. WSMC board minutes, September, 1947.

58. WSMC board minutes, May 5, 1950.

were approximately $67 per Sunday. This information was to be put in the church bulletin and sent to absentee members in an attempt to generate more revenue.[59]

In spite of the financial trouble and the constant need for funds, there remained a strong mission emphasis at Warren Street. Lowell and Mary Troyer, members of Warren Street who were serving in a mission church in McKinley, Michigan, received a car from Warren Street to be used in their work. Foreign mission projects were desperately in need of funds and appealed to the GC churches.

Since there were five different projects to support, the Warren Street board decided to take a special offering each month and emphasize each particular project separately. Home mission projects, such as Bluffton College and Camp Friedenswald, were also part of the church board's decision to increase mission giving.[60]

The Korean War brought an interesting situation to Warren Street Church. One member of the congregation, Donald Mockler, who joined in the early 1950s, speaks for several others who joined during this time for the same reason:

> I was just a kid during world WW II, and I used to sit in the balcony at First Mennonite Church. I'd see these guys that came home from the service get up in front of the congregation. They'd beg to be let back into church. Then and there I made up my mind that I would never beg anyone to let me in church. So when the Korean War came and I decided to go into the military, I left First Mennonite and started attending Warren Street. They didn't make a big deal about this.[61]

Rev. Thiessen resigned in 1955 and a search began to find a replacement. Three candidates were considered. Two of the candidates, Elmer A. Wall and a Rev. Regier, were from the same hometown—Mountain Lake, Minnesota. Regier did not want to be in competition with anyone he knew personally so he withdrew his name. The third candidate was a retired missionary from Kansas, and the board felt it would be too expensive to bring a candidate that distance to preach a trial sermon. So, without further considering other candidates, Elmer Wall was recommended by the church board to the congregation.[62]

Elmer Wall[63] had grown up in the First Mennonite Church in Mountain Lake, Minnesota and went to Bethel College. Before coming to Warren Street, Elmer had served as a volunteer with Mennonite Central Committee in Gulfport, Mississippi,

59. WSMC board minutes, June 14, 1951.

60. WSMC board minutes, June 30, 1955.

61. Donald Mockler interview with VonGunten, January 29, 1984. Donald Mockler contributed much to the life of the congregation over the years, serving in many capacities. His first wife, Marcia, died at age twenty-eight. Subsequently Don married Marlene who also was very involved in the work of the church.

62. WSMC board minutes, July 28, 1955.

63. Elmer Wall was born October 30, 1929, to Abram and Mary Wall in Mountain Lake, Minnesota. After leaving Warren Street, he married Winifred Mumaw of Elkhart, Indiana, on December 17, 1960.

and had attended two years of seminary, one year at the Mennonite Seminary in Chicago and one year at Goshen Biblical Seminary.

This was Elmer Wall's first pastorate and he was licensed to the ministry at Warren Street by R. L. Hartzler on October 15, 1955. He was then ordained in his home congregation in Mountain Lake by Willard Wiebe on August 12, 1956. During one school year while at Warren Street, Elmer traveled by train to Chicago each week to complete his seminary degree at McCormick Seminary.

When the first Warren Street Yearbook was printed in 1956, pastor Wall wrote:

> The publishing of this yearbook marks a forward step for the congregation. We seek constantly to operate on a more informative and effective level. May this venture be symbolic of our desire to improve and grow, and together go forward for Christ.[64]

Later pastor Wall wrote: "What [the yearbook] is unable to record is the spiritual growth of individuals and the witness by word and deed."[65] He remembered Warren Street as a fine, active little church.[66]

In January 1954 the church board decided to make the next project remodeling the basement of the church building. At the February board meeting, a report was given by the trustees. Nothing further was done with the report at that time. The Women's Bible class, which represented the older women of the church, began to hold discussions about the appearance of the church building. Part of their class offering was designated to be used to finish the outside entrance to the back room.[67] With much volunteer labor, the church basement was remodeled to create a usable Sunday school room, the sanctuary walls and windows repaired and painted, and a used oil furnace installed.[68]

Elmer Wall remembered that the Warren Street building was very close to the street. The only place on the property where there was grass was a narrow strip between the church building and the hardware store. However, the church people didn't need to mow that grass, as the hardware employees would mow it while demonstrating lawn mowers to potential buyers!

In 1958, Ellsworth (E. A.) Troyer, a charter member of Warren Street, was recognized for his faithful service to this congregation. He had been a board member since the beginning of this congregation. Two of his sons, Lotus and Lowell, were GC ministers. His health no longer permitted him to be an active member of the church board; and in order to show appreciation, E. A. was named an honorary member of the Warren Street Church board.[69]

---

64. *WSMC 1956 Yearbook*, 1.
65. *WSMC 1959 Yearbook*, 1.
66. Elmer Wall in phone conversation with Hartzler, February 15, 2012.
67. Women's Bible Class minutes, August 15, 1957.
68. *WSMC 1959 Yearbook*, 4.
69. WSMC board minutes, December 8, 1958.

A small item appeared in the February 1958 board minutes that would ultimately change the entire course of the Warren Street congregation. The item read, "We helped fill out a survey of the membership of our congregation that was sent to Elmer Wall by Leland Harder, student at Chicago Mennonite Seminary." Harder was doing a sociological survey of many GC churches. Considering the low growth potential of the Middlebury community, the decline in membership and lack of financial support at Warren Street, the future of this congregation did not seem good, according to Harder's survey. The members of Warren Street did not share this dismal assessment. J. O. Yoder and other leaders dared to think a radical thought: build a new church! The future at the deteriorating building with no room to expand was hopeless. But a new church building would make the future more hopeful.[70]

A DREAM MADE INTO REALITY (1960–1964)

In August 1960 Elmer Wall left the Warren Street Church to accept a pastorate with the Church of the Brethren in Middletown, Ohio. Deep regret was expressed upon pastor Wall's leaving. Samuel J. Blough wrote in the 1961 *Yearbook*, "Rarely do you find a person so devoted and sincere in his work, for which we are indeed grateful." For the remainder of the year the pulpit was filled with guest ministers.

In January 1961 Raymond Yoder[71] was hired as a part-time pastor, and Bernard ("Bernie") Wiebe, a college student, was hired as the associate pastor. Keeping in mind the vision of a new church, it was known to these church board members that Raymond Yoder was a strong leader, not afraid of confrontation, and definitely in favor of building a new facility.

Raymond Yoder is remembered for a vivid sermon illustration. He said, "Christ coming to earth in the form of human would be like us taking on the form of a mouse and trying to teach something to other mice!" Yoder was described as a jolly kind of guy. He taught school in Millersburg along with being pastor of WSMC for a year. He had been ordained to the ministry in 1939 and served at the Chicago Home Mission and the Congerville (Illinois) Mennonite Church before coming to Warren Street.

The February 1961 board meeting was the first meeting Raymond Yoder attended. After considerable discussion on the problems of further remodeling and long-range planning, pastor Yoder made a motion "that the trustees bring a recommendation to the board on two plans." Plan one would be to remodel the present church to meet needs. Plan two, as pastor Yoder recommended, would be to research building an entirely new church building. These plans should be presented to the board in four weeks with cost estimates of each plan included. Robert Wortinger, trustee, seconded the motion, and it carried seven to two.

70. J. O. and Leona Yoder interview with VonGunten.

71. Raymond Yoder (March 28, 1914–April 6, 1983) was the son of Samuel A. and Nora Stutzman Yoder, members of College Mennonite Church.

At the March 1961 board meeting, the trustees' report was read by Bob Wortinger. Plan one gave a list of things that needed to be done, but "in the opinion of the trustees, it would be uneconomical and impractical to remodel." Donald Hershberger, trustee, further clarified this position by stating that the present location of the church had no land for building expansion or parking facilities. Congregational growth just could not occur under these conditions. Plan two stated that the trustees would not secure an estimate on a new building until more information was available, but Donald Hershberger did state that building costs were $10–15 per square foot.

Preschool class at Warren Street in 1965. Clockwise from left: Doneta Burkhardt, Cindy Mockler, Michael Krehbiel, Mary Yoder, Richard Yoder, David Mockler, Kelly Tahara.

Bob Wortinger, acting chairman, presented plans one and two to the congregation. A third plan was suggested—to do nothing. He stated that twenty families indicated they would be willing to pledge $27,000 over a five-year period, and five families were unwilling to commit themselves. J. O. Yoder, deacon, reported on several churches he had visited. Most of these churches were built with a lot of volunteer labor to keep the cost lower. Donald Hershberger made a motion, seconded by J. O. Yoder that: "We start a new church building program." The motion carried. The remainder of the meeting was spent appointing committees to carry out the building program.[72]

72. WSMC congregational meeting minutes, April 9, 1961.

Inside Warren Street Mennonite Church in 1965.

The Sunday morning attendance had been in the 30s and 40s at that time. Not everyone agreed with the building program, and some families left the church. At the May 1961 meeting of the church board, the chairman and the secretary both resigned from their respective positions due to their opposition to the building program. Concern was expressed that the building program was moving too rapidly and not enough attention was being paid to the objections expressed by some of the members.

While members were discussing the future of the congregation, apparently a variety of options were being considered. Even though the decision to build had been made at the April 1961 congregational meeting, someone from Warren Street apparently sent a letter to Silver Street in early May. On June 6, 1961, a letter was sent to pastor Bernie Wiebe from Louis Koerner, deacon and chairman of the Silver Street Mennonite Church board. It follows:

> Dear Brethren in Christ:
>
> Greetings in Jesus' name.
>
> In reply to your letter of May 9, 1961, our church board has convened and discussed the propositions concerning our two churches. We, the deacons, have been asked to send a reply to the two topics stated in your letter.
>
> Concerning the possibility of sharing one full-time minister in two locations we feel that both churches would lose somewhat of the personal contact needed with the minister since he would not be able to be at both full services.

However, we feel that the possibility of consolidating the two churches is quite feasible and also desirable. We would like to extend an invitation to the members of the Warren Street Church to join us. The Silver Street Church is already quite centrally located and the structure is more than adequate to care for our combined membership.

We trust you will give this matter some very careful and prayerful consideration.

Sincerely, in His service,
Louis Koerner

The time was not right for a merger of Silver Street and Warren Street churches. Instead, Warren Street committees began to work, and by February 1962 the building committee reported that a timetable was established as follows: June 1962, a building site would be chosen and a rough draft of the proposed building would be ready. These rough drafts would be done by Keith Plank, an architect for United Air Lines and an inactive member of Warren Street. Within a year, by June 1963, the final plans and blueprints should be completed by an architect. The projected starting date for building would have to be determined by available finances.

The Finance Committee projected an income of $20,000 from pledges, and $15,000 from the sale of church property. The balance needed would be borrowed at building time.[73] For his annual report, J. O. Yoder, building chairman, spoke to the frustrations of putting a vision into reality:

> It is somewhat difficult to summarize the past year's efforts. . . . Early in the year, delay and interruptions were created by church membership withdrawals leaving some committees nearly deplete. (This) prevented a smooth and orderly development of the overall building program. . . . It is encouraging to note increasing interest . . .[74]

In the midst of all the plans and activity, in June 1962 the congregation called Myron Krehbiel to be pastor for a three-year term. Myron had grown up in the Eden Mennonite Church in Moundridge, Kansas, and graduated from McPherson College, a Church of the Brethren college in Kansas. He had attended seminary in Chicago before coming to Middlebury, and his long term plan was to be a missionary to Colombia, South America.[75] Myron accepted a three year term at Warren Street. He came with his wife, Jean, and their son, Michael John, who had been born in November 1961. During the three years at Warren Street, a son, Timothy Leon, was born to them on December 1, 1964.

Jean Marie (Noffsinger) Krehbiel had been born in Dayton, Ohio. Her father, Paul Noffsinger, was a minister in the Church of the Brethren. Jean graduated from North

73. WSMC *Newsletter*, February 15, 1962.

74. Ibid.

75. JoAnn Krehbiel Funk (sister of Myron) in phone conversation with Hartzler, April 2, 2012.

Manchester High School and studied at Manchester College before entering nursing training at Swedish Covenant Hospital in Chicago. She became a registered nurse in 1959. Jean and Myron had met in Chicago and were married September 26, 1959. Their first home was in the parsonage at Pulaski, Iowa. There Jean joined with Myron in work in the Mennonite Church. Her musical talents included vocal, piano, and organ.[76]

The Warren Street leaders continued pursuing the dream of a new location. After many meetings to find the best site at a cost that was affordable, Tom Tahara, treasurer, reported to the church board on September 9, 1963, that a contract for six acres adjoining the west side of Twin Oaks subdivision on County Road 16 was ready to be signed. A down payment of $300 was made to owner Dewey Gingerich[77] with a balance of $3,500 due.[78]

The Warren Street Church building was sold in 1964 for $10,000. The group who bought it was led by Jonas D. Miller. They had previously been members of the Riverside Mennonite Conservative Church. An interesting sidelight of this transaction was given by Don Hershberger, a trustee at the time. The group had very little money and had decided to inform the Warren Street Church that they would not be able to purchase the building. On his way to Middlebury with this news, Miller stopped at someone's home and at that home received the financial resources needed. Therefore, when Mr. Miller arrived at Don Hershberger's home, he had good news and completed arrangements to buy the opera-house-turned-church-building.[79]

Since a new church building was not yet available to the Warren Street congregation, the two groups shared the building. Each group conducted their own church services and Sunday Schools until April 1965.[80]

Very careful planning was done by each committee. Details of rooms were combined to create warmth and togetherness. These ideas were given to the Executive Committee and then to the architect. By February 1964 the final drawings were being made, and work on the new building began in April 1964. A building fund kick-off dinner brought the total in the building fund to $8,026.11. (Payment for the land had been made.) In June the trustees were authorized to borrow $12,000 for a period of four years. At last, three years after the motion to build a church was passed, the

---

76. Jean Noffsinger Krehbiel (September 22, 1936–April 11, 1965) obituary, WSMC/POMC archival material that will go to the Central District Conference Archives at Bluffton University.

77. Dewey Gingerich was an Amish man whose grandson Matthew Gingerich became a member of Pleasant Oaks in 2005. For three months in 2006 Matt served as youth pastor.

78. WSMC board minutes, September 9, 1963. The exact size of the purchased lot remains somewhat of a mystery in 2010. According to J. O. Yoder, the land was purchased at $500 per acre and the total cost was $3500.

79. Donald Hershberger interview with VonGunten, January 29, 1984.

80. According to Don Hershberger, when the new Pleasant Oaks congregation moved into their new facilities, the Warren Street Church Chapel (with Jonas Miller as leader) could not support the facility financially, so it was soon sold to Varns and Hoover Hardware in Middlebury. Within a short time, the building was torn down and the lot was then used as storage space for the hardware store.

construction began. Donald Hershberger, a building contractor, consented to be the supervisor of volunteer labor.[81]

The small group of church members, men and women, all volunteers, worked every weekday evening and all day most Saturdays. Some of the children came along with their parents to play or to help. When the group finished work in the evenings they often headed for the Curve Inn (now the Essenhaus) because some came straight from working at their jobs all day and were hungry. At times some of the women brought food to eat and the group ate at the new building. Sometimes they had watermelon to eat and would have a contest to see who could spit watermelon seeds the farthest. Later watermelon vines grew in the yard!

Women carried bricks and mixed mortar right along with the men. Everyone worked hard, and gradually the dream of a new church building became a visible reality. By November Don Hershberger reported that the building was enclosed; plumbing, heating, and septic systems were completed; staining and painting were progressing.[82]

In 2009 Don Hershberger reflected back on the building of the church. He said, "The weather was always good. We were never rained out." Apparently during the summer of 1964 the rains always came early in the day, at night, or on Sundays![83]

Don and his wife, Doris (Kline),[84] were very involved in the Warren Street Mennonite Church throughout their long marriage. Doris served as church secretary for two or three years in the mid-1970s and then worked at AMBS as a receptionist for about four years. Don spent his adult life working as a contractor, first working with his father in "Hershberger and Sons" and then continuing the business with his brother Calvin and employing up to twenty men. Don was the general contractor who supervised the construction of the Pleasant Oaks building in 1964–65 as well as the educational wing on the east side of the building, beginning in September 1969, and the front entrance in 1984.[85] Thus, Don feels much invested in the building as well as in the life of the congregation.

Doris and Don raised three daughters in the church, Linda, Judy, and Cathy. It was their daughter Judy who at age twelve submitted the winning entry in a contest to name the congregation and new building in 1964: Pleasant Oaks Mennonite Church. The church board moved that the new name be officially used starting January 1, 1965.[86]

---

81. WSMC *Newsletter*, February 28, 1964; WSMC board minutes, April 14, 1964; WSMC board minutes, June 9, 1964; WSMC *Newsletter*, May 1, 1964.

82. WSMC *Newsletter*, November 3, 1964.

83. Don Hershberger conversation with Hartzler, May 2009.

84. Doris grew up as a Methodist in nearby Sturgis, Michigan. She and Don were married on July 1, 1945.

85. Don volunteered his time for the 1964–65 building project, running his business by day and supervising the volunteer church members on evenings and weekends. He and his crew were hired to build the additions in 1969–70 and in 1984.

86. WSMC board minutes, October 13, 1964.

When spring arrived, the building was ready for occupancy. John Burkhardt made a large cross that was placed on the front panel of the sanctuary. The sanctuary was built to seat 125. The educational wing included seven classrooms, one of which also served as the pastor's study and three that could be converted into a fellowship hall. The entire structure cost $45,000.

Doris Hershberger remembers that on the evening before Palm Sunday some of the members were laying the tile on the floor of the foyer, while others were busy working in other parts of the new church building. They were working hard to finish the building. The church board voted to have Maundy Thursday Communion in the new church with Easter Sunday (April 18, 1965) the first Sunday morning worship service.[87] Palm Sunday (April 11, 1965) was the last service for the congregation in the building that had been their home since 1923.

On Palm Sunday the congregation left the morning worship service with joyful anticipation, but before the day was over, unimaginable devastation swept over Elkhart County. What became known as the Palm Sunday Tornados tragically claimed the lives of dozens of people including the pastor's wife and infant son, Jean and Timothy Krehbiel. A wide outbreak of forty-seven tornados in Ohio, Michigan, and Indiana killed 271 people (137 in Indiana) and injured 1,500 (1,200 in Indiana). From the South Bend area east to LaGrange there were sixty-five deaths, many injuries, and scores of homes damaged or destroyed.[88]

Many people from Pleasant Oaks remember the day vividly. Each year on Palm Sunday the five sister churches (of the Central District Conference) in the area would combine choirs to perform a musical program. The program was scheduled at the church in Nappanee that evening. Doris Hershberger remembers that all afternoon there were tornado warnings on the radio and television. Perhaps because it had been a long time since a tornado had occurred in this area, the warnings were not taken seriously. Doris told the following story:

> Donald and I, along with our three daughters, started for Nappanee and went by way of Elkhart. On the way over we saw a tornado traveling parallel to us. It was far enough away from us, and as long as it didn't change direction, we thought we weren't in any danger, so we kept driving.
>
> Shortly after we arrived at the church in Nappanee, everyone was told not to leave but to go down into the basement because of the tornado warning. Jean Krehbiel, the wife of our pastor, Myron Krehbiel, and their two young sons (Michael John, age three and one-half, and Timothy Leon, four and one-half months) had planned to come later, because Jean had stayed in Middle-bury to practice in a quartet. Myron had come with someone else. Since Jean did not arrive at the church as expected, we told our pastor that we could take him home. When the all clear was given and we were finally allowed to leave,

87. POMC board minutes, April 6, 1965.
88. http://en.wikipedia.org/wiki/1965_Palm_Sunday_tornado_outbreak.

we went home by way of Goshen. At that time we didn't know the extent of the damage caused by the tornados, so we were surprised when we kept hearing sirens and seeing ambulances and police cars as we were routed around different streets in Goshen.

When we finally got back to Middlebury we dropped off Myron at his house and went home. I turned on the television to see if we could get any news about what had happened. As we were listening to reports of all the destruction that had taken place and were being told that phone service was out, we were startled to hear our phone ring. The caller was Doris Wortinger, a nurse at Goshen Hospital who was allowed to make an emergency call. (Mrs. Wortinger was a former member of Warren Street.) She asked us to get Myron and bring him to the hospital. She said that Jean and the baby were brought to the hospital because they were hit by the tornado as they drove through Jefferson en route to Nappanee. Mrs. Wortinger didn't know what happened to Michael. She also said that Jean's leg had been amputated by the tornado and that her heart had stopped three times, but was started again each time, and that she and Baby Timothy were still alive.

We went to pick up Myron, but he was not at home. We soon found him walking toward his house. He had been to a bridge where someone was killed by the tornado. We told him that Jean was in the hospital but did not tell him all that we had heard about her and the children. He got into the car and we left immediately for the hospital. When we went into the hospital we were shocked to see so many wounded people lying on cots in the halls waiting until someone could take care of them. Many had visible cuts and bruises and were covered with dirt and blood.

Jean was still living but in critical condition. Inquiring about three-year-old Michael, Doris was told that an unidentified child was on the second floor. She found Michael, not seriously hurt, but shaking and wide-eyed with fear. Doris and Don waited with Myron at the hospital. Timothy died at midnight, and Jean died thirty minutes later. These deaths still cause people to shudder and wonder how our loving God allows natural disasters to happen. Or does God allow this? If God is all powerful and all loving, how can bad things happen?

Jean had been driving south on State Road 15 and was close to the Jefferson School when her car was engulfed by the tornado, recklessly tossing her and Michael and Timothy about in the car. Living in Colorado in 2012, Michael reflected on the tornado and accident. Although only three and one-half at the time of his mother's death, Michael retains memories of riding his tricycle around their small apartment and brushing against his mother's wool plaid skirts.

In addition to Myron, Michael, and her parents, Jean was survived by a brother and a sister. A vivid memory that continues in the minds of those who were there is that of a precious baby in the arms of his mother in the casket. The Krehbiels had been at Warren Street for nearly three years, and they were dearly loved by the congregation.

A description of Jean on the back of the funeral bulletin said, "Her ministry in the healing arts was exceeded only by her dedication to the Master Physician."

Instead of the first worship service in the new Pleasant Oaks building being a joyful Easter service, the first service was a double funeral on Maundy Thursday. The funeral sermon, "Living in Trust" was preached by Vernon F. Miller, a minister from Goshen City Church of the Brethren. A men's quartet sang "Safe in the Arms of Jesus" and "Still, Still with Thee." Myron's brother-in-law, Walter Davis, remembers that they also sang, "How Great Thou Art," Jean's favorite hymn that was just becoming familiar at that time. Wilbur Yoder, bishop and pastor of First Mennonite Church, officiated at the graveside service. A memorial fund in memory of Mrs. Krehbiel and Timothy was established for relief for tornado disaster victims.

Some POMC members have no memories of Easter in 1965; memories were squelched by the immeasurable grief. Others remember that on that Easter Sunday the congregation gathered at the Warren Street location for prayer and then drove to the new location in caravan. Driving up the hill to Pleasant Oaks felt like going up the hill to Calvary, rather than going to the garden to find the empty tomb.

A communion service was held in the new sanctuary on Easter Sunday. Doris Hershberger remembers that former pastor Raymond Yoder preached the sermon and that when he went to the platform to preach, he first fell to his knees and prayed.

These two deaths had a profound effect on the Pleasant Oaks congregation, not only in the immediate time following the accident. In the 2000s when the story of the new building was told by those who had been there in 1965, mention was usually made of the tornado and double funeral.

A special service was held in June 1965 to dedicate the new piano in the new sanctuary. It was "dedicated to the glory of God and in memory of the faith shown us by Jean Krehbiel." Somehow, by the grace of God, Myron Krehbiel continued to serve as pastor into the beginning of August. At that time, Krehbiel, who had submitted his resignation before the tragic deaths, left POMC and (along with his son, Michael) proceeded with his plans to be a missionary in Cali, Colombia, South America.[89]

The Pleasant Oaks congregation did what people often do when they have experienced loss; they reached out to others. Later in 1965, the Krehbiel Memorial Fund of $1,000 was given to the Andrew Boone family of Goshen. Their only child was killed and the mother severely injured in the Palm Sunday tornado.

---

89. After a time of teaching in Colombia, Myron Krehbiel returned with Michael to the United States and worked in Indiana, Ohio, and Michigan and got a second degree in teaching. He never pastored another congregation. He taught in many different schools in the Midwest and in missionary schools in Juhaka and McAllen, Texas. According to family members, in many ways Myron floundered the remainder of his life. His best natural gift was thought to be improvising music on the piano, but in spite of encouragement from family, Myron did not pursue a career in music. He married Betty Jamieson in 1970, and when Michael was twelve, they adopted John who was also twelve; Betty died in car accident in 1982; in 1996 Myron married Allie Heck who died in 2009; Myron moved to Sterling, Colorado, and lived with his son Michael before his death in 2011.

PLEASANT OAKS EXPANDS (1965–1975)

**Dedication of Pleasant Oaks Mennonite Church building, November 14, 1965,
outside and in the sanctuary.**

The year 1965 was one of great losses in Middlebury, but it was also one of new beginnings at Pleasant Oaks. Floyd Quenzer came to POMC as a candidate on June 20, 1965. Thinking a "trial" sermon seemed unfair, Floyd read inspirational poetry instead of preaching a sermon. He was hired and began his pastorate at POMC on September 5, 1965, installed by conference minister Gordon Dyck. Floyd came with his family, his wife, Ruth, and daughters, Shirley (age five) and Sheryl (age two). Floyd was a graduate of Pacific Bible Institute and had been pastor at Spring Valley Church from 1961 to 1964; he had been ordained in Henderson, Nebraska, by Lester Janzen in 1962.

The new church building was dedicated on November 14, 1965. Lotus Troyer returned to give the main address, "Temples of God." A. E. Kreider, J. Herbert Fretz, Raymond Yoder, and Ernest Bohn, all GC ministers, also participated in the service. Olen Yoder (senior) gave a history of the congregation. Even though Olen was more than seventy years old, he had contributed 800 hours of hard physical labor to the building of Pleasant Oaks![90]

Through the remaining years of the 1960s, the financial picture of POMC was good. One significant boost came when the members built a duplex apartment at the Associated Mennonite Biblical Seminaries in Elkhart in the summer of 1966. The income from this project helped pay what was owed on the Pleasant Oaks building. In January 1967 a debt of $8470 was owed on the church, and the general fund was in sound shape. Unprecedented growth took place in the new church building. Sunday attendance was forty-nine in 1966, the first full year in the new facilities. How gratifying that the average attendance more than doubled (to 104) by 1969! Treasurer Donald Mockler suggested appointing a committee "to look into the needs in regard to additional space for the Education Department."[91] The committee's report was given in December 1968. It was thought that eight additional rooms and an enlarged fellowship hall were needed.

In April 1969 the Building committee met with the architect to draw up a set of preliminary plans. The congregation approved the project in June, and a groundbreaking service was held September 21, 1969. With the growing membership, suddenly the Pleasant Oaks congregation faced new problems: How can members of the church get to know each other better? Would forming small groups be a solution? More social activities? Shall there be stricter membership requirements?[92]

The decade of the 1960s ended with an educational wing being added to a four-year-old building. This decade, which began with a small membership, ended with a spurt of growth never known before. Ten years earlier the situation appeared hopeless to many persons, but a determined core of members did not allow the church to die. New members included Lowell and Mary Troyer who had returned to the Middlebury

90. Olen Yoder (senior) personal interview with VonGunten, March 7, 1984.

91. POMC board minutes, October 10, 1968.

92. POMC board minutes, April 8, 1969.

area after serving at the McKinley Mission church in Michigan. They were both employed at the Mennonite Biblical Seminary in Elkhart.

The educational wing of the church was dedicated on October 10, 1971. This wing included three new classrooms, a secretary's office, pastor's study, kitchen facilities, and a large group room known as Fellowship Hall. Since the facilities were now available, an idea of starting a church-sponsored nursery school was presented to the church board. The idea was approved, and a nursery school for four-year-olds began in September 1971. Charlotte (Weldy) Hurst, member of POMC, was the first teacher. Steven Quenzer, son of pastor Floyd and Ruth Quenzer, was the only POMC child who attended the first year.[93]

A fiftieth anniversary celebration was held at Pleasant Oaks on October 21, 1973. Former member Lotus Troyer brought the message titled "The Voices We Listen to— Yesterday, Today and Tomorrow." There was a lot of singing, and interestingly, all the songs that were sung that morning were songs that POMC sang thirty-five years later around the time of the eighty-fifth anniversary celebration. They were "Holy God, We Praise thy Name," "To God be the Glory," "We are One in the Spirit," "Rise Up, O Men of God," and "Unity." This might suggest that the songs of the earlier years became part of the DNA of the congregation.

All charter members who were living and could be contacted were invited. Those who attended shared informally following a fellowship meal. Many came and others sent letters. A few letters in response to the invitation have been saved. S. S. Yoder's daughter Mable Yoder Hershberger sent a letter from Sarasota, Florida, saying, "I visited the church about seven years ago and was much impressed with the church, its members and their enthusiasm. At the time I remarked as to how thrilled my father would be to see the active and useful congregation."

During the early 1970s the neighborhood around POMC began to change. Das Dutchman Essenhaus opened across the street in 1971. The Northridge High School building was erected in 1969, and the Heritage building (then Junior High) was added in 1976. School traffic increased dramatically when an additional elementary school, Orchard View, was built in 1994. Activity behind the church building increased in 1974 when a community family garden was begun by church members. Members continued gardening in that space for many years.

Later, when the Essenhaus Inn and Conference Center opened across the street from the POMC building, members began to invite guests from the inn to attend worship services at POMC by placing bulletins on the receptionist's desk at the inn. Over the years, travelers were often welcomed to worship services, traveling Mennonites as well as people from other denominations.

There was an increase in Sunday morning worship attendance during the first six years in the Pleasant Oaks building. Records indicate that in 1965 there were thirteen households actively involved in congregational life, consisting of twenty-nine members

93. More information about the nursery school/preschool is included in chapter 6.

and twenty-two children who were not members. Three more people became members the following year, and the average Sunday morning attendance was forty-nine. The average attendance continued to go up: fifty-two people in 1967, seventy-eight in 1968, 104 in 1969, and 108 in 1971. However, beginning in 1972 there was a six-year general decline in Sunday attendance, decreasing to seventy-nine people in 1978.[94]

The Quenzer family helped to fill the children's Sunday school classrooms. In addition to arriving with two young daughters, son Stephen was born during their years in Middlebury. Floyd Quenzer also served the Silver Street congregation from August 1972 to June 1975. Near the end of 1974, Floyd resigned as pastor of POMC. His pastorate officially ended June 1, 1975. A farewell was given for the Quenzer family before they moved to Fresno, California where Floyd had accepted a pastorate at Fresno Mennonite Community Church.

A NEW CONCEPT IN MINISTRY (1975–1984)

The pastoral selection committee recommended a new idea to the Pleasant Oaks congregation. The idea was new, not only for this congregation, but for the entire GC denomination. The new idea was a team ministry. Ken and Anne Neufeld Rupp, both seminary graduates, wished to share one full-time job. Ken was an ordained minister; Anne was a licensed minister. They would divide the responsibilities as they wished. There were no other team ministries in the General Conference in 1975, so the idea seemed strange. Anne tells the story of how she and her husband came to this concept of ministry:

> In 1966, Ken and I were married (after we had both graduated from seminary). I continued to teach piano, and also began to take writing more seriously while Ken served churches in Turpin, Oklahoma; in Beatrice, Nebraska; and in Kansas City, Kansas. One son, Byron, joined our home in 1971.
>
> The church has always been important in my life, and I've always been involved in music, teaching or speaking. Our Western District minister frequently said, "Have you two ever thought of going into a team, to make use of both of your gifts?" . . . It didn't seem right at that time. In 1974 we both did some career assessment testing with a Presbyterian career system and the director said, "Have you two ever thought of going into a team—your gifts complement one another." Somehow the Lord spoke to us that day. We walked out of that session, both of us with the conviction, "We're going into a team." It was a leap of faith.[95]

---

94. More detailed information regarding attendance and membership is in appendix R.
95. Anne Neufeld Rupp in letter to VonGunten, received April 1, 1984.

Ken[96] and Anne Neufeld Rupp[97] were hired for a team ministry. Anne had grown up in a German-speaking Russian Mennonite family on a farm in southern Manitoba without running water or electricity. She went to a one-room school through grade nine and then worked in a hospital to earn enough money to finish high school. She graduated from Canadian Mennonite Bible College in Winnipeg with a degree in Sacred Music and Christian Education. She then attended Bethel College in Kansas and earned a teaching certificate and prepared to go to Africa as a missionary. Instead she was sent to Mexico where she taught children of Old Colony Mennonites for three years. Unable to return to Mexico after a furlough, she attended Associated Mennonite Biblical Seminary (AMBS) in Elkhart and graduated in 1966 with a Masters degree in Religious Education. Even though her father and his father had been ministers, Anne did not consider pastoral ministry because that was not an option for a woman in the mid-1960s. Instead she became a pastor's wife after marrying Ken Rupp whom she had met in seminary. However, her role changed when they came to Middlebury.

Ken Rupp had grown up in Mountain Lake, Minnesota. He graduated from Bethel College with a degree in sociology. Later he earned a degree from AMBS in Elkhart where he met Anne. Ken had served several GC congregations in Nebraska, Oklahoma, and Kansas before coming to POMC.

At Pleasant Oaks Anne's areas of responsibility were Christian education, pastoral care, and outreach. Ken was in charge of worship and administration. Both Anne and Ken preached, sharing that responsibility about equally; Ken often led adult Sunday school classes and Bible studies.

On November 7, 1976, Anne was the second woman to be ordained in the General Conference Mennonite Church and the first woman ordained in Central District Conference. This service took place at POMC with Anne's father, Abraham Neufeld, a pastor from Manitoba, Canada, preaching the sermon. He told of how Anne had nearly died during childhood. Anne's mother and he dedicated Anne's life to God during this illness. For her mother and father, Anne's ordination was a special occasion—seeing Anne's life dedicated to God's work. Another interesting note of that day was that Abraham Neufeld, first generation Canadian from the German Mennonite colonies in Russia, had never preached a sermon in English. He normally preached to German-speaking Canadian congregations. Anne spoke of his hesitancy to preach such an extended time in English—he would have been much more comfortable speaking German!

Perhaps it should not come as a surprise that a congregation that began because young women rejected an old tradition was the second congregation in the denomination to ordain a woman. The following statement was made: "The unusual situation of ordaining a woman as pastor was not as important as being faithful to the Biblical

96. Ken Rupp (April 23, 1941–April 27, 2010) was born to Emil and Marie (Rahn) Rupp in Mountain Lake, Minnesota.

97. Anne Neufeld was born March 5, 1932, to Abram G. and Margaret (Duerksen) Neufeld in Manitoba. Her parents had both been born into Mennonite families in Russia and immigrated to Manitoba as young people.

mandate of discerning gifts and affirming those gifts so clearly seen and appreciated in her ministry in the congregation."[98] In his 1976 deacon report to the congregation, J. O. Yoder described Anne's ordination as high point in the spiritual life of the congregation.[99]

Anne and Ken Rupp shared pastoral tasks including in the pulpit.

Anne and Ken did a great deal to emphasize Christian education. In 1977 a new Sunday school curriculum, *The Foundation Series*, was released. This was a cooperative project of five peace churches: Brethren in Christ, Church of the Brethren, General Conference Mennonite Church, Mennonite Brethren Church, and "old" Mennonite Church. This was adopted for the Sunday school program at POMC.

Anne noted the keen interest in adult Christian education, remembering that sometimes there were more people present for the education hour than for the worship service. She and Ken arranged for people from AMBS to come and speak to classes. According to records, the average Sunday morning attendance remained steady (averaging between eighty-five and ninety-two) during the seven years the Rupps were at Pleasant Oaks.

The Central District Conference Executive Committee requested that POMC host the Central District Conference annual meeting in 1982. POMC agreed to do this and invited the other GC churches in northern Indiana to assist. These included Assembly, Eighth Street, First Mennonite (Nappanee), Hively Avenue, Silverwood,

98. Rich, *Walking Together in Faith*, 147. It is not clear who made this statement; J. O. Yoder was chair of the Deacons in 1976.

99. POMC annual report, 1976.

South Side Fellowship, and Topeka. POMC made arrangements to rent the First Mennonite Church facilities in order to accommodate the expected 400 conference guests.

Yes, this was the same congregation that fifty-nine years earlier Warren Street charter members had left! In 1982 these two congregations were in different Mennonite denominations, but the memory and repercussions of the painful 1923 split were still alive in many members. Lotus Troyer, who had been a young boy when the split occurred, realized when he attended the 1982 conference that he had not been inside First Mennonite Church since the split in 1923. "It was a strange feeling, but a good one too," he commented. "It wasn't long after the split that Middlebury Mennonite ladies were bobbing their hair too and not wearing hoods! It was all rather stupid."

In retrospect conflict does seem stupid. But disagreements are a fact of life, even in congregations where many things go well. Ken and Anne worked very hard at the various aspects of congregational ministry and provided extensive lists of their activities in annual reports. These included the usual planning, leading, and preaching in worship services at POMC and other places in the community; leading communion services and Bible studies; teaching Sunday school and Bible school; counseling and preparing youth for baptism; visiting in homes, nursing homes, hospitals, and their own home; leading retreats and a divorce support group; attending and leading committee meetings; going to ministers' meetings and other conferences; planning and officiating in funerals and weddings; doing the administrative work of the church, and much more.

Although Ken and Anne received much affirmation for their work, especially in their early years, some people were not satisfied with their ministry. During her retirement years Anne looked back and reflected on the importance of God's grace. She wrote, "Breaking new ground was hard work. I had no role model [for a woman in pastoral ministry]. There is no doubt in my mind that I made many mistakes, yet God's love surrounded me."[100] Anne chuckled as she remembered comments she heard when she was a pastor.[101] One was, "We like everything you represent, if only you did not have to preach!" Seeming to disregard the growth and enthusiasm in the majority of church members, one person said, "You just don't fit! You should be teaching in a university somewhere."[102]

Ken and Anne Rupp resigned their POMC positions in 1982 and accepted a call to the Alexanderwohl Church in Goessel, Kansas. After *Hymnal: A Worship Book* was published in 1992, Anne Neufeld Rupp was fondly remembered when the congregation sang #26, "Holy Spirit, Come with Power," a hymn text that Ann wrote and had copyrighted in 1970.[103]

---

100. From Anne Rupp correspondence with VonGunten, January 13, 2012.

101. These comments were not necessarily made at Pleasant Oaks.

102. Rupp correspondence, January 13, 2012.

103. Published conjointly by Brethren Press, Faith and Life Press, and Mennonite Publishing House, 1992.

Two interim pastors, David L. Myers and Clarence Sink, served the congregation from 1982 to early 1984. In February 1984 John Reeser, originally from Meadows Mennonite Church in Illinois, became the full-time pastor. John had been baptized as a youth by Lotus Troyer—then pastor of Meadows who had grown up at Warren Street. In 1964 John had married Connie Manier and they had three children: Martin, Gretchen, and Jason. John graduated from Illinois State University in 1966 with a degree in education after which he taught school for eleven years. From 1975 to 1982 John and his family had a touring singing ministry called "The Reeser Family Singers." John experienced a "spiritual reawakening" in 1976, and the singing ministry became full time work in 1978.[104] John became a student at AMBS in January 1983 and the following year began his ministry at POMC.

The congregation connected with John Reeser in various ways, from his child-hood in a GC sister congregation and his early association with Lotus Troyer, to his musical gifts and his association with AMBS. It seemed Pleasant Oaks was ready for the next stage of congregational life.

---

104. Estes, *Mountains to Meadows*, 154.

6

A Congregation Thriving through Growth and Decline, 1984 to 2006

"The Lord gave, and the Lord has taken away;
blessed be the name of the Lord."

Job 1:21

By 1984 Pleasant Oaks had had a face lift. A new front entrance with two sets of glass double doors opened into an enlarged foyer. The Don Hershberger Construction Company did the remodeling that included a peaked roof in place of the flat roof over the original classrooms.

Pleasant Oaks Mennonite Church building about 2000. The carved wooden church sign was created by Phil Troyer.

A gable above the entrance offered a space for a cross, and one was designed and provided by Elizabeth and Norm Mattocks from a large hickory tree that had fallen in their yard during a storm on Easter Sunday 1984. The tree seemed to have some special meaning, as it had fallen on the area where Elizabeth and Norm's seventh and eighth grade Sunday school class had enacted a play, "The Week that Shook the World," three weeks before Easter. The slide production of the play was being shown on Easter Sunday when the storm hit. The cross that had been used in the production of the play remained standing in the Mattock's back yard, unharmed and nestled among the branches of the fallen tree.

Over the years Pleasant Oaks was the home church for many gifted, generous and passionate people. While a few were noticed, many worked quietly behind the scenes. Affirmation sheets were initiated at POMC in 1983 with the purpose of affirming gifts in others in the congregation. The gifts of many members helped to carry the congregation through times of transition during the following years.

PASTORAL CHANGES

A rapid turn-over of pastors at POMC followed the relatively long pastorate of Floyd Quenzer (1965–1975) and the seven-year pastorate of Ken and Anne Neufeld Rupp (1975–1982). David Myers, a seminary student, served as interim pastor for the summer months in 1982. In November of 1982, Clarence Sink, a retired Church of the Brethren pastor, began a fifteen-month interim assignment followed by the installation of John Reeser as pastor in February 1984. The congregation had high hopes for another long-term pastorate with this gifted man who had grown up in a General Conference sister congregation in Illinois, Meadows Mennonite Church.

A priority for pastor Reeser was learning to know the members of POMC by visiting in their homes or having them in his home. An initiative during his time at POMC was a special love offering collected at the Thanksgiving Sunday Service. The funds were to be held in reserve for special needs in the community of which members would become aware. This was the beginning of the Samaritan Fund that continued during the remaining years of the congregation. It was a "beyond budget" fund that the deacons and pastor distributed for pastoral care needs, using the criteria, "What would Jesus do?"

Sadly, all did not go well; conflict arose between pastor Reeser and some members regarding theology and style, and sixteen months later the Reesers left. The congregation accepted his resignation even though there was great reluctance from those who appreciated his ministry.

The congregation was without a pastor from July 1985 until February 1986 when another General Conference pastor, Virgil Gerig, came to serve for an interim period (February to June 1986). Virgil was a very seasoned pastor, having served numerous General Conference congregations in Ohio, South Dakota, and Hively Avenue Mennonite Church in nearby Elkhart. He and his wife, Mary Kay

(Ramseyer), brought many gifts to POMC. It was a time to evaluate, mourn losses, and heal from the hurts of the previous years.

Pleasant Oaks sanctuary in the late 1980s or early 1990s.

Earlier in 1986 while the search committee worked, the leadership invited the entire congregation to make a commitment to set aside four Sunday evenings for a new experience: Harold Bauman (secretary for congregational leadership with the "old" Mennonite Board of Congregational Ministries) led the series of meetings around the following themes: Ways to Build Community, Dealing with Diversity and Differences, Spiritual Gifts in a Ministering Body, and Goals. It was somewhat novel to utilize the resources of an agency of the "old" Mennonite Church.

During Virgil Gerig's time at Pleasant Oaks, he became a mentor to Barry Schmell, who first came to POMC as a visitor, then as an AMBS student, and then began serving as a student intern in January 1986. When the pastoral search committee accepted names of candidates for a permanent pastor, Barry was considered. After careful discernment, the committee called Barry Schmell and he began his pastorate July 1, 1986.

A FULL HOUSE: THE "SCHMELL SWELL"

Pleasant Oaks members felt relief and eager anticipation when Barry Schmell was installed as pastor on July 13, 1986. Barry had grown up in the Deep Run West Mennonite Church in Bedminster, Pennsylvania, an Eastern District Conference congregation where J. Herbert Fretz had been pastor from 1945 to 1953. Barry attended Bluffton University where he majored in Sociology and Religion and began studies at AMBS in 1980. Barry and Deb (McCoy) married in Dunlap, Indiana, on September 18, 1982. He and Deb then moved to Quakertown, Pennsylvania where Barry served as youth pastor to the West Swamp Mennonite Church from 1982 to 1985.[1]

Following his time at West Swamp, Barry and Deb, along with their two-year-old daughter, Rebekah, moved to Elkhart in 1985 so that Barry could finish the MDiv program at AMBS. Barry was ordained at Pleasant Oaks as a Minister of the Gospel in the General Conference Mennonite Church on Sunday afternoon, June 7, 1987. Walter Fry from West Swamp Mennonite Church brought the afternoon message. Mark Weidner, conference minister for Central District Conference, presided over the service.

Barry brought passion, creativity, and imagination to his pastoral work. As the second year of his pastorate was coming to an end, there was a shortfall in the church finances. On December 13, 1987, the church still needed $4366.44 to meet the budget. Barry announced that if the budget was met by the end of the year, he and the finance committee would eat a meal on the roof of the church building. In the remaining two weeks of 1987, $5200.70 was collected. On the following June 12, as the congregation ate a carry-in meal in the fellowship hall, pastor Barry and Don Mockler ate their meals sitting on the peak of the steep sanctuary roof!

1. West Swamp is the congregation where John Oberholtzer was pastor and organized Bible instruction classes in 1847. This led to the division that was the beginning of the General Conference Mennonite Church.

There were no strings attached to Barry Schmell and Don Mockler as they ate a meal sitting on the peak of the roof of the sanctuary in 1988.

Barry became very involved in the life of the congregation and community. He was a school bus driver for the Middlebury Community Schools during the twelve years of his ministry at POMC, getting to know many families that lived in the community. With his outgoing personality, Barry lived his Christian testimony and engaged in conversation with many people.

Barry was instrumental in starting a community-wide recycling program that was very rare in the late 1980s and early 1990s. The church's interest in this was in response to the policy of General Conference that was encouraging recycling and saving earth's resources. In 1990 it was reported that "in the past year over 62,000 pounds of waste suitable for recycling has been collected." For a time the bins were located behind the POMC church building. Eventually the town of Middlebury took over the recycling program as it had grown beyond what the church could manage.

There was a remarkable swell in church attendance and membership at POMC while Barry was pastor. Although the average Sunday morning attendance between 1965 and 1971 had gradually increased from forty-nine to one hundred eight, from 1971 to 1978 there had been a general decline in Sunday average attendance back to seventy-nine in 1978. When Barry began his pastoral assignment in 1986, the average Sunday attendance was seventy-four. The numbers in attendance increased every year through 1993 when an all time high was reached with the annual average Sunday attendance at one hundred eighteen. This could be called the "Schmell Swell."

According to church records, the monthly average Sunday attendance was 135 for two months during the "Schmell Swell": November 1991 and April 1993. The highest ever Sunday morning attendance at POMC was 168 on November 10, 1991. The only other Sunday when more than 160 people were present was April 11, 1993, with 163 present.[2]

The sanctuary was nearly bursting at its seams, so a plan to expand was approved. The small rooms in the front of the sanctuary, one on each side of the platform, were removed. The organ and piano were moved into the newly-created space, and two more benches were added on each side in front of the previously existing benches.

Signs of growth were everywhere. The church library grew and more shelving was needed. Ben Kauffman responded by building and donating an additional shelving unit. Earlier pastor Ken Rupp had built shelves for the expanding library. A garage was built behind the church building in 1997. This was utilized for storage and a variety of other uses, including a place to park the lawnmower tractor and a meeting space for the youth for a period of time.

Reading excerpts from newsletters and bulletins from the 1980s and 1990s is like reading about a hive of busy bees.

- Friend and Neighbor Day was initiated in August 1987. This included a continental breakfast before the worship service and a noon carry-in picnic followed by recreation. This was continued for several years. Some years the meal was followed by an ice cream social. At least once the carry-in meal was held at River Bend Park.

- With the support of the deacon board, in the fall of 1987 Barry began leading Bible studies on Wednesday evenings and Friday mornings. Parents of preschool children were given special invitations to the morning studies that also included informal worship. Several families with preschool children subsequently became involved in the life of the congregation.

- The men's group planted two pin oak trees along the east driveway in 1987. After all, the name of the congregation was Pleasants Oaks!

- At least six small groups met in the late 1980s. The purposes were to share the joys and sorrows of life, for support, and fellowship.

2. A table showing the monthly average attendance from 1986 to 2009 is in appendix S.

Marvin Miller, Neil Yoder, and Jordan and Barry Schmell welcome church-goers and direct them to the east entrance during construction on the front entrance.

- Bible School continued each year, sometimes held by POMC alone and sometimes jointly with other churches in the community. The 1984 Bible School Project was to purchase life jackets for Camp Friedenswald; $274.53 was collected. In 1984 a Summer Bible Institute study of the book of Colossians was held at

POMC on Sunday evenings.

- Christian education was valued, and beginning in 1992, scholarships were made available to church members and their families who attended Mennonite colleges and seminaries.

- Vision 2000 was initiated in 1992, a fund for a building project that was anticipated.

- In December 1992 Barry led a service that included "Cookie Communion."

- The Women in Mission group continued service projects, often alternating annual garage sales and craft auctions to raise money for missions.

Members of POMC were also involved in prison ministry with the leadership of Abe[3] and Martha Peters, who had begun to regularly attend Pleasant Oaks in the 1970s following Abe's pastoral assignment at nearby Topeka Mennonite Church. Abe had been active in prison ministries, working with the Mennonite Steering Committee on Corrections when they lived in Kansas (where Abe was a pastor in a General Conference congregation), and continuing when they moved to Indiana. His passion to reach those in prison continued as he worked at Michigan City State Penitentiary.

Martha Peters died in 1977. Abe married Emma Schmucker Miller on November 23, 1978. Emma joined Abe in his passion to reach those in prison. In 1980, Abe discontinued working under the Mennonite Steering Committee and accepted the job of Protestant Chaplin at the Michigan City Penitentiary. Abe regularly shared with the congregation about his prison ministry. Often other men from the congregation accompanied Abe to assist with the Saturday night services. Others from the congregation joined in by offering canned or boxed food for the "House of Hope" prison ministries. When Abe became ill, Emma continued correspondence with many inmates, remembering them at Christmas and birthdays. Both Abe and Emma were members of POMC for the remainder of their lives, Abe dying in 1996 and Emma in 2003.

Over the years, Pleasant Oaks had close ties to Associated Mennonite Biblical Seminaries in Elkhart. Because of this, numerous people were student interns at the church: Boyd Snider (1968), Eldon Epp and Sue Schantz (1979), Debbie Schmidt (1994), Craig Friesen (1995), Anita Schroeder Kipfer (1996), and Lillian Elias (1998). In addition, a ministry inquiry Bluffton College student, Lowell G. Evans of Elida, Ohio, served as an assistant during the summer of 1994. Each of these made positive contributions to the life of the congregation.

Barry and his family were at POMC for twelve years. Again, dissension between members and with the pastor became a major concern. Many deacon/pastor meetings and meetings with the congregation, pastor, and deacons could not resolve issues that

---

3. Abe Peters (September 22, 1916–December 22, 1996) had been born in Henderson, Nebraska, and served as a minister in the General Conference throughout his adult life, first in Oklahoma and Kansas and then from 1966 to 1972 at the Topeka Mennonite Church in nearby Topeka, Indiana.

became divisive. Barry resigned in 1998, completed his assignment in July, and accepted a pastorate at Maplewood Mennonite Church in Fort Wayne, Indiana.

GROWTH TO CELEBRATE AND LOSSES TO LAMENT

Judy, Don, and Doris Hershberger, Tom Tahara, 1995.

John King, a retired "old" Mennonite pastor residing in Goshen, Indiana, became the interim pastor after Barry's departure. Once again, the congregation worked to become a body that could reach consensus and agreement. Membership was declining and people were discouraged.

The congregation was blessed with John King's leadership for about eighteen months. One of the rituals that John introduced during his time at Pleasant Oaks was celebrating birthdays each month with a special song. People with birthdays that month were invited to bring forward an offering to a designated project while the congregation sang a birthday song to the tune JEWELS (a familiar text that uses this tune begins with "When he cometh . . ."). In March 2000 a farewell dinner was given in honor of John and his wife, Edith, who had done a great deal to help the congregation become united. Perhaps John and Edith's presence also helped to prepare the way for growing connections with "old" Mennonites.

Robin La Rue was welcomed as the new pastor in April 2000. Robin had been born in Goshen and had served in GC sister congregations as associate pastor of First Mennonite Church in Berne, Indiana, and as pastor of First Mennonite Church in Nappanee. He had an interest in evangelism and youth ministry. The congregation was grateful to have been led to a pastor who could help them grow in those areas. Robin brought a lot of energy and enthusiasm to his work at Pleasant Oaks. He also emphasized that the members were crucial to the growth of the congregation.

A financial boost was given to the congregation in 2000 when a strip of land sixty feet wide along the west length of the property was sold to a developer who needed access to the land behind the Pleasant Oaks facility. In 1999 POMC had sold a smaller five-foot strip of land (totaling .04 acres) along County Road 16, used to create a bike path between the public school campus and downtown Middlebury.

Waiting for a carry-in meal to begin, Neil Yoder and Evan Stahly interact with a young friend while Robin and Rosemary La Rue, Sanford Yoder, and Ken VonGunten wait.

By the beginning of 2001, a Vision and Purpose Group was ready to begin their task. Four people from the congregation along with Marv Borntrager and Robin La

Rue formed the group. Their task was to look at the future of Pleasant Oaks with two basic questions in mind: "Who are we as God's people?" and "What is our mission?" Members joined in new initiatives as well as maintenance activities.

In 2001 Eileen Yoder Miller made new curtains for the fellowship hall and foyer. A new computer, printer, and overhead projector were purchased. Many people helped with the construction of the new and improved playground area in 2002. Gerri Beachy was acknowledged for his extra time and effort on the playground. In 2003 a new church sign board with lights and panels for short announcements or quotes was installed.

Christian education of children and youth was always important at Warren Street and Pleasant Oaks. The newsletters are sprinkled with notes about Bible School over the years. The first reference to Bible School with First Mennonite Church is in 1994. Again in 1999, 2000, and 2001, Pleasant Oaks and First Mennonite worked together to offer Bible School to children in the congregations and the community.

Robin La Rue, who had been assigned to develop the youth program, worked to establish Mennonite Youth in Action that soon became known as MYIA. Contact was made with two other small Mennonite congregations in the Middlebury area—Forks and Bonneyville.[4] Robin worked with pastors of these congregations to jointly hire a youth pastor. In his late fifties, Robin playfully said that the youth didn't really respond to an aging pastor like himself; someone younger with more energy was needed. Consequently, Bonneyville, Forks, and Pleasant Oaks jointly hired Michael Miller as youth pastor. Michael had grown up at Waterford Mennonite Church where he was baptized as a youth. As a young adult, he became involved in church ministry and was ordained in the spring of 2000 by Foundation Ministries.

In September 2002 Michael began his ministry in the Middlebury area. He led Wednesday night meetings that included games and Bible study. Youth without church affiliations, youth who chose to not attend the church of their parents, and youth from families in the three congregations came for the Wednesday evening events. Michael's energy was enormous. He planned outings to professional ballgames, youth conventions, and summer mission trips, including trips to Puerto Rico and Mexico.

A big event for the summer of 2002 was a "Summer Family Fun" weekend. Saturday afternoon family games preceded a meal under a canopy. A few families stayed overnight. An outdoor worship service was held on Sunday morning. Hopes were high for this to be an annual event that would bring in more people from the community.

In July 2003 Ken Livengood, pastor at Bonneyville and strong supporter of MYIA, was killed in a motorcycle accident. This was a great loss to not only his family and congregation, but also to the MYIA program. Unfortunately, support and interest from the Bonneyville and Forks congregations diminished, and by 2004 POMC was the only congregation supporting Michael. The larger plan of small congregations

---

4. By 2002 the GC and MC denominations had merged into MC USA. The collaboration of these congregations from both traditions is an indication that the merging was working on the local level.

banding together did not materialize on a long-term basis. However, MYIA continued to attract many youth and they met at POMC.

Robin La Rue and his wife, Rosemary, were at Pleasant Oaks until August 2004. Robin made the decision to retire from pastoral ministry and accept a position with Heartland Home Health Care and Hospice in Fort Wayne, Indiana. He had always had a deep interest in Alzheimer's and elder care. A farewell dinner was held to honor Robin and Rosemary.

Eugene Bontrager, who, along with his wife, Barbara, had been attending POMC following years of pastoring at near-by Forks Mennonite Church (1985–1996), agreed to serve as interim pastor for a year. Michael Miller continued as the youth pastor. Due to the decline in membership and low attendance (average of forty-one on Sunday mornings in 2004), Eugene was hired for a half-time position beginning September 2004.

Not only was the life of the congregation sustained during the months that Eugene served as pastor, there were numerous signs of hope. On July 1, 2005, the attendance soared to fifty-four on a Sunday with a hog roast designated as "Visitors' Day."[5] Eugene led three young people through instruction classes, and they were baptized on September 18, 2005. It was a time for rejoicing! Seventy people came to worship and celebrate the baptisms that Sunday, bringing the average attendance that month to forty-three.[6]

Gerri, Connie, and Cami Beachy at a fellowship meal.

5. The average monthly attendance had dropped to thirty in October 2004, apparently the lowest attendance in the life of the congregation to that date.

6. However, the average monthly attendance was never greater than forty-three in the remaining years of the congregation's life. A table showing the monthly average attendance from 1986 to 2009 is in appendix S.

A social committee planned events such as Valentine dinners, an all church pool party, and on one occasion, a hayride at the Hooley farm. The girls and women in the church frequently had special events during May, usually with an interesting guest speaker. Bridal showers and baby showers also brought together the girls and women of the congregation.

In addition, many of the traditional activities of the church continued: annual cleaning of the church building and grounds followed by homemade ice cream, Christmas programs, and taking a turn at hosting the Middlebury community Ministerium-sponsored Lenten services, the community World Day of Prayer service, and the Easter sunrise service.

There were many significant losses for Pleasant Oaks in the late 1990s and early 2000s. A trend throughout North America was people leaving traditional denominational churches for larger congregations with many appealing programs. Many of the new congregations were not associated with a denomination; some were described as mega-churches. Numerous people left POMC for other congregations, including several families transferring to other Mennonite congregations in the area. Those who remained deeply felt each loss.

Several deaths between 1985 and 2002 compounded the losses. Especially the deaths of Charlotte Hurst, Lynn Rheinheimer, Marlene Mockler, and Ken VonGunten seemed very untimely.

Charlotte (Weldy) Hurst and her husband, Tony, and sons had been part of the Pleasant Oaks family since 1970. It was Charlotte and Sara VonGunten who had envisioned the nursery school/preschool, and the first class began in September 1971 with Charlotte as the teacher. She continued her involvement with the nursery school classes through 1977, serving as teacher and director. On November 8, 1985, Charlotte, at age forty-one, was tragically killed in a car crash caused by a drunken driver. Both Charlotte and Tony had been very involved at POMC in the 1970s and early 80s, Tony having served a term on the board of deacons. However, by the mid-1980s they had begun to explore other church possibilities, and by the time of Charlotte's death, they were involved at Zion Chapel, a "charismatic" fellowship in Goshen. Nevertheless, this did not minimize the great loss. Not only had the Hursts left POMC, but now it was clear that Charlotte would not be coming back.

At the time of her death, Charlotte was employed at Goshen College, and her memorial service was held at College Mennonite Church. Officiating ministers were Bob Detweiler (pastor of Yellow Creek Mennonite Church), Steve Chupp (pastor of Zion Chapel), and John Reeser, who returned from Pennsylvania for the service. Money was donated to POMC in memory of Charlotte. Sculptor John Mishler was commissioned to create an original carved wooden piece that was placed in the sanctuary. In raised letters the plaque proclaims "I am the resurrection and the life." To all who knew Charlotte, this was a reminder of her abbreviated although well-lived life.[7]

---

7. This memorial and other memorial gifts to WSMC/POMC are listed in appendix M.

Lynn Rheinheimer and Darlene Helmuth joined Pleasant Oaks before they were married in September 1968. It became the home church for their children, Gayle (later married to Keith Roth) and Craig. Lynn grew up in a family that raced trotter horses. Early in their marriage Lynn got involved in horse cart racing, and soon trotter horses became a family project. Sadly, in January 1993 Lynn was found to have lung cancer. After undergoing chemotherapy, Lynn felt much better in May and went on to have the best race season he had had in years. However, the cancer returned, and Lynn died October 28, 1993, at the age of forty-seven, leaving Darlene with two young adult children. The POMC family surrounded Darlene, and she remained involved in the life of the congregation. Money given in memory of Lynn was used to purchase NIV Bibles for the church pews. The absence of another young member was keenly felt at POMC.

In addition to being mother for a large blended family, Marlene (Mishler Baker) Mockler was actively involved in the life of Pleasant Oaks. She was director of the preschool for eight years and served on the preschool board for many more years. In 1996 Marlene retired from eighteen years of secretarial work for POMC, during which time she had edited the church newsletter. Marlene died from cancer in February 1998. Memorial money was designated for the preschool. In addition, Marlene's husband, Don, contributed playground equipment and a much-appreciated laminator for preschool use to the memory of Marlene.

Sara and Ken VonGunten raised their three children (Amy, Doug, and Peter) at Pleasant Oaks. They both taught in the Middlebury School system, Sara in elementary and Ken in the high school. They were very active lay leaders at POMC all the years they attended. Sara was very involved in Central District Conference activities as well as in the local congregation. Both served as Sunday school teachers and on the deacon board and church board, each taking a turn at chairing these boards. Ken retired from school teaching at age sixty-three with lots of energy. It was almost unimaginable that a healthy, relatively young man like Ken would have a stroke, but that is what happened on August 16, 2002. Ken was put on life support, and the congregation surrounded Sara and their children as they waited day after day for signs of hope. When there was evidence of severe brain damage, Sara made the agonizing decision to stop the life support, and Ken died on September 1, 2002.

Hundreds of stunned people came to pay respect and offer condolences to Sara, her children, and the extended VonGunten family. Ken's memorial service was at the First Mennonite Church, which was filled with relatives, friends of all the family members, current and former church members, students, faculty, and staff from Northridge, and other community people.

The death of a spouse causes great turmoil for most people, complicated at times by an identity crisis and the need for new beginnings. For Sara VonGunten, it was returning to the church of her childhood, Eighth Street Mennonite in Goshen. For Pleasant Oaks, this meant the loss of two more very important people, and the congregation stumbled over these losses.

Other significant losses were the leadership gifts of Marvin and Ruth Miller, another couple with many gifts and willing hearts. They had been members since 1985, and both served in many capacities. Following a stroke in 2001, Marvin participated in worship but could no longer lead, and Ruth was fully occupied in Marvin's care.

And then there were the losses of pastors. It is interesting to note that only one pastor at WSMC/POMC remained with the congregation for longer than 10 years. That was Barry Schmell, who stayed at POMC for twelve years, from July 1986 to July 1998. While it is not unusual for pastors to remain in one congregation for short periods of time, it seems noteworthy that most served for relatively short times, and all the "regular" pastors (not including interim or student pastors) between 1975 and 2004 left on unhappy terms. The contract for Ken and Anne Rupp was not renewed. The next non-interim pastor, John Reeser, stayed just sixteen months. Barry Schmell was much loved and admired in the early years of his pastorate, but everyone seemed to acknowledge that things did not go well near the end of his time. Although Robin La Rue worked hard at the mandate given to him—build up the youth program and the over-all church attendance—he left POMC after four years sprinkled with conflicts. One member described pastoral transitions as rough sailing.

It's hard to imagine what might have happened to POMC when Robin La Rue left in 2004, had Eugene Bontrager not been available and willing to carry on with pastoral responsibilities. Eugene was a lifesaver for the little congregation where the attendance was decreasing with each passing year. Eugene agreed to fill the pastoral position for a year.

By the grace of God, the energy was found for another pastoral search committee to find the next pastor. In the fall of 2005 the committee interviewed Rachel Nafziger Hartzler who was looking for a half-time pastoral position. As the possibility of hiring a female pastor was discussed among the leadership, youth pastor Michael Miller stated that because of his understandings of scripture, he would find it difficult to work with a female pastor. Rachel's name was dropped and other candidates were pursued. How interesting that the question of women in pastoral leadership was raised in 2006 in this congregation that had thirty years earlier ordained the first woman in the Central District Conference in 1976![8]

Even though Eugene had agreed to serve as interim pastor through September 2005, he reluctantly agreed to continue through the end of 2005, but no longer. Without a permanent pastor in the offing, the church board asked Michael Miller to assume the role as lead pastor for an interim period of time beginning in January 2006. He continued the active youth program, planned Sunday morning worship services, and preached many Sundays.

After several months, not finding a suitable and available male candidate to fill the role of lead pastor, the POMC leadership group had more discussions with Michael Miller, after which the search committee invited Rachel Nafziger Hartzler

8. See chapter 5 for information about the ordination of Anne Neufeld Rupp.

into conversation again. On April 30, 2006, Rachel preached a sermon on forgiveness, "Witnesses of the Resurrection." The recommendation to hire Rachel passed with a vote of twenty-seven to three.

One description of the congregation early in 2006 is that they were fatigued and discouraged, but they held onto a cautious hope that things would improve. In April 2006 Rachel Nafziger Hartzler was hired to become Pleasant Oaks' lead pastor. She agreed to begin on May 16. Could the energy and enthusiasm of a new pastor help to turn around the discouragement and declining attendance patterns of the previous few years?

A THRIVING NURSERY SCHOOL/PRESCHOOL

One of the most delightful sounds in the world is the music of young children, happily singing and playing in a pleasant and safe environment. Some of the most beautiful structures in the world are church buildings, places where God is worshiped. Of all the work places imaginable, one of the most wonderful is a church office that is adjacent to a preschool. Blessed are those who have this opportunity, for they will be reminded daily that with each child that is born, God is offering new hope to the world! Numerous pastors of Pleasant Oaks have had this pleasant privilege.

For more than forty years preschool children have been nurtured on weekdays at Pleasant Oaks Mennonite Church in Middlebury, Indiana. In May 1971, two educators in the congregation, Charlotte Hurst and Sara VonGunten, had presented the church board with a plan to use the church facilities for a nursery school. The board approved, and in September 1971, a nursery school for four-year-olds was begun with Charlotte Hurst as the teacher. The voices of children could be heard at Pleasant Oaks three days each week.

Pleasant Oaks Nursery School was the first nursery school program of its kind in the Middlebury community. It is a not-for-profit, church-sponsored program that is considered an outreach endeavor by the congregation. The overall goal for the nursery school has been to provide a motivated learning atmosphere that emphasizes Christian living through social play in the areas of sharing, self-esteem, motor skills, and world view. The school was dedicated to the Christian nurture of young children and to the glory of God.

The first class of twelve four-year-old students[9] began on September 14, 1971. By December there were fifteen children in the class. Steven Quenzer, son of pastor Floyd and Ruth Quenzer, was the only POMC child who attended the first year. The mornings were filled with planned activities and supervised free play and frequent field trips into the community.

9. Although often referred to as the "four-year-old class," the children were four when school began and turned five during the following year.

The enrollment at the nursery school varied from twelve to fifteen children during the first three years. Eighteen children began the fourth year the nursery school was in session (1974–75), and two more were added by Christmas. By 1975 the nursery school had grown to twenty-five children and had to turn away a number of applicants. Six of the children were from POMC. The increased numbers certainly indicated growing support in the community and emphasized the need for the program.

The annual report indicates that 1976 was a year of introspection, growth, and change for the nursery school. POMC decided to make the nursery school an arm of the church, and Charlotte Hurst was named as director. A climbing structure was donated by the Exchange Club of Middlebury, and a sand table was purchased.

Charlotte Hurst was the teacher for three of the first five years and then became the director for the 1976–77 school year. POMC member Marlene Mockler became the nursery school director the following year and continued in that position for a total of eight years, through the 1984–85 school year.[10] This continuity was certainly a factor in the success of the nursery school during those early years.

A nursery school board of members of POMC, and occasionally parents of preschool children, gave direction to the nursery school from the beginning. The board established policy, hired staff, and supported the program with fundraisers, encouragement, and prayer.

The 1977–78 annual nursery school report listed the following activities: father-grandfather night, Christmas party, a mothers' tea, Halloween parade, Valentine party, and an open house for the community. A library was started for the nursery school that year, and a speech and hearing test was given to each child. Each day a volunteer (a mother or other interested person) assisted in the classroom, following a monthly cycle. These are typical of the activities that have been repeated over the decades.

Subjects listed for the 1978–79 school year include ourselves, our families, the Thanksgiving and Christmas seasons, our town, our helpers, and ways of transportation. There were seventy in attendance for the father-grandfather night and twenty for the mothers' coffee discussion. Sonya Beasley was the only POMC child attending for this school year, the others being children from the community. Shirley Wingeart began as teacher and Norma Modlin as assistant, the first of many years of working as a team.

Twenty-two children began nursery school in 1979 with five from the Pleasant Oaks congregation: Gunner Beck, Jason Delcamp, Angie Hostetler, Eric Risser, and Jodi Rychener. The children helped to make noodles for the thanksgiving feast. They also made doughnuts and snacks for the father-grandfather night. A highlight near the end of each school year was taking the children on a train ride from Elkhart to South Bend and back.

---

10. Marlene Mockler had served on the nursery school board for one year before becoming the director and later served on the board for an additional six years, bringing her total years of service to fifteen years.

Twenty-four four-year-old children were accepted for the 1980–81 school year with four from POMC: Jared Beasley, Keri Troyer, Peter VonGunten, and Russell Yoder. The children were introduced to shapes, colors, alphabet, numbers, following directions, playing together, and sharing with the group.

Peter VonGunten and Cindy Kauffman in preschool.

The same staff of Marlene Mockler (director), Shirley Wingeart (teacher), and Norma Modlin (assistant), welcomed twenty-four children for the 1981–82 school year, including five from POMC: Kathy Miller, Stacy Miller, Tim Troyer, Jason Wogo-man, and Anita Yoder. The usual activities, field trips, mothers' discussion, and father-grandfather night were repeated. New families in the community continued to bring children to nursery school.

Grant Miller and friend in preschool.

Three POMC children were in the 1982–83 nursery school class: Noelle Beck, Kelle Hostetler, and Robin Yoder. A ring toss game was made during the annual fa-ther-grandfather night this year. Homemade noodles and applesauce were part of the Thanksgiving feast. Sprinkled through the annual reports is gratitude for prayers and acknowledgement of God leading the ongoing nursery school program.

A parents' information meeting preceded the opening day of nursery school in 1983–84. The roster of twenty-one children included three from POMC again: Jenny

Johnson, April Nofziger, and Travis Wiesman. Field trips included going to the public library, teacher's home, post office, civil defense building and the fire station. Classes continued to meet three days a week (Tuesday, Wednesday, and Thursday) from mid September through mid May.

After six years of teaching at Pleasant Oaks Nursery School, Shirley Wingeart resigned due to personal reasons and family obligations. The congregation expressed appreciation to Shirley for the many hours and years of service she had given to the nursery school. Norma Modlin also resigned; Sue Abbott was hired as teacher and Cathy Wiesman as the assistant for the 1984–85 school year. Marlene Mockler continued offering her gifts as director for one more year. However, for the first year since 1974, there were fewer than twenty children enrolled. The school year began with fifteen students, none of whom were from POMC families. In February Connie Reeser began working as a teaching assistant, preparing to become director for the next school year.

Unexpected events occurred in 1985. Pastor John Reeser resigned and left Middlebury in June along with his wife, Connie Reeser. Only eleven children were registered for nursery school in September, so the board decided to eliminate the position of director and have the head teacher (Sue Abbott) absorb some of the duties of director. Cathy Wiesman began the year as the assistant, but she moved to Florida in October. POMC member Elnora Yoder was hired to fill out the year as the assistant. Because of the sharp decrease in enrollment for a few years and the financial problems that presented, the board asked the congregation's counsel about whether to continue operation of the nursery school.

Most shocking and painful was the death of Charlotte Weldy Hurst on November 8, 1985. As noted above, Charlotte was killed in a car crash caused by a drunk driver. The nursery school made a donation of $100 to the Charlotte Hurst memorial fund.

The congregation decided to continue the nursery school even with the new challenges. Sue Abbott was teacher for the third consecutive year, and Elnora Yoder continued as the assistant for the 1986–87 school year. The usual activities of field trips, parties, mothers' tea, father-grandfather night, and speech and hearing tests continued.

Reminiscent of what the Warren Street congregation had done when their membership dwindled in the early 1960s, the nursery school board recommended and the church board approved an expansion. A three-year-old play group was added to the existing program. Twenty-three families attended the open house on March 29. The congregation worked hard to prepare for the 1987–88 school year, holding fundraisers and developing policies and guidelines on class times, sizes, and programming. The service-stewardship committee sponsored a harvest table to benefit the nursery school, a place for members to bring extra produce from their gardens to share with others. The produce was taken in exchange for a donation to the nursery school. Both classes were filled to capacity when nursery school began in September, twenty children in the class of four-year-olds and twelve children in the class of three-year-olds.

The following children were from POMC families: Chelsea Haarer, Kyle Herschberger, Derek Jackson, Michelle Jones, Noah Lederach, Rebekah Schmell, and Ryan Smeltzer.

Sue Abbott resigned her position in October. POMC member Lisa Lederach, mother of two and expectant mother of one, was hired and began working on November 2. She began a maternity leave on November 25, and Carolyn DeWilde was hired temporarily. Lisa attended each class once every week with Baby Isaac and resumed her responsibilities on January 4. Everyone helped to make these transitions smooth, especially teaching assistant Elnora Yoder. In order to achieve greater consistency and continuity with the nursery school program, the POMC church board asked that a nursery school board member join the church board as an ex officio member, a practice that continued for the remainder of the life of the congregation.

A second class of four-year-olds was begun on Monday, Wednesday, and Friday afternoons, in addition to the morning class of four-year-olds, and the Tuesday and Thursday class for three-year-olds. In the summer of 1988, a session on dinosaurs was held as an opportunity for children and their parents to try out the nursery school program. Fundraisers (the harvest table and Current products—stationery, gift wrap, and greeting cards) brought in money to update classroom supplies and equipment. Also, several scholarships were given to families who were in need of help with tuition because of specific hardships.

The nursery school had turned around. Three classes ran at or near capacity for the 1989–90 school year, with the majority of spots reserved already by the previous April. Lance Jackson, Laura Renaud, Natalie Stalter, Tristan Tahara, and Brittany Yoder were from POMC families. Lisa Lederach returned to teaching in the public school system, and Teresa Irelan was hired as teacher. Teresa had six years of experience as the teacher/ director of the Bristol community preschool held at Bonneyville Mennonite Church. Nean Smeltzer returned as teaching assistant for the second year. Activities continued much as in the past with another fundraiser of Current products. A Pleasant Oaks Nursery School book bag was given to each child at the Christmas program.

The congregation's ongoing support kept the nursery school running well, including helping to add two swing sets to the playground. Nursery school board members continued to be people from the congregation, with a number of different individuals taking a turn on the board. Again the school ran at near capacity for the 1990–91 school year, with Teresa Irelan as teacher and Nean Smith as the teaching assistant. Students from POMC families included Mandy Herschberger, Lance Jackson, Laura Renaud, and Natalie Troyer.

Barry Schmell, POMC pastor from 1986 to 1998, supported the preschool in numerous ways. He and his wife, Deb, came to Middlebury with a preschool child, Rebekah. Within the next few years, two sons, Jordan and Jacob, were born into the family, and the Schmell children all attended the Pleasant Oaks Nursery School.

In addition to preschool children in his family, pastor Barry got very involved with children and families in the community. He initiated and led a Bible Study one day a week while the nursery school was in session. Mothers of enrolled children attended the Bible study, and families began attending Sunday morning worship services at POMC. Four families, whose initial contact was through the nursery school, became very involved in the life of POMC: the Stalters, the Hooleys, the Morgans, and the Renauds.

Kim Bitting began her long relationship with the nursery school, first as teaching assistant, during the 1991–92 school year. Teresa Irelan continued as lead teacher and maintained the various programs and field trips as in the past. Erin Haarer, Megan Jackson, John Renaud, and Shawn Smeltzer were the children from POMC.

The nursery school was filled to the capacity of forty-six students again in the 1992–93 school year. POMC families brought the following children: Caitlin Kuykendall, Brittany Herschberger, Jackson Hooley, Isaac Lederach, Jeramiah Morgan, John Renaud, Jordan Schmell, and Brian Yoder. The board was extremely pleased with the contributions of both Kim Bitting and Teresa Irelan and gave them good raises. A carnival was held in May 1993 to raise funds for the nursery school and other noteworthy church programs. Nursery school staff, church youth, and congregational members worked together, helping members to better understand the nursery school program that was thought to be one of the greatest ministries the church had to offer. The funds raised were donated to the congregation's Vision 2000 fund.

The enrollment of fifty children for the 1993–94 school year hit a record high up to that date. There were fourteen in the three-year-old playgroup, and seventeen and nineteen in the nursery school morning and afternoon classes. Of these, the following were from POMC families: Kelsey Herschberger, Jordan Hooley, Stephanie Jones, Caitlin Kuykendall, Rosemary Morgan, and Jordan Schmell. Teresa Irelan and Kim Bitting continued as the teaching team. The men's group assembled an "Eagle's Nest" play climber for the children to enjoy.

During each of the following years, three children from POMC families were in the nursery school: Courtney Herschberger, Rosemary Morgan, and Neil Yoder in 1994–95, and Courtney Herschberger, Clinton Kuykendall, and Weston Morgan in 1995–96.

Two of the forty-five children were from the Pleasant Oaks congregation during the 1996–97 school year: Clinton Kuykendall and Weston Morgan. All the classes had fall parties, Thanksgiving feasts, Christmas parties and programs, and Valentine and Easter parties. In addition to the two nursery classes and the playgroup, the Elkhart County Special Education Coop sent a speech therapist four days per week, giving speech therapy to fifteen children from the community.

During the 1997–98 school year, Jacob Schmell was the only child of POMC members enrolled. After being the teaching assistant for seven years, Kim Bitting became the nursery school teacher in 1998, a position she held through the 2008–09 school year. Kim's gifts of organization, creativity, sensitivity, flexibility, and love of children were greatly appreciated by children, parents, staff, and church members alike. During the years of her work at Pleasant Oaks, Kim and her husband, Jim, were active members of the Jefferson Brethren Church north of Goshen, and their three children grew to adulthood.

The Pleasant Oaks congregation supported the preschool from the beginning, providing the space, paying the utilities, and holding fundraisers to help meet the expenses. The income from student tuition paid the salaries for the teacher and teaching assistants, and some classroom supplies.

A variety of fundraising events were held over the years. Fundraisers helped to fill in any budget gaps and keep the tuition affordable, often the lowest of similar programs in the community. Typical fundraisers were spaghetti dinners/suppers on an annual basis from 1998 to 2003. The congregation was involved in these events, even elementary age children on some occasions. Doug Morgan, a preschool parent and POMC member who taught the fifth grade Sunday school class in 1998 and 1999, organized and led the fifth grade children in bussing tables.

In an evaluation completed by parents during the 1998–99 school year, children revealed that they especially liked the book loft, monkey bars, songs, sharing time, new friends, painting, field trips, crafts, teachers, games, play-doh, snacks, and the whole program. The children didn't like rainy days and going home! The positive values highlighted by parents were teachers, Christian values, respect, and sharing taught, parent/teacher conferences, opportunities for parents to be involved, and children learning phone numbers and letters, learning to share, positive attitudes and manners, the fun learning environment, and preparation for kindergarten. This was confirmation that the program was going well and strong motivation to continue the program without significant alterations.

In keeping with the trend in describing preschool programs like the one at POMC, the name was changed from Pleasant Oaks Nursery School to Pleasant Oaks Preschool (POPS) around 2003–2004. Grant Miller was the only child from a POMC family during the 1999–2000 school year. In 2000–01, Grant and Morgan Stahley attended. Although there were fewer preschool children at POMC after 2000, there were more families in the community who wanted to send their children to POPS than could be accepted. Waiting lists were started, sometimes as early as the April before the following school year.

Along with so many other lessons about life, the preschool children had opportunities to experience sharing with those less fortunate. Both preschool families and members of the congregation brought donations for Christmas baskets that the church youth then packaged and delivered to needy people in the community. In the following years, donations were received in the weeks before Christmas and delivered to the Middlebury Food Pantry.

In 2006 a Potato Bar/Hot Dog event was held. Krispy Kreme doughnuts, which the congregation had sold to raise money for the Friedenswald weekend in 2004 and 2005, were sold as a preschool fundraiser in March and again in November 2007: 460 dozen doughnuts were sold in the spring and a similar number in the fall.

The benefit of fundraisers in which the congregation participated multiplied when Mennonite Mutual Aid (headquarters in Goshen) provided grants through their sharing fund. The congregation needed to be involved in the fundraiser, and a minimum of $500 needed to be raised to qualify for a maximum grant of $500. The preschool was awarded this grant numerous times.

POMC hosted a festival for preschool families on Sunday afternoon, September 9, 2007. This was a gesture of goodwill and an opportunity for members of the congregation to learn to know families in the community who send their children to preschool. New members Jan and Bill Swartzendruber and Thelma and Glen Horner took the lead in planning the festive event. Activities included face or arm or knee painting by Char Swoveland and Miss Kim; Amish horseshoes by Bill Swartzendruber who built the frame; and bean bag toss for which Thelma Horner made bean bags and Sandy and Gary Bjornson built boxes. Prizes were given to each child as they participated in each game: POMC pencils furnished by Horners, small plastic animals, and wrapped candies.

Happy sounds of celebrating the beginning of another school year filled the air as approximately 100 people (POMC members, preschool families, and staff) moved in and out of the fellowship hall throughout the afternoon of the festival. Balloons (blown up with helium from a rented tank) drifted up to the ceiling and into the sky. Bags of freshly-made popcorn were freely shared, along with twelve dozen cookies and ice cream with toppings. Cookie donors complied with the new important consideration: no nuts or peanut oil because of allergies among preschool children.

Local eateries, Rulli's and the Essenhaus, supported the preschool by offering "give back" coupons in 2008. Many people showed their support for the preschool and gratitude to the restaurants by participating. A second successful preschool festival was held in October 2008.

The year 2009 was a year of change for the Pleasant Oaks Preschool. Kim Bitting retired as lead teacher after serving the preschool for seventeen years, seven years as the teaching assistant and ten years as lead teacher. There was standing room only at the Spring Program in May when Kim was recognized and honored with gifts, seventeen red roses from the congregation (one for each year that she served at Pleasant Oaks) and a mantle clock from the preschool board and congregation. An extra surprise for Kim was the appearance of her husband and son just before the gifts were presented. Many families expressed great admiration and deep gratitude for the positive influence "Miss Kim" had had on the lives of their children.

Kim notified the preschool board of her decision to resign early enough for the board to update the job description for the lead teacher and to search for a replacement. Rachel Scroggins, who had a son in the preschool program and had experience in running a private preschool in her home, was chosen and began orientation with Kim before school dismissed in May 2009.

The other big change in 2009 was POMC deciding to re-unite with First Menno-nite Church of Middlebury, the congregation from which they had come in 1923. The well-being of the preschool was a major factor for the congregation in choosing which course of action to take. The members of FMC entered into the agreement of forming a new congregation with POMC and keeping the operation of the preschool a priority for the future. And it was agreed to keep Pleasant Oaks as the name of the preschool.

Preschool Board members, 2007: Char Morgan Swoveland, Nan Stalter, Viv Schlabach, Juanita Yoder, Robin Tahara Miller, Elnora Yoder, and Kim Bitting.

As lead teacher, Rachel Scroggins maintained much of the good programming that carried the program through more than forty years of serving preschool children and their families in the Middlebury community. A new activity in the autumn of 2009 was the preschool classes of four-year-old children singing "This Little Light of Mine" in the downtown Middlebury park on the evening of September 21, the International Day of Prayer for Peace.

The preschool board of talented, dedicated, and generous people has provided a continuum of attention to the overall management and philosophy of the school. Dan Flager, preschool parent and spouse of former POMC member, and Karla Beasley, member of FMC and spouse of former student, have served on the board since 2009, each bringing an additional set of skills and new energy to the board.

Several women who were part of the Pleasant Oaks congregation for many years have given the board stability through the changes of recent years. There is no question that some of the success of the Pleasant Oaks preschool program is rooted in the deep commitment, dedication and generosity of many people. Some deserve special acknowledgement: Nan Stalter, who has served at least twelve years as board member and often as nurse consultant; Viv Schlabach, who has served twelve years, most of those years as treasurer; Elnora Yoder, who served eight years as assistant teacher and board member; and Char Morgan Swoveland, who served seven years as assistant teacher and board member.

The person who has served the preschool the most years is Robin Tahara Miller, a woman who has been involved at POMC all her life. Robin is now in her twentieth year as a board member, having chaired the board since 2000. Robin's dedication and hard work, her positive attitude and passion for Christian service, her confidence that God has led throughout the years, and her ongoing trust in God have all helped to inspire the school board and the staff to make the Pleasant Oaks Preschool be all it can be. Although Robin deserves much credit, the greatest acknowledgment for the success of the program goes to God, the one who inspires, equips, and fills with love those who dedicate their lives to making the world a better place by attending to children.

7

Music, Mission, and Mennonite Youth

IT'S TIME

It's time to plow
to turn over new ground,
to bury the debris, and begin all fresh.

It's time to drag out the old weeds that pester us,
and destroy them so that new growth may begin.

It's time to cultivate those strong, faithful
who have wintered with us,
and to nourish them with our tender loving care.

It's time to transplant,
and bring new life to a distant place.

It's time to plant the seeds
that God has entrusted to our care.

It's time we learn to do our tasks,
but only God can make our garden grow.

Time is short,

for all too soon
it will be time for harvest.

DORIS E. HERSHBERGER
MAY 1981[1]

---

1 Doris Hershberger was a long-time member of WSMC/POMC. This poem was first published in the August 25, 1981, issue of *The Mennonite*. Reprinted with permission.

Make a joyful noise to the Lord, all the earth.

Worship the Lord with gladness;
come into his presence with singing.

PSALM 100:1–2

MUSIC AT WSMC AND POMC

DURING THE TWENTIETH CENTURY, Mennonites became known for their excellent *a cappella* four-part singing. However, Mennonites didn't always sing in four parts. One of the reasons for excommunicating Daniel Brenneman from the Yellow Creek Church in 1872 was his insistence on singing bass. At the same time, singing schools were emerging among Mennonites in Virginia, first at the initiative of gifted Mennonite musician and publisher, Joseph Funk,[2] who compiled the *Harmonia Sacra*,[3] but singing in parts was not yet permitted at Yellow Creek in 1872.

Most Mennonite groups who emigrated from Europe to North America had a tradition opposed to musical instruments in the church. In 1875 the "old" Mennonite Indiana conference officially stated that musical instruments foster "pride and display" rather than leading toward "humility."[4] Nevertheless, singing in parts and musical instruments gradually came into the Mennonite Church. Some Warren Street members were playing orchestral and band instruments in the twenties, thirties, and forties.[5] A piano and organ were used at Warren Street Mennonite Church in the 1940s.

As a young teenager at Warren Street, Margaret Kauffman Sutter longed to play an organ.[6] Margaret had a first cousin, Evelyn Hartzler (now Bushong), who attended Eighth Street and played the organ there, and Margaret wanted to do the same. An adult at Warren Street, Helen Litweiler Plank, heard of Margaret's desire and said, "There's no reason that we can't have an organ here." With Helen's encouragement, the fund was started. Margaret herself made the little cardboard church that received donations to the organ fund.[7]

The following announcement was made in the bulletin on January 14, 1944:

> The Organ Fund: A word of commendation needs to be spoken of the splendid efforts of the young people's group in the securing of funds for the purchase of a new Hammond pipe organ. Already their organ fund stands at well over

2 This Joseph Funk (1778–1862) is not to be confused with his cousin John F. Funk, minister and publisher in Elkhart, Indiana.

3. T. Schlabach, *Peace Faith Nation*, 63–69.

4. Pannabecker, *Open Doors*, 178; T. Schlabach, *Peace, Faith, Nation*, 64.

5. See beginning paragraphs of chapter 4.

6. Margaret was the daughter of Rollo (founding member of WSMC) and Mary Bohn (sister of Ernest Bohn) Kauffman.

7. Margaret Kauffman Sutter in phone conversation with Hartzler, May 29, 2012.

$150. Of this amount, $140 was initially begun by the young people. It took an active membership of only eight young people to accumulate that much in two months. Their goal is "an organ by next Christmas." They have plans for the money needed, and they are very serious about this project. But they also need help. The little white church at the rear of the church was presented as a symbol of their endeavor at the candle light service New Year's Eve, and it now stands ready to receive the gifts of the members of the congregation. Margaret Kauffman will also receive offerings from those who prefer to give it personally. All financial facts and interesting data about the project and its progress will be posted regularly near the little church. Take a look at it frequently and encourage our young people by a personal interest in the fund.

When $1,000 was raised, the organ was purchased for $2,167 from Lyon and Healy, Inc. in Chicago. The contract, agreeing to pay the balance in twelve equal monthly installments, was signed by Margaret Kauffman, treasurer of the organ fund, and Mrs. Alden Plank, adult advisor. The Hammond organ was delivered in April 1946.

Margaret was the regular Warren Street organist from the beginning. During her high school years she had after-school jobs in downtown Middlebury (hand-folding the Middlebury Independent and sewing Amish pants at Gohn Brothers), and then she walked over to the little church building on Warren Street and practiced the organ. Bernita Miller was the substitute organist when Margaret was a student at Goshen College and came home to Middlebury only part of the time. Margaret's first teaching job was in the Middlebury Elementary School, and she regularly played the organ again. After two years she married Earl Sutter, and they moved away for Earl's CPS assignment and later, moved to Illinois.[8]

In addition, the congregation purchased a piano from pastor Regier in June 1947. Whether this was the first piano at Warren Street is not known. A new piano was purchased in 1965 (and dedicated to the memory of Jean Krehbiel). The 1946 organ was moved from WSMC to POMC in 1965, and both instruments served the congregation well through 2009.

Even in the presence of organ and piano, vocal music was always important at WSMC/POMC. In 1944 seventy-five new copies of the *Mennonite Hymnary* were purchased.[9] These were used until 1970 when they were donated to Camp Friedenswald. *Sing and Rejoice* songbooks were added to the POMC collection in the spring of 1981. The following appeared in the "Pleasant Oaks Sharing Tree."

> Orlando Schmidt, professor of church music and worship at the Mennonite
> Biblical Seminary in Elkhart, is the compiler and editor of a new song book
> for the congregations. . . . *Sing and Rejoice.* The music committee has received

8. Margaret and Earl Sutter returned to Goshen in 1994 and joined the Eighth Street Mennonite Church.

9. These were published by the Board of Publication of the General Conference of the Mennonite Church of North America in Berne, Indiana, 1940.

copies of these books at specially reduced prices from the Central District Conference. The committee picked up fifty of these books at $2.60 each. . . .

Only 10 percent of the material in today's standard hymnals was produced in the twentieth century. Less than 5 percent was created during the past fifty years. *Sing and Rejoice* is an attempt to supplement the rich heritage of the past with texts and tunes from recent decades. The present generation has witnessed an explosion of creativity in church music, and this book enables us to enjoy this movement in our worship services.

Some of the songs you will already know, some you will have heard before, and some will be new. Surely some will become part of future church hymn books. The songs in this book have all been selected with the congregation in mind. We think you will learn to enjoy this new addition to our church pews.

The *Sing and Rejoice* books were in the hymnal racks along with *The Mennonite Hymnal,* 1969 for many years. POMC began using the 1992 *Hymnal: A Worship Book* when it became available. According to records kept, the hymns most often sung from the 1969 and 1992 hymnals were in the following order: "I sing the mighty power of God," "To God be the glory," "How great thou art," "Great is thy faithfulness," "For God so loved us," "Amazing Grace," "Lift you glad voices," and "Praise, I will praise you, Lord." During the last year at POMC, members were invited to list their favorite hymns, and all of those listed were sung at least once. Nearly all of the thirteen people who responded named at least one of the eight most frequently sung hymns.

Easter Sunday 2009 with DeRoy Kauffman at the organ.

Singing was almost always accompanied at Pleasant Oaks, usually by organ or piano. Sally Miller was the organist in the late 1960s and early 70s. Dorcas Summerton became the regular organist in the 70s and early 80s. At that time, most of the singing was accompanied by the organ. When Dorcas was not available, Sara VonGunten accompanied on the piano. Sometimes an organist was hired. Isabelle Eby Miller of Middlebury Church of the Brethren served as part time organist during the 1980s. DeRoy Kauffman began serving as a part-time organist and pianist in 1988. DeRoy, a professional-quality organist and pianist and member of First Mennonite Church, accompanied about half the worship services beginning in the late 90s and was the regular accompanist in the final years of Pleasant Oaks.

Having both an organ and piano since the 1940s, WSMC/POMC was sometimes blessed with piano and organ duets. The mystery of instrumental music lifting spirits heavenward was felt at the Eighty-fifth Anniversary Celebration on August 8, 2008, and at the final POMC worship service on November 22, 2009, as former member and pianist Sara VonGunten and POMC organist DeRoy Kauffman played preludes and offertories.

Tony Hurst was the regular song leader in the 70s. Dale and Viv Schlabach began attending POMC in 1973, and soon Dale became an alternate song leader. After Tony left POMC, Dale was the regular song leader for the remaining years. There was a time in the 1990s when an interest in contemporary Christian music developed and a worship team led the singing. Mary Yoder Kuykendall played guitar and led the worship team.

Contemporary Christian singing continued while Robin La Rue was pastor, accompanied by guitars and percussion instruments purchased with funds donated to POMC in memory of Ken VonGunten. The cross on the front panel of the sanctuary was raised toward the ceiling, and a screen was installed so that words for contemporary songs could be projected. Red loose-leaf notebooks, filled with songs not in the hymnals, were added to the hymnal racks. This collection of songs appealed especially to the younger set who attended for a period of time. The "traditionalists" in the congregation joined with the youth in singing new songs.

There were many excellent vocalists among the members over the years. One Christmas in the early 70s, pastor Floyd Quenzer directed a choir that sang several choruses from Handel's Messiah, no mean feat for a small church. DeRoy Kauffman and a few others sang solos occasionally. Periodically, an ensemble or choir would assemble for special occasions or particular seasons of the church year. After Floyd Quenzer left, Dale Schlabach directed the choir and assisted with numerous ensembles.

And of course there was the music of children over the years. Some years Christmas pageants were presented by the children.

Christmas pageant, 1999 or 2000. Front row: Grant Miller, Morgan Stahley, Cory Smith, Weston Morgan; second row: Rosemary Morgan, Katie Stahley; third row: Jeremiah Yoder, Jordan Hooley, Cody Yoder; fourth row: Brian Yoder, J.D. Morgan, Neil Yoder, Jackson Hooley, John Renaud; back row: Brittany Yoder, Laura Renaud, Natalie Stalter, Shawn Smeltzer, Austin Miller, Evan Stahley.

Paul Yoder, Viv Schlabach, Dale Schlabach, Eileen Miller in 2007.

One of the pleasant musical gifts offered repeatedly at POMC came from Don and Doris Hershberger. Doris played her portable keyboard and Don played harmonicas. They played familiar hymns primarily as preludes and offertories. A special presentation that was requested from time to time was "Footprints in the Sand." Doris played "How Great Thou Art" on the keyboard while Don recited from memory the poem that describes in first person the dream of someone who recognized the footprints of Jesus walking with him throughout life and then discovered that during the most difficult periods of life, Jesus carried him, leaving one set of footprints in the sand. There were often tears in the congregation during and after this recitation.[10]

Another memorable musical gift was Jim Mishler's *a cappella* singing of *The Lord's Prayer* from the back of the sanctuary following the pastoral prayer one Sunday. The congregation regularly recited or sang one of the numerous versions of *The Lord's Prayer*.

MEMBERS IN CHURCH SERVICE

Although WSMC/POMC did not send out traditional foreign missionaries, mission emphases and mission activities were present. Robert and Alice Ruth Ramseyer were regular presenters during their US furloughs from their missionary assignment in Japan.[11] The congregation also supported numerous individuals over the years, and often those who served brought back stories that enriched others. Names of some who served in church-related assignments follow:

- POMC helped to support Stacy Miller (now Edwards) in several assignments. She took leadership training with Great Commission Ministries in 1996 and then took a college-level mission course with New Tribes Mission in Papua, New Guinea, in 1999. Stacy went to Sanford, Florida, in 2001 to do a one-year volunteer assignment in graphic design at the New Tribes Mission Headquarters.

- In September 1980 POMC blessed associate member Judi Miller as she left for a Mennonite Voluntary Service assignment in London, Ontario, for two and one-half years. She worked at Teen Girls' Home.

- Robin Tahara began a voluntary service assignment in Washington, DC, in 1978 and remained there through 1983. She served with the Fellowship Foundation, a "quiet" organization that supports those who have been called to lead our country, including the president, members of congress, and judges. She worked at a house along Embassy Row that had many international visitors.

- In 1977 Dave, Carolyn, Scott, and Tonya Sherck were sent with the congregation's blessing into voluntary service in Canton, Oklahoma, working with a GC Mennonite Church project among Native Americans.

10. This poem can be found at http://www.footprints-inthe-sand.com.
11. Robert is a grandson of Simon S. Yoder, the first pastor of Warren Street.

- Gary Yoder did two years of 1W service at Prairie View Hospital in Newton, Kansas.

- Richard Kauffman and Ken VonGunten served in PAX overseas. Richard, son of Rollo (founding member) and Mary Bohn Kauffman, was in Greece. He taught for two years in a school located on the island of Crete. The school was started when Richard and a German boy named Clouse were available as teachers for the school, and the school was then named Richard-Clouse School. Ken served in PAX from 1959–61, helping to build homes for people in postwar Germany.

- Lowell Troyer and his wife, Mary, lived in McKinley, Michigan, some one hundred miles north of Flint beginning in 1951. Lowell served as minister at the McKinley Mission Church for fifteen years. In 1952 the Warren Street congregation purchased a car for Lowell and Mary as a way of supporting this mission project that was under the Central Mennonite Conference.

- Lowell Troyer and his brother Lotus Troyer both served in Civilian Public Service (CPS) as described in chapter 5.

- J. O. Yoder served with the Brethren Service Committee (of the Church of the Brethren) and the United Nations Relief and Rehabilitation Administration (UNRRA)[12] as a seagoing cowboy from December 1945 to February 1946. He was one of more than 7,000 men and boys from across the United States and Canada who volunteered to tend livestock shipped to war-devastated countries after World War II between June 24, 1945, and mid-1947. J. O. has told his story in his self-published diary, *Crossing to Poland: From a Farm Background Anywhere USA to Danzig, Poland, and Return.*

As a twenty-six-year-old with a college degree and significant farming experience, J. O. was designated leader of the group of thirty-two Mennonite and Church of the Brethren young men, most of whom were younger and just off the farm. These "seagoing cowboys" cared for the 744 horses aboard the *S. S. Clarksville Victory.* Their duties included feeding and watering the horses, cleaning the seven areas where they were held, and disposing of the dead horses, which totaled fifty-six during the sixteen days of crossing to Danzig, Poland.

The experience at sea was absolutely new for J. O., and the contrasts between the smooth sea and the raging storms were dramatic. The group celebrated Christmas aboard ship in a harbor of the Kiel Canal in Germany on the approach to Danzig. On Christmas Eve "good old Christmas hymns" were played on the radio. These were wonderful to hear, and J. O. found himself thinking about the Germans, who for the first time in many years could really celebrate Christmas—if they could afford it.

---

12. UNRRA was created by forty-four nations in November 1943 to provide postwar relief. This organization is not to be confused with the later twentieth and twenty-first century United Nations.

Arriving in Danzig on December 27, the group was startled to see the devastating effects of the war. J. O. wrote, "All the buildings, trees, roads and just everything are shot up! It really looks and sounds like 'hell'! There is shooting going on continuously—one can hear shots ring out every so often from any direction." Numerous dramatic interactions occurred both on and off the ship through January 7 while they were in Danzig: unloading the 688 horses that were distributed to farmers in Poland; distributing candy brought from the United States; shopping and preparing for the return journey.

There were not horses to attend on the return trip across the Atlantic so the cowboys read, played checkers, and reflected on what they had experienced. Not all the cowboys were pacifists or even Christians, but most groups did have worship services on their ships on Sundays. Many men were transformed into more sensitive and caring world citizens by being seagoing cowboys.[13]

MISSION AND OUTREACH ACTIVITIES

While some people went far from Middlebury and even overseas to serve, others engaged in mission and outreach activities close to home.

Women in Mission

Women have always been involved in the life of Warren Street and Pleasant Oaks Mennonite Church. There are notes from 1932–35 indicating that the "Ladies Aid" was active, serving food and providing canned fruits and vegetables for missions. Central Conference had organized a Ladies Aid Society in 1925, and Warren Street had a local group at least by 1932.[14]

In 1948 the women's group was called Women's Christian Service (WCS); their project one month was to bring food for relief—dry foods as beans, cereals, raisins, and sugar—to be sent to Mennonite Central Committee (MCC). A church bulletin note in 1949 indicates that sixty-seven pounds of used clothing had been sent to MCC, and already in July the women were thinking about preparing Christmas bundles to be sent through MCC.

By 1966 the women's group was called the Women's Missionary Association (WMA) at POMC.[15] From 1962 to 1987 the district WMA published "Women at Work" as part of the *Central District Reporter*. Ferne (Yoder) Ramseyer, a charter member of Warren Street, was the first editor of "Women at Work." In 1974 the WMA adopted a new constitution and changed its name to Women in Mission (WM).[16] Another

13. Peggy Reiff Miller has more information on her website: www.seagoingcowboys.com.

14. Pannabecker, *Open Doors*, 289.

15. It is likely that the group had been called WMA earlier, such as when the Central Conference and the Middle District Conference became the Central District Conference in 1957.

16. Rich, *Walking Together*, 151.

change occurred in 1997. WM, the women's organization of the General Conference Mennonites, and WMSC, the Women's Missionary and Service Commission of the "old" Mennonite Church, merged to become Mennonite Women or MW. However, the women at Pleasant Oaks continued to think of themselves as "women in mission."

POMC Women in Mission 2003 Christmas Party: Standing: Laura Hooley, Rosemary La Rue, Reidun Yoder, Sara VonGunten, Elnora Yoder, Eileen Miller; Kneeling: Robin Tahara Miller, Juanita Yoder, Rachel Stahley.

The women knotted comforters, rolled bandages, and made baby blankets. In 1974 seven comforters were donated to the Michiana Relief Sale; twenty-five pounds of bandages were rolled, and seventeen layettes were made and sent to Zaire. For many years the POMC WM had garage sales and craft auctions to raise money. With funds taken in, they purchased supplies and items for the church kitchen—a stove and banquet tables in 1969, and a new refrigerator and approximately 180-place settings of china in 2000. Also in 2000 the women agreed to pay for the Bibles given to the youth.

Women were also involved in other aspects of church life at POMC. As early as 1962 there are women on the church board. Doris Hershberger, Leona Yoder, and Doris Wortinger were some of the board members in the 1960s, although they were referred to by their husbands' names—Mrs. Don Hershberger, etc. Gradually women's first names were listed, although the yearbook reports that in 1972 a baby shower was held for Mrs. Phil Wogoman and infant son, Jeffrey, and in 1974 Eric Ryan was born to Mr. and Mrs. Dennis Risser.

POMC women knotting a comforter in 2007: Doneta Burkhardt, Viv Schlabach, Anne Yoder, Rosie Miller, Juanita Yoder, Elnora Yoder, Eileen Miller, Ruth Miller.

Michiana Mennonite Relief Sale

A long running mission project of Pleasant Oaks was the sausage and onion sandwich booth at the annual Michiana MCC (Mennonite Central Committee[17]) Relief Sale held annually in September in Goshen starting in 1967. Reference to the sandwich booth is first noted in the POMC 1977 annual report. Church records include the names of the coordinators for the MCC booth beginning in 1989. Continuing annually through 2009, the POMC congregation did the work to make this popular booth happen on the fourth weekend every September. The hard-working and efficient volunteers developed the process until it was down to a science, beginning with the POMC representative(s) attending planning meetings and ordering supplies.

On Thursday afternoon of sale week, a group gathered at the church to cut and bag onions—250 pounds of onions were cut in the last several years. Onion-cutting happened on the lawn outside the back door of the fellowship hall whenever the weather permitted. This process became more and more streamlined over the years

---

17. MCC is a faith-based relief and development organization that was created in 1920 through a partnership between the Mennonite and Brethren in Christ churches. Their goal is to respond to basic human needs and work for peace and justice both in the United States and abroad. Relief sales are among the MCC's largest and most wide-spread fundraising efforts. Dozens such sales occur throughout the United States and Canada each year.

with a food processor cutting the onions and electric-skillet-size portions of onions being saved in plastic bags overnight.

A few POMCers went early in the day on Friday to set up the booth and begin cooking onions to be ready to serve when customers arrived in the late afternoon. Again on Saturday morning volunteers arrived at the crack of dawn to be ready for the early morning crowd. Yes, some people do enjoy sausage and onions for breakfast! The sweet sautéed onions were spread onto a long sandwich roll, and one and one-half links of beautifully cooked whole hog sausage[18] was laid on top. The assembly line included wrapping the sandwiches and placing them in a warming unit to be ready for the lines of people who returned every year for their tasty relief sale favorite—as well as the newcomers.

Pleasant Oaks people happily signed up to take work shifts at the relief sale. The booth and adjacent pavilion area took on the flavor of a family reunion as current and former members came to work and/or eat. There were opportunities to answer questions brought by newcomers—the reason for the sale and the purpose and vision of MCC: sharing God's love and compassion for all in the name of Christ by responding to basic human needs and working for peace and justice.

The record high income for the Michiana MCC Relief Sale was $453,626 in 1998.[19] Complete records of the sausage and onion sandwich booth project were not kept at Pleasant Oaks, but a few highlights are: in 2006, 148 *dozen* sandwich buns were used, and income from the 2009 booth was $5525.

Responsibility for organizing the project was rotated among people in the church. Records show the following people coordinated the sausage and onion sandwich booth:

1986	Sanford and Shirley Yoder	1999	Ben and Gert Kauffman
1989	Terry and Anne Herschberger	2000	Marvin Borntrager
1990	Paul and Elnora Yoder	2001	Paul Yoder
1991	Jack and Sue Riegsecker	2002	Gerri Beachy
1992	Ben and Gert Kauffman	2003	Gerri Beachy
1993	Marvin and Linda Borntrager	2004	Paul and Elnora Yoder
1994	Gary and Nean Smith	2005	Paul and Elnora Yoder
1995	Bob and Sue Troyer	2006	Dale and Viv Schlabach
1996	Dave and Mabel Yoder	2007	Dale Schlabach, Paul Yoder, Gerri Beachy
1997	Dan and Loretta Mast	2008	Dale Schlabach, Paul Yoder, Gerri Beachy
1998	Gerri and Connie Beachy	2009	Dale and Viv Schlabach, Paul and Elnora Yoder, Gerri Beachy

18. For many years Mishler Packing Company in LaGrange, Indiana, provided the labor and processing of the sausage used in the sandwich booth and in the sausage and pancake breakfast barn.

19. This figure does not include the sale of the Shalom House from which profits were included for a number of years.

It became clear to the Pleasant Oaks people early in 2009 that this year would be the last year to host the sausage and onion sandwich booth. Again, active members and former members, some who had grown up at Pleasant Oaks, came to work and eat. If tears were shed that day, blame might have been placed on the onions, but a few people described the day as bittersweet. People who came to the relief sale in 2010 looking for sausage and onion sandwiches were disappointed. But beginning in 2011, the new re-united Mennonite Church of Middlebury assumed responsibility for the sausage and onion sandwich booth, and new volunteers were pleased to discover the great popularity of these sandwiches.

Middlebury Community Food Pantry

There was a church-sponsored food pantry in Middlebury beginning in 1983 or before. It started as a project of First Mennonite Church (FMC) within the church building. The location of the pantry has been in the next-door former parsonage of FMC since about 1993 when Robert Martz organized the pantry and helped move it out of the church building. Sometime in the 90s the Middlebury Ministerium accepted responsibility for the pantry, and members of many congregations in the community took turns staffing the pantry on Saturday mornings.

With the economic repression of 2008, the unmet needs of many people in the community became greater, and the program rose to meet the challenge. Pam Bingaman (a member of First Mennonite) became the volunteer director, and hundreds of people were served weekly. Pleasant Oaks became more aware of community needs and stepped up the pattern of filling a grocery cart with pantry items. Leona Yoder and Jan Swartzendruber helped to coordinate the POMC participation in this important ministry.

Other Mission Projects

Over the years bulletins were periodically taken to the Essenhaus Inn across the street from Pleasant Oaks. Because of this, the congregation enjoyed frequent tourists and visitors to the community coming to worship services.

In 1984 the congregation adopted a Mennonite Central Committee (MCC) project in Somalia, raising money for two oxen to be used for agricultural projects. Lyn and Lois Miller worked under Mennonite Voluntary Service in San Antonio, Texas, for a month in 1995.

In 2005 Eugene Bontrager and Dale Schlabach spent a week in Florida helping repair a home damaged by Hurricane Charlie. The family did not have funds to make the repairs themselves, but their income was too high to qualify for grants. The Mennonite Women of POMC made a knotted "throw" for them and sent it with Eugene and Dale. "It was a token and reminder of our caring and that our church was praying for them."[20] Pleasant Oaks participated in a Habitat for Humanity building project in 2006 and in 2008 the church supported a Foods Resource Bank growing project, described in chapter 8.

Supporting students in Mennonite Colleges and Seminaries was part of the mission of the church. In 1986 a Student Financial Aid Plan was begun. For many years POMC designated an organization each month to receive mission offerings. These included Mennonite Mission Network, Camp Friedenswald, Bluffton University, AMBS, Central District Conference, Mennonite Church USA (MC USA), Habitat for Humanity, Chicago Mennonite Learning Center, Golden Rod of Mennonite Disabilities Committee, Middlebury Food Pantry, Middlebury Ministerium and Elkhart County Jail Chaplaincy Program, Menno-Hof, and POMC's Samaritan Fund. The December mission offering varied from year to year. In 2007 it was divided between local food baskets and a MEDA (Mennonite Economic Development Associates) project: anti-malaria mosquito nets for Tanzania. During a worship service, Rose Mtoka, a Tanzanian woman living in Goshen, told about the need for such mosquito nets.

MENNONITE YOUTH IN ACTION

From the beginning of the Warren Street Mennonite Church the youth were valued and given attention, although records from the early years are scant. In 1971 the youth group met on a regular basis with youth from Silver Street Mennonite Church. Robert and Nancy Koehn from the Mennonite seminary led the group with Sara and Ken VonGunten assisting. In June 1979 the youth class of Dena Bloss, Keith Gingerich, Cindy Miller, Gayle Rheinheimer, and Mary Yoder spent a week working in Oklahoma with Dave and Carolyn Sherck who were serving among Native American people. Lois and Lyn Miller and Marlene and Don Mockler accompanied the youth.

A Youth Sunday was held in March 1980. The stated purpose was "to make our youth program more vital," and Jim Amstutz, Central District Youth Director, facilitated. In July 1986 seven of the senior youth and Lois Miller went to General Conference in Saskatoon, Saskatchewan, Canada. There were also activities for junior youth. In December 1987 they collected food for eleven families that included twenty-five children. In June 1993 the senior youth did a service project at Sunshine Children's Home in Toledo, Ohio.

In 2001 Pleasant Oaks joined with Bonneyville Mennonite Church in youth ministry. The team of ministry leaders included three people from Bonneyville, Ken (Bonneyville pastor) and Gale Livengood and Ellis Bontrager, and three from POMC, Mike and Rachel Stahley and Juanita Yoder. The youth were invited to submit names for the new youth program, and the name chosen was Mennonite Youth in Action or MYIA. Robin La Rue described the most significant aspect of MYIA as the fact that new youth were reached, youth who had not had a youth group or church home.

20. Story as told by Leona Yoder.

The vision of MYIA was to provide a ministry environment for spiritual growth and opportunities for Christian service through a Mennonite perspective. "We seek this in an attitude of joyous fun," reported Robin. Watching youth interact with each other and with scripture and develop their own Christian perspective is both rewarding and challenging. Attendance in 2001 varied from thirteen to twenty-two. The decision was made to more clearly separate junior and senior youth for 2002. A "new" youth center was also opened in 2002; that is, the free-standing garage behind POMC was turned into a youth center![21]

Wes Yoder, pastor of Forks Mennonite Church, joined the team of MYIA leaders, and in 2002 the pastors of the three churches (Forks, Bonneyville, and POMC) hired Michael Miller as youth pastor of the combined youth ministry. Although not openly discussed in the congregations, Michael did not hold to a traditional Mennonite position of non-participation in military services. Some of the members who were aware of this were assured that the lead pastors would teach the youth on this issue and Michael would not try to persuade the youth of his position. Other people left POMC because they could not support a Mennonite congregation who hired a non-pacifist youth pastor.

Nevertheless, Michael did lead MYIA with evangelistic zeal and missionary passion. In the summer of 2003, MYIA went on a mission trip to Puerto Rico and went to the MC USA youth convention in Atlanta, Georgia. J. D. Morgan, Katie Stahley, and Brittany and Brian Yoder were the youth from POMC who participated that year and adults included Michael, Sandra Bjornson, and Ken Livengood. Subsequent trips included a service trip to Mexico in 2004; trips to Sarasota, Florida, in April 2005 and 2006 to "reach the beach"; the 2005 MC USA youth convention in Charlotte, North Carolina, which included a ministry to homeless people in Charlotte; another mission trip to Mexico in June 2006; and a mission trip to Jamaica in July 2006. Michael Miller and Susan Hull were the adults on the Jamaica trip, and the nine youth included three from POMC families: Weston Morgan, Jake Troyer, and Jeff Troyer.

Michael also took some of the youth to "Acquire the Fire" events, a weekend youth convention held in major cities across the United States. "Acquire the Fire," part of Teen Mania Ministries, has been described as a mix of pep rally, rock concert, and church service. Some of the youth were "on fire" following this experience and invited friends to church.

MYIA highlights from 2006 included the following: On the first weekend in January, the MYIA senior high youth went on a retreat in Syracuse, and on the last weekend of the month, the junior high youth had a retreat in Syracuse. In February there was a MYIA Super Bowl party, and another time the MYIA youth provided babysitting services at the church. Outings to Ft. Wayne included a "Winter Jam" concert and a hockey game.

21. Minutes of MYIA planning meetings are in the POMC archival collection that will be in the Central District archives at Bluffton University. However, these were not reviewed for writing this summary.

MYIA Christmas party, 2005; front row: Susie Drust, Caitlin Hull; second row: Nicky Steele, Bre Irving, Aleigha Bourdon, Brittany Parker; third row: James Gingerich, Weston Morgan, Jordan Troyer, Jacob Troyer; fourth row: Jordan Bontrager, unidentified guest, Jeff Troyer, Jeremy Drier; back row: Matthew Gingerich, Michael Miller.

Wednesday evenings at POMC typically included outdoor activities in warm weather (such as volleyball on the lawn), followed by a Bible study, prayer, sharing, and refreshments. Because of three mission trips in the spring and summer of 2006, extra fund raisers were held, with Nelson's barbecued chicken being sold on numerous Saturdays.

POMC youth in 2007: Rose Morgan, Brian Yoder, Neil Yoder, James Gingerich, Jordan Hooley.

Michael seemed to have unlimited energy, and he poured himself into the youth and the youth program. His passion, zeal, and love for the youth were appreciated by many people at Pleasant Oaks and especially by some of the parents of youth who had not been involved in a church youth program before participating in MYIA.

CAMP FRIEDENSWALD

The Central Conference of Mennonites and the GC Middle District Conference began providing retreats and camps for their young people in the 1920s and 1930s, first at Bluffton College and then at the Brethren Retreat grounds on Lake Shipshewana just east of Middlebury. Quaker Haven on Dewart Lake near Syracuse provided the location in 1940–41, and then from 1942 through 1950 the retreats were held at Camp Alexander Mack, a Church of the Brethren camp on Waubee Lake near Milford, Indiana. These week-long camps provided youth with opportunities to renew or make new faith commitments.[22]

By the late 1940s the conference had expanded the program to include junior high as well as high school students for several weeks each summer. Because of the growing vision for camping as a setting for spiritual nurture, a movement to purchase and operate a camp within the Central District gained momentum.

22. Marge Graber, *Friedenswald*, 1–4.

Thus a camp board was formed, and a group of men, including J. O. Yoder from Middlebury and Robert Hartzler from Goshen, scouted out a wooded acreage covered with trees and sumac bushes on a shore of Shavehead Lake near Cassopolis, Michigan. In 1949 forty acres were purchased and Camp Friedenswald was born. J. O. Yoder was hired as the on-site manager for the development of the grounds and buildings and led in transforming the dream of a campground into a reality. Dozens of conference people volunteered time during the summer and fall of 1950, and the first ten cabins were built.[23] Other projects included improving road access to the camp, creating a level three-acre area of solid footing next to the lake, drilling a well, and installing outdoor sanitation. Pastor Harold Thiessen from Warren Street had worked on a hookworm project during his CPS days, and he assisted in the "building of a substantial privy."[24]

J. O. was again the site director in 1951, and with the decision to cancel the reservation for use of Camp Mack, the pressure was on. Lists of tasks accomplished are in *Vision, Faith, Service* as well as lists of volunteers who helped ready the camp for the first campers on July 23, 1951. Two Warren Street "alumni" helped to lead the first camp: Lotus Troyer, then from Carlock, Illinois, was the dean and camp pastor, and his brother Lowell came from Fairview, Michigan, to teach classes with his wife, Mary.[25]

In 1953 J. O. returned to manage the camp and oversee the construction of the building to be used as a dining hall, kitchen, and offices. Don Hershberger, member of Warren Street, was in charge of building operations for the structure. J. O. Yoder had a design idea to furnish the dining room. Ernie Yoder (from Eighth Street) took J. O.'s idea and figured out the dimensions for special table units from which the table tops could be removed and stacked against the wall. Thus, the benches could be used for regular seating. Ernie Yoder cut the pieces for eight units from knotty pine, and members of the Warren Street Mennonite Church assembled the tables and benches, sanded them, and finished the units with numerous coats of varnish in the Warren Street basement.[26]

J. O. continued serving as camp director through 1958. In 1954 Leona Doell came from Henderson, Nebraska, to serve as camp nurse at Friedenswald. She returned the following four years in this capacity; however, in 1956 she did not come from Henderson. The winter before, Leona and the camp director were married, and she came from Middlebury with her husband! In 1957 and 58 Leona and J. O. came to camp with their daughter Sherry who was born in February 1957.

The camp program expanded greatly over the years. New programs included family camps, outpost camps in tree houses, trip camps, winter retreats for youth, parent/child retreats, and a program that reached out to the surrounding community. The camp also was used by local elementary schools for outdoor education programs.

23. Cabin 8 still holds the first cornerstone inscribed "Dedicated to the Glory of God—1950".

24. Marge Graber, *Friedenswald*, 10.

25. Ibid., 17–22.

26. These were used through the 1995 camping season when the dining hall was enlarged and remodeled.

WSMC/POMC supported Camp Friedenswald from the camp's beginning. The congregation sent children to camp, for many years using a camp scholarship fund that provided half of the cost of camp. Members volunteered at the camp, and they held annual congregational camping weekends on the grounds. The last time that POMC rented space for a weekend retreat was in October of 2008.

Brain Yoder, Jeramiah Morgan, Jackson Hooley at Camp Friedenswald about 1994.

Many Warren Street and Pleasant Oaks people will always hold fond memories of Camp Friedenswald. In a review of the year 1968 it was said that all the events of the year were significant, yet the weekend at Camp Friedenswald seems to stand out above them all. "It was then that a significant change of spirit came over our congregation." Experiencing God in the natural setting of Friedenswald has led countless people to make faith commitments, to grow in faith in Jesus Christ, and to participate more fully in the reign of God.

8

Lament and Celebration, 2006 to 2008

Becoming God's People

Turn, O Lord! How long?
Have compassion on your servants!
Satisfy us in the morning with your steadfast love,
so that we may rejoice and be glad all our days.

Psalm 90:13–14.

IN ORDER TO TRULY celebrate the goodness in life and authentically praise God, we must first lament our losses, that is, somehow express to God our deep sorrow or pain. Doneta Hershberger Burkhardt, a POMC member who lived at Greencroft Retirement Center, knew this. One of the first things Doneta told Rachel upon meeting in the spring of 2006 was that her vision was deteriorating. Her lament was, "When I moved to Greencroft I told God that I wanted to be a witness for Jesus. But how can I be a witness if I can't see?" At first Rachel took Doneta at face value, telling her that she was a witness by talking about Jesus, including talking about how she felt. Doneta asked the same question nearly every Sunday, and as her memory diminished, sometimes she asked it more than once in the same conversation. Rachel finally heard this as Doneta's lament. Little by little she was losing her independence and her capabilities.

Rachel began to join Doneta in her lamenting. When visiting at Greencroft, they first lamented by talking about her losses, expressing disappointment that she couldn't be a witness in the way she wanted to be, and then often went for a walk. When Doneta became unsteady on her feet, they held hands on their walks. Sometimes Rachel would say, "I feel like a school girl when I walk with you," then Doneta would say something very funny, and they would laugh like school girls. Times with Doneta were times of weeping with those who weep and laughing with those who laugh. Lamenting and celebrating would become a pattern over the next three years in Rachel's visits with Doneta and in the Pleasant Oaks congregation.

CHANGES IN THE CONGREGATION

In May 2006, Pleasant Oaks had waited nearly two years to have a new pastor settle into the pastor's pleasant office on the southeast corner of the church building. The previous lead pastor, Robin La Rue, left in August 2004, and Rachel Nafziger Hartzler began her ministry at Pleasant Oaks on May 16, 2006. A big change was that while Robin La Rue's position was full time, Rachel was now employed half time. The interim pastor, Eugene Bontrager, had modeled that a part-time pastor for Pleasant Oaks was adequate since the congregation was smaller.

2006 POMC high school graduates: J. D. Morgan, Brian Yoder, Jackson Hooley, and Matt Gingerich.

Rachel jumped right into the life of the congregation. On her first Sunday Rachel and youth pastor Michael Miller arranged for a blessing for the graduating high school seniors. As had been the tradition for many years, the women of the church had made comforters for the 2006 graduates. Four graduates from Northridge High School were honored: Matthew Gingerich, Jackson Hooley, Jeramiah D. Morgan, and

Brian Yoder. Matt was from an Amish family and had quit school after eighth grade. While he worked for Rich Yoder and Tanglewood Farms, he had done high school studies part time, and he had just completed requirements for graduation.[1]

On May 28, 2006, a licensing and installation service was held for Rachel. Lloyd Miller, conference minister for CDC (Central District Conference), officiated, and Janeen Bertsche Johnson, AMBS minister for community life, brought the sermon, "Defined by God." A mixed octet (Barb and Eugene Bontrager, Rex Gleim, DeRoy Kauffman, Eileen Miller, Viv and Dale Schlabach, and Juanita Yoder) brought additional music to the joyful and hopeful service of worship. A bountiful carry-in meal was enjoyed after the worship service, and then it was off to graduation at Northridge High. The following day, Memorial Day, was a day for graduation open-house events. Rachel took this opportunity to visit and celebrate in homes of graduates.

Soon after Rachel's arrival at POMC, Michael Miller resigned his position as youth pastor but offered to continue serving for the remainder of the summer months. The church board accepted his offer and continued his salary. Although Michael traveled many weeks during the summer for mission trips and Bible Memory Camps, he continued to meet with local youth on Wednesday evenings whenever he was in Middlebury.[2] Rachel filled in for Michael on a few Wednesday evenings, taking the youth to Menno-Hof in Shipshewana on June 28.

A search for a one-fourth time youth pastor was initiated. Matt Gingerich accepted a call to become youth pastor and served from September through November, 2006. Matt had grown close to the Rich and Juanita Yoder family during the years he worked as a farm hand. He became even more endeared to the Yoders when in a barn fire in 2002, Matt risked his life by going back into the barn to save one more calf. Matt and his younger brother, James, became good friends with Rich and Juanita's sons, Brian and Neil. They began coming to the Pleasant Oaks youth group (MYIA) and to Sunday morning services. In 2005, Matt had taken the preparation-for-baptism classes led by Eugene Bontrager, and was baptized and received as a member on September 18, 2005 (along with Rosemary Morgan and Jeff Troyer).

Although she had served four months as an interim pastor at the Florence Church of the Brethren/Mennonite in Constantine, Michigan, Pleasant Oaks was Rachel's first "regular" pastoral assignment. After graduating from Goshen College and a long career in nursing and parenting four children, Rachel began seminary in 2000 following the sudden death of her husband, Harold E. Hartzler. Rachel graduated from Associated Mennonite Biblical Seminary (AMBS) in 2004 with a Master of Arts in Christian Formation. Since graduation she had served as interim pastor, worked as a spiritual director with Goshen College students and others, led retreats, and finished editing her

---

1. Matt's grandfather, Dewey Gingerich, had owned the acreage where the Pleasant Oaks building stands. He sold it to the congregation in May 1963.

2. Michael was the camp pastor and Bible teacher for Bible Memory Camps at Camp Azusa (of The Apostolic Bible Students Association) in Syracuse, Indiana, and Camp Buckeye in Holmes County, Ohio.

MA thesis for publication. The thesis was titled *Loss as an Invitation to Transformation: Living Well Following the Death of a Spouse*. Later in 2006, Herald Press published the book with a new title: *Grief and Sexuality: Life after Losing a Spouse*.

As Rachel began to hear and experience the multiple stories of loss at Pleasant Oaks, she gained clearer understanding as to why she was called there. God had prepared her to walk with people mourning various kinds of losses. In addition to Doneta Burkhardt's diminishing health, there had been many losses in the congregation over the years, especially in the previous six years.

Marvin J. Miller, a retired minister who had held many leadership positions in the church from the time he and Ruth became members in 1985, had a debilitating stroke in 2000. Marvin suffered from aphasia following the stroke, and although he continued to sing hymns and recite scripture, he could no longer communicate well enough to fill a leadership role.

In 2002 Ken VonGunten had a stroke and died two weeks later. Ken had served in many leadership positions at Pleasant Oaks since becoming a member in 1971 and had just retired from teaching school. The congregation anticipated his ongoing lay leadership in the church, and along with Ken's family, felt crushed by his death that seemed very untimely.

Three more deaths of members in their 80s and 90s followed (Emma Peters, Lowell Troyer, and Sanford Yoder).[3] These deaths did not seem untimely, but funerals do nevertheless take a toll on a congregation, and in the case of Sanford Yoder, his widow, Shirley, remained and valued pastoral visits.

Another couple who had been very involved in the life of POMC had an employment change that took them to Florida in 2002. Linda (Hershberger Wogoman) Borntrager had grown up at Pleasant Oaks, and her husband, Marvin Borntrager, had become a member after they married in 1981. All together, these losses had a crippling effect on the congregation.

MEMBERS REMEMBERED

In the final years of Pleasant Oaks, three more members died, each of whom had earlier been significant leaders.

Tom Tetsuo Tahara

The declining health of Tom Tahara affected the lives of all the participating members in 2006. Tom was a servant leader in the congregation. While he had good health, it seemed like Jesus had been physically moving around in the village of Middlebury. A widow's overgrown hedges were trimmed. Groceries were found by the back door

3. A list of funerals/memorial services at Pleasant Oaks or in which Pleasant Oaks ministers officiated is in appendix L.

of a family whose bread-winner had lost his job. Newlyweds who were struggling financially discovered their water bill was paid by an anonymous donor. While the church ladies shared faith stories with each other in the living room, the dishes from the luncheon seemed to wash themselves. Teenage boys were welcomed to church by a Japanese man with a warm smile and an outstretched hand and discovered dollar bills in their hands when the hearty grip loosened.

The stories sounded remarkably like those in the New Testament gospels—stories about Jesus who went around feeding hungry people, healing the sick, giving hope to the hopeless and proclaiming peace. In Middlebury there were occasional sightings of a small man with dark hair just disappearing around the corner. And someone saw a truck that looked a lot like Tom Tahara's pulling away from the house where the bags of groceries were found.

Throughout his adult life, Tom Tahara helped an untold number of people. He never preached a sermon from the pulpit in front of a congregation, but his sermons were lived out. Stories about Tom were all the more extraordinary when one knew about his earlier life. His family had emigrated from Japan before Tom was born, so he was a US citizen. Nevertheless, during World War II, Tom's entire family was held at Tule Lake Center internment camp in California along with approximately 120,000 other Japanese and Japanese-American people.

The Tahara family had been living in the Olympia, Washington, area where they were strawberry farmers. Tom's father, Matsutaro, died at home before the war, so the family in camp included Tom, his mother, brother Paul, and sisters Kime, Tara, and Mary. Kime was a good friend of Jeanne Schrock, living in Olympia at the time, and they corresponded while Kime was in camp.

In 1945, Jeanne's father, Mark Schrock, then pastor at the Middlebury Church of the Brethren, and his wife, Mabel, sponsored Tom and his mother and siblings to resettle in Middlebury. Tom was sixteen years old. He was forever grateful to the Schrock family and kept in touch with them during the remainder of his life.

Perhaps it was in part the love of God, extended through the Schrock family that allowed Tom the courage and wisdom to not become bitter. Tom finished high school in Middlebury, became a Christian and was baptized at the Middlebury Church of the Brethren, fell in love with and married Sandra (Sonie) Buchtel, and joined POMC. But it wasn't smooth sailing for Tom. Numerous times he was unfairly discriminated against, especially by people who had family members who fought in World War II. But like Jesus, Tom did not seek vengeance. Instead he turned the other cheek and continued living like Jesus, blessing many people. Along with the unique career as a poultry sexer,[4] Tom was an outstanding golfer.

4. The techniques used in chicken sexing (a method of distinguishing the sex of chicken and other hatchlings) were developed in Japan in the 1920s and the knowledge and skills of the job were often passed down through the generations. Tom taught the skill to women because he thought they had smaller hands and better dexterity.

In 1988, Congress passed and President Reagan signed legislation that apologized for the internment on behalf of the US government. The legislation said that government actions were based on "race prejudice, war hysteria, and a failure of political leadership." Respect for Tom grew over the years. Two indicators that many in the Middlebury community learned to love and respect Tom came in 1994, when Tom won the Book of Golden Deeds from Middlebury's Crystal Valley Exchange Club and Tom and Sonie were selected as parade grand marshals for the Middlebury Festival.

Tom was very involved in the life of POMC as a Sunday school teacher, treasurer, deacon, trustee, board member, and moderator of the congregation. He also worked behind the scenes and is remembered as the first person to begin washing dishes after a carry-in meal. He and Sonie raised four loving, responsible, and gifted children, and were dearly loved by their grandchildren, from the oldest to the youngest, Grant Tetsuo Miller.

Unfortunately, Tom suffered from back problems, rheumatoid arthritis, and side effects from medication. He continued to put others ahead of himself, but he was severely physically limited in the last few years of his life. Rachel Hartzler had only six or seven pastoral visits with Tom. They had a minimum of conversation, but one day Rachel told Tom that she wanted him to help preach a sermon. He became more alert than usual and said, "You've got to be kidding!" She explained that she wanted to use examples of his life to illustrate the ministry of Jesus. Tom had little to say about that, and Rachel concluded that his actions spoke louder than his words.

Tom expressed to Rachel that he thought he was near death but that he was not afraid to die. However, when they talked about heaven, Tom said he didn't know if he would see some of his loved ones there because they were Buddhist. This presented a challenging pastoral quandary. Finally Rachel simply said, "God is gracious," and the two sat in reflective silence.

As Tom's body continued to weaken, family members, close friends, other caregivers, and Rachel were present, often in silence, quietly praying, or reading Psalms. Tom died peacefully on June 4, 2006, surrounded by his loving wife, Sonie, and children: a daughter, Robin, member of POMC, and three sons, Terry, Tim, and Kelly, who had grown up at POMC. Many relatives, friends, and church and community members came to the Miller-Stewart funeral Home for visitations, to his funeral service at the Middlebury Church of the Brethren on June 9, and burial at Grace Lawn Cemetery. Eugene Bontrager, former interim pastor, neighbor, and friend of Tom and Sonie, preached the funeral sermon, and Rachel assisted with the funeral and graveside service. Pleasant Oaks provided a meal for the family, close friends, and out-of-town guests that included Julian Schrock and other members of the Mark Schrock family. Pleasant Oaks purchased a tree in memory of Tom that was planted at the Krider "World's Fair" Garden the following June.

Rachel later shared this reflection on Tom's life:

Yes, it was Jesus moving around Middlebury. It was God made flesh, incarnate, living in the aging, crippled body of Tom Tahara. Yes, ". . . the Word was made flesh and lived among us, full of grace and truth" in the first century in the land of Palestine, *and* in the twentieth century in the state of Indiana.

Sandra ("Sonie") Buchtel Tahara

Sonie was grief-stricken when her beloved Tom died, but with the comfort and love of God, her family, and her church, she continued to live. Sonie's church family made a pledge to walk with her. She had been born into the congregation,[5] was baptized there, had helped with the construction of the Pleasant Oaks building, and was involved her entire life. Sonie was a warm, generous, and loving person, and she was dearly loved by all who knew her.

Sonie had often missed church during the last months of Tom's life as she cared for him, but she immediately began attending regularly after his funeral. However, as the months went on, Sonie had some health issues. Her treatment included surgery in November that was followed by complications and a slow recovery. She was able to return to church by the end of December, and was present on most Sundays and for congregational meetings through April. Sonie seemed to always have loving words of appreciation and encouragement, and there was usually a sparkle in her eyes.

Sadly, health issues resurfaced, leading to open heart surgery on May 1. She was well enough to go home for a short time, but her recovery went poorly. Before the end of May, she was back at Elkhart General Hospital. Sonie felt God's presence, but her body didn't heal. During the regular visits with Rachel, Sonie expressed her faith in God and her confidence that all would be well. She was aware of the prayers of many people and expressed deep appreciation.

There were two special events to which Sonie looked forward: the wedding of her granddaughter Megan, and the dedication of trees in memory of Tom at Krider Garden. A cloud of sadness hovered over those who gathered on June 7 for a short service of dedication of the American Beech tree donated by POMC[6] and a row of White Pine trees donated by the Tahara grandchildren. Grandchildren Morgan Tahara and Grant Miller shared memories and a poem written by their uncle Tim Tahara.

Sonie's absence was keenly felt at the park as she remained in the hospital. Although it was difficult for her family to talk about death, Sonie eventually began to talk to her pastor about dying, and before she was put on a ventilator in mid-June, she released herself anew into God's care. For several weeks Sonie held together the

5. Sonie's grandparents, Freed and Nina Hershberger, were founding members of WSMC and her mother, Lois Hershberger Buchtel Tyson, had also been born into WSMC, was baptized there and remained for life.

6. The words on the plaque by the beech tree are "Dedicated by Pleasant Oaks Mennonite Church in memory of Tom T. Tahara (1929– 2006), a friend to all".

mysteries of life and death—of wanting to live but also being ready to die, anticipating the joys of heaven and the comfort of eternal life.

The Tahara children hovered over their mother like angels, lovingly doing all they could to make her as comfortable as possible and arranging for her to never be alone. At the end of June, Sonie was transferred to Our Lady of Peace Hospital in South Bend, Indiana.

Sonie's spirit was peacefully released from her body, and she was totally healed on Thursday, July 5, 2007. She was led by Jesus into the presence of her great and wondrous God. When the Pleasant Oaks congregation gathered on Sunday, they began the worship service by remembering Sonie. Based on the belief that when grieving a loss, lament to God is necessary before authentic praise of God can happen, the service began with lament. Sonie's funeral would occur on Tuesday, but it was necessary to remember Sonie that day. After a brief remembrance and prayer led by Rachel, there was a time of silence, and then the congregation sang "Let hope and sorrow now unite" as a way to consecrate the mixed feelings about Sonie's death before shifting to praise of God.

Sonie's children planned a meaningful funeral service, with Eugene Bontrager and Rachel officiating. Her son Tim spoke eloquent words about his mother's wonderful heart. Proverbs 31:10–31 was read, a beautiful passage that describes an ordinary woman transformed by the grace of God into a woman of great strength and clear purpose. That described Sonie. She was a woman who loved deeply and lavishly; she left a wonderful legacy of a life well-lived and filled with love.

Marvin J. Miller

A significant loss at POMC was the active participation of Marvin J. Miller following bypass surgery and a stroke in 2001. Marvin and Ruth Miller were another couple with many gifts and willing hearts. They moved to Middlebury in 1978 after Marvin retired from his pastoral assignment at Walnut Hill Mennonite Church in Goshen where they had been the founding pastoral couple in 1957. Both Ruth and Marvin accepted many assignments at POMC. Soon after becoming members in 1985, Marvin was called to serve as a deacon. Over the next sixteen years Marvin served as a deacon, trustee, Sunday school teacher, choir member, worship leader, and preacher in the pastor's absence. In addition, Barry Schmell asked Marvin to be the official church photographer. Ruth sang in the choir and in ensembles, served as Sunday school superintendent, and taught Sunday school. She helped plan worship services, led worship, and read scripture. Ruth also offered the gift of hospitality, quietly, graciously, and sincerely.

Following his stroke, Marvin suffered from physical limitations and aphasia and was no longer able to contribute to the life of the congregation in the same way. Ruth cared for Marvin, and as long as possible, brought him to church where he continued to join in the singing. In October 2006 Marvin moved to a health care room at Greencroft in Goshen where he watched baseball games, listened to music and *The Mennonite* on tape, spent time in prayer and meditation, and received visitors, sometimes singing and reciting scripture with his visitors. He joyfully and solemnly participated in communion when a small group of POMCers gathered at Greencroft for communion services.

Plaque at Pleasant Oaks in memory of Marvin J. Miller.

Marvin's health deteriorated in early June 2008, and he was hospitalized in Goshen. There he and Ruth were surrounded by their family, three of their five children and several of their ten grandchildren, and their pastor. Remembering Marvin's love of music, on June 14 Rachel suggested that grandson Kevin bring his guitar and the family sing together. The family gathered that evening, prayed, sang "Amazing Grace," "Jesus loves Me," and "You are my Sunshine," and spoke loving words of release to husband, father, and grandfather. Later that evening Marvin peacefully left this world and entered the glory of his Lord whom he had faithfully loved and passionately served.

Marvin's was the last Pleasant Oaks funeral, held at the Miller-Stewart Funeral Home in Middlebury. All Marvin and Ruth's children, all but one grandchild, and all of Marvin's living siblings gathered to mourn his death and celebrate his life. Burial in the Clinton Union Cemetery was followed by a meal and sharing in the POMC fellowship hall. The loss of Marvin was felt by the congregation over a period of several years: from the time he had the stroke through the years of his attending worship services but communicating less and less; during his months in health care at Greencroft in Goshen; and then again at the time of his death in 2008.

Ruth designated Pleasant Oaks as a recipient for memorial money and later chose a hand-crafted wooden sculpture to be hung in the front of the POMC sanctuary, a twin piece to the one dedicated in memory of Charlotte Weldy Hurst. The Hurst sculptured plaque has the words, "I am the resurrection and the life." The words on the Miller piece are, "Jesus said 'Believe in me.'" Both pieces were hand carved from solid cherry by Sculptor John Mishler of Goshen, Indiana. Mishler, a nationally known art sculptor, had been Associate Professor of Art at Goshen College since 1985.

LOSSES AND LAMENT

Along with joy and hope, were many losses during the last four years of the Pleasant Oaks congregation. The presence of Gale Livengood in POMC worship services during 2006–2007, including her piano accompaniment, was greatly appreciated. However, her presence was a reminder of the fact that she was a woman in transition. Her husband, Ken Livengood, who had been pastor of Bonneyville Mennonite and a strong supporter of the MYIA program, had tragically died in a motorcycle accident in 2003.

Michael Miller's last Sunday as youth pastor at POMC was August 27, 2006. He preached a sermon titled "Where there is No Vision, the People Perish," and the congregation gave him a blessing. A collection had been taken earlier to give Michael toward buying a laptop computer to help him maintain connections in his next ministry.

The MYIA summer activities ended with a good-bye party for Michael Miller and Susan Hull hosted by Brittany Parker at her grandparents' home north of

Middlebury. The evening included a hot dog roast, games in the yard, and a circle of prayer and conversation during which the MYIA "mantle" was passed from Michael to Matthew Gingerich.

The following Sunday was a celebration of hope and expectation. Loren Johns preached on "Jonah and the Scandalous Grace of God," and Matthew Gingerich was commissioned as POMC youth pastor. The congregation took responsibility in calling an unusually young youth pastor, answering in the affirmative the following questions: Do you accept your role in setting apart Matthew for leadership? Will you honor Matthew's calling and also your own? Will you search the Scriptures and pray with and for Matthew? Will you speak the truth in love? Will you join Matthew in the mission to youth in this congregation and in this community? Matt was then given a copy of the Mennonite Church USA *Minister's Manual*, a token of the congregation's affirmation of him as youth pastor.

Nevertheless, during the final months of 2006, more sadness crept among the participants of Pleasant Oaks. Michael Miller's absence was felt. The new energy that Matt Gingerich brought to the youth program was like a breath of fresh air, and it looked as though the youth program that Michael had helped to build might continue. Sandi Bjornson and/or Rachel joined Matt in the Wednesday evening activities as community youth gathered at POMC for games, Bible study, and food. However, a number of the youth wanted to meet with leaders in the congregation to express their concerns.

The deacon council, church board, and numerous other interested people gathered on October 4, to listen to the youth. Anger was expressed at Rachel since it was because of her that Michael Miller left POMC, choosing to leave rather than serving with a female pastor. A POMC member pointed out that it was the congregation that had invited Rachel to come, and then there were accusations that the congregation didn't care at all about the youth. POMC members were not defensive, even though the congregation as a whole and many individuals had given much support in time, money, and prayers over the four years that Michael had been paid to do youth ministry. Although faltering attempts were made to biblically support the idea that women should not be in church leadership, those present who supported women in church ministry were patient and gracious. The meeting ended with cider and donuts and a moderate tone.

Many laments and prayers during the late autumn of 2006 were for the youth. Five of the MYIA youth were in a car crash on November 12, 2006. Brittany Parker and Kim Courtney were in a Ft. Wayne hospital after the car in which they were riding hit a tree in Middlebury. Aleigha Bourdon, Matt Lehman, and Brett Robinson were also in the car and were hurt, but not hospitalized. Brittany remained in critical condition in intensive care for an extended period of time and then remained in the hospital for a few weeks to recover from liver damage, a dislocated hip, and severe burns.

As a symbol of support and a reminder to pray, a candle was lit at Pleasant Oaks whenever the church office was open, when a meeting took place, and when the congregation gathered for worship. Matt Gingerich was a very supportive youth pastor to these young people. He made many trips to Ft. Wayne and kept Rachel and the congregation updated. The congregation prayed regularly and gave financial support.

Sadly, Matt's leadership was short-lived. When Matt ended his assignment as youth pastor at the end of November, the young people involved with MYIA at the time said they would not continue meeting at Pleasant Oaks, even if another youth pastor were hired. So this important ministry officially came to an end in late 2006— another loss for the congregation. Rachel continued to keep in touch with a few of the youth from the community and the youth whose parents were members of Pleasant Oaks. The group was no longer called MYIA, but she met with the Pleasant Oaks youth occasionally and arranged for them to have monthly Sunday noon meals to-gether, often in the homes of generous members.

And then came a loss so tragic that it felt like a bomb dropped on an already suffer-ing village. On December 1, Caitlin Kuykendall died. Caitlin was the seventeen-year-old daughter of Mary Kuykendall (daughter of Leona and J. O. Yoder) and Steve Kuykendall. Mary had grown up at POMC and was known by most of the members in 2006, and loved by all who knew her. The Kuykendalls lived in the Middlebury area when Caitlin and her brother, Clinton, were born, and they were each dedicated to God in a parent/baby dedication service at POMC. When Caitlin was nine and Clinton was six, the fam-ily moved to the Dallas, Texas, area. They were actively involved in a spirited, evangelical congregation there with both Caitlin and Clint participating in youth activities.

Caitlin had been sick with mild flu-like symptoms for a month and then became seriously ill on November 21. She was care-flighted to Dallas Children's Hospital where she was diagnosed with acute myeloid leukemia and brain hemor-rhaging. The next day Leona, her daughter Anita Miller, and granddaughters Brit-tany Yoder and Rachel Wenger, flew to Dallas to be with Caitlin and her family. A website (Grace4Caitlin.org) gave daily updates, and people around the world prayed fervently for her. Her parents described her as calm and beautiful, letting the love of God shine through her, even in her dying.

Caitlin, who would have been eighteen on December 13, had attended Pleas-ant Oaks on her regular visits with her grandparents, aunts, uncles, and cousins—in-cluding in the summer of 2006. The hearts of Pleasant Oaks ached for Mary, Steve, and Caitlin's fifteen-year-old brother, Clint, as well as for Leona, J. O., Rich, Juanita, Brittany, Brian, Neil, and other family members. The extended family flew to Texas for Caitlin's funeral at Grace Church of Ovilla on December 5, where her death was mourned and her life was celebrated.

In addition, Nan Stalter, who had been involved at Pleasant Oaks since first bring-ing her daughter Natalie to preschool from 1988 to 1990, had triple losses in her family. Nan's "dad", Phillip H. Kane, Jr., died on December 3, in Newport, Rhode Island. Phil was technically Nan's uncle, but he and his wife raised Nan from the time she was three years old, and he was a father to her. Nan was grateful that she was able to go to Rhode Island and spend time with him before he died. This was the third death within five months of a significant person in Nan's life. Her brother, Eddie Fougere, died from cancer at age fifty-six in July 2006. Then on November 9, Nan's father-in-law, Earl Stalter, died. There was a good friendship between Nan and Earl, a member of First Mennonite of Middlebury. Members of POMC grieved along with Nan.

An additional Pleasant Oaks family had been dealing with a chronic illness. Jon and Kelly Troyer and their son Jordan had been diagnosed with a liver disease in the spring of 2005. Jon and Kelly had had a year of rigorous treatment but saw no improvement in their viral counts. Jordan was still in a treatment plan. While awaiting the results of Jordan's treatment and waiting to see if more treatment might be available for Kelly and Jon, the couple asked for an anointing service at the church. This was held on Sunday morning, December 17. Rachel led the anointing service with the assistance of Eugene Bontrager. The congregation recited Romans 8:38–39 and then gathered around the family and sang the old hymn, "The love of God is greater far than tongue or pen can ever tell . . ."

Another loss for Pleasant Oaks in 2006 was that Eugene and Barbara Bontrager were gradually leaving. Eugene had been pastor at Forks Mennonite Church from 1985 to 1996. He and Barb worshiped at Pleasant Oaks from 1999 through 2005. They graciously returned to Pleasant Oaks at Rachel's request for some specific tasks and preaching assignments during 2006 through 2009, but for Eugene and Barbara, it was time to return "home" to Forks Mennonite Church, the congregation where they had both grown up. In addition, Eugene had the specific assignment of writing the Forks church history for their Sesquicentennial anniversary in 2007.

Two members who had been attending other churches made requests for letters of transfer during 2006: Brittany Yoder to the Middlebury Church of the Brethren and Sara VonGunten to Eighth Street Mennonite. Although happy that they had each found places that better met their needs, people at POMC greatly missed them both.

A very tangible loss in the fall of 2006 was the theft of the church office computer. Although there were hard copies of much of the data on the computer, there was some information that was not duplicated elsewhere. The mystery of who took the computer was not solved, so the congregation felt uneasy. Who would do this? Was this done in anger? POMC prayed for the person who had taken the computer and then went about the task of purchasing another computer and re-keying the exterior doors and the door to the church office. Even with the distribution of a limited number of keys, people remained on edge.

How did the congregation cope with all these losses? At times members felt empty with little hope, but by the grace of God, they were adequately nourished in times of worship and fellowship. For five Sundays during the summer they worshiped around biblical themes of bread, especially passages from the Gospel of John with Jesus' teachings about "the bread of life." Someone from the congregation provided bread each Sunday. POMC enjoyed communion in the broad sense of the word, and celebrated the Lord's Supper on one of the Sundays. People were fed and sustained.

The congregation took another proactive step in the midst of this series of losses. During the worship service on November 26, POMC commemorated Eternity Sunday by remembering Sanford Yoder and other loved ones who had died. At the time of Sanford's death (February 25, 2005), memorial monies were designated for Pleasant Oaks, and the family wished to buy books for the church library. Many new books for the library were purchased along with fifty copies of *Sing the Journey*, a supplement to the Mennonite *Hymnal: A Worship Book*.[7]

On Eternity Sunday many members of the Sanford and Shirley Yoder family were present to help dedicate the books to the service of God. In her sermon that morning, Rachel led the congregation through the rituals of remembering loved ones who died, lamenting, giving thanks, and proclaiming hope. Most of the fifty-two people present came forward to light votive candles in memory of loved ones who had died. After a time of lament, the congregation praised God by singing one verse of the very familiar "Praise to God, Immortal Praise" followed by the last four verses, never sung before at Pleasant Oaks, at least not in recent memory.

> Lord, should rising whirlwinds tear from its stem the ripening ear,
> should the fig tree's blasted shoot drop her green untimely fruit;
> should the vine put forth no more, nor the olive yield her store,
> though the sickening flocks should fall, and the herds desert the stall;
> should thine altered hand restrain the early and the latter rain,
> blast each opening bud of joy, and the rising year destroy;
> yet to thee my soul should raise grateful vows and solemn praise,
> and, when every blessing's flown, love thee for thyself alone![8]

After giving thanks in spite of losses, the congregation then proclaimed hope by singing "I'm Pressing on the Upward Way," and exited to a lively rendition of "When the Saints Go Marching In!"

LOVE'S REVELATIONS

Pleasant Oaks followed the Mennonite Church (MC USA) theme for Advent, Christmas and Epiphany, "Love's Revelations," and a song from the new *Sing the Journey* books became the theme song, "Love came down at Christmas." Indeed, it was God's love that sustained the congregation through the darkness of illness, loss, and grief,

7. *Sing the Journey*, Faith and Life Resources, 2005. Many new songs as well as some old familiar songs in this book were sung in worship services throughout the following three years. After the last service at POMC, the church board agreed to donate twenty copies to the new emerging Mennonite Fellowship of Asheville, North Carolina, a church plant of the Central District Conference where Rachel Nafziger Hartzler served as pastor from January through June of 2010.

8. Anna L. Barbauld, "Praise to God, Immortal Praise," verses 6–9. *Hymns for Public Worship*, 1772. Based on Habakkuk 3:17–18: Though the fig tree does not blossom, and no fruit is on the vines; though the produce of the olive fails and the fields yield no food; though the flock is cut off from the fold and there is no herd in the stalls, yet I will rejoice in the Lord; I will exult in the God of my salvation.

and into the light of hope offered in Jesus. A large white star shimmered from the front on the sanctuary on the large banner designed and loaned to the congregation by Rosanna Eller McFadden, a free-lance artist, student at AMBS, and member of Creekside Church of the Brethren in Elkhart.

Many people participated in the Advent/Christmas/Epiphany services. Children and youth lit candles, presented dramatic readings, and recited words of prophets. Sandi Bjornson and Laura Hooley led creative and instructive times for the children during worship services. Dale Schlabach and DeRoy Kauffman led and accompanied more than the usual number of carols and hymns, and many other people made important contributions. Working behind the scenes, Laura Hooley coached the dramatic readers; Char Osborn Morgan and Doris Hershberger (with the help of Gerri Beachy and Ed Swoveland) created and displayed visuals that enhanced worship services; Doris Hershberger used her creative talents to build a podium that was the right height and angle for her scripture reading!

On the Wednesday before Christmas, the youth and young adults visited Brittany Parker and Kim Courtney and sang Christmas carols for these two who were still recovering from injuries of the accident of November 12. The birth of Christ was celebrated, and the year ended with hope—along with a sigh. Another couple decided to leave Pleasant Oaks.

In the January 2007 newsletter the following appeared:

> The year 2006 has ended and 2007 has begun. When something new begins, something old usually dies. And when something dies, something new often emerges. In the life of our congregation, MYIA has ended. . . . We have lamented that loss and are now moving on, ready for something new to develop. . . . Let us pray that God will continue to move among us and that new things will emerge—programs or activities that will capture the interest and attention of the youth . . .

Members continued to pray on Sunday mornings and Wednesday evenings, asking God to send more people. On January 8, 2007, the church board decided to name "the elephant in the room." People were wondering if the church could continue, but the fear of that possibility was so great that the concerns were expressed in barely more than a whisper. With the board's prompting, Rachel talked with Lloyd Miller, CDC conference minister. Lloyd gave suggestions for Rachel to bring back to the board.

On February 12, Rachel presented the board with a summary of Sunday morning attendance:

> Pleasant Oaks Mennonite Church has gone from a membership of well over 100 people to an average attendance of approximately thirty. Within the past month one more couple has left the congregation, bringing us to a point of needing to ask the difficult question of whether we can survive as a congregation. We have forty-five active participants (including seven unbaptized

children and youth) who have attended services regularly (at least numerous times) during the past three months (except for two Greencroft residents). This does not count those who have recently left or those who have not attended in the past six months but are technically still members.

The monthly average attendance of Sunday morning services was reviewed from the beginning of 1986. From October of 1987 through May of 1998 the average attendance was over eighty every month, and over ninety most months. The average attendance was 135 in November 1991, 133 in December 1992, 135 in April 1993, and 133 in November 1993. The average attendance was seventy-nine in June 1998, and from that point on a decline in attendance was experienced.[9]

Rachel continued with suggestions from Lloyd Miller: Invite ten to twenty people from sister congregations "to come over to Macedonia and help us" by participating in our worship services and fellowship for six to twelve months to give us a "jump start"; or consider a merger with First Mennonite of Middlebury. Rachel made initial inquiries with other pastors about plan one, but no one responded positively.

Lloyd attended a congregational meeting on February 26, to give a historical perspective on churches facing similar circumstances and to help the group think about options.

1. Lloyd noted that the last decade has not been kind to POMC. It's not that we have failed doing a good job, because we have had good visioning. Churches have peaks and valleys. POMC has a wonderful history! Our beginnings were tough, breaking away, making sacrifices and building the church building. We have an enviable preschool program and facility.
2. Something new is being called for from the church now and it's a scary thing to us. Our pastor Rachel cannot make decisions about it. The decisions need be come from us. She loves us.
3. POMC is going through a Spiritual discernment right now (Ephesians 1). Picture an image: "the eye of your heart," which requires a different kind of seeing than using our logic. This is how we need to look at our present circumstance with regard to future decisions.
4. Lloyd described POMC as being at a "tipping point."
5. Lloyd responded to the idea of re-uniting with First Mennonite by saying that if we would do that, we should do that from our strength, not our weakness.[10]

The idea of re-uniting with First Mennonite was one of many options brought to the discussion. Considering many ideas, the congregation agreed to take intentional steps during the Lenten season and committed to: praying specifically about Pleasant Oaks; listening to each other; and sharing thoughts and visions. Being reminded that

9. A table showing the monthly average attendance from 1986 to 2009 is in appendix S.
10. POMC board minutes, February 26, 2007.

the congregation had met weekly to pray back in the early sixties as the POMC building was being planned, the group decided to meet at 9 a.m. before worship services each Sunday. (Sunday school had been temporarily discontinued.) In addition, some members gathered to pray every Wednesday evening.

Answers to prayer during Lent gave great incentive to maintain hope for POMC. Thelma Horner offered to support the work at Pleasant Oaks with her attendance and piano accompaniment if needed. Bill and Jan Swartzendruber visited in March and reported they would be moving from the Chicago area to Middlebury later in the spring and were looking for a congregation where their gifts could be used.

At the same time, having heard that POMC was exploring options for the future, the leadership group at First Mennonite Church of Middlebury (FMC) picked up the ball and went into action. With positive responses from the staff, elders, and church council to the idea of "testing the waters" regarding some kind of merger with POMC, the decision was made to inform the entire FMC congregation of the discussion. A copy of the memo from FMC lead pastor Linford Martin to the FMC members was placed in POMC member's boxes on March 2, the same day it was distributed at FMC. The memo gave information and asked questions: Might this be an opportune time to re-unite, to come together to form one Mennonite congregation in the Middlebury community? "Might this be a time to combine our gifts, our abilities, and our energy to shape a new future together? Might this be a time when we could express caring, experience reconciliation, and envision new possibilities?" The memo invited reflection, comments, and observation.

Pleasant Oaks celebrated the Resurrection of Jesus on April 8. Even though the celebration was joyful, there was the paradox of joy and sorrow, death and new life. In addition to the deaths of 2006, Eileen Miller's mother, Florence Yoder, died on January 1, 2007, and three members experienced the death of siblings in early 2007: Dale Schlabach's sister Eudean Broni, and Paul Yoder's brother Sam Yoder, both in their sixties, died in January; an older sister of J. O. Yoder, Verna Weaver, who had grown up at Warren Street, died in March. The congregation gave Easter lilies to these families in memory of their siblings. In keeping with a long-time tradition, others had ordered Easter lilies in memory of loved ones, so the sanctuary was filled with these symbols of new life.

With the fragrance of Easter still in the air, members met for a congregational meeting on Easter Monday, April 9. Since the last meeting, conversations with the leadership of FMC had occurred, and a formal letter had arrived from Linford Martin, inviting POMC to dialogue about the possibility of merging with FMC. Copies were distributed to POMCers on April 8. The letter reported an overwhelmingly positive response from FMC members to the idea of ongoing dialogue about the possibility of re-uniting with POMC.

The April 9 discussion began with a question from Dale Schlabach, board chair and acting congregational chair. Who would be open to our merging with First

Mennonite Church? Much discussion followed with honest and open comments as to future dreams and plans. Some commented that there are other area Mennonite churches that may be of interest, such as Bonneyville and Clinton Brick, since they are smaller. A number said they are more comfortable in a small church that feels more like a family. FMC had around 220 attending regularly. POMC had around forty-five active attendees. Gratefully, there was not a sense of "camps" vying for power within the group. This had not always been true in POMC's history.

The preschool, POMC's community outreach, was a big concern for all. The POMC church board had already decided that the next school year (2007–2008) would be supported with POMC money, regardless of the status of the congregation. Children were already registered, and families were counting on that. But what about after that?

Several times during the April 9 meeting it was said that the POMC church board should meet with the FMC church council before their next congregational meeting. Discussion on how to become better acquainted with FMC members and their worship style on Sunday mornings, ended with a motion that for one Sunday morning POMC close the doors in order for all to visit another church of choice. The presence of God's Spirit was acknowledged, and appreciation was expressed for the honest, respectful, and helpful sharing that occurred throughout the meeting.

Two POMC board members attended the FMC church council meeting on May 3, 2007. They indicated that maintaining the preschool was a high priority for POMC. The FMC council agreed that they would support the continuation of the preschool if the congregations would re-unite. They also agreed on a desire to continue the dialogue with POMC. May 6 was attend-a-different-church Sunday for POMC. When the members gathered to share their experiences, it was surprising to note that nobody visited FMC.

For a number of reasons, the discussion about re-uniting with FMC came to a halt, and other things took precedence. Conversations with land-developer Edgar Miller had come to the board a few times in early 2007. In 1998, a sixty-feet-wide tract of land along the west edge of the Pleasant Oaks property had been sold to Miller for access to property he owned behind the church building. Earlier he had planned on a residential development. Now he was negotiating with Martin's Super Markets to build a store on the property.

In May, the POMC head trustee, Gerri Beachy, received an offer from Edgar Miller of $600,000 for the church property. He polled the POMC board members who unanimously agreed that this was too low to consider. Edgar then returned with a proposal to purchase the back half of the church property. Although the congregation had decided several years earlier to not divide the property, the board decided to take the question to the congregation again. A congregational meeting was scheduled for June 10.

On one hand, some wondered if this offer was an answer to prayer. At the same time, other answers seemed to be emerging. Bill and Jan Swartzendruber had moved to Middlebury and expressed great interest in joining with POMC. Thelma Horner had been attending regularly since April and indicated that her husband, Glen, was planning to join in at the end of August when he finished a Sunday-school-teaching commitment at Bonneyville. Four recently-retired, gifted, experienced, and enthusiastic new members certainly seemed like a quadruple blessing from God! The congregational vote was again to not divide the property.

GIFTS FROM GOD

Along with the losses of 2007, there were also many gifts to POMC. After the Horners and Swartzendrubers became involved at POMC, Thelma and Glen (both retired Mennonite ministers) each preached several times a year, Bill preached a few times, and Jan very capably and creatively led worship on a regular basis. These were received as gifts from God and answers to prayer. Open discussions about ending the congregation ceased. POMC was on the map to stay—at least for the time being.

One benefit of having a half-time pastor who preached only two or three Sundays per month was having regular guest preachers. Those who preached several times in 2006 through 2009 were Elmer Wall, former pastor; Eugene Bontrager, former interim pastor; Joe Yoder, physical neighbor and director of Menno-Hof; Galen Johns, retired pastor and conference minister; John D. Rempel, AMBS professor of historical theology; Ron Kennel, retired pastor who last served at Clinton Brick Mennonite Church; Rhoda Schrag, retired Mennonite pastor; John Heyerly, interim conference minister for CDC during 2007–2008; Larry Hicks, retired pastor and Navy chaplain; and Don Blosser, Goshen College professor emeritus of New Testament.

Others who preached once during 2006 were James Waltner, former pastor of College Mennonite Church in Goshen; John King, former interim pastor at POMC; Loren Johns, academic dean at AMBS; Matt Gingerich, POMC youth pastor at the time; Ken Hawkley, development director of Chicago Mennonite Learning Center; and Marlene Kropf, AMBS associate professor of spiritual formation and worship and minister of worship for Mennonite Church USA.

In addition to the regular guest preachers, others in 2007 were: Vic Stoltzfus, Goshen College president emeritus; Joe Richards, retired missionary and Mennonite pastor; Alice Roth, representative of CDC; Robert Martz, Mennonite pastor between assignments, later pastor of Topeka Mennonite Church; Heidi Regier Kreider, member of the board of Mennonite Mission Network (MMN) and pastor of Bethel College Mennonite Church in North Newton, Kansas; Todd Taylor, licensed minister in the Church of the Brethren; Keith Swartzendruber, director of the Anabaptist Peace Center in Washington, DC; and Adam M. L. Tice, musician and writer of hymn texts. Adam, a student at AMBS at the time, wrote a hymn text specifically for April 15 at Pleasant Oaks. The text weaves together John 20:19–31 and Psalm 150, two of the lectionary texts for the day (http://www.giamusic.com). The hymn, titled "Peace be with you" to the tune written by Chris Ángel and titled Pleasant Oaks, is in appendix T.

A visit from former pastors Anne and Ken Rupp and their family was a special blessing on July 8, 2007. Forty-eight members and former members gathered to worship. Anne brought greetings and Ken preached about "Lessons from Life." For people who had been at POMC between 1975 and 1982, it was a joy to see Anne and Ken, and their son, Byron, and his family. Byron had been a child in the congregation during those years. A carry-in meal offered time for fellowship.

Another gift in the summer of 2007 was a children's time during the worship service led by Rose Morgan and Jim Mishler, titled "The Thrill of the Race" and based on verses from Hebrews:

> . . . let us run with perseverance the race that is set before us, looking to Jesus the pioneer and perfecter of our faith, who for the sake of the joy that was set before him endured the cross, disregarding its shame, and has taken his seat at the right hand of the throne of God. Consider him who endured such hostility against himself from sinners, so that you may not grow weary or lose heart. . . . Therefore lift your drooping hands and strengthen your weak knees . . . (Hebrews 12:1b–3, 12).

Both Rose and Jim were racers—Rose as a cross country runner and Jim as a horse cart racer with trotter horses. They each told stories, responding to questions about what kind of racing they had done. Is racing easy or hard? Why do you do it? What are some of the thrills? What are some of the difficult things about racing? Rachel then preached a sermon on this text and ended with reciting Hebrews 12:12–13 from *The Message*: "So don't sit around on your hands! No more dragging your feet! Clear the path for long-distance runners so no one will trip and fall, so no one will step in a hole and sprain an ankle. Help each other out. And run for it!"[11]

The vision, energy, and enthusiasm of the Swartzendrubers and Horners had a positive impact on POMC. Understanding the high value placed on the preschool, the four envisioned an all-church and all-preschool event. They led in planning and implementing a "Preschool Festival" in September 2007. Approximately one hundred preschool children and their families and Pleasant Oaks members enjoyed the Sunday afternoon event of games on the lawn, visiting, and food. Four gallons of lemonade, four gallons ice cream, twelve dozen cookies, and seventy-five bags of popcorn were enjoyed.

Gerri Beachy served many years as a trustee, very capably and conscientiously caring for the building and grounds. He asked to be relieved of the responsibility in 2007. With deep gratitude for all that Gerri had done, the church board invited Bill Swartzendruber, a retired engineer, to assume that task. Bill asked for time to think and pray about the request and then came back saying he would rather work with the youth. It was another unexpected answer to prayer! Beginning in September 2007, and continuing

---

11. Scripture quotation from *The Message*. Copyright © by Eugene H. Peterson 1993, 1994, 1995, 1996, 2000, 2001, 2002. Used by permission of NavPress Publishing Group.

through 2009, Bill led a Sunday school class for junior and senior youth. Even though attendance was low, Bill's enthusiasm and love for youth was a great blessing.

The adult Sunday school class had been temporarily suspended early in 2007, and in its place, the hour prior to Sunday morning worship became a gathering time for coffee and fellowship. While this time was highly valued by many, some members missed the Christian nurture that Sunday school provided. Again, a gift was offered, this one from Glen Horner, Sunday school teacher extraordinaire. Glen's love of the Bible and gift of teaching came through in classes as the group used the quarterly study of the Bible from an Anabaptist perspective from Faith and Life Resources. Beginning in the fall of 2007, the class met twice each month so that the gathering time events could also continue.

Additional gifts over the years were creative visuals for the worship space, items that enhanced worship and pointed to God. Char Morgan Swoveland's imaginative and artistic creations were highly valued and greatly appreciated. Beginning in late 2007, Juanita Yoder and Jan Swartzendruber often prepared the sanctuary for God-focused worship, using visual arts to help proclaim God's Word, helping worshipers to see, smell, taste, and touch the glory of God.

For more years than most people remember, the Middlebury Ministerium has been an active group of pastors from most of the denominations in Middlebury. The ministerium arranged for a pulpit exchange during the Week of Prayer for Christian Unity between January 18 and 25. In 2006, Wes Yoder from Forks came to POMC. In 2007, POMC did not participate because of a conflict. The "Bound 4 Glory" men's quartet from the Agape Church of the Brethren in Ft. Wayne led the worship service on Unity Sunday. In 2008, Gordon Henke, lead pastor of River of Life Fellowship north of Middlebury, preached at POMC, and Rachel preached at Bonneyville Mennonite Church. In 2009 Rachel exchanged places with Linford Martin, pastor of First Mennonite of Middlebury.

The ministerium also organized Sunday evening worship services during Lent, Good Friday services, and sometimes an Easter morning breakfast. For many years the Good Friday noon service was at POMC. In 2007, Linda Craig, pastor of the Methodist Church was the preacher; in 2008, Scott Miller, pastor of Pathway Assembly of God preached on Good Friday; and in 2009 Rick Lambright preached at the Good Friday service at POMC.

In addition to the regular preachers, guest preachers in 2008 included: Vic Hildebrand, pastor at Kempsville Presbyterian Church in Virginia Beach, Virginia; Norm Braksick, a volunteer with Foods Resource Bank; Chuck Tayler, retired Church of the Brethren pastor; Clair Hochstetler, chaplain from Goshen General Hospital; Glen Miller, retired physician and program manager of MC USA Healthcare Access; Sarah Thompson, student at AMBS, Mennonite Voluntary Service worker in Elkhart and former North American representative of AMIGOS of Mennonite World Conference; John Driver, retired life-long Mennonite missionary and author; Andy Alexis-Baker,

Christian activist and student at AMBS; and Marlin Jeschke, author and Goshen College professor emeritus of philosophy and religion.

Other gifts to the congregation were the office secretaries who worked part time behind the scenes, often going beyond the call of duty. Doris Hershberger and Patti Whetstone Beck served in this capacity in the late 70s and early 80s. Marlene Mockler worked in the office for many years in the 80s and 90s, followed by Juanita Yoder who served from 1996 to 2003 except for a short interval when Kristi Yoder served. Shannon Cramer, Char Morgan, and Alyson Kerezman each worked for shorter periods of time. Leasa Worley was the last POMC secretary, serving from June 2005 through October 2009.

"THE WORLD IS ABOUT TO TURN"

POMC followed the 2007 MC USA theme of Advent that was bursting with expectation. The subthemes were: Get ready! Take heart! Rejoice! Be restored! Praise the Lord! Part of preparing to praise God was dealing with more losses. Another theft occurred; again a telephone was stolen from the church kitchen. The POMC leaders tried to respond like Jesus would, seeking restorative justice. What could a small congregation in Middlebury do to join in the work that God was doing in the world? How do the respective gifts of individual POMC members come together into what God makes into the "gift" of POMC to the world to help bring about the reign of God?

Peace and Ecumenical Initiatives

Rachel brought a strong peace emphasis to POMC. Nonresistance and pacifism were distinctly and clearly taught in the congregation and Mennonite community of her childhood and youth (Tedrow Mennonite Church in Fulton County, Ohio), at Goshen College and AMBS, and at College Mennonite Church in Goshen where she had been an active member for many years. Rachel was aware when she came to Pleasant Oaks that the peace emphasis was not as great in many former General Conference congregations as she had experienced. She came with an openness to learn more about another way of understanding military participation and invited those men who had served in the US military services to tell their stories.

With respect for their stories and support of others in the congregation, attention was given annually to nonresistance and the Anabaptist peace position. For several years the "historic peace churches" of Middlebury co-sponsored a peace booth at the annual Middlebury Summer Festival, and POMC joined in that venture. The peace booth, staffed by volunteers from the supporting churches, offered activities for children and youth, and literature and conversation options for everyone.

Each year on September 21, the same churches sponsored a candle-light prayer walk and peace vigil in the Middlebury Memorial Park. Groups walked carrying candles from three locations (POMC, Middlebury Church of the Brethren, and First Mennonite Church) and converged in the park. The International Day of Prayer for Peace was commemorated with prayer, song, scripture, and stories, and often a motivational speaker.[12]

Linda Pieri from FMC worshiped with POMC in 2007. Linda and her family were very involved in peace initiatives in many places, and she was a leader in the interchurch peace events. Linda had the vision for collecting 1000 paper cranes as part of the peace booth activities at the Middlebury Summer Festival that year. At POMC, she demonstrated and assisted in making paper cranes during children's time. Linda also brought along her handcrafted peace pole. A peace pole is an eight-foot monument pole displaying the message and prayer "May Peace Prevail on Earth" in different languages on each of its four, six, or eight sides; it stands as a silent prayer and message for peace on earth. Linda created this in keeping with a worldwide tradition with information from www.peacepoles.com. There are more than 200,000 Peace Poles in 180 countries all over the world serving as constant reminders to visualize and pray for world peace.

Along with teaching Sunday school for youth, Bill Swartzendruber became somewhat of a roving ambassador for POMC. It was soon noted that Bill approached faith and church life with more energy than most people! He regularly brought imaginative ideas to Rachel for consideration. One idea that Bill and Jan helped to implement was an invitation to our neighbors at St. Paul's Lutheran Church, just 350 yards east of Pleasant Oaks, to see the movie *Luther*, a dramatic biography of the life of Martin Luther, on Reformation Sunday, October 28, 2007. In her sermon that morning, Rachel used a text from Romans 3, one of Luther's favorite passages; reflected on the life and faith of Martin Luther; and reported on Lutheran-Mennonite conversations, making reference to the document: *Right Remembering in Anabaptist-Lutheran Relations*. On that Sunday evening, a number of members of St. Paul's joined POMC for a time of food and fellowship and the viewing of the DVD. The guests included Erin Pergram, director of youth and family ministry, and her confirmation class.

Bill was also behind a December meeting of board members, deacons, and their spouses, called together to discuss some next steps in determining the mission and vision of the congregation. Leaders and their spouses were invited with the hope of prompting a common point within each household for discussion and discernment around these issues. Bill's invitation said "this is the work of the church, and we can best discern God's will where two or more of us are gathered in the name of Christ." Joe Richards, retired missionary and minister (and who along with his wife, Emma, had formerly pastored Bill and Jan), had preached at POMC in November. Bill's conversations with Joe had sparked a lot of ideas that Bill used to guide the discussion.

12. The September 21, 2009 event is described at the beginning of chapter 2.

Becoming God's People

In 2008 Dean Heisey, Networking/Partnership Coach from Mennonite Mission Network (MMN), led in a series of sermons and interactive meetings with the congregation to help discern and articulate God's vision for the group. It was decided to use the theme "Becoming God's People" and base Bible studies and sermons on the book of Ephesians from Pentecost through August 10, when the 85th anniversary of WSMC/POMC would be celebrated.

Dean led the church board and deacon council in an introductory session where he asked a question to begin the discussion: "Who is running the church?" On May 25 Dean preached on "Glory, Success, and Fruitfulness." The congregation continued the study of Ephesians and most Sundays were invited to join in the closing benediction, together blessing God and reflecting God's glory while saying Ephesians 3:20–21: "Now to God, who by the power at work within us, is able to accomplish abundantly far more than all we can ask or imagine, to him be glory in the church and in Christ Jesus to all generations, for ever and ever! Amen."

The congregation gathered with Dean in a retreat at POMC on July 14–16 to study, imagine, and discern. Dean said, "Visioning is about defining how to inch our way toward the picture of the ultimate reign of God." He asked, "How does Pleasant Oaks imagine intentionally discovering new ways of not being alone and of doing God's work together with others?" In a passionate Sunday morning sermon, Dean confirmed that the congregation is God's living Word and sign, and called the group to translate individual calls into corporate acts of collaborating with God on a mission that is *God's* mission for POMC.

Dean was a good advocate for healthy conversations that led to greater respect and trust within the group. Dean challenged individuals to tell deep personal painful stories to at least one other person in the congregation before the end of the year. Although this was an individual assignment, opportunities for story-telling were offered every other Sunday morning, alternating with Sunday school classes led by Glen Horner. A few people used the Sunday morning time to tell personal stories, and the bonds between members became closer.

In addition, Dean asked all active members to complete a "Discover Your God-Given Gifts" assessment form. This process was for the benefit of the congregation and greater self-awareness of members. The 2008 October Friedenswald retreat was a time for members to continue discerning together with Dean Heisey's leadership. A few people went on Saturday, and a group of twenty-one assembled on Sunday. Along with enjoying the beauty of creation, the company of each other, and a meaningful worship service, the group had an interactive session in the afternoon with Dean again leading the group in exploring gifts and thinking about the congregation's mission, vision, and goals. With the help of an "outside" leader, members expressed feelings that aren't easily spoken during more routine times.

Three statements were proposed after times of praying, brainstorming, sharing, and discerning: The mission statement was: "POMC, by the power of the Holy Spirit, exists to continue Jesus' work as we fully learn, live and proclaim God's Good News of healing and hope." The proposed vision statement was: "POMC will discover ways to share life together in an atmosphere of celebration, hospitality, and caring so that an expanding circle of people follows Jesus' way of shalom." The following three year goals were proposed:

> In order to attain that vision, POMC commits to these three-year priorities: 1. Intensify our life together through intentional community building; 2. Initiate new patterns of decision-making, accountability, and reporting (adjusting structures to fit what works); 3. Implement a gifts-based model of ministry engagement for all participants; 4. Involve at least 50 percent of attendees in defined "mission" roles.

The proposed written document was intended for further reflection and discussion. Leaders asked, "How might this document be changed to better reflect who we are and where we think God is calling us as a congregation?"

An additional outcome was recognizing the importance of working at more effective communication within the congregation. Bill Swartzendruber offered a document that the church board reviewed and presented to the congregation in November 2008. Bill reviewed the principles of the protocol at a later congregational meeting, and people agreed to implement the principles as much as possible. This useful document was adapted from a similar document used at Lombard Mennonite Church (LMC) in Illinois, brought to POMC by Bill Swartzendruber. It is included in appendix N with permission from Todd Friesen, pastor of Lombard. The year ended with renewed hope!

CELEBRATIONS

Times of celebration are built into the church year. In addition to Christmas, Epiphany, Easter, and Pentecost, regular celebrations of the Lord's Supper, baby dedications, baptisms, and weddings take place. Celebrations were also a part of the Sunday school program throughout the life of WSMC and POMC. Although careful records of POMC Sunday school activities were not retrieved, there are records of 116 people who made faith commitments, were baptized, and became members at POMC. This list is in appendix K. During 2008 a series of celebrations brought balance to POMC after so many losses of the previous years.

Eighty-five Years of God's Faithfulness

The idea of an anniversary celebration began sometime during 2007. A committee of Leona Yoder, Robin Tahara Miller, Sara VonGunten, and Rachel Nafziger Hartzler worked together, and a theme was chosen: "Celebrating Eighty-five Years of God's Faithfulness." With the assistance of church office secretary, Leasa Worley, addresses of former and inactive members were compiled, and invitations were sent. On August 10, 2008, a wonderful day of celebration occurred with one hundred three people gathering. The celebration included times of worship, remembering, storytelling, and eating together the carry-in meal that Viv Schlabach and Elnora Yoder organized.

Leona and J. O. Yoder at a fellowship meal.

Seven former pastors attended the events, including Elmer Wall, pastor from 1955 to 1960, who preached in the morning service. The sermon, titled "God's Faithfulness to All Generations," was a pastoral summary of the book of Ephesians. Additional features of the worship service were vocal numbers by a small choir of current and former members led by Dale Schlabach; piano and organ duets for the prelude, offertory, and accompaniment by Sara VonGunten and church pianist/organist DeRoy Kauffman. Lu-Etta Friesen was present, representing First Mennonite Church of Middlebury.

Other former pastors in attendance were Herbert Fretz, Barry Schmell, John King, Michael Miller, Eugene Bontrager, and Matt Gingerich.[13] The former pastors each had an opportunity to share memories and current activities after the carry-in meal. Robin Tahara Miller and Dale Schlabach led the time of sharing in the fellowship hall. Greetings from additional former pastors were read: Floyd Quenzer, Anne and Ken Rupp, and John Reeser.

13. The dates of service and other information about the former pastors are in appendix H.

Sharing time included storytelling, sharing of highlights, funny and quaint memories, and challenges of the past. Many of the guests were former members or people who had been children in the congregation. Old photos were posted around the church building, and photo albums were passed around, evoking precious memories from the past. Sharing recent and long-ago stories helped the congregation to embrace an identity shared by all, even though not everyone experienced the events when they occurred.

This celebration was a spiritual boost for POMCers who had been prayerfully trying to pay attention to where God was at work and seeking to follow Jesus, joining in God's mission in the world. Themes were remembering the past, living joyfully in the present, and looking to the future with hope. God's faithfulness does not mean that everything is always smooth and pleasant. It does mean that God walks with people, prompts them to action, and helps them find a way through their troubles. The anniversary celebration was a highlight in the process of moving toward a newly articulated vision of where God was leading.

A Harvest Festival

J. O. Yoder was eager to share from the bounty of good crops with less fortunate people around the world. Rachel joined J. O. in his quest to make connections and learned about a partnership between Mennonite Central Committee (MCC) and Foods Resource Bank (FRB).

FRB, a Christian response to world hunger, is a non-government humanitarian organization committed to supporting food security efforts in the developing world through sustainable small-scale agricultural production, and it does so in a unique way. FRB works on behalf of its member organizations (fifteen of the mainline Christian denominations or their agencies, including MCC) to mobilize and increase the resources needed to support smallholder, agricultural food security programs in some of the world's poorest villages. FRB's goal is to engage the grassroots agricultural community in the United States, and along with individuals, churches, and urban communities, to grow solutions to hunger problems in our world.

J. O. and Rich Yoder and Bill Swartzendruber together embarked on a growing project on eighteen acres of farmland that J. O. donated. Several farm dealers in the area donated seed, fertilizer, pesticide, and drying of the crop; Rich Yoder and neighborhood farmers donated the equipment and labor to plant, cultivate, and harvest the crop. POMC members also donated funds toward the cost of the project. In addition, numerous corporate sponsors and members of other local churches participated in the project, making it a community project.

**Bill Swartzendruber from POMC and Norm Braksick
from Foods Resource Bank at the harvest celebration.**

The FRB growing project harvest celebration was held on November 1, 2008. The sun was shining as two huge combine harvesters made their way into the field of ripened corn. Rich Yoder drove the red Case-International combine, and Steve, Barry, and A. J. Kauffman of Deer Grove Farms and the Pleasant View Mennonite Church provided the green John Deere combine. An ample supply of cider and doughnuts greeted POMC members, a few preschool families, and others from the community. At 10 a.m., the harvest paused for a prayer service and reading from Psalm 65. Verses 9 and 10 were especially relevant: "You visit the earth and water it, you greatly enrich it; the river of God is full of water; you provide the people with grain, for so you have prepared it. You water its furrows abundantly, settling its ridges, softening it with showers, and blessing its growth." The harvest then resumed while horse-drawn Amish wagon rides, corn-shelling, and conversation continued. A highlight for numerous people was crawling up into the combine cabs to watch the harvest from that vantage point. The harvest was indeed bountiful, and after being dried, the corn was sold for $6,569. These funds supported an MCC program in Sincelejo, Colombia, creating new possibilities for families relocated by civil unrest. The goal of the FRB/MCC program is to assist people in developing countries to grow their own food and to support a common fund for resources and training to improve food security.

Jim Mishler, Steve Kauffman, and Glen Horner watch the corn harvest. Jan Swartzendruber, Juanita Yoder, Norm Braksick, and J. O. Yoder chat in the background.

Steve Yoder was a community member who attended the harvest festival on November 1. Steve was a brother of POMC's Juanita Yoder and had become a friend to many POMC folks. It was the last time many POMCers saw Steve as he tragically died on December 19 after shoveling snow. In the face of this untimely death and the "economic wilderness" of 2008, the congregation prayed a psalm of lament on December 21.

> Lord, hear our prayer; let our cry come to you.
> For our days are full of questions; anxiety hovers around us like fog.
> Our hearts are burdened with sadness and worry; there is no security in the workplace and loved ones have died untimely deaths.
> Have mercy on us, O Lord; have mercy.
> The assurance of a weekly paycheck is no more; and hope for a job vanishes like the wind.
> Our future is shrouded in doubt and darkness; we worry for our children, ourselves, our retirement.
> Yet you have been our dwelling place in all generations. From everlasting to everlasting you are God.
> We give thanks for your mercy, O Lord; we give thanks.
> We wait now in a wilderness of unknowing; security has faded and our hearts are heavy.
> This recession has come upon us though we had not forgotten you.

We wait with tightened belts and thinning wallets, though we had not departed from your way.

Have mercy on us, O Lord; have mercy.

You have been our refuge through all generations; through the valley of shad-
ows you have comforted us.

There are many around us who grieve the deaths of loved ones. For some the
suffering is almost unbearable.

Rise up and help us—and all those whom we love, O Lord; and we will rise up
in praise to you.

Turn your face toward us, that we may turn our faces toward each other.

In your mercy, O Lord, help us show mercy.

You are our strength, O Lord; we wait upon you; our hearts take courage, for
we trust in you through Jesus Christ, the Messiah.[14]

Ordination of a Pastor

In MC USA, ministers are licensed for specific assignments for a period of time. After the licensing period, ordination is often considered. POMC and Rachel Nafziger Hartzler completed the discernment process and interviews, and Rachel was ordained for pastoral ministry in the Central District Conference at POMC on November 23, 2008. The theme of the Sunday morning service was thanksgiving with Elmer Wall preaching.

After a carry-in meal, the congregation, CDC representatives, and family and friends of Rachel gathered for the afternoon ordination service. In addition to the participation of many POMC members and joyous singing of the congregation, a choir of Pleasant Oaks people and some of Rachel's dearest friends and mentors led in praise to God, and John D. Rempel preached on "Bearers of Hope," reminding the congregation and Rachel of their shared calling— "the magnificent but fragile ministry of declaring hope." He went on to explain that "Hope is the trembling confidence that God is faithful, and because of that, there will always be enough love to go around." Lois Johns Kaufmann, CDC conference minister, officiated over the ordination. The congregation responded with a litany including the refrain, "May your spirit rejoice in God who does great and marvelous things."[15] The ninety-two participants were then invited to a dessert buffet provided by POMC in the fellowship hall where the celebration continued.

This was the third ordination of a minister at POMC. Anne Neufeld Rupp was ordained in 1976 and Barry Schmell in 1987.

14. Adapted from a lament written by Lois Johns Kaufmann.
15. John Rempel, *Minister's Manual*, 161–62.

PART II: History of Warren Street and Pleasant Oaks Mennonite Church

Church Year Celebrations

Scanning the chronological list of events throughout the years of WSMC and POMC gives glimpses into numerous celebrations. Members often spread Christmas goodwill by making Christmas bundles or packing food boxes and going Christmas caroling. Christmas programs, sometimes with candlelight, often included a Christmas pageant. Some years there were Christmas Eve services. Pastors sometimes hosted a holiday breakfast or open house.

Although Mennonites have not celebrated Epiphany widely, many Amish groups commemorate "Old Christmas" on January 6. In recent years, especially with resources for planning worship services available in the MC USA *Leader* magazine, many Mennonite churches have added services for Advent, Epiphany, Lent, Eastertide, and Pentecost to the traditional church celebrations of Christmas and Easter. Epiphany focuses on God's light in Jesus being revealed to the whole world, remembering the coming of the Magi. "Beautiful Star of Bethlehem" is a favorite old song that resounded at POMC on Epiphany.

For many years the Middlebury ministerium organized joint Sunday evening worship services and Good Friday services during Lent, and POMC participated.[16] In addition, Maundy Thursday was commemorated at POMC with an evening meal together. However, the traditional practice of footwashing had not been enacted at POMC. The old footwashing buckets had been left at the Warren Street building when the congregation moved to the Pleasant Oaks location in 1965. J. Herbert Fretz reported that the first time he participated in footwashing was when he was a student pastor at WSMC in 1942. Olen Yoder (senior) had invited him to be his partner in footwashing, and it was a very spiritual experience. Whether the church observed footwashing between 1942 and 2007 is unknown. Rachel reintroduced footwashing on Maundy Thursday services at POMC, and some members participated in this ritual of servanthood for the first time. Rachel emphasized that rituals help to express enormous realities in simple gestures.

Worship resources from *Leader* helped POMC celebrate Eastertide as a season rather than just a single day in the church year. Celebrating the risen Christ continued on Sunday mornings from Easter until Pentecost. The coming of the Holy Spirit and the birthday of the church was celebrated on Pentecost by members wearing red and with the flames of many candles, sometimes red, orange, and yellow. Celebrating Pentecost keeps alive the belief that that the experience of Jesus is as possible in the twenty-first century as it was to those who met Jesus in the first century!

16. Charles Yoder, former member of First Mennonite, said the community Lenten services began in the 1930s or 1940s.

9

Reconciliation and Re-union, 2009

Retying the Strings that Bind in Christian Love

"I ask not only on behalf of these,
but also on behalf of those who will believe in me through their word,
that they may all be one.
As you, Father, are in me and I am in you,
may they also be in us,
so that the world may believe that you have sent me."

JESUS IN JOHN 17:20–21

THE FIRST BUSINESS MEETING of the 2009 calendar year could have been like any other—except the report from the treasurer was so startling that the day suddenly became a pivotal event in the life of POMC (Pleasant Oaks Mennonite Church). The February 15 meeting was scheduled on a Sunday afternoon to follow a noon carry-in meal. The morning service was titled "Continuing the Work of Jesus: Healing and Hope." Following a sermon that included the story of Naaman from 2 Kings, Rachel had offered a "water blessing" to all who came forward, using water that she had brought back from the Jordan River in 2008—and had strained and boiled.

The meal was bountiful and tasty as usual, but the report from church treasurer Rich Yoder jolted the members into a new reality. There was not enough money for the church to continue. A harsh halt came to any memory of the lyrical lines from "O Healing River" sung an hour earlier. The church board and deacon council had previously received this information, but it was new to some members of the congregation. The announcement and discussion were summarized in the minutes recorded by Juanita Yoder:

- We have been using $6500 from the land sale money each year to pay bills. Part of those funds were used other ways in the past, such as a salary for our youth pastor for four years. The land sale money is pretty well used up. Rich wants the church to be aware, and even though he has been given authorization to use other funds to pay the bills, he wants to ask if the congregation wants him to go ahead and dip into the Vision 2000 money. That account in the past has been protected for the possible future expansion of the church building.

- Discussion time was opened to anyone who had a question or opinion. With our finances in mind a question was asked whether the continuation of our being a "church" within this building is still feasible. Several said it bothered them about having more expenses than income and using our investments to pay the bills. The question was asked if we are being selfish in continuing to use our investments to pay bills for such a small church, when that money could be used to help those in need? Pastor Rachel responded by saying that she doesn't see continuing to be a congregation as necessarily being selfish. We did raise over $6000 for overseas missions (Foods Resource Bank) last year, and we support the preschool. She said she continues to see hope for the congregation to continue, but if God leads us to end our life as a congregation, she wants to pastor us through that process. Dale suggested that this be discussed in our next congregational meeting. Bill mentioned that we need cash flow now to pay bills. Since many are on "set incomes" it would be difficult or impossible to increase our giving.

- Bill made a motion for Rich to be authorized to sell shares of the Vision 2000 Mutual funds to pay our bills as the needs arise. . . . a show of hands passed the motion unanimously.

The meeting ended with an agreement to ponder and pray about the future of Pleasant Oaks and to be prepared to continue discussion at the next congregational meeting in March. A Communication Protocol Document, which had earlier been approved by the church board, had been placed in members' mailboxes a week before the February 15 meeting. Everyone was encouraged to read and study the document and be ready to discuss it. How timely for this document to be ready for the congregation's use just as the need to communicate about its future became so critical![1]

The financial dilemma felt like a curve ball after recently welcoming a new member into the group. Lucy Miller attended her first Pleasant Oaks service in January, and before leaving that day, she announced she had found her new church. However, it seemed apparent that a number of people in the congregation thought it was time to end Pleasant Oaks. Others fervently and even vehemently resisted the idea. Would there be any way to reach something even close to consensus for this dilemma? No, not except for the transforming work of God through the Spirit of Jesus.

1. The Communication Protocol document is Appendix N.

CONGREGATIONAL DISCERNMENT

The POMC church board faced the tough questions prayerfully and head on. The board invited Lois Johns Kaufmann, CDC conference minister, to become involved in the process that began to unfold. Lois attended several board meetings and congregational meetings. The board decided that three members would form a "triumvirate" to jointly lead the congregational meetings: Robin Tahara Miller, a life-long member with family roots going back to the congregation's beginnings; Dale Schlabach, a member for thirty-five years; and Bill Swartzendruber, representing relatively new members of POMC. This was presented to the congregation and was approved.

The March 8 congregational meeting again followed a Sunday noon carry-in meal. Robin led in a remembering and reflecting exercise during which "positives and negatives" from the previous few years were named and listed. Then ideas of how the congregation might save money and continue were named. These activities were modeled after ideas from Dr. Edward de Bono's "Six Thinking Hats," which Lois Kaufmann recommended for brainstorming, gathering information, and weighing pros and cons. The "Six Thinking Hats" in six different colors represent different modes to use in group discussions. The colored hat response guide was not strictly followed, but using the various designations seemed to help members listen better to each other. For example, at times, the intention was to get all possible options on the table without pausing to evaluate the options when suggested. At a later time the pros and cons were considered. In this system, the white hat calls for information known or needed; the red hat signifies feelings, hunches, and intuition; the black hat is judgment, focusing on why something will likely not work. The yellow hat symbolizes brightness and optimism; the green hat focuses on creativity: the possibilities, alternatives, and new ideas. Finally, the blue hat is used to manage the thinking process.[2]

Near the end of the March 8 meeting, Lois Kaufmann encouraged members to stay in the "uncomfortable gray area" of "wandering in the wilderness" in order to explore all options, all pros and cons, all creative possibilities. In addition, she urged prayerful reading of the Communication Protocol document (which Bill had summarized earlier in the meeting), perhaps reading it before sleeping and inviting God to work in the sub-conscious mind.

A resource consulted for discernment is Sally Weaver Glick's *In Tune with God: The Art of Congregational Discernment*. Glick uses the evocative image of the community of believers listening for, hearing, and then entering God's song, thus joining in holy music-making. Discernment is distinguishing between God's music and our own static and noise. Undergirded with scripture, Glick clarifies that congregational discernment is intertwined with worship, is a communal activity, and is an ongoing

---

2. Dr. Edward de Bono thinking systems are described at http://www.debonothinkingsystems. com/tools/6hats.htm.

activity. Good discernment lets God's song "sing through us and shape us, so that we can join in harmoniously, responding to God's love and mercy."[3]

As the leadership group planned for meetings for congregational discernment, they discussed the value of symbols as reminders of God's presence and abiding care. Although candles can effectively symbolize the light and presence of God, some people have unpleasant sensitivities to candles, so the symbol of flowing water was chosen. A small water fountain owned by Viv Schlabach was placed in the center of the circle of members. The trickle of water that was heard during periods of silence was a reminder of the flow of God's movement among the group. This was one way in which the group listened for God's song.

While some POMC members were eager for a decision about the congregation's future, others needed more time to deal with feelings evoked by the process. Lois Kaufmann advised against making an abrupt decision, and added that praying and thinking individually is not the same as processing, discussing, and discerning together such a significant decision. Lois also helped POMC leaders to see that the implications for the future of the congregation involved more than the few active members in 2009. The essence of POMC was long and wide—there was a long history to consider as well as a wide group of people, particularly the Central District Conference.

The group at POMC knew they must discern options that looked to the future, and at the same time cherish resources of the heritage and respond to current needs. They knew that "traditional religious community does not offer shelter from the winds of change."[4] Change is difficult, and yet change is necessary. Standing still is not an option, and it was obvious that POMC was not standing still. If one measured by numbers of people attending on Sunday morning, the direction was backward. But God calls people to faithfulness, not to success by the world's standards.

As the members of POMC listened to each other and to God, a list of creative ideas emerged. These included renting the sanctuary to another group and continuing to meet at alternate times or spaces within the building; considering a possible merger with another small Mennonite Church in the area; and hiring a one-quarter-time pastor, perhaps one currently working part time in another congregation. One thing was abundantly clear: everyone agreed that whatever option was chosen, it needed to include the great likelihood of the Pleasant Oaks Preschool continuing. It was as though that was a string attached!

During one of the meetings that spring, Dale Schlabach asked, "What would be your response if I would say it is time to close Pleasant Oaks?" Without even a moment's pause, Don Hershberger said, "Over my dead body!"[5]

---

3. Glick, *In Tune with God*, 43.

4. Kniss, *Disquiet in the Land*, 18.

5. In 2010 Don gave permission to Rachel to publish his statement and the follow-up conversations over the subsequent months.

Don Hershberger often told jokes, repeating some too often, and it was not un-usual for him to occasionally startle people with off-the-wall statements, but this was no joke, and it was not a casual statement. "Over my dead body" was embedded with deep meaning, and the response of nervous, light laughter was an indication that no-body was quite ready with an appropriate response to Don's gut reaction. After some awkward moments, a few more people shared deep regrets about needing to consider closing the church, and a subtle shift to deeper honesty in sharing began to emerge.

At another congregational meeting when the idea of making a connection with First Mennonite Church was on the table, Don Hershberger was quieter than usual. When everyone was urged to speak, Don made another statement that got people's attention. He said that because of something that had happened many years earlier, he didn't think he could attend First Mennonite Church. A few days later Don shared with Rachel the story that lay behind his strong feelings. After ninety minutes of story-telling and reflection, Don conceded that if people were "nice," he might be willing to *consider* attending First Mennonite.

Don had an enormous attachment to the Pleasant Oaks building. He had been the construction manager for the crew of volunteers when the original structure was built. "I don't think anybody has an attachment to that building like I do," he said. "J. O. had chores to do. But I was there every evening and every Saturday. I never knew how many would show up to work on those evenings. But I used whoever came." Don and his crew also built the addition. A piece of history that had been lost to the family was that Don's paternal grandfather, Jacob C. Hershberger, became deacon of the Middlebury Mennonite Church in 1911 *and* built the meetinghouse on Lawrence Street during that same year. Learning this in 2012 was a consolation to Don and Doris as they continued to adjust to attending the newly-formed con-gregation that met on Lawrence Street.

Pleasant Oaks congregational meetings continued once or twice monthly in 2009, often after a Sunday noon or Wednesday evening meal. Using the colored hat types of thinking, the congregation decided to drop the option of dissolving the congregation and pursue other possibilities. Many options were discussed and explored, including a proposal designed by Bill Swartzendruber for a "one church, two campuses" relation-ship with another congregation. With this model POMC would partner with another congregation for pastoral care and administration but remain a separate congrega-tion. Significant discussion was given to this concept.

With the ongoing support of Lois Kaufmann, Rachel worked on behalf of POMC to explore the ideas of sharing a pastor with another congregation and employing a one-quarter-time pastor. As the discernment process continued, Rachel had the clear sense that she would soon be ending her pastoral work in Middlebury. She was trans-parent about this with the entire congregation and with FMC when she was asked. She was confident that God would be calling her to a new place, so there was no question about finding a place for her to minister in a new structure in Middlebury.

POMC leadership group met with a leadership group from FMC who expressed interest in "one church, two campuses" and in more conversation. Discussions at POMC congregational meetings continued. As members sat at tables facing each other at one meeting that spring, Dale Schlabach asked for a show of hands of those who would be willing to at least consider attending First Mennonite. Quiet gasps could be heard in the circle as both Don Hershberger and his wife, Doris, promptly raised their hands. It was becoming abundantly clear that God was at work at Pleasant Oaks!

On July 19 POMCers began the congregational meeting with "green hat thinking," focusing on creativity, possibilities, alternatives, and new ideas. Two ideas that came to the forefront were:

1. To enter into a six-month pilot experience with First Mennonite in a "one church, two campuses" model, recognizing that to make this workable, it will take more people than have currently expressed a desire to continue worshiping together at POMC.

2. To merge or re-unite with First Mennonite Church: by some of our members joining First Mennonite; by passing on to the organization the Pleasant Oaks Preschool and its vision; and by also passing on the Pleasant Oaks property, buildings, and furnishings, with the understanding that First Mennonite would continue the preschool program (and hopefully retain the name Pleasant Oaks Preschool), with arrangements agreed upon by both congregations.

One reservation expressed at POMC regarding joining with FMC related to being members in two different district conferences within Mennonite Church USA. Lois Kauffman took these concerns seriously and reflected on some of the differences in the Indiana-Michigan and Central District conferences. She emphasized that both congregations adhered to the 1995 *Confession of Faith in a Mennonite Perspective.*

FMC invited POMC to attend their worship service on July 26, eat a carry-in meal together, and then join in a "talk about." The invitation was to discuss "the topic of how Pleasant Oaks and First Mennonite can relate/work together and support each other." This was a time for discussion, not decision making. At the "talk about," Dale Schlabach gave a presentation about POMC—a brief history and a summary of the process of discernment in the preceding months. During the discussion that followed, there was much affirmation from members of both congregations for joining together. Near the end of the "talk about," Don Hershberger from POMC asked for the microphone and said he was ready to join in! This is the same man who a few months earlier had said, "Over my dead body."

By the end of July, many people sensed God leading toward a re-uniting of Pleasant Oaks and First Mennonite Churches. POMC members made a deliberate choice to *not* say that the church was *dying*. And it was not denial. It was the firm belief that the life of the congregation will go on, not only in the memories of the past, but in the lives of those who were formed and transformed at Pleasant Oaks. Both Pleasant Oaks and First Mennonite made official decisions to re-unite with votes in congregational meetings in September and October, and the legal steps began. POMC would live on in the new body formed by the re-uniting of the Pleasant Oaks and First Mennonite congregations. Members of both congregations recognized that it was God's action that brought them together. The human action was a response to what God had already done.

FOR SUCH A TIME AS THIS

The memory of weekly prayer times at Warren Street during 1963–64, prompted POMC members to place an increased value on meeting to pray every Wednesday evening during 2009. Gathering to worship together also continued to be very important for the members of Pleasant Oaks. Even though references were often made to the discernment process, the "elephant" of dwindling numbers in worship services was not always mentioned. Sometimes people stammered to say what was difficult. But worship continued with regular prayers for the needs of members, and the Lord's Prayer was spoken or sung nearly every Sunday—as had long been a POMC tradition. Singing seemed as important as ever. It has been said that tradition is the vessel in which our spiritual practices are carried. In some ways, singing was the practice in which faith and hope were best expressed. While considering re-uniting with FMC, POMC began to regularly sing "Unity" regularly in worship services. Earlier, "Unity" had been sung at the conclusion of every worship service.

"The Welcoming Face of God" was the theme that began on Epiphany 2009. Guest preachers and preachers from within the congregation through Epiphany and Lent included: storyteller Mary Klassen from the AMBS staff who told stories of allegiance; Leroy Mast, director of Menno-Hof; Glen and Thelma Horner; Linford Martin; and Joe Yoder. The theme for Lent was "Our Lives are in Your Hands," very apt during congregational discernment. Beginning on Easter and continuing through Pentecost on May 31, the theme was "None Can Stop the Spirit." Preachers in addition to Rachel were Don Blosser, Eugene Bontrager, Rhoda Schrag, and Bill Swartzendruber.

A new theme began on June 7 and continued throughout the remaining months of the congregation's life: "For Such a Time as This." The theme was initiated by two sermons from the book of Esther, with Rachel and Glen Horner preaching. Rachel's sermon was on Vashti, the queen who preceded Esther. Rachel suggested that Vashti's refusal to obey the king's command to dance in front of his drunken guests was an example of radical courage. Vashti's audacious, unexpected "no" to the king was a life-affirming "yes" to a higher power. Vashti was dangerous in the same way that Jesus was dangerous, a threat to the religious authorities of his day, and the same way that the early Anabaptists were dangerous, choosing to follow the Jesus of the New Testament rather than the traditions of a corrupted church. Pleasant Oaks members were finding similar courage to face an unknown future.

A focus on the life and teachings of Jesus, especially the Sermon on the Mount, carried the theme through the summer. Guest preachers included Leonard Beechy, local high school teacher and writer of Mennonite Sunday school materials; Jeff Newcomer Miller, admissions counselor at AMBS; and Leonard Wiebe, retired Mennonite minister. On June 21, Ron Kennel preached Jesus' most famous sermon. He recited "The Sermon on the Mount" from memory. The congregation sat in awe as if hearing it for the first time.

Beginning in July 2009, worship services took on a different flavor at POMC. The group decided to conclude the years as a separate congregation on November 22, and boldly chose to continue celebrating the goodness of life during the interim, while also lamenting what was being lost. A transitional board (consisting of Robin Tahara Miller, Dale Schlabach, Bill Swartzendruber, Leona Yoder and Rich Yoder) was put in place, and it didn't take long to find several celebration-worthy events.

The oldest active member who had been in the congregation from the beginning was J. O. Yoder, and his ninetieth birthday was August 29. (Shirley Yoder was older, but she lived at Greencroft in Goshen and came to church about once each year between 2006 and 2009.) On August 30, approximately fifty people worshiped together and celebrated J. O.'s birthday. In her sermon, Rachel gave a summary of the Shema, Jesus' new love commandment, and the Great Commission, as ways of underscoring the importance of remembering, loving, and doing. J. O. had requested that people tell their stories of how being part of this congregation had nurtured them spiritually and influenced them in the events of their lives. Various members and guests (which included numerous former members and Yoder relatives—many of whom were former members) told stories after the carry-in meal.

As summer days passed, many people sensed God leading toward a re-uniting of Pleasant Oaks and First Mennonite. POMC members had attended FMC worship services twice during the summer months and invited FMC members to worship at POMC, thus experiencing the "Pleasant Oaks style" of worship and fellowship. This was a way of beginning to blend into a new congregation. Starting times were adjusted so that FMC members could attend their worship service and then attend POMC during their Sunday school hour. There was not adequate space in the POMC sanctuary for all FMC members to attend on the same Sunday, so three Sundays (September 6, 13, and 27) were selected for FMC members to attend. Some groups of FMC folks came as Sunday school classes. With many visitors, the POMC attendance soared to eighty-two on September 6 and eighty-five on September 13. Each of the September services was special in its own way. Bill Swartzendruber preached on the Gospel of John on September 6. The earliest living former pastor, Elmer Wall, preached on September 27 on the theme of reconciliation.

The baptism of Grant Tetsuo Miller was celebrated on September 13. Grant, the son of Mike and Robin Tahara Miller, had been born into the Pleasant Oaks Mennonite Church as a fifth generation "child of the church." Grant's parents had grown up in the congregation, and both sets of grandparents (K. Marion and the late Betty Miller and Tom and Sandra Tahara) had been leaders in the church for many years. One set of great-great grandparents (Freed and Nina Hershberger) were founding members. Being a very congenial child in addition to having many relatives in the congregation, Grant had in some ways become the darling of Pleasant Oaks. Whenever other children were present, Grant graciously shared the attention he received. He enjoyed relating to adults and children: his peers, those older, and those younger. He also found pleasure in interacting with preschool children and assisted in preschool events.

In the last few years of the congregation's life, there were often only a few families with children present for worship services. Rachel believed strongly in having something special for children in every service, even if only one child was present, so there was almost always "children's time" during worship. When Grant was the only elementary age child in a service, the teenagers would join Grant for children's time so that he wouldn't be alone. So it was, when Grant was baptized on September 13, 2009, Grant's relatives, the teenagers—now many of them young adults—and the junior high Sunday school class from First Mennonite came to participate in the service.

The theme of the day was "Come and Follow Me" with the scripture from John 1 (the calling of Andrew, Simon Peter, Philip, and Nathanael) being dramatically presented by several adults in the congregation. In her sermon, Rachel emphasized that God has created, formed, redeemed, and called by name, Grant and every other person present. She said that baptism incorporates the believer into the community of kingdom citizens—the church—there to be accountable to and for others in all matters of faith and life. That is why in the Mennonite tradition, baptism and church membership are inseparable.

Following Grant's statement and his baptism, the congregation sang one of Grant's favorite hymns, "How Great Thou Art." Then all present were invited to respond to Grant and renew baptismal covenants with the following:

> As we now receive you into the fellowship of the church, we make this covenant with you as we renew our own covenant with God: to bear each other's burdens, to assist in times of need, to share our gifts and possessions, to forgive as Christ has forgiven us, to support each other in joy and sorrow, and in all things to work for the common good, thus making known Christ's presence among us to the glory of God. As we unite with each other now, may we all be joined with Christ, our Lord.[6]

Grant's baptism was special, first of all, because another child of God made a commitment to be a follower of Jesus. It was noteworthy because he was the first fifth generation person of WSMC/POMC to be baptized, and his would apparently be the last POMC baptism. Although records of baptisms at Warren Street had not been saved, there is a record of 116 baptisms at Pleasant Oaks beginning in 1965. How

---

6. This response is from *Hymnal: A Worship Book,* 777.

wonderful that at least 116 people made public commitments to follow Jesus Christ and received Christian nurture at POMC![7]

In addition to worshiping together, members of POMC and FMC engaged together in new ways in the community. On August 9 the Middlebury summer festival ended with a community worship service in a tent adjacent to Memorial Park, and a mixed octet of members from Pleasant Oaks and First Mennonite sang during the service. The octet also sang in Shipshewana at the Menno-Hof Singspiration on September 20. At the Middlebury celebration of the International Day of Prayer for Peace on September 21, Rachel Hartzler and Linford Martin told the story of reconciliation that was happening with the two congregations. In addition, Pleasant Oaks Preschool and all preschool alumni were invited to sing "This Little Light of Mine."

The two congregations celebrated communion together on World Communion Sunday, October 4. Linford and Rachel jointly served communion in a Spirit-filled service that also included footwashing.

During a time of musing about the Pleasant Oaks folks not meeting together regularly after 2009, it was mentioned that Doris and Don Hershberger would celebrate their sixty-fifth wedding anniversary in July of 2010. Somehow the idea of an early celebration came into the conversation, and that quickly developed into the idea of celebrating all the marriages in the congregation. When Doris and Don's daughters got wind of the proposal, they wanted to be involved.

The theme of the October 18 worship service was "Celebrating Covenanted Relationships." Fifty-four members and guests gathered that morning, and following introductions, marriages in the congregation were acknowledged. The following appeared on the back panel of the bulletin.

> Today we celebrate marriages. We especially honor the longest married couple in our congregation, Doris and Don Hershberger, who are in their sixty-fifth year of marriage. There are numerous other "extra special" wedding anniversaries in 2009 for members of our congregation:
>
> | | |
> |---|---|
> | Shirley and (the late) Sanford Yoder | 70 years |
> | Gert and Ben Kauffman | 60 years |
> | Connie and Gerri Beachy | 40 years |
> | Laura and Brad Hooley | 25 years |
> | Sandra and Gary Bjornson | 15 years |
>
> In 2010 the following couples will celebrate "extra special" anniversaries:
>
> | | |
> |---|---|
> | Doris and Don Hershberger | 65 years |
> | Thelma and Glen Horner | 55 years |
> | Leona and J. O. Yoder | 55 years |
> | Eileen and Ray Miller | 40 years |
> | Elnora and Paul Yoder | 40 years |

7. The list of those who were baptized and became members at POMC is in appendix K.

Jan and Bill Swartzendruber	40 years
Nan and Rich Stalter	35 years
Juanita and Rich Yoder	25 years

Other Pleasant Oaks marriages that we celebrate today are:

Doneta and (the late) John Burkhardt	67 years
Ruth and (the late) Marvin Miller	57 years
Anne and Adin Yoder	53 years
Viv and Dale Schlabach	43 years
Rachel and (the late) Harold Hartzler	38 years
Kelly and Jon Troyer	21 years
Leasa and Myron Worley	18 years
Robin T. and Michael Miller	17 years
Darlene and Jim Mishler	12 years
Char and Ed Swoveland	2 years

Doris Hershberger read the wedding song, "Your love, O God, has called us."[8] The song acknowledges that God is the source of all love. As had become the custom, before praising God the congregation lamented, expressing to God the disappointment of unanswered prayers. The group read Psalm 24 responsively:

> As a deer longs for flowing streams, so my soul longs for you, O God. My soul thirsts for God, for the living God. When shall I come and behold the face of God? My tears have been my food day and night, while people say to me continually, "Where is your God?"

Following the psalm, Don Hershberger again recited "Footprints," the powerful poem that is in some ways a lament. In the poem God is accused of forsaking one who loves God, but then follows a beautiful resolution as God reveals the truth of always being present, carrying the beloved during the darkest hour. The congregation then sang a well-loved favorite, "Come, let us all unite to sing, God is love."

Along with celebrating marriages, the congregation pondered the upcoming "marriage" of two congregations. In her sermon, "Union with God and Each Other," Rachel said:

> I have been asked on a few occasions if FMC and POMC are enough alike to become one congregation, and I have answered with a confident *yes.* I recognize that there are many differences, but this makes our testimony even stronger. Because of the love of God, expressed to us in Jesus and his love for the church, and because of the bond of unity created by the Holy Spirit, we can live in loving relationships even though we don't agree on everything. We may be as different as night and day in some areas, but we can still respect each other. In our families and in the church, our human nature tempts us to argue

8. This song, written by Russel Schultz-Widmar in 1981, is number 625 in *Hymnal: A Worship Book.*

and fight and act disrespectful, but the grace of God empowers us to love each other and to transform us into loving people. In our confession of faith we state that the church of Jesus Christ is one body with many members, ordered in such a way that, through the one Spirit, believers may be built together spiritually into a dwelling place for God.

The congregation heartily sang "The love of God" after the sermon. The ending song was "In the bulb there is a flower," and the congregation sang the benediction, "The Lord bless you and keep you," with the sevenfold amen. A carry-in meal followed the service, and people enjoyed gathering around the display table where couples had brought wedding photos to share with the group.

ENDINGS AND BEGINNINGS: BLESS'D BE THE TIE THAT BINDS

The last worship service for the Pleasant Oaks Mennonite Church was filled with a mixture of lament and celebration. Again the service began with a time of lament. Doris Hershberger read part of Psalm 86, and then the group listened to a song of lament: "Nothing is lost on the breath of God."[9] The words express a mixture of feelings that was experienced that day. The end had come, and yet existence had not been futile. The song proclaims that God's love will remain and hold the world together; that all of creation is counted and told as part of God's story. Nothing is lost on the breath of God, or to the eyes or heart of God. Beginnings and endings are gathered and known in God's goodness. Warren Street and Pleasant Oaks Mennonite Church had accomplished a purpose, perhaps not all that God had called the congregation to do, but many young people had been nurtured in the congregation and were baptized into the Christian community. The ensemble of members from both POMC and FMC sang the words from the back of the sanctuary, hoping people would be able to better reflect on the words when faces were out of sight.

The sanctuary was nearly filled with eighty people present, members and former members, conference officials, guests from FMC, and numerous members of the family of Marvin Miller. Marvin had died in June 2008, and monetary gifts had been given to POMC in his memory. Before the decision was made to re-unite with FMC, Marvin's widow, Ruth, had suggested commissioning a plaque with a Bible verse to compliment the one on the front wall of the sanctuary, one that had been made in memory of Charlotte Hurst. The POMC church board approved and ordered a complimentary plaque to be made by the same artist, John Mishler. By the time the plaque was finished, the decision had been made to re-unite with First Mennonite. However it was the wish of Ruth to have the plaque dedicated at POMC, realizing it might find a new home sometime in the future. The Miller family and congregation read together:

9. Colin Gibson wrote the text and a tune for "Nothing is lost on the breath of God" in 1994. It appears in *Sing the Story*, Faith and Life Resources, 2007.

"With gratitude to God for the life and teachings of Jesus and the life and teachings of Marvin J. Miller, we dedicate this plaque to the glory of God, trusting that it will always witness to the truth of Jesus Christ."

DeRoy Kauffman, long-time church organist and pianist, and former member and pianist Sara VonGunten filled the worship space with three awe-inspiring organ-piano duets as the prelude, interlude, and offertory. Conference minister Lois Johns Kauffman brought the sermon. She said, "Many of us are feeling a profound sense of loss—of an ending. And many of us are leaning forward into the future with thanksgiving. Today we will find grief and gratitude weaving back and forth as we both remember and look ahead, as we embrace the hard work of letting go and laying hold."

A responsive reading with recognition of ending, release, thanksgiving, and blessing was spoken near the end of the service. The reading concluded with the congregation praying together:

> Eternal God who, like a Mother, broods over her children, we commend one another into your care as we move now into new directions. We give thanks for cherished memories, for spiritual refreshment shared together, for a renewed sense of who we are and are meant to be. We ask for the comfort of the Holy Spirit who intervenes for us with sighs too deep for words. And we trust that you are guiding all of us, in this parting, for the work of the Gospel. Through the name of the Risen Christ we pray. Amen.[10]

The worship service ended with Linford Martin, representing FMC, giving words of welcome to POMC members, the enthusiastic a cappella singing of an anthem version of the Doxology, "Praise God from Whom All Blessings Flow," and a sung benediction, "The Lord bless you and keep you."

Many joined in a carry-in meal which was followed by sharing from numerous members and former members. Some of the sharing was solemn, and some was light. Before the sharing ended, Rachel slipped out of the fellowship hall and returned wearing a hat that she had borrowed from Rachel Weaver Kreider. It was a hat with "strings" that could be tied under the chin.

"Bless'd be the tie that binds our hearts in Christian love" is an old familiar hymn that was often sung at POMC, at least twice during most of the recent years.[11] During 2009 it was sung more often than usual, particularly at the end of congregational meetings or times of sharing. It happened that on November 22 there was also a congregational meeting at First Mennonite Church following a carry-in meal. The First Mennonite event ended a few minutes before the sharing at POMC ended. Tom Bontrager, an FMC member who was very interested in the developments at POMC, left the downtown meeting after the group there sang, "Bless'd be the tie that binds." He arrived at POMC just as that group was beginning to sing the same sending/ending

---

10. The responsive reading is appendix P.

11. Words by John Fawcett (1740–1817), minister in Wainsgate, England.

hymn, leaving no question in the minds of those who heard this story that God was clearly at work in bringing the two congregations together!

What is the "tie that binds" the hearts of Christians together in love? Or we might ask, what are the strings that are attached? We *are* bound together, knit together in Jesus, and as the song declares, "joined in heart."

Rachel Nafziger Hartzler put on a "bonnet with strings" while talking about the history writing project during the sharing time following the last Sunday morning worship service at Pleasant Oaks Mennonite Church, November 22, 2009.

CLOSING THE POMC OFFICE

After the decision was made to re-unite with FMC, Leasa Worley, church office secretary and maker of colorful flyers for all sorts of occasions, sent out notices to stop the mail. Ordering of new supplies came to a halt, and after September, only two more bulletins were needed. The monthly pastor-secretary lunch sessions ended with an exit interview to complete Leasa's four and one-half years of part time work in the church office.

Happy to be relieved of the weekly task of changing the words on the outdoor church sign, Leasa lamented that she would miss the regular interactions with Pleasant Oaks members and preschool teachers and children. Leasa's last day in the office was October 23. The congregation gave Leasa a small gift, and she and her family joined in the final worship service. Juanita Yoder served as a volunteer interim office staff person.

Upon guidance from the church board, Rachel, along with Leona Yoder and Juanita Yoder, combed through files to attend to membership concerns. Attention had not been given to the membership file for several years, and there were technically 134 members after Grant Miller was baptized in September 2009. The records indicate that when the Pleasant Oaks building had been inhabited in 1965, there were fifty-six members. Pastor Floyd and Ruth Quenzer soon joined bringing the number to fifty-eight. During the years following 1965, an additional 302 people joined the church. Many of the 360 people had died; others voluntarily withdrew from membership. In 1991 nine people were removed from the role by "deacon termination."

Thirty people were active members of POMC in 2009. Leona Yoder helped find addresses for nearly all of the one hundred four inactive members, and Rachel composed a pastoral letter that began to go out on October 17. Because of the belief that a pastor represents not only a congregation but also the church of Jesus Christ, the letters were personalized when possible and were warm and inviting, not strictly business-like. A typical letter is in appendix O. Fifty-eight people responded.

The transitional board took action at the November 19 meeting to approve: certificates of membership to be sent to forty-four inactive members as documentation that they had been members; the removal from the membership list of the fourteen people who asked to have their names withdrawn (either because of being involved in a congregation that does not keep a membership list, or because of not being involved in a congregation at the time); and the removal from the membership list of thirty-eight people who did not respond to the letter. These names were posted on the bulletin board, and the congregation was encouraged to pray for these former members, many of whom were still friends.

After the action of November 19, 2009, there were thirty remaining active members of POMC. These are listed in appendix I. In addition, eight inactive members requested that their membership be automatically transferred to First Mennonite. As directed by the transitional board, Rachel wrote letters of transfer for these eight members and sent them to FMC for their leadership to act upon.

Two nursing home residents (Doneta Burkhardt and Shirley Yoder) automatically became members of FMC. Attention was given to Doneta and Shirley during the transition. On November 19, a small group of members and Linford Martin gathered with Doneta and Shirley in the Manor 3 Garden Room at Greencroft Goshen for a pizza lunch. After pizza the group sang old favorite hymns; Shirley joined in with her strong alto voice, and Doneta listened, occasionally humming quietly. In December Linford Martin and Pamela Yoder, FMC pastors, led a communion service at Greencroft with Doneta and Shirley and some of Shirley's family members. The pastors gave a special invitation to Rachel to attend, hoping her presence might make the transition smoother for these two senior members.

Since Rachel concluded her pastoral care assignment on November 22, files on POMC members who were currently active were turned over to FMC lead pastor Linford Martin that day. With the guidance of the deacon council, Rachel completed and distributed the transfer of church membership documents for the remaining twenty-eight active members. Of these, eight intended to transfer to other congregations, and twenty considered becoming part of FMC. Those who chose to retain their membership with Pleasant Oaks Mennonite Church in order to help make final legal decisions, were instructed to hold the document until the legal process of re-uniting with First Mennonite was complete. The document states that the person is a member of the "sending" congregation until confirmation is received from the "receiving" congregation.

Having completed her official role as pastor, Rachel withdrew from participating in congregational meetings. The other twenty-seven members were eligible to participate in the remaining decisions to be made while POMC was still a legal entity. Following the last worship service, Rachel, Leona Yoder, and Juanita Yoder worked many hours in the office to update the membership book and prepare materials to go to the Central District Conference Archives at Bluffton University.

Two members of POMC died before the re-uniting with FMC was complete: Doneta Burkhardt and Jim Mishler both died on February 5, 2010. Shirley Yoder died on May 9, 2012.

CELEBRATION OF RE-UNIFICATION

It takes nine months for a human baby to grow and develop in a mother's womb. Similarly, it was nearly nine months after the final worship service at Pleasant Oaks until the legal proceedings of the re-uniting of the two congregations were complete. Early in August 2010, Dennis Rheinheimer, chair of the church council of First Mennonite Church, received official notice that The Articles of Merger of Pleasant Oaks Mennonite Church, Inc. and First Mennonite Church of Middlebury, Indiana, Inc. had been filed with the Indiana Secretary of State on July 29.[12] The legal work dissolved the two former entities (or corporations) and formed a new entity, a new Mennonite congregation in Middlebury.

The celebration of re-unification was held on August 8, 2010. Verses from Colossians 3 were the scriptural focus of the day.

---

12. Included was the Certificate of Merger which indicated that POMC members cast thirteen votes with thirteen in favor of the merger and FMC members cast 171 votes with 171 in favor of the merger.

... as God's chosen people, holy and dearly loved, clothe yourselves with compassion, kindness, humility, gentleness and patience. Bear with each other and
forgive whatever grievances you may have against one another. Forgive as the
Lord forgave you. And over all these virtues put on love, which binds them all
together in perfect unity (Colossians 3:12–14, NIV).

Dozens of colorful balloons and fresh flowers set the stage for a worship service
in the sanctuary of the church building on East Lawrence Street. Adding to the visual
features of the morning were the elements of communion, dozens of clear plastic cups
holding an eye-catching array of colored sand, and an empty clear glass cylinder at the
front of the sanctuary. Songs of praise to God for the marvelous work of reconciliation began the worship service as 185 worshipers raised their voices. Colorful bulletin
covers designed for weddings added to the festive ambience of the morning. Lead
pastor Linford Martin brought a biblical, thoughtful, and passionate sermon, "Two
Became One." Associate pastor Pamela Yoder and many lay people from both former
congregations assisted with the service.

As worshipers had entered the sanctuary, three of the youth, Katrina Pieri,
Grant Miller, and Bryce Rheinheimer, had given each person a small piece of colored paper. Children, youth and adults were all instructed to write their names on
the papers, and they were collected with the morning offering. Following the sermon Grant and Bryce, representing both former congregations, came to the front
of the sanctuary and inserted the small papers, each with a name, into the "history
capsule" in the center of the clear glass cylinder.

A ritual of unity was then enacted by pouring of sand, symbolic of pouring one's
life into the mix that is now a new congregation. The ritual began with pastor Linford
inviting Rachel Nafziger Hartzler, the last pastor of the former Pleasant Oaks Mennonite Church, to join him in pouring the first cups of sand into the cylinder. Lay leaders
from both congregations followed, and then long lines were formed as the everyone
present was invited to walk up the side isles, select a cup with colored sand, and in
concert with another worshiper, pour it into the clear cylinder.

The Spirit of Jesus was almost tangible as music from the worship team filled the
air while children, women, and men, young and old, added to the escalating multi-
colored layers of sand. After the children added their sand, they were each given a
brightly colored balloon to take with them, spreading the symbols of celebration
throughout the sanctuary. A few of the helium-filled balloons danced to the ceiling as
the music continued, and the cylinder was filled with the colors of the rainbow.

A second ritual followed the first. Baptized members and guests were offered
bread and then a small cup of grape juice, in both cases holding the elements of communion until all had been served. The pastor invited everyone to partake together,
increasing the sense of communing together as the symbols of the body and blood of
Christ were received by the "Body of Christ," the church.

In his sermon Linford said he wished that Simon S. Yoder could have been present to see the two congregations re-unite. Simon was one of the pastors of the Middlebury Mennonite Church at the time of the communion service in the spring of 1923—when this story began.

As was described earlier, the original Middlebury Mennonite congregation remained with the Indiana-Michigan Mennonite Conference, which was part of the Mennonite Church denomination. The group that became Pleasant Oaks Mennonite Church joined the Central Conference of the General Conference Mennonite Church denomination in 1926. In 2001 these two denominations decided to merge, and in 2002 the legal work was completed, forming a new denomination, Mennonite Church USA. Even though First Mennonite and Pleasant Oaks became part of the same denomination, and for the past few decades had collaborated in various worship, educational, mission, and outreach experiences, they had remained in two different area conferences.

It is believed that these are the first two congregations that have split in an unhappy situation and then have re-united at a later time. Even though the former Pleasant Oaks congregation was much smaller than the former First Mennonite congregation, Pleasant Oaks brought to the newly formed congregation a church building on six acres of very accessible property, a thriving preschool, and a rich history in addition to thirty members, fourteen of whom were present for the August 8 celebration.

The August 8 worship service ended with a cappella singing of an anthem version of the Doxology, "Praise God from Whom All Blessings Flow," sometimes called the "Mennonite Anthem." Again voices filled the worship space with praise to God, ending the service as it had begun—with a focus on praise to God.

PART III

Imagining the Future of the Mennonite Church

God calls us to be followers of Jesus Christ and,
by the power of the Holy Spirit,
to grow as communities of grace, joy, and peace,
so that God's healing and hope flow through us to the world.
Vision of Mennonite Church USA

Grace Hildebrand and Juna Hartzler learn about the past and imagine the future
at Menno-Hof in Shipshewana, Indiana, 2010.

10

Reflections Regarding Strings and Boundaries

The boundary lines have fallen for me in pleasant places;
surely I have a delightful inheritance.

PSALM 16:6 (NIV)

How very good and pleasant it is
when kindred live together in unity!
It is like the precious oil on the head,
running down upon the beard,
on the beard of Aaron,
running down over the collar of his robes.
It is like the dew of Hermon,
which falls on the mountains of Zion.
For there the Lord ordained his blessing,
life for evermore.

PSALM 133

FOR MANY YEARS PLEASANT Oaks Mennonite Church participated in the week of prayer for Christian unity between January 18 and 25. The Middlebury ministerium organized a Sunday morning pulpit exchange and a joint Sunday evening worship service. Since 1908 Christians around the world have remembered the words of Jesus in John 17 and have joined together to pray during January. On January 18, 2012, Pope Benedict XVI explained how this initiative brings together Christians who "invoke that extraordinary gift for which the Lord Jesus prayed . . . 'That they may all be one.'"

He also said that "lack of unity among Christians is an obstacle to a more effective proclamation of the Gospel, because it endangers our credibility," and noted that "the fundamental truths of the faith unite us far more than they divide us."[1]

Unity is a high value in the Judeo-Christian tradition. Unity is rooted in the love of God. We are united as we respond to God's love for us—by loving God with heart, soul, mind, and strength and by loving our neighbors as ourselves. As Christians, we are further united in Jesus.

In the preceding pages, the story of a congregation in Middlebury, Indiana, first called Warren Street and then Pleasant Oaks Mennonite Church, serves as a case study in an inquiry into varying patterns of Christian responses to differences. The WSMC/POMC story is set within the larger framework of the ebb and flow of Mennonite congregational life within the past 150 years, from about 1860 forward. This has included formation of congregations by immigrants primarily from Europe, divisions and realignment of Mennonite groups, and the merger in 2002 of the two largest Mennonite subgroups within the United States.[2]

The reconciliation and re-uniting of two earlier-estranged congregations in Middlebury in 2009 was like reattaching body parts. André Gingerich Stoner says that because Mennonites and other Christians are part of the same body of Christ, we can't be satisfied simply existing next to each other. We are parts of the same body—arms and legs, stomach and brain, eyes and ears—and it is important that blood vessels and nerves connect all the parts. If we live side by side but don't discuss what is important and how we differ, we are like amputated body parts scattered about. If we are *not* connected, we are not the living body that God intends us to be.[3]

We *can* be united even when we don't agree on all things. We often discuss and debate issues with the assumption that resolution comes only when one side is proven right and the other proven wrong. The church is called to dialogue instead of debate, "to build relationships and engage in dialogue . . . because we have gifts to give and receive that help us be more faithful to Jesus." Stoner goes on to explain that "the assumption of dialogue is that none of us has the full truth. As we listen and speak carefully with each other, together we can discover God's greater truth. We enter these conversations in the name and spirit of Christ."[4]

David Boshart clarifies that unity is not sameness, agreeing, toleration, or the result of coercion. The body of Christ includes diverse people, not people who are all the same; we agree to disagree—but always in love; unity calls for embracing, not simply

1. http://www.vatican.va/holy_father/benedict_xvi/audiences/2012/documents/hf_ben-xvi_aud_20120118_en.html.

2. Mennonite Church Canada was also formed in 2002 by the merging of the General Conference Mennonite Church and the "old" Mennonite Church in Canada. By 2002 there were many members in both MC USA and MC Canada with genetic roots that are not European.

3. André Gingerich Stoner is director of holistic witness and director of interchurch relations for Mennonite Church USA. http://www.mennoworld.org/2011/4/4/reattaching-body-parts/?print=1.

4. Ibid.

for toleration, which places one person above the other—one who tolerates and one who is tolerated. Christian faith and unity cannot be coerced. Early Anabaptists gave their lives on the principle that faith must be *chosen* by individuals, not coerced. John D. Roth says that the challenge for the church today is "to align ourselves with God's unsettling and surprising movement in the world while also being faithful stewards of a 'goodly heritage' (Psalm 16:6)."[5]

Nancy Kauffmann, denominational minister for Mennonite Church USA (MC USA), calls the church to not impose conformity . . . but to "maintain the unity of God's Spirit, wherever that might lead or whatever shape it might take." Rather than a "spirit of unity," which can become a "smothering conformity," we can maintain the unity of God's Spirit as we find sanctuary (a place where heaven and earth meet when we worship and discern together), pray, study scripture, and offer others the same love and grace that God gives us.[6]

ON THE RE-UNITING OF TWO CONGREGATIONS

The re-uniting of Pleasant Oaks Mennonite Church and First Mennonite Church of Middlebury is a unity that was not achieved by the leaders of the two groups. Clever minds, creative imaginations, and hard work cannot create unity. Unity is a gift of God, given rather than manufactured. The images of unity in Psalm 133 may seem odd at first (oil flowing from the head and down onto the beard of a newly ordained high priest and dew from the northern mountains), but oil is the pleasant fragrance of something soothing and tangible that comes from God; dew is that mysterious refreshment that God offers to those who awaken to the reality that God created us for loving relationships and empowers us to live in love. Unity comes from God, not from human initiative.

Unity occurred in Middlebury in 2009 when leaders and members of two congregations joined in the work that God had already been doing. The task was to prepare to receive and then maintain the unity for which Jesus had prayed. People with diverse beliefs and ideas and needs found unity by worshiping together, dialoguing, and nurturing friendships. Unity is challenged by our cultural context that encourages individualism, supports polarization, and promotes mistrust. Boshart urges the church to prepare "to receive and maintain the unity of the body by drinking deeply of the one Spirit in which we are baptized and by cultivating practices among us that result in humility, gentleness, yieldedness, patience, and forbearance."[7]

One reason the re-union of First Mennonite and Pleasant Oaks was possible is that there was *more* than good communication. The two groups had communion together.

---

5. Boshart, "Becoming a United Church." David Boshart is executive conference minister of Central Plains Mennonite Conference; John D. Roth in foreword to Kanagy, *Road Signs*, 10.

6. Kauffmann, "Sanctuary," 89–92.

7. Boshart, "Becoming a United Church."

Communion is an experience that goes beyond words. It acknowledges and confirms the unity that exists because of our unity with God through Christ. The two congregations together participated in the Lord's Supper on World Communion Sunday on October 4, 2009. During the celebration of reconciliation and re-union on August 8, 2010, a celebrative communion service was shared by the re-united congregation.

Traditional ecumenical dialogue has often been concerned with refining doctrinal expressions to discover points of agreement and disagreement. Conversations among various Mennonites might also be described in this way. While some Christians may try to recover a unity that was lost because of human misunderstandings and limitations, Thomas Merton described a unity that had never been lost, "because it is beyond the reach of human weakness. This unity is discoverable only at the level of the religious experience—something that can never be adequately expressed in doctrinal formulations."[8] In our doctrinal statements we recognize our differences; within sacred encounters we experience unity. This helps to explain the power of communion.

Although the differences between the two Mennonite congregations in Middlebury were much smaller in 2009 than they had been fifty or eighty years earlier, the differences still existed: in a different history, in varying understandings of biblical interpretation, and in a different congregational polity, particularly in how decisions were made. But thanks be to God, remembering and believing and behaving differently has not prevented Middlebury Mennonites from treating each other respectfully, and from becoming a community of grace, joy, and peace, and together offering healing and hope to each other and to the world.

The merging of the General Conference Mennonite Church and the "old" Mennonite Church in 2002 is, in part, a result of what GC Mennonites began in 1860 at West Point, Iowa; that is, working for a union of all Mennonites in America. There were differences in the various groups of Mennonites then, and some of those differences appeared to be even greater in the intervening years. But in the mid-1900s, distinctions became less divergent. To some extent this was due to the work of Erland Waltner, who as a GC leader had helped to bring the Mennonite Biblical Seminary from Chicago to Elkhart, Indiana. Erland was the third president of the seminary (which had begun in 1945), the first president in Elkhart. Through Erland Waltner's respectful listening, pastoral patience, and undaunted courage, he led the seminary in joining with Goshen Biblical Seminary to become Associated Mennonite Biblical Seminaries (AMBS) in 1958.[9]

The coming together of the two seminaries was one of the very significant steps in moving the two Mennonite bodies toward the 2002 transformation into one new

---

8. Merton, *Hidden Ground of Love*, x.

9. James C. Juhnke, "Preparation of a Leader: Erland Waltner from Dakota to Elkhart," and Cornelius J. Dyck, "President of Mennonite Biblical Seminary," in Yoder, *The Work is Thine*. Associated Mennonite Biblical Seminaries became Associated Mennonite Biblical Seminary and then in 2012 the name was changed to Anabaptist Mennonite Biblical Seminary.

denomination, Mennonite Church USA. There were many challenges, numerous misunderstandings, and abundant blessings in the journey of two denominations becoming one, and by the grace of God, it happened. And now the reconciliation and reunification of the two Middlebury congregations is an example of the good fruit that has come from the 2002 merger.

"Part of what Mennonite Church USA is, in my understanding, is a logical result of the 150 years preceding," said Jim Schrag when he retired from his position as the first executive director of MC USA. "The distinctions between us are blurring—not just between Mennonite groups but also between [denominations]." The church is called to move beyond traditional cultures and communities.[10]

It seems that historically there has been more cheerfulness and buoyancy to some aspects of life in the GC denomination. A Mennonite moved from Ohio to Goshen in 2010. Although he lives a stone's throw from College Mennonite Church and has children who are members there, he decided to attend Eighth Street Mennonite Church. "It's General Conference," he said, well aware of the merger that took place in 2002. "What is the difference?" Hartzler asked him. "Oh!" he said. "We have fun when we get together!" He reminisced about an occasion when the GC Central District Conference had a joint annual meeting with an "old" Mennonite conference. "We always concluded our annual meeting with communion, but when we met with the Ohio Conference, we were told we couldn't have communion. Some of them had never had communion together so they certainly could not have communion with another denomination!"

He continued, "We went to annual meetings as families. Our children looked forward to this special event. It was like a family reunion for us. But the Ohio conference was attended only by ministers and a few other church leaders—all male back then. We had a good time, and they seemed to come out of a sense of duty. Has that changed yet?" he asked.

DIFFERENT UNDERSTANDINGS REGARDING THE BIBLE

Within MC USA there are different understandings of scripture. Some sisters and brothers hold fast to the Bible as the inspired, inerrant, and infallible[11] Word of God. Others believe that the Bible was certainly inspired by God, but since it was written by human hands and translated by human minds, there are some small discrepancies.[12] Mennonites tend to agree on divine inspiration, declaring with 2 Timothy 3:16–17 that all Scripture is inspired by God, or as Peterson translates in *The Message*, "Ev-

10. James Schrag quotations in Krehbiel, "Leader looks back." http://www.mennoworld. org/2009/12/7/leader-looks-back-time-change/?page=3.

11. "*Infallibility* usually means that the Bible will not fail to accomplish its purpose of revealing God's will and salvation. . ." Marlin E. Miller, "Inerrancy of Scripture."

12. Two examples of discrepancies are 2 Samuel 24:1 and 1 Chronicles 21:1,where there is not agreement on who caused David to take a census; and Matthew 10:9–10 and Mark 6:8 and Luke 9:3, where there is not agreement on what the disciples should take with them.

ery part of Scripture is God-breathed and useful one way or another—showing us truth, exposing our rebellion, correcting our mistakes, training us to live God's way. Through the Word we are put together and shaped up for the tasks God has for us."[13]

The Bible was central to the life and faith of early Anabaptists, and Jesus is at the center of the Bible. Menno Simons said, "All Scripture must be interpreted according to the Spirit, teaching, walk, and example of Christ and the apostles." Reading the Old Testament through the lens of Jesus' life and teachings clarifies many questions. The Anabaptist way is to give elevated status to the New Testament, especially the life and teachings of Jesus, rather than holding to a "flat Bible," which places equal weight on all the books of the Bible. To give Jesus superior status means to give the highest priority to the greatest commandments: "Love the Lord your God with all your heart, and with all your soul, and with all your mind, and with all your strength. . . . [and] love your neighbor as yourself." Jesus himself took the lead in identifying that some parts of the biblical message are more important than others. He presented a "new covenant."[14]

There are numerous issues in both the Old and New Testaments about which Christians today believe differently from Christians a few decades and/or centuries ago. One example is slavery, once thought by many Christians to be appropriate. Also, circumcision of males was an important practice in Judaism and the very early church, but it no longer has religious significance in most Christian circles. The Acts 15 story of the discussion about the necessity of circumcision for first century Christians has some interesting parallels to the dialogue about homosexuality for twenty-first-century Christians.

Solo scriptura was a foundational principle of the Protestant Reformation—the belief that "by scripture alone" Christians can discern how to live. Since the 16th century, Mennonites have emphasized the authority of the Bible for faith and life, meaning that the Bible is the supreme guide for decision making. The Holy Spirit guides a believing community in discernment that is in harmony with the scripture. A question for today centers on how much authority the gathered community holds in interpreting the Bible. The discernment process at the Jerusalem conference in Acts 15 led to the conclusion that circumcision was not required for salvation. Does the church today have authority to do that kind of discernment? A congregational polity, more common among former General Conference congregations, creates a more likely setting for community discernment.

---

13. 2 Timothy 3:16–17. Scripture quotation from *The Message*. Copyright © by Eugene H. Peterson 1993, 1994, 1995, 1996, 2000, 2001, 2002. Used by permission of NavPress Publishing Group.

14. John Horsch, *Menno Simons*; Mark 12:30–31; also Matthew 22:37–39 and Luke 10:27; Luke 22:20.

DIFFERENT WAYS OF MAKING DECISIONS

Have the members of the new congregation in Middlebury found enough common ground for the church to grow and thrive? Might it be a challenge for people from two different traditions to become one? Numerous people whose early years were in the "old" Mennonite tradition came to Pleasant Oaks because of conflicts or unhappiness within their congregations.

Sources of Authority

Rachel Weaver Kreider describes the sixteenth-century Reformation as the time when an infallible Bible was substituted for an infallible pope. Even though claiming the Bible as authoritative, the radical reformers who became Anabaptists recognized that the Bible was interpreted in various ways and therefore believed that community discernment was crucial. Examples of Michael Sattler (d. 1527) consulting with his community of believers are given in chapter 2. However, there are occasions when Anabaptists have returned to the system of hierarchical authority that occurs in the Catholic Church and many Protestant churches. There are also examples of church leaders who called the church to be the "priesthood of believers" that an Anabaptist theology promotes. Joseph Stuckey and Simon S. Yoder are two historic examples of ministers who, in a sense, "rejected authority" by not giving in to the demands of their superiors; at the same time, they continued to be faithful followers of Jesus.[15]

Historically there were phenomena that occurred around the turn of the twentieth century that pulled in opposite directions. The Chicago World's Fair in 1893 was a significant turning point, a time when the influence of secular culture on Mennonites began to increase rapidly. There was a fear among some church leaders that religious life and tradition were so bound together that without the trappings of tradition (such as uniform clothing), true religious experience might be lost or at least compromised. Daniel Kauffman led in an authoritarian direction and basically took the "old" Mennonite church with him.[16]

From another direction, individualism was sneaking its way into the church. Whereas in traditional Anabaptist communities, the good of the community was a higher value than the good of an individual, the individual was gradually given greater esteem in some circles. It seems that individualism found a more tolerant home in churches with a congregational polity than in congregations where authority was held by the leadership.

---

15. Joseph Stuckey's story is in appendix G and Simon Yoder was the first pastor of WSMC.
16. Details about Daniel Kauffman and his work are given in chapter 3.

Authority in the Leadership

As author and editor of the *Gospel Herald*, Daniel Kauffman was the authoritative voice for the "old" Mennonite Church for more than thirty years, from 1898 to 1930. We might wonder how one person generated so much authority. Great numbers of Mennonites accepted his doctrinal methods, in part because of the concern that "worldliness" was creeping into the church. Some feared that worldliness would kill the Mennonite church, so Bible doctrine as described by Daniel Kauffman was widely accepted.[17] Without question, Kauffman was a capable leader and was dedicated to Christ and the Mennonite Church. He was the leading energy behind the creation of the "old" Mennonite Church denominational organizational body in 1898, which brought a new approach to denominational structure for Mennonites, including the idea of a central authority, which, in practice, transcended the authority of the area conferences.[18] Kauffman was then the first moderator of the organization and served three additional terms.

From the time of the publication of Kauffman's first edition of *Bible Doctrine* in 1898 and for the next twenty-five years, "old" Mennonite church theology became more conservative, influenced by Protestant Fundamentalism that swept over North America. Fundamentalism made a claim of inerrancy of scripture, and this doctrine of inerrancy became the decisive test for orthodoxy. In general, doctrinal theology does not mesh well with Anabaptism, which traditionally has had a strong emphasis on discipleship.

An example of a church leader who apparently changed with the times is Daniel J. Johns from the Clinton Frame Church south of Middlebury. John C. Wenger says, "As a bishop he was rather mild in his discipline as a middle-aged leader, but became stricter in his later years." Johns had been ordained preacher in 1882 and bishop in 1887, before the strong emphasis on doctrine and clothing styles had begun.[19] Daniel D. Miller is an example of a bishop being required (or at least expected) to act in ways more restrictive that he preferred. At a meeting at College Mennonite Church in 1923, bishop Miller said that he needed to work with the conference rules even though he did not agree with all of them. Additionally, D. D. Miller's son Ernest revealed in his biography of his father that, although it was not well known, "at one point he decided to leave the Old Mennonite Conference. Only considerations about his family and his own future usefulness kept him from taking this step."[20]

17. As noted in chapter 3, other church leaders wrote sections of the second edition of *Bible Doctrine*.

18. The organization was the General Conference *of the* Mennonite Church, not to be confused with the General Conference Mennonite Church. This was not at all a creative name, considering that the General Conference denomination already existed!

19. Wenger, "Johns, Daniel J." Bishop Johns had oversight of the Middlebury Mennonite congregation when it began in 1094, officiating at the first communion service. He was bishop at Middlebury until 1913 when D. D. Miller took over that responsibility. See chapter 4.

20. T. Schlabach, "The Past in Perspective," 26; Ernest Miller, *D. D. Miller*, 34.

Many of those who could not tolerate the heavy hand of authoritarian leaders left the "old" Mennonite Church. There were a number of Goshen College faculty members who left Goshen and went to Bluffton College. Others, not as free to change locations, were disciplined, often with reinforcements from other conservatives. At the beginning of the twentieth century, program boards and denominational agencies were dominated by influential men who established and extended conference authority over issues in congregations. These local leaders regularly brought in third parties to make judgments about conflicts. Third parties were often conference leaders or respected bishops from other areas who were usually somewhat sympathetic to the agenda of the local leaders, and their agenda was consequently reinforced. The simultaneous expansion of institutions and consolidation of traditional religious authority in boards and conferences had a huge effect on conflicts among "old" Mennonites in the early twentieth century.[21]

Authority in the Congregation

In spite of the schisms in Mennonite groups throughout the centuries, a strong sense of community was part of Anabaptism from the beginning. In general, decision making was done within the group. The "priesthood of all believers" was an important feature in Reformation thought. Although this concept became less important in the development of many denominations, it has remained, in varying degrees, a significant element in Anabaptism. Therefore, decision making in early Mennonite and Amish groups leaned toward being congregational. Amish and groups that came to be part of the General Conference Mennonite Church tended to be congregational in polity.

Congregational autonomy seemed to work quite well in GC churches and continues to be the mechanism by which the Central District Conference (CDC) operates. It was the familiar way of making decisions at Pleasant Oaks and informed the process of the last months of functioning as a congregation. The church board was transparent in its work; minutes of meetings were readily available to members. An essential role of the pastor was to listen to how God was moving among the people and to invite the congregation to join in the action, not to be the decision maker. Three conference ministers in the CDC supported the pastor and congregation during the final years: Lloyd Miller, John Heyerly (as interim), and Lois Johns Kaufmann, each a valuable resource without being imposing or controlling.

A mission of the church is to be in tune with God's Holy Spirit. Congregationalism expects that the primary place where God's Spirit moves is in congregations. Members meet beyond congregations in settings like area conferences for inspiration and support, but that is not the primary place of decision making when a congregational polity is in place. The executive committee of MC USA made a statement on June 13, 2012, which confirms that although ministers are credentialed by conferences,

21. Fred Kniss, *Disquiet in the Land*, 37.

congregations make decisions about members. The national body does not have the authority to control discussions or decisions of area conferences or congregations. The executive committee concluded their statement by calling the church to pray that the denomination may keep "the bond of peace" as described in Ephesians 4:3 and to remember that "There is one body and one Spirit, just as you were called to the one hope of your calling, one Lord, one faith, one baptism, one God and Father of all, who is above all and through all and in all" (Ephesians 4: 4–6).[22]

Individualism versus Community

Individuals within the church and congregations are uniquely created and led by God, but at the same time are dependent upon the gathered community to fully discern God's leading. It is important to distinguish between individuality and individualism. Individuality is the qualities or characteristics of a person that distinguish that person from similar people; it is the sum of those characteristics that set a person apart from other individuals. Individualism is the principle that the interests of the individual are of utmost importance. In short, it places the individual over and above community. Individualism runs counter to the greatest commandments as Jesus defined them, love of God and neighbor.[23] Individualism does not harmonize with the importance of community that Anabaptism emphasizes.

And yet, individualism was promoted by three important leaders in the General Conference. C. Henry Smith[24] began his teaching career in 1898 at the Elkhart Institute and Goshen College before going to Bluffton College in 1913. Although highly respected as a historian, Smith described the essentials of Anabaptism incorrectly. He wrote, "The Anabaptists insisted that each individual must decide the Bible message for himself. The greatest degree of liberty must be granted the individual conscience in spiritual matters. Anabaptism was the essence of individualism."[25]

J. E. Hartzler was an MC and then a GC leader who "defended his loyalty to the essence of Mennonite faith, but a faith defined more in terms of individual rights than Anabaptist tradition."[26] In his 1925 book on education Hartzler wrote that a foundational principle of Mennonitism is "faith in an open Bible for all men with freedom of interpretation; a faith which urges entire freedom of conscience, and yet honors Divine authority."[27] The missing ingredient in J. E. Hartzler's statement is community.

---

22. http://www.themennonite.org/uploads/File/EC_statement_2012Jan13.pdf

23. Mark 12:30–31; also Matthew 22:37–39 and Luke 10:27.

24. See footnote 37 in chapter 3 (page 72) for more information on Smith.

25. Smith, *Story of the Mennonites*, 21.

26. J. Denny Weaver, "Hartzler, John Ellsworth (1879–1963)." See footnote 13 in chapter 1 (page 8) for more on Hartzler. In 1925, J. E. Hartzler was president of Witmarsum Theological Seminary at Bluffton.

27. Hartzler, *Education among the Mennonites*, 7–8.

It has been said that "community without grace breeds legalism, and grace without community leads to individualism."[28]

A third GC leader who promoted individualism was Samuel K. Mosiman who chaired the General Conference "Committee of Seven," a committee that considered a denominational position against participating in warfare. In 1920 Mosiman reported "neither Committee nor Conference could speak for the individual conscience of the drafted men."[29] Giving prominence to individual choices seems to have in some cases trumped the Mennonite traditional teaching on Jesus' teaching on love and nonviolence. Indeed, a specifically named characteristic of the General Conference was the emphasis on freedom for the individual. In describing GC characteristics for the 1956 *Mennonite Encyclopedia*, Edmund G. Kaufman[30] explained a conference emphasis on freedom and autonomy, stating that each believer stands before God "in faith as a free individual, uncoerced by other believers." It was spelled out that each individual is "competent and responsible to deal directly with God through Christ, without intervention of parent, priest, sacrament, church, or state."[31]

In discussions about serving in the military versus being conscientious objectors, numerous former GC people have emphasized that everyone must choose for themselves. While this is obviously true, an eighteen-year-old conscience needs significant guidance, especially if the young person has not been thoroughly grounded in the teachings of Jesus from the Sermon on the Mount. Without some checks and balances, it seems that a congregational polity can slide toward individualism.

The congregational polity that was common among Amish groups and among the General Conference and Central Conference groups from the beginning has many positive features. However, the connection between congregationalism and individualism must not be overlooked. Emphasizing individual rights at the expense of others violates not only the commitment to community, but also the common good of others outside the community.

Did the progressives who left the Middlebury church in 1923 do so because they valued the right of the individual to make decisions more than they valued the community cohesiveness that exists when the expected practice of the community is followed? That is difficult to say, especially since the congregation from which they came apparently didn't allow for discernment within and by the community. And it may be that there was inadequate grace in the Indiana-Michigan Conference system

28. John Rempel, "Mennonite Communion Practice."

29. Juhnke, *Vision, Doctrine, War,* 212.

30. Edmund G. Kaufman was a General Conference Mennonite missionary to China (1917–1925) and president of Bethel College in Kansas (1932–1952). He earned degrees at Bethel College, Witmarsum Seminary, Garrett Biblical Institute, and the University of Chicago. He was described as a vigorous teacher, administrator, churchman, and intellectual leader.

31. Kaufman and Poettcker. "General Conference Mennonite Church."

of authoritarian bishops at that time. If there had been true community discernment in the Middlebury congregation in 1923, how might the story have been different?

Although the following may seem like legalism to some, a dramatic example of giving up individual rights for the benefit of community is described in *Amish Grace*:

> On bended knees at baptism, Amish individuals agree to follow Christ, to place themselves under the authority of the church, and to obey the *Ordnung*, the unwritten regulations of the church. Here the key words are self-denial, obedience, acceptance, and humility—all of which require yielding to the collective wisdom of the community. This doesn't mean the individual withers away, but it is constrained. Rather than making their own way alone, Amish people must yield to the authority of the church community and ultimately to God.[32]

When an abundance of grace is involved, this is a beautiful picture of community.

The Practice of Giving and Receiving Counsel

Accountability is an important feature of Christian living, necessary for all members of a healthy Christian community, including leaders. Being human and sometimes under great pressure, leaders can become especially vulnerable to sin. Giving and receiving counsel is a practice that provides accountability for members of a group. In a hierarchical system where giving and receiving counsel is expected, a leader is accountable to the supervising person or group. When this system works well, misbehavior in a leader will be addressed.

Placing a high value on individualism tends to minimize the emphasis on giving and receiving counsel that has long been at the heart of Anabaptism. The 1995 *Confession of Faith in a Mennonite Perspective*, article 11 clarifies that in baptism people "commit themselves to follow Christ in obedience as members of his body, both giving and receiving care and counsel in the church." When the current MC USA *Minister's Manual* is used at the time of baptism, the baptismal candidate promises to give and receive counsel in the congregation.[33]

When a brother or sister in the congregation has offended or seems to be out of tune with God's ways, the instruction provided by Jesus in Matthew 18 gives guidance. First, one talks with the individual in question. If the individual doesn't hear the concern, one goes back with another person from the community. If that attempt for reconciliation is not received, the concern is then taken to the leaders of the congregation. When the concern is with a leading minister, the third step would be to go to the conference minister, overseer, or bishop.

---

32. Kraybill et al., *Amish Grace*, 93.

33. http://www.mcusa-archives.org/library/resolutions/1995/1995–11.html; John Rempel, *Minister's Manual*, 48.

Daniel Kauffman was often called upon to hear concerns and responded with the Matthew 18 principle. An example of his typical response is given in his biography. A question arose among certain church leaders about a young man with considerable responsibility in the church, questioning his loyalty to the church. The leaders went to Daniel Kauffman, ready to remove the man from his position, and Kauffman's response was for the church leaders to first go to him in kindness and talk with him about the implications of his actions. This was done, and the young man was "shown to be mistaken in methods rather than in principle and his shortcomings were the result of inexperience rather than disloyalty." Kauffman said, "It was a mistake of the head, not the heart."[34]

Church conflicts are usually complicated, but many quarrels could be avoided or minimized if the Matthew 18 principle were followed. However, it can be challenging for the giver of counsel to show love, and it is often difficult to receive counsel without being defensive. Here is where grace is essential. Thank God for amazing grace!

DIFFERENT TRADITIONS

Historically the Mennonite Church has been a group "separated from the world" for the sake of purity and preservation, but that has changed in recent decades, at least in MC USA, as more attention has been focused on observing God's activity in the world and attempting to join in God's activity. Once, happy to be "the quiet in the land," Mennonites are now being encouraged to actively share their faith, especially the way of peacemaking, with a world hungry for an alternative to violence.

As noted above, around the turn of the twentieth century Mennonites were faced with the effects of acculturation, especially on young people who were leaving home for education and mission work. Earlier the German language had helped to keep people in community. Among "old" Mennonites, the shift to English came earlier than for Russian Mennonites and their descendants. Perhaps one reason that the need for boundaries—by restrictions on dress and headwear—felt more urgent to "old" Mennonites is that part of their identity as a separate people was lost as they no longer spoke primarily German in their congregations and families. Most of the GC churches in the west continued to speak German until the First World War. Their nonconformity was expressed in the language they spoke.

Speaking German became a problem for many folk during World War I, as the language raised the suspicion of supporting Germany. In *Vision, Doctrine, War*, James Juhnke tells stories of the persistent and sometime severe persecution of Mennonites (particularly German-speaking Mennonites) during the First World War.[35] At that time, those Mennonites in the United States who still spoke German began to use it less in public places, and the distinction between Russian Mennonites and "old" Mennonites began to diminish.

34. A. Gingerich, *Daniel Kauffman*, 50.
35. Juhnke, *Vision, Doctrine, War*, 208–210, 218, 222–227, 239–240.

In addition, during and following World War I, the cooperative efforts of leaders of numerous Mennonite and Amish groups to arrange for alternative service for conscientious objectors, and then to begin relief efforts through Mennonite Central Committee (MCC), helped to bring people from the different Anabaptist traditions together. This continued as various Mennonite men (and a few women) served together in Civilian Public Service (CPS) during World War II and then worked side by side in programs to rebuild Europe after the war.[36]

Although working together for world relief and alternatives to participating in war, there was a basic difference in the way unity was perceived in the GC and MC traditions. From the beginning, the General Conference stated purpose was to unify all Mennonite groups in North America. On the other hand, Daniel Kauffman, essential spokesman for the "old" Mennonite Church for many years, did not favor a union among all Mennonites. He wrote in a 1913 *Gospel Herald* editorial, "As a rule, this kind of meeting fosters the spirit of compromise through the emphasis of 'unity' at the expense of things which are essential to be united upon."[37]

An additional distinct difference existed between the reactions of "old" Mennonites and GC Mennonites in response to World War I. MCs were clear on their position. GCs could not come to a conclusion.[38] Within both the MC and GC traditions and now MC USA, there have been differences in expressions of worship, but unity in that all respond to God's faithfulness, generous grace, and steadfast love.

DIVIDED INTO DENOMINATIONS

In 1925 J. E. Hartzler said, "The only justification for any denomination is on the condition that it makes some unique contribution to the Kingdom of God."[39] Dividing into many different denominations is counter to the unity that Jesus prayed for in John 17 and that the Apostle Paul begs Christians to, as they bear one another in love and maintain the unity of the Spirit of Jesus. Unity is the hope of Jesus as well as the hope of Paul for the church.

A question that J. O. Yoder has repeatedly raised is, "Why are there so many Christian denominations?" He reports that when he was in college in 1938, there were 280 denominations in the United States. In 2010, there are about seventy different

---

36. Stories from CPS are on a website: http://civilianpublicservice.org. A renowned postwar program initiated by the Church of the Brethren and United Nations Relief and Rehabilitation Administration (UNRRA) is commonly referred to as the "seagoing cowboys." Many Mennonites also joined in this effort, which is detailed at http://www.seagoingcowboys.com . Also see Peggy Reiff Miller, "Coming of Age on a Cattle Boat: The Mennonite Seagoing Cowboys." *The Mennonite*, January 10, 2006.

37. D. Kauffman, "The General Mennonite Convention at Berne," 338.

38. Juhnke, *Vision, Doctrine, War*, 212–214. This is further explored below under Nonresistance, Pacifism, the Gospel of Peace.

39. Hartzler, *Education among the Mennonites*, 7–8.

denominations within easy driving distance of Middlebury, and estimates claim that there are more than 30,000 Protestant denominations worldwide.[40]

The foolishness of church divisions is illustrated in a story that J. C. Wenger is remembered telling: An Amish man died and met Saint Peter at the gates of heaven. Peter welcomed the man into heaven and then told him to walk down a long corridor until he came to the Amish door. The man was surprised that there were different rooms in heaven, but as he walked he thought that God probably had this well planned out. He walked past the Lutheran door into heaven, the Methodist door, the Mennonite door, the Presbyterian door and kept walking. Finally near the end of the corridor he came to the Amish door. He entered and saw family and friends who had died before he had, and then, as he started looking for Jesus, he noticed that this was a very expansive room, and that all the denominational doors opened to the same place—heaven!

More troubling than many Protestant denominations may be the fact that there are more than 300 different Anabaptist-Mennonite fellowships and "denominations."[41] How can a movement that began with a strong peace emphasis become so fractured? A Mennonite-turned-Catholic offers an answer. Gerald Schlabach points out that the movements within the Reformation

> shared a commitment that the church constantly needs renewal and reform. This has come to be known as the Protestant Principle. But the virtue of protest has all too often become the vice of schisms, splits and splinters. The Protestant Principle has become the Protestant Dilemma. Mennonites are deeply infected by the Protestant Dilemma. The issues of the day have repeatedly ripped us apart—whether matters of dress, Sunday schools and revival, women in leadership or how we understand differences in sexual orientation.[42]

Drawing from years of experience at the intersection of Anabaptism and Catholicism, Schlabach writes: "What all of us need are the practices and virtues that make it possible to reform, protest and even dissent out of love for one's Christian community—even while sustaining a doggedly loyal commitment to hang in there with those among whom we disagree."[43]

Reconciliation is happening around the world, wherever people confess wrongdoing and are granted forgiveness. And reconciliation is happening among the denominations that are rooted in the Protestant Reformation. In recent decades, people in the European historic state churches (Catholic, Lutheran, and Reformed) have become aware that their spiritual ancestors conspired with their governments to force

40. A website reports that in November 2007 the number exceeded 43,000. http://www.philvaz.com/apologetics/a120.htm.

41. Stoner, "Who wants to hang in there," http://www.mennoweekly.org/2012/2/20/who-wants-hang-there.

42. Stoner reporting on G. Schlabach, *Unlearning Protestantism,* http://www.mennoweekly.org/2012/2/20/who-wants-hang-there.

43. G. Schlabach, *Unlearning Protestantism,* 32.

dissenting members of their societies to believe what the state and its official church believed. Anabaptists refused to comply, and thousands of Anabaptists were persecuted and killed in Europe in the sixteen and seventeen centuries.[44]

In the 1980s Lutheran and Mennonite conferences in Germany and the Alsace met to see if they could recognize each other as faithful churches. Lutherans expressed regret for persecution. Old prejudices were overcome, and they agreed on open communion toward each other.

From 1998 to 2003 the Vatican and Mennonite World Conference held a dialogue to address historic prejudices and antagonisms between them. The primary goal of that process was the healing of memories. The Catholics expressed remorse for persecuting and killing Anabaptists.

In 2004 the Reformed Church of the canton of Zurich (with the support of the whole Swiss Reformed Church) made a public apology to a cross section of descendents of Anabaptists (from mainstream Mennonite to Beachy Amish) for persecuting and killing their ancestors because of what they believed. Hundreds gathered in the main church of Zurich where the church president arose, confessed his church's wrongdoing and asked for forgiveness. Within a year there were two other gatherings (in the United States and Switzerland) in which charismatic Reformed and charismatic Anabaptists met to pray for the Holy Spirit to help them forgive one another because both sides had sinned.

In 2005 the Evangelical Lutheran Church in America (ELCA) approached MC USA (but included all Anabaptist groups in their intention) with remorse for persecuting and killing Anabaptists because of what they believed. They asked for a process aimed at reconciliation in which the two bodies would try to understand and overcome historical convictions and actions that had divided them. The Lutheran World Federation (LWF) took this process to the global level. On July 22, 2010, the LWF and Mennonite World Conference (MWC) experienced what LWF general secretary Ishamel Noko described as "God's work toward unity and reconciliation."

At their best, all denominations hold deep convictions and want to preserve the integrity of the Gospel. It is, therefore, painful when we realize that sometimes we cannot agree which beliefs and practices are at the heart of the Bible. However, a new age seems to be upon us when we can talk about our differences in loving dialogue. Thanks be to God!

NAMING WHAT DIVIDES US

Nearly fifty years ago Mennonite sociologist Cal Redekop said that "rapid social change leaves people insecure and confused. People vary in the manner by which

---

44. *Martyrs Mirror*, the classic 1660 Dutch religious history by Thieleman Van Bragt, memorializes the godly lives and deaths of thousands of early Christians, especially European Anabaptist martyrs between 1524 and 1660. It is available online at: http://www.homecomers.org/mirror/index.htm.

they can adapt themselves to new situations. Those that are more adaptable will be willing to adopt the new, while those not so adaptable will resist."[45] Is it our adaptability that is tested by innovations?

This simple study of schisms in Mennonite churches has led to numerous observations and a few probing questions. Many of the major divisive issues in the past 100 years had to do either directly or indirectly with issues of sexuality. For men to decide what women should wear on their heads has raised concerns in many Anabaptist congregations during the past century. This was followed by many Anabaptist women discovering a new way to understand the Apostle Paul's directives to the Corinthian church, and as a consequence, deciding to not cover their heads for worship. Some believed their hair was the only covering needed. Others rebelled against the idea that the devotional covering was a sign of women being subordinate to men.[46]

Not necessarily following in this sequence, additional issues related to sexuality have demanded attention in many Mennonite congregations: women cutting their hair, remarriage following divorce, women in leadership roles in the church, abortion, and homosexuality. From head coverings to homosexuality, there are scriptural references that some understand to be clear about how to respond to each of these. To come to accept any of these practices as permissible requires looking at scripture through lenses other than literal ones.

At one time head coverings were part of the wardrobe of most women. As fashions changed, some held to the customs of earlier years. As many women began to question the necessity of the covering in the 1960s and 1970s, some congregations did in-depth studies of this issue, sometimes spread out over a period of years. On the other hand, there is a story about the decision being made within a week in one congregation— without any formal church discussion. One Sunday one of the women came to church without her covering. The next Sunday only one woman wore a covering. All the other women left their coverings at home, and further discussion was not needed!

In 1968 a large group of high school youth at College Mennonite Church in Goshen had taken the preparation for baptism classes. The boys in the group were ready to be baptized. The girls were also ready to be baptized—except that they did not want to wear head coverings. Many women in the congregation were no longer wearing coverings, but College Church had never baptized a female who was not wearing the prayer veiling. A study was underway to determine if the policy would change, but studies like this can take years, especially in large congregations. The pastors had a dilemma. After much hand wringing, they proposed a compromise. If the girls would wear coverings for their baptism, the ministers would ignore their uncovered heads

---

45. Redekop, *Brotherhood and Schism*, 18.

46. Although subjection to men is the position that many have understood Paul to call for, other Pauline passages make clear that men and women are to be equally valued and mutually accountable within marriage.

following that Sunday. The girls graciously accepted, and the entire group was baptized and joined the church together, but the girls didn't wear coverings after that day.

In 2012 only a few women in MC USA wear head coverings. Most have come to understand that Paul's teaching for the Corinthians regarding head coverings for women was for that specific time and culture, where only women with loose morals would appear in public with an uncovered head. That the style of covering should matter and be an issue large enough to merit excommunication seems nearly unbelievable to many Mennonites today. A similar pattern developed regarding women cutting their hair. As with head coverings, Amish girls and women and some conservative Mennonite women continue to have uncut hair today, but length of hair has not been a concern for many decades in most MC USA congregations. In the GC tradition length of hair or clothing were not religious symbols or marks of faithfulness.

Remarriage following divorce has been a more difficult issue to process in most Mennonite congregations. Jesus did not address coverings and hair length for women, but he did speak directly about divorce, speaking against both divorce and remarriage following divorce. A young man in Goshen had grown up in a Mennonite family and was a member of College Mennonite Church in 1965 when his marriage ended in divorce. He knew the teachings of the church on divorce, so he left the Mennonite Church; in fact, he left the church altogether. Now as he is aging and facing health concerns, he has no congregation. Five years after he left the church, two couples, each of which included one person who had been divorced, sought acceptance for their marriages at College Church. The congregation did an in-depth study and finally in 1972 accepted both couples as members. Theron Schlabach has told this story in detail in the 2003 history of that congregation.[47]

Schlabach identified the congregational decision about divorce and remarriage as a turning point at College Mennonite Church, writing:

> In that treatment the congregation made decisions about how to read the Bible and about accepting a measure of situation ethics. It tried new approaches to accountability and church discipline. It shifted the balance between biblical teaching and doctrine on the one hand and relational considerations on the other.[48]

How does a faithful church approach issues that threaten to divide? Traditionally, confessions of faith have provided boundaries or parameters within which the church did discernment. But is seems that something more is needed today. A four-layer template that might guide our discerning is scripture, Spirit, church, and context. God's love, mercy, and wisdom can flow as believers together look at issues through the lens of scripture, giving priority to the life and teachings of Jesus; through the guidance of

47. T. Schlabach, "The Past in Perspective," 66–75.
48. Ibid., 75.

God's Holy Spirit; by holding the issue(s) in light of the traditions and practices of the church; and by considering the context in which we live.

Chuck Neufeld, conference minister for Illinois Mennonite Conference, suggests four questions that should be asked of both sides that have a conflict within the church: "Is Jesus Christ Lord and Savior in your life and in your congregation? Is scripture authoritative for your life? Is the *Confession of Faith in a Mennonite Perspective* your foundation? Are you gathering as a people of faith to pray for and discern the Holy Spirit's guidance?" Neufeld believes that if both parties can answer yes to these questions, the way will become clear.[49]

In *Slavery, Sabbath, War and Women*, AMBS New Testament Professor Emeritus Willard Swartley suggests that

> the appropriate (God-intended) biblical word is more likely heard on controversial issues when:
>
> 1. The historical and cultural contexts of specific texts are considered seriously.
>
> 2. Diversity within Scripture is acknowledged, thus leading to a recognition that (a) intracanonical dialogue must be heard and assessed, and (b) the Gospels in their direct witness to Jesus are . . . taken as final authority.
>
> 3. The basic moral and theological principles of the entire Scripture are given priority over specific statements which stand in tension either with these principles or with other specific texts on the subject.
>
> Conversely stated, the appropriate (God-intended) biblical word is least likely heard when:
>
> 1. Numerous texts, occurring here and there through the Bible are sewn together into a patchwork quilt with disregard for the different cultural fabrics and historical textures of each patch.
>
> 2. The interpreter assumes a "flat view" of biblical authority; i.e., all texts are of equal significant to us and must be harmonized into one, rational, propositional truth.
>
> 3. Specific texts on a given subject are used legalistically—for example, 1 Timothy 6:1–6 on slavery—to silence the spirit of pervasive moral emphases, such as "Love your neighbor as yourself."[50]

The Bible is an authoritative guide, especially the teachings of Jesus where the love of God and neighbor is the foundation for right living. Christians may be sincere, faithful, and totally committed to following Jesus, but all humans make mistakes. The life of Jesus is an invitation for the church to err on the side of being inclusive. It may

49. Chuck Neufeld in table group conversation with Hartzler in Pittsburgh, July 2011.

50. Swartley, *Slavery, Sabbath, War and Women*, 23.

sound simplistic, but if the church includes brothers and sisters that God for some reason finds unacceptable, God will surely forgive us. However, if the church excludes those whom God has blessed, we haven't done a good job of representing the love of God to the world.

Although greater forces unite us than divide us, there are issues that divide or threaten to divide the Mennonite Church in the twenty-first century. The stories in this book suggest that different ways of understanding or interpreting the Bible are at the heart of most, if not all, divisions. The two most divisive issues in MC USA in 2012 are homosexuality and pacifism.

Homosexuality

Homosexuality is a concern in most churches, probably all but the most liberal and the most conservative. The issue may not get attention in some of the most conservative groups where there is agreement that people with a homosexual orientation do not belong in the church. It is not an issue in the most liberal congregations because gay and lesbian people are not singled out, but are treated with the same love and respect as others. All members are expected to behave lovingly, respectfully, and responsibly in all areas of their lives.

A young adult from Middlebury went to his Mennonite pastor. Although having roots in the Mennonite Church, Mike and his family had been attending a free evangelical church where most things were black and white and there was little tolerance for diversity in beliefs. Mike was concerned about his housemate, Bill.[51] They had been housemates for a few years and had become very good friends and regularly spent time with each other's families of origin. At a recent family event a member of Mike's family began talking about homosexuality. This family member had rigid beliefs about homosexuality and especially about any same gender sexual activity and made numerous judgmental comments. Others around the table joined in with similar derogatory comments as Mike and Bill became more and more uncomfortable. What nobody else at the table knew is that Bill is gay.

Mike and Bill became good friends and then housemates before Mike knew that Bill has a homosexual orientation. Mike is heterosexual, but loves Bill as a brother and was embarrassed by what his family member said in Bill's presence. Mike told his pastor, "I don't know how my family member who is a devout Christian can be so judgmental. It is so unlike Jesus!" Mike went on, "Furthermore this person takes literally the stuff about homosexuality in the Old Testament law but ignores lots of other stuff in the Hebrew law. And what really doesn't make sense, is how this same person supports US wars. Why does this person take the Old Testament literally and not the words of Jesus?"

51. Names have been changed to protect these two people from harassment.

The fact that young people are leaving the traditional church because of the intolerance of homosexuality on the part of conservative folk in the church is *not* in itself a reason to change the position of the church. It is, however, a reason to give attention to this issue.

Some people believe that it is sinful to experience any kind of sexual attraction to a person of the same gender. Others differentiate between a homosexual attraction and homosexual sexual/genital activity, understanding that while behavior can be controlled, heterosexual and homosexual people alike do not have control over their basic attractions. Some members of MC USA (and people in other denominations) are sure that one's sexual orientation is *not* chosen by the individual, but is part of God's creation. This group would hold the same standard of responsible moral behavior for homosexual and heterosexual people, believing that promiscuity is sinful whether heterosexual or homosexual. Intimate sexual/genital experiences are for covenanted relationships.

The Anabaptist way is to place an emphasis on the life and teachings of Jesus, especially the Sermon on the Mount. The Old Testament and the New Testament epistles are understood through the lens of Jesus' life and teachings. Doing a scriptural analysis of homosexuality is beyond the scope of this book. There are numerous books by Mennonite presses including Bible studies, personal stories, and dialog about homosexuality. Several are listed in appendix Q.

Many members of MC USA are engaged in prayer, dialog, and discernment regarding concerns related to homosexuality: from people in the pew to leaders at congregational, conference, and denominational levels; from heterosexual people to celibate people with a homosexual orientation to same-sex couples in committed monogamous relationships; from youth who don't understand why homosexuality is a big deal, to middle age and other people who think that accepting homosexuality is going too far, to maturing people who see a broad picture of God's revelation and love. Using the principles of "Agreeing and Disagreeing in Love," the conversations continue with the hope that the reign of God will continue to come to earth.[52]

Special sensitivity is needed to process questions about homosexuality. Forty years ago the issue got almost no attention in North America, and it continues to be an extremely difficult topic for people in many cultures where the Mennonite Church has spread. Issues related to sexuality often prompt an initial gut response, and it may take years until enough stories and experiences can move a person from a gut response to a head response, until the Holy Spirit might help to reopen and reevaluate a previously held understanding of scriptural interpretation.

Although homosexuality was rarely referenced and seldom discussed at Pleasant Oaks, one can imagine a trajectory of acceptance based on the pattern historically observed at WSMC/POMC and other GC congregations. WSMC/POMC was referred to as a "do as you please church" when it came to women cutting hair or not wearing

---

52. A document titled "Agreeing and Disagreeing in Love" is used in Mennonite Church USA and is available at http://mennoniteusa.org/resources/agreeing-and-disagreeing-in-love.

a specific prayer veiling, or when couples could marry even though one or both had been previously married and divorced. Most of the practices that were at one time thought to be out of line by more conservative folk, at a later time became common practice among those who earlier thought they were holding to something essential.

Is this a slippery slope? Will the church continue to accept more and more behaviors and practices once thought to be sinful? Some have feared that would happen. And to some extent it has. A question asked in 1923 is a question still asked in 2012: What are the essentials for faithful Christian living?

Nonresistance, Pacifism, the Gospel of Peace

The traditional Anabaptist peace position is an issue in some Mennonite congregations where secular culture (and "God and Country" religiosity) has eroded the foundation of the unconditional love of God and allegiance to Jesus Christ. Beginning in the 1500s, Anabaptists understood the love commandments of Jesus to clarify that hate of enemy and killing are against the will of God. The teaching of Jesus, especially the Sermon on the Mount, is the foundation for the peace position that includes love of enemy, nonresistance, and nonviolence. Today many Mennonites talk about the "gospel of peace" rather than nonresistance or pacifism. Of course this is not a new concept. In his *Manual of Bible Doctrines* published in 1898, Daniel Kauffman made clear that the gospel of peace was an inextricable part of the gospel.

For nearly 400 years this position was taught and adhered to by almost all Anabaptist groups. One of the primary reasons for European immigrants to come to North America was to escape military service. On numerous occasions, Anabaptists fled to places where there were promises of exemption from military service, only to be eventually disappointed when promises were retracted. In the United States, many Mennonite and Amish men found various ways to avoid participating in the Civil War, but others enlisted. Some of these stories are told in Theron Schlabach's *Peace, Faith, Nation*.

There was a noteworthy change in the peace position among some Mennonites in the early 1900s when certain groups began to show less resistance to US military operations. Schlabach identifies a beginning shift in articles published in John Funk's *Herald* as the nineteenth century neared its end. There are fewer articles written by pacifists and more by "Evangelical Christians" who were not pacifists. It seems that Mennonites who had been "quickened" by spiritual revival were at risk of losing the Anabaptist concept that peace is at the very heart of the gospel.[53]

Schlabach observes that from early in the existence of the General Conference Mennonite Church, there was not absolute clarity about participation in war. In the first two chapters of *From Nonresistance to Justice: The Transformation of Mennonite Church Peace Rhetoric 1908–2008*, Ervin Stutzman provides excellent historical

---

53. T. Schlabach, *Gospel Versus Gospel*, 50.

summaries of GC and MC (and MC USA in 2002–2008) peace theology and practice. Early in the twentieth century some Mennonites embraced national political progressivism by accepting patterns of thought outside the traditional Anabaptist teaching.[54] People who grew up in the "old" Mennonite Church in the last half of the twentieth century may have difficulty grasping how this developed. Some observations follow.

Samuel (S. K.) Mosiman (1867–1940), president of Bluffton College (now University) for twenty-five years (1910–1935), had significant influence on more than a generation of students, some of whom became pastors and other leaders in the GC Mennonite Church. Compared with conservative traditionalists in northern Indiana, Mennonite progressives associated with Bluffton College did not resist acculturation, but welcomed and accepted outside innovations such as higher education. Bluffton educators and scholars tended to adopt mainstream intellectual and cultural life during Mosiman's presidency. Bluffton historian and author Perry Bush describes Blufftonites marching "to the beat of the reform-oriented national progressivism that dominated American culture and politics in the first two decades of the twentieth century."[55]

In addition to faculty statements and writings, periodically outside speakers promoted disconcerting attitudes. "One chapel guest lectured in 1918, for example, on the beneficence of California's anti-alien land laws that upheld Japanese exclusion. Another the next year advocated isolating foreigners from the 'pure blood of civilization.'"[56]

Bush summarizes his comments by saying that "in electing to embark on the cultural-political current of progressivism, the college would come to some strange and questionable positions." In 1913 campus chapters of the YMCA and YWCA began at Bluffton. While these seem to increase the devotional activities of students, the Y organizations also connected Bluffton students with "thousands of students across the country, combining warm Christian devotion and missions fervor with a heady American nationalism . . . During World War I the Ys would also work to funnel prowar sentiment onto campus."[57]

When the United States entered the Great War in 1917, there was a vicious offensive against anyone in the country who appeared to not support the war. Most of the Mennonites at Bluffton (and other places in North America) descended from a Germanic-derived religious group whose theology was rooted in pacifism, making them doubly suspect of not supporting the war effort. Some Mennonites were victims of violence, imprisonment, and church-burning.

How were church leaders to advise the young men of draft age during World War I when there was not an alternative service option? Some advised noncombatant service, and others encouraged young men to stick with Mennonite teaching and "stay firm in rejection of all military service and orders. Draftees who accepted this advice

54. T. Schlabach, *Peace, Faith Nation*, 137.

55. Bush, *Kobzar*, 67. More information about S. K. Mosiman is in chapter 3, pages 79 to 81.

56. Ibid., 68.

57. Ibid., 69, 76–77.

found themselves paying a high price. Isolated in army camps, they were raked raw with brooms, beaten with fists, and court-martialed to lengthy prison terms when they disobeyed directives from officers."[58]

Although there was mob action against pacifists in the area around Bluffton, the college largely escaped danger, likely because "it mostly rang with War enthusiasm."[59] Bush explains further that:

> Mosiman defended traditional Mennonite pacifist principles where he thought they applied. He was proud that by May 1917, at least, no Bluffton College man, Mennonite or not, had enlisted for regular combatant service. . . . On the other hand, believing his nation's effort "the cause of righteousness and justice," Mosiman threw himself and the college . . . behind the war in every way short of contributing to actual combat. . . . The college would join the president's fight for "Christianized democracy" with only a slight and qualified nod to Mennonite peace principles. "I have consistently urged our boys to be patriotic, and have told them that every citizen owed his country some service in war-time," he assured an assistant secretary of war in Washington. . . . He likewise extended this kind of advice to a wholesale embrace of noncombatant activities at home, enthusiastically backing the extensive Red Cross activities and war bond sales at the college.[60]

In a sociological study of Mennonites published in 1975, Kauffman and Harder indicate that of the 507 respondents from the GC denomination, 66 percent agreed that "The Christian should take no part in war or any war-promoting activities." Of the 1084 "old" Mennonite respondents, 87 percent agreed that participation in war and war activities was wrong for Christians.[61] Although there have clearly been some strong pacifists among GC Mennonites, Delbert Gratz acknowledges that a firm stand for the peace position was not popular in the mid-twentieth century. One fine exception was Lloyd Ramseyer who, during his presidency at Bluffton College (1938–1965), was a courageous advocate of truth, forthrightness, and practicality in all of life and a strong supporter of the Mennonite peace position.[62] Perhaps the influence of Ramseyer helped to bring some change in the following statistics of MC USA Mennonites attitudes about participation in war.[63]

---

58. Ibid., 84.

59. Ibid.

60. Ibid., 84–85.

61. Kauffman and Harder, *Anabaptists*, 133. See chapter 5 for more information about military service for members of Warren Street Mennonite Church and other General Conference Mennonites.

62. Gratz, Delbert. "Ramseyer."

63. Statistics of the two groups (MC and GC) before the 2002 merger were not accessed. In addition, since there are far fewer former GCs than former MCs in the new denomination, these figures may not indicate a significant change of beliefs about participation in war.

Mennonite sociologist and minister Conrad Kanagy summarizes his 2006 sociological survey of MC USA members in *Road Signs for the Journey*. He reports that 85 percent of respondents indicate that "complete nonviolence as a way of living is very important to me," and 93 percent of respondents agreed that "peacemaking is a central theme of the gospel." However, at the same time, 21 percent would choose regular or noncombatant service, and 10 percent were unsure of what they would do.

Thanks be to God, there is renewed interest among many Mennonites to clarify and vigorously teach the traditional Anabaptist peace position. Central District Conference (CDC), a former GC area conference, has supported a pledge through a resolution at their annual meeting in June 2012: "A Congregational Peace Pledge: A call to intentionally encounter the realities of war." Speaking for the resolutions committee, pastor David Moser said, "This resolution is an invitation to reflect deeply on the society in which we live." It invites congregations to commit themselves to actions such as the following: (1) Send members to conflict zones with Christian Peacemaker Teams, Witness for Peace, Fellowship of Reconciliation, Mennonite Central Committee, Mennonite Mission Network, or other organizations dedicated to providing a nonviolent presence nationally or internationally; (2) Sponsor events that ask youth to question participation in war; and (3) Bring speakers to congregations who have worked at peace building with victims of war, are former combatants, or are persons who did alternative service during a previous war.[64]

In addition, the CDC provides information about and resources to respond to military recruitment for young people, helping them prepare informed responses when contacted by recruiters and also to be prepared should a draft be reinstated. The most vulnerable youth are those in communities with low economies. When life options are limited, youth become more vulnerable to military recruiters. The church is also encouraged to take responsibility to provide information and alternative options to the youth in our communities beyond our church walls.[65]

The Anabaptist understanding of peace is a gift that Mennonites in 2012 have inherited from their spiritual ancestors. It is a precious gift and a gift to share with people around the world, people from other faiths, other Christian denominations, as well as other Mennonites who have not yet recognized that peace is at the heart of the gospel of Jesus Christ.

BOUNDARY LINES IN PLEASANT PLACES: IMAGINING A MORE FAITHFUL FUTURE

We are at a crucial time in the history of the church. For the past two decades mainline churches in the United States have experienced a mass exodus, and Mennonite

64. The complete resolution is in appendix R and at the conference website: http://centraldistrict. mennonite.net.

65. http://centraldistrict.mennonite.net/Resources/Alternative_to_Military_Recruitment.

churches have seen similar patterns. Mega churches grew rapidly, and now some are also declining. Many young people and some older ones are cynical about the organized church.

This pattern is the beginning of what church observer Phyllis Tickle calls "the Great Emergence," an event in history with parallels in the Reformation in the sixteenth century, and the Great Schism in the eleventh century. She points to a major change or upheaval every 500 years, with Gregory the Great holding the church together largely through the development of the monastic system in the sixth century; and of course the coming of God in Jesus and the establishing of the church in the first century.[66] In her 2008 book, Tickle says Christians should not fear the massive changes that are sweeping through the church, but seek to understand and identify where to fit into the great thing that is happening. She says, "Always without fail, the thing that gets lost early in the process of a reconfiguration is any clear and general understanding of who or what is to be used as the arbitrator of correct belief, action, and control." Until that question is answered, Tickle expects people will stumble and fall and the "empowered structures of institutionalized Christianity" will be shattered so that renewal can again occur in the church. From looking at history, Tickle has hope that a new more vital form of Christianity will emerge again as it always has when reconfigurations occurred in the past.[67]

Mennonites are a people who have been inspired by and received hope from prophetic imagination. As Christians in the Anabaptist tradition, it seems good and right to continue imaginative visioning of God's work in the world, and as followers of Jesus to enter into that work as individuals and especially as communities. Hope is expressed in Isaiah 11:6: "The wolf shall live with the lamb, the leopard shall lie down with the kid, the calf and the lion and the fatling together, and a little child shall lead them." David Boshart calls the church to partner with God, and to be "united as a faithful and obedient church" so that we can "move toward the world's brokenness to announce that redemption, forgiveness, and reconciliation are possible."[68]

In the first few decades of the twentieth century, Mennonites were caught between two religious streams—fundamentalism and liberalism. Historical theologian Karl Koop explains how Harold Bender's Anabaptist vision illuminated a third way for Mennonites, a way that focused on the New Testament Church that was the model for the sixteenth century Anabaptists. An Anabaptist identity and vision is shaped by scripture, which offers information, and is "a fundamental source of inspiration,

66. Tickle, *The Great Emergence*. Phyllis Tickle is founding editor of the Religion Department of Publishers Weekly. A lay Eucharist minister in the Episcopal Church, she is the author of more than twenty-four books and one of the most respected authorities and popular speakers on religion in the US today.

67. Tickle, *The Great Emergence*, 45.

68. Boshart, "Becoming a United Church."

imagination and courage. . . . Examining our tradition is an opportunity to join in a conversation about the essentials and nonessentials of the faith."[69]

Believing, belonging, and behaving are a triplet of terms that have been used by theological theorists and teachers for several years to describe relationships within religious communities. Two common positions have been identified: "believing without belonging" and "belonging before believing." The first describes people who don't belong to a church but identify themselves as Christians, believing similar concepts to those who do belong. The second position describes those who participate in church before identifying themselves as Christians or decide what they believe.[70] Our traditional Mennonite churches have tended to expect that believing and behaving are necessary before one can belong.

In an article in *Canadian Mennonite*, Henry Neufeld suggests a different order of making disciples than has typically been practiced by most churches. We have wanted people to believe in Jesus, then to behave in a Christ-like way, then to join the church and belong. Believe, behave, and belong. But Neufeld says that is backwards, like a "formula for selling heavenly insurance."[71] Instead,

> it should be belong, behave and believe, because that's Jesus example. When Jesus called his disciples, he did not give them a test about their beliefs, about their theology, about their faith. He didn't ask them if they believed the Ten Commandments and the Mosaic Law. He simply said, "Follow me." We would say, "Hang out with me for a while. Join up with me. Watch what I do."

British theologian and author Stuart Murray adds to the discussion. He says that the church today

> dare not ignore "behaving." In a skeptical culture, faith must be lived if it is to be believed. In a culture moving away from both residual Christian values and distorted Christendom patterns, churches have new opportunities and responsibilities to incarnate the gospel authentically. This does not mean legalism or moralism . . . but countercultural churches that live out the attractive but provocative implications of the story they proclaim. . . . Believing, belonging and behaving are not separate stages but different dimensions of the journey on which all followers of Jesus are pilgrims.[72]

Growth in one dimension leads to growth in the others. Belonging has an effect on belief and behavior. Believing leads to changes in behavior and deepens bonds of belonging. Behaving increases identity with a community and strengthens belief.

69. Koop, "Requisite Conditions," 19–21.

70. Murray, *Church after Christendom*, http://www.anabaptistnetwork.com/node/260.

71. Henry Neufeld, "Believe Behave Belong," *Canadian Mennonite*, Volume 13, No. 9, Apr. 27, 2009.

72. http://www.anabaptistnetwork.com/node/260.

Thriving churches of the twenty-first century are communities where belonging, believing, and behaving are in process simultaneously rather linear steps on a journey.[73]

Although the Anabaptist commitment to peacemaking and reconciliation stretches back almost five hundred years, the history is tarnished with the reality of inner conflicts and outer divisions. Many have involved pain. Where is the hope of blending the goodness of each of these traditions—the "old" Mennonite and the General Conference Mennonite traditions? Perhaps the hope lies in the same place wherein lies the challenge—agreeing and disagreeing in love! Instead of thinking about boundaries that are pleasant (Psalm 16) or even those boundaries that make us squirm, we can focus on the center. Jesus is at the center of faith and life for the Christian. Following Jesus in daily life has been an Anabaptist theme from the beginning.

Mennonites have a delightful heritage: the New Testament church reestablished 500 years ago, with a history of peacemaking for these five centuries and a history of courage to stand for nonviolence—the only reasonable and effective way to respond to violence in the world today. "Following Jesus" is the theme for Christian discipleship. Discipleship is living out the ways of Jesus in daily life, lives lived out and tested in community, where individualism takes a back seat to what is best for the community. Community is people gathered in the name of Jesus for the purpose of bringing glory to God and helping to bring about the reign of God on earth as it is in heaven as Jesus instructed his followers to pray.

How is the Mennonite Church moving forward? As believing communities, large and small, members discern together what, in God's gracious purpose under the lordship of Jesus Christ and by the power of the Holy Spirit, they can be and do while participating with God in bringing about God's reign. May the Church of Jesus Christ, and specifically the Mennonite Church, continue to live and reflect the essence of God—which is love, known most fully through the life and teachings of Jesus. Where communities of believers keep Jesus at the center of their faith and worship, God's Spirit will draw people in, and the boundaries will naturally fall in sometimes unrecognizable but pleasant places.

73. Ibid.

Appendix A

The Emergence of Anabaptism

John D. Rempel

RADICAL REFORM WAS IN the air in German-speaking Europe in the early 1520s. The most famous instance of reform for Anabaptism occurred in Zurich. Ulrich Zwingli (1484–1531) led the official Reformation. It was Zwingli's intention to create a truly Christian social order to be implemented by the city council. Conrad Grebel (1498–1526) and Felix Mantz (1498–1527) were the best known of Zwingli's radical followers. From the New Testament they had re-discovered the baptism of believers and sought a church based on a personal profession of faith in Christ. From their reading of the gospels they had seen in the teachings of Jesus, especially the Sermon on the Mount, a new light. They became convinced that the love of enemies belonged to the heart of the Gospel. After much soul-searching and debate, the Radicals baptized one another into a church of believers.

The term "Anabaptist" literally means "re-baptizers." It was first used by opponents of the movement as an uncomplimentary term for those who baptized believers rather than baptizing infants as the church and state required.

The beginning of the radical reformation in Zurich is merely the best known of a host of far-reaching dissent across much of Europe. Some forms of dissent were biblical and pacifist, like the community in Zurich, while others turned in an apocalyptic direction and in some occasions resorted to violence.

In South Germany it was mystics who were first attracted to the radical vision. Persecution was immediate, and many of the new believers dispersed across Europe as missionaries and refugees. One of these was Hans Hut (d. 1527) who included community of goods in his vision of the church. With many of the other missionaries, he took refuge in Moravia (today part of the Czech Republic) where radical groups were tolerated by local rulers. In the ferment, communal as well as non-communal forms of Anabaptism quickly arose. Jakob Hutter (d. 1536), after whom the Hutterites are named, was the first leader of communal Anabaptism. Thriving communities emerged during toleration and later weathered the storms of persecution.

New expressions of the Anabaptist spirit emerged in German-speaking territories, stretching east to Moravia and west to Strasbourg (on the German-French border today). One of them was a peaceful form that arose primarily in cities. It was the least separatist of the Anabaptist experiments. Its most significant leader was Pilgram Marpeck (1495–1556).

Melchior Hoffmann won radicals emerging in the Netherlands and bordering states to the Anabaptist cause. Using the books of Daniel and Revelation he developed a teaching that God would call politicians and 'true' believers to bring in the kingdom of God. A peaceful version of this vision developed in Strasbourg, led by prophets, of whom Ursula Jost was the most prolific writer and one of the few Anabaptist female public leaders. Militant versions developed in Amsterdam and Münster (1534–35). In Münster the leaders, in a bitter irony, resorted to brutal violence to bring about their vision. This experiment in utopianism was brutally exterminated and left Anabaptism with a notorious reputation.

Menno Simons (1496–1561, who left his post as Catholic priest in Witmarsum in 1536) had increasingly been convinced that a pacifist believers church faithfully expressed the apostolic pattern. But it took the disarray of the movement following the events at Amsterdam and Münster for him to emerge as a leader, as the keeper of the peaceful vision. Menno and his wife, Gertrude, undertook a traveling ministry to groups of persecuted believers, building them up into disciplined pacifist communities. Menno's works are the most published of any Anabaptist leader. His followers were first called Mennists, then Mennonists, and eventually Mennonites. This name was gradually applied to most of the descendent movements of Anabaptists other than Hutterites, although some groups retained the name "Baptism-minded Christians."[1]

1. Used with permission from John D. Rempel; sent to Hartzler via email April 7, 2012.

Appendix B

Dordrecht Confession of Faith

Adopted April 21, 1632, by a Dutch Mennonite Conference held at Dordrecht, Holland

ARTICLE XVI. OF THE ECCLESIASTICAL BAN, OR SEPARATION FROM THE CHURCH

WE ALSO BELIEVE IN, and confess, a ban, Separation, and Christian correction in the church, for amendment, and not for destruction, in order to distinguish that which is pure from the impure: namely, when any one, after he is enlightened, has accepted the knowledge of the truth, and been incorporated into the communion of the saints, sins again unto death, either through willfulness, or through presumption against God, or through some other cause, and falls into the unfruitful works of darkness, thereby becoming separated from God, and forfeiting the kingdom of God, that such a one, after the deed is manifest and sufficiently known to the church, may not remain in the congregation of the righteous, but, as an offensive member and open sinner, shall and must be separated, put away, reproved before all, and purged out as leaven; and this for his amendment, as an example, that others may fear, and to keep the church pure, by cleansing her from such spots, lest, in default of this, the name of the Lord be blasphemed, the church dishonored, and offense given to them that are without; and finally, that the sinner may not be condemned with the world, but become convinced in his mind, and be moved to sorrow, repentance, and reformation. Jeremiah 59:2; 1 Corinthians 5:5, 13; 1 Timothy 5:20; 1 Corinthians 5:6; 2 Corinthians 10:8; 1 Corinthians 13:10.

Further, concerning brotherly reproof or admonition, as also the instruction of the erring it is necessary to exercise all diligence and care, to watch over them and to admonish them with all meekness, that they may be bettered, and to reprove, according as is proper, the stubborn who remain obdurate; in short, the church must put away from her the wicked (either in doctrine or life), and no other. James 5:19; Titus 3:10; 1 Corinthians 5:13.

ARTICLE XVII. OF SHUNNING THE SEPARATED

Concerning the withdrawing from, or shunning the separated, we believe and confess, that if any one, either through his wicked life or perverted doctrine, has so far fallen that he is separated from God, and, consequently, also separated and punished by the church, the same must, according to the doctrine of Christ and His apostles, be shunned, without distinction, by all the fellow members of the church, especially those to whom it is known, in eating, drinking, and other similar intercourse, and no company be had with him that they may not become contaminated by intercourse with him, nor made partakers of his sins; but that the sinner may be made ashamed, pricked in his heart, and convicted in his conscience, unto his reformation. 1 Corinthians 5:9–11; 2 Thessalonians 3:14.

Yet, in shunning as well as in reproving, such moderation and Christian discretion must be used, that it may conduce, not to the destruction, but to the reformation of the sinner. For, if he is needy, hungry, thirsty, naked, sick, or in any other distress, we are in duty bound, necessity requiring it, according to love and the doctrine of Christ and His apostles, to render him aid and assistance; otherwise, shunning would in this case tend more to destruction than to reformation.

Therefore, we must not count them as enemies, but admonish them as brethren, that thereby they may be brought to a knowledge of and to repentance and sorrow for their sins, so that they may become reconciled to God, and consequently be received again into the church, and that love may continue with them, according as is proper. 2 Thessalonians 3:15.[1]

---

1. http://www.gameo.org/encyclopedia/contents/D674.html#XVI; http://www.gameo.org/ency-clopedia/contents/D674.html#Commentary

Appendix C

Statement of Doctrine

Presented to the General Conference Mennonite Church at its twenty-ninth session held in Souderton, Pennsylvania, August 17–22, 1941

ACCEPTING THE FULL BIBLE AND the Apostolic Creed:

1. We believe in one God, eternally existing and manifest as Father, Son, and Holy Spirit.

2. We believe in the deity of Jesus Christ, the only begotten of the Father, full of grace and truth, born of the Virgin Mary, in His perfect humanity, His atoning death, His bodily resurrection from the dead, and His personal triumphant return.

3. We believe in the immortality of the soul, the resurrection of the dead, and a future state determined by divine judgment.

4. We believe in the divine inspiration and the infallibility of the Bible as the Word of God and the only trustworthy guide of faith and life.

5. We believe a Christian is one saved by grace, whose life is transformed into the likeness of Christ by His atoning death and the power of His resurrection.

6. We believe that Christ lived and taught the way of life as recorded in the Scriptures, which is God's plan for individuals and the race; and that it becomes disciples of Christ to live in this way, thus manifesting in their personal and social life and relationship the love and holiness of God. And we believe that this way of life also implies nonresistance to evil by carnal means, the fullest exercise of love, and the resolute abandonment of the use of violence, including warfare. We believe further that the Christian life will of necessity express itself in nonconformity to the world in life and conduct.

7. We believe in prayer as fellowship with God, a desire to be in His will and in its divine power.

8. We believe that the Christian Church consists of believers who have repented from their sins, have accepted Christ by faith and are born again, and sincerely endeavor by the grace of God to live the Christian life.

9. We believe in the brotherhood of the redeemed under the fatherhood of God in Christ.[1]

1. General Conference Mennonite Church, "Statement of Doctrine (1941)."

Appendix D

Confession of Faith in a Mennonite Perspective, 1995 Summary Statements

1. We believe that God exists and is pleased with all who draw near by faith. We worship the one holy and loving God who is Father, Son, and Holy Spirit eternally. God has created all things visible and invisible, has brought salvation and new life to humanity through Jesus Christ, and continues to sustain the church and all things until the end of the age.

2. We believe in Jesus Christ, the Word of God become flesh. He is the Savior of the world, who has delivered us from the dominion of sin and reconciled us to God by his death on a cross. He was declared to be Son of God by his resurrection from the dead. He is the head of the church, the exalted Lord, the Lamb who was slain, coming again to reign with God in glory.

3. We believe in the Holy Spirit, the eternal Spirit of God, who dwelled in Jesus Christ, who empowers the church, who is the source of our life in Christ, and who is poured out on those who believe as the guarantee of redemption.

4. We believe that all Scripture is inspired by God through the Holy Spirit for instruction in salvation and training in righteousness. We accept the Scriptures as the Word of God and as the fully reliable and trustworthy standard for Christian faith and life. Led by the Holy Spirit in the church, we interpret Scripture in harmony with Jesus Christ.

5. We believe that God has created the heavens and the earth and all that is in them, and that God preserves and renews what has been made. All creation has its source outside itself and belongs to the Creator. The world has been created good because God is good and provides all that is needed for life.

6. We believe that God has created human beings in the divine image. God formed them from the dust of the earth and gave them a special dignity among all the works of creation. Human beings have been made for relationship with God, to live in peace with each other, and to take care of the rest of creation.

7. We confess that, beginning with Adam and Eve, humanity has disobeyed God, given way to the tempter, and chosen to sin. All have fallen short of the Creator's intent, marred the image of God in which they were created, disrupted order in the world, and limited their love for others. Because of sin, humanity has been given over to the enslaving powers of evil and death.

8. We believe that, through Jesus Christ, God offers salvation from sin and a new way of life. We receive God's salvation when we repent and accept Jesus Christ as Savior and Lord. In Christ, we are reconciled with God and brought into the reconciling community. We place our faith in God that, by the same power that raised Christ from the dead, we may be saved from sin to follow Christ and to know the fullness of salvation.

9. We believe that the church is the assembly of those who have accepted God's offer of salvation through faith in Jesus Christ. It is the new community of disciples sent into the world to proclaim the reign of God and to provide a foretaste of the church's glorious hope. It is the new society established and sustained by the Holy Spirit.

10. We believe that the mission of the church is to proclaim and to be a sign of the kingdom of God. Christ has commissioned the church to make disciples of all nations, baptizing them, and teaching them to observe all things he has commanded.

11. We believe that the baptism of believers with water is a sign of their cleansing from sin. Baptism is also a pledge before the church of their covenant with God to walk in the way of Jesus Christ through the power of the Holy Spirit. Believers are baptized into Christ and his body by the Spirit, water, and blood.

12. We believe that the Lord's Supper is a sign by which the church thankfully remembers the new covenant which Jesus established by his death. In this communion meal, the church renews its covenant with God and with each other and participates in the life and death of Jesus Christ, until he comes.

13. We believe that in washing the feet of his disciples, Jesus calls us to serve one another in love as he did. Thus we acknowledge our frequent need of cleansing, renew our willingness to let go of pride and worldly power, and offer our lives in humble service and sacrificial love.

14. We practice discipline in the church as a sign of God's offer of transforming grace. Discipline is intended to liberate erring brothers and sisters from sin, and to restore them to a right relationship with God and to fellowship in the church. The practice of discipline gives integrity to the church's witness in the world.

15. We believe that ministry is a continuation of the work of Christ, who gives gifts through the Holy Spirit to all believers and empowers them for service in the church and in the world. We also believe that God calls particular persons in the church to specific leadership ministries and offices. All who minister are accountable to God and to the community of faith.

16. We believe that the church of Jesus Christ is one body with many members, ordered in such a way that, through the one Spirit, believers may be built together spiritually into a dwelling place for God.

17. We believe that Jesus Christ calls us to discipleship, to take up our cross and follow him. Through the gift of God's saving grace, we are empowered to be disciples of Jesus, filled with his Spirit, following his teachings and his path through suffering to new life. As we are faithful to his way, we become conformed to Christ and separated from the evil in the world.

18. We believe that to be a disciple of Jesus is to know life in the Spirit. As the life, death, and resurrection of Jesus Christ takes shape in us, we grow in the image of Christ and in our relationship with God. The Holy Spirit is active in individual and in communal worship, leading us deeper into the experience of God.

19. We believe that God intends human life to begin in families and to be blessed through families. Even more, God desires all people to become part of the church, God's family. As single and married members of the church family give and receive nurture and healing, families can grow toward the wholeness that God intends. We are called to chastity and to loving faithfulness in marriage.

20. We commit ourselves to tell the truth, to give a simple yes or no, and to avoid the swearing of oaths.

21. We believe that everything belongs to God, who calls the church to live in faithful stewardship of all that God has entrusted to us, and to participate now in the rest and justice which God has promised.

22. We believe that peace is the will of God. God created the world in peace, and God's peace is most fully revealed in Jesus Christ, who is our peace and the peace of the whole world. Led by the Holy Spirit, we follow Christ in the way of peace, doing justice, bringing reconciliation, and practicing nonresistance, even in the face of violence and warfare.

23. We believe that the church is God's holy nation, called to give full allegiance to Christ its head and to witness to every nation, government, and society about God's saving love.

24. We place our hope in the reign of God and its fulfillment in the day when Christ will come again in glory to judge the living and the dead. He will gather his church, which is already living under the reign of God. We await God's final

victory, the end of this present age of struggle, the resurrection of the dead, and a new heaven and a new earth. There the people of God will reign with Christ in justice, righteousness, and peace for ever and ever.[1]

1. *Confession of Faith in a Mennonite Perspective,* 93–98.

Appendix E

Discipline in the Church

Commentary for Article 14 from Confession of Faith in a Mennonite Perspective[1]

1. Anabaptists and Mennonites in sixteenth-century Europe saw discipline as vital for pastoral care and for the well-being of the church. Indeed, they considered discipline to be as important for church renewal as believers baptism and participation in the Lord's Supper. Mennonites have traditionally emphasized church discipline. Discipline has sometimes been neglected in many Mennonite congregations, in part because of some misuses, in part because of cultural and social influences. Both the misuse and the neglect of discipline undermine the church's life and witness. Both misuse and neglect work against the important correcting, renewing, and redemptive purposes of church discipline in pastoral care, nurture, and congregational life.

2. In some church traditions, responsibility for church discipline has been limited to particular ministerial offices, such as pastor or bishop. From a Mennonite perspective, discipline is related, first of all, to the mutual care of members for one another. According to the rule of Christ (Matthew 18:15–18), all believers are to offer mutual encouragement, correction, and forgiveness to each other. For that reason, it is good to include a promise to give and receive counsel when persons are received into church membership. Pastors and other church leaders have a special responsibility to give guidance and to carry out discipline in the life of the church (Acts 20:28–31; Titus 1:5–11; 1 Peter 5:1–4; Hebrews 13:17). They are to exercise their responsibility lovingly, in gentleness of spirit, and without partiality.

1. *Confession of Faith in a Mennonite Perspective* (Scottdale, PA: Herald Press, 1995), 56–58 and http://www.mennolink.org/doc/cof.

3. Pastors and other church leaders who move away from faithful discipleship or are overtaken by sin are not exempt from discipline in the church. Because of their representative ministries, their teaching and conduct can greatly help or hurt members of the church and the church's witness in the world. They are therefore accountable to the congregation which they serve and to the broader church. Pastors, teachers, and other church leaders may sometimes be victims of gossip and unjust accusations. Allegations against them should be tested carefully (1 Timothy 5:19). Not only do the failures of ministerial leaders damage the church's life and witness; unfounded accusations against them also do injury to them and the church.

4. The New Testament gives several reasons for suspending fellowship or for excommunication: denying that Jesus Christ has come in the flesh, persisting in sinful conduct without repentance, and causing divisions in the church by opposing apostolic teaching (for example, 1 John 4:1–6; 1 Corinthians 5:1–13; Romans 16:17–18).

5. For more discussion related to church discipline, see also "Discipleship and the Christian Life" (Article 17) and "Christian Spirituality" (Article 18).

Appendix F

Peace, Justice, and Nonresistance

Commentary for Article 22 from Confession of Faith in a Mennonite Perspective[1]

1. The biblical concept of peace embraces personal peace with God, peace in human relations, peace among nations, and peace with God's creation. The Old Testament word for peace (shalom) includes healing, reconciliation, and well-being. Peace is more than the absence of war; it includes the restoration of right relationship.

   Justice and peace belong together, since right relationship involves both. According to Greek and Roman ideas of justice, people should get what they deserve. According to the Bible, justice involves healing and restoring relationships. That is a reason for the special concern for the poor and the oppressed evident in the Bible (Deuteronomy 24:10–22; Matthew 20:1–16; James 2:5).

   Nonresistance means "not resisting." Our example is Jesus, who endured accusation and abuse without retaliating. Jesus did sometimes confront wrongdoers (Matthew 23:1–36; John 2:13–22), but he did so in a nonviolent way that shows us how to overcome evil with good (Romans 12:21; see 1 Peter 2:21–24).

2. Peace and justice are not optional teachings, counsel that Christians can take or leave. They belong to the heart of gospel message. Sometimes the Mennonite peace position has been based only on the teachings of Jesus. A biblical understanding of peace is also based on the atoning sacrifice of Christ: the atonement is the foundation for our peace with God (Romans 5:10) and with one another (Ephesians 2:13–16).

   Similarly, justice is based not only on Jesus' teachings (Luke 4:18–19), but also on his atoning death. Jesus' death on the cross accomplished justice. His

---

1. *Confession of Faith in a Mennonite Perspective*, 82–84 and www.mennolink.org/doc/cof.

crucifixion brought forgiveness and thus restored sinners to right relationship with God. On the cross Jesus cried out to God on behalf of a world mired in sinful, unjust relationships. This cry was amplified by the shedding of his blood, which creates a just, forgiving community of the new covenant (Hebrews 5:7–10).

3. In continuity with previous Mennonite confessions of faith, we affirm that non-participation in warfare involves conscientious objection to military service and a nonresistant response to violence. Our peace witness also includes peacemaking and working for justice. Peace witness is needed even when the nations in which we live are not at war. Ministries of mediation, conciliation, and nonviolent resolution of everyday conflict can express our commitment to Christ's way of peace.

4. There is no simple explanation for the practice of war in the Old Testament. The Old Testament repeatedly points toward peace (Exodus 14:13–14; Judges 7:2; Ps. 37; Isaiah 31; Hosea 2:18). Both the Old and New Testaments proclaim the vision of a coming peaceable kingdom (Isaiah 9:1–7), preached and revealed by Jesus Christ (Acts 10:36).

Appendix G

Joseph Stuckey

(June 12, 1826–February 5, 1902)
Monologue written by Rich Bucher[1]

GUTEN MORGEN. (GOOD MORNING.) I'm "Choseph" (Joseph) Stuckey. I've heard that some of you remember me—or at least some stories about me. I've even heard that your conference today still bears the touch of my convictions. Ach, my Barbara would be surprised!

Vell, let me tell you! I have lived a full and exciting life. I have seen many things in my life-time. I find it amazing that I have spent most of my life in Illinois. Did you know that my grandparents lived in Bern, Switzerland, along with many other Amish and Mennonite families that later moved to America? But then my parents fled to the Alsace-Lorraine area of France because of persecution, so I grew up speaking French.

I was born in 1826 and when I was five years old my parents decided to come to America. When we got on the ship to cross the Atlantic Ocean there were lots of Amish boys and girls on the ship. So I learned German from them as we played together. Ach, what a long boat ride! We got to a place called New Orleans and then sailed up the Mississippi River and the Ohio River to Butler County near Dayton, Ohio.

I never had the chance to go to school, but my mother and father taught me to read German. I was baptized and joined the church when I was seventeen, and then I got married the next year to Barbara Roth. In 1850 I got what you call "itchy feet." I wanted to move out west. So Barbara and I and our two children got on a boat and traveled down the Ohio River to the Mississippi and then the Illinois River and came

1. Monologue written by Rich Bucher, Pastor of North Danvers Mennonite Church. Used with permission from Rich who wrote, "History is to be told and retold. I think that Joseph Stuckey would feel honored to have his story told, and I count it a privilege to have been able to tell part of his story." Email to Hartzler, October 25, 2010. Recited by Mick Sommers at the annual meeting of Central District Conference in Bluffton, Ohio, on June 25, 2010. Information was gathered from Weaver, *History of the Central Conference Mennonite Church*; Estes, *A Goodly Heritage: A History of the North Danvers Mennonite Church*; and Pannabecker, *Faith in Ferment: A History of the Central District Conference.*

to Peoria, where I worked in a meat packing plant to make us some money. Then in March of 1851 we made the big move to Danvers Township where I started farming. I loved the earth, the good soil. I enjoyed farming. I was a good farmer and did well. People often came to me for advice about money.

The world was changing fast. I knew that I needed to learn to read English. I could speak English, but not read it. I remember one day in 1856 I went to Bloomington and bought an English newspaper. I decided that I was going to learn to read English. And I did! Barbara thought I was *verecht*—excuse me, she thought I was crazy. I really enjoyed reading and studying my Bible. The ministers in the congregation were getting older, and so they voted me in as a minister in 1860. Being ordained really made me want to dig into the scriptures. I always carried a Bible with me. Barbara used to get so upset with me because I was always losing my Bible when I was plowing! I wonder if any of you Illinois farmers ever found my New Testament in the ground.

Soon after I became a minister the Civil War began. That was not a good time. Some of our young men served in the war. Such pain the war caused! I must say, though, it was good for us farmers. We got some very high prices for our corn and wheat. The prices were so high it made it possible for me to retire from farming when I was only forty-two. Oh, I helped my son-in-law when he needed help on the farm, but God had other plans for me. The church took a lot of my time—preaching, marrying and ordaining. Would you believe I married 256 couples and baptized 1,328 believers?

I didn't have many books. I just read the scriptures. When I would preach I didn't have many notes, I just trusted God to give me what I needed to say. Sometimes the congregation wished God wouldn't give me so much. *Ach, der lieber,* sometimes I preached for almost two hours. I preached about discipleship, you know, that we need to follow Jesus Christ in our everyday life, but I also thought it was very important that we have a new birth experience.

Barbara was so patient with me. I was always going to a meeting someplace. I traveled to other counties in Illinois. . . . And I went to Iowa and Indiana a lot. I even traveled way out east to Ohio and Pennsylvania and west to Missouri to meet with other ministers. Lots of travel, lots of miles, lots of time—but we knew we needed to get together lest we forget who we are and what we believe.

Some of the other ministers just wanted to talk about rules and more rules, but that's only part of it. I got into trouble sometimes. Did you know that I could be stubborn sometimes? At least that's what Barbara said. And she was usually right. I didn't like all the rules that some of the bishops said were so important. I remember in about 1865 some of the men in the Rock Creek congregation began to wear buttons, and the younger men began to wear neckties. That raised a ruckus! We had a lot of meetings about rules.

Ministers meetings and more ministers meetings. We would get together and try to decide which was the proper method of baptism, the responsibility of the deacon's office, and the extent to which the ban should be observed, especially in such cases as between husband and wife. We talked about the use of such worldly innovations as insurance, photographs, lotteries, meetinghouses, lightning rods, and musical instruments. And then came 1872.

In 1872 my congregation built a meetinghouse at North Danvers. Did you know that it is the oldest church building in McLean County that still has the same congregation worshiping in it? But those were not good years for me. I had a lot of trouble with some of the rules that we Amish bishops had, like excommunicating someone from church. That's telling someone they can't worship with you anymore. The straw that broke the camel's back came when my friend, "Choseph Joder" (Joseph Yoder), wrote a poem that I didn't like and other bishops didn't like either. His poem talked about how God would let all people go to heaven because God wouldn't send anyone to hell. Even though I didn't agree with Joseph, I didn't think he should be excommunicated. How are you ever going to get someone to change their mind if you don't talk to them anymore?! What really didn't settle with me was having people who didn't know him decide he should be excommunicated. They didn't understand him; they didn't know what motivated him; they didn't know what the rest of his life was like. How could others decide to excommunicate him?! So I told the other ministers, "He is still my brother." That did not please the bishops.

It was a sad time. Many of the bishops said that I had failed the church, and so they disfellowshipped me. They refused to speak to me anymore. But the other ministers at North Danvers stood beside me. And soon other ministers and bishops let me know that they agreed with me. That helped me get through that sad time. Pretty soon we became known as the "Stuckey" Amish.

I was really helped during those hard years by the many good *Mennonite* friends that I had in the area. We often talked about the church and God's Word. There were a lot of like-minded congregations that asked me to be their bishop—some in Indiana, Illinois, Iowa and other places. People said we had a "Stuckey Way" of Christianity. We agreed that some things were more important than other things. We were more concerned for what people have in their heads and hearts—rather than for what they have *on* their heads. We wanted the emphasis on heart attitudes rather than on outward forms. We felt called to be ambassadors of Christ through the will of God. And we wanted abundant opportunity for young people to accept responsibility in the church.

As an old man, I saw the Central Conference of Mennonites formed. Creating the conference was a practical way to help churches solve problems, find preachers, and start new Sunday schools in our area. I didn't do much to design the conference. I let that to younger ministers. But we organized the conference to help our churches be strong, not to decide on rules. And we always stayed in fellowship with the ministers of the Middle District and were encouraged by their efforts to be faithful as well.

Vell, it wasn't easy! I know there were others besides Barbara who thought I was stubborn. I did have strong convictions, but I always tried to be very considerate of the views of others. Some said I was unorthodox because I was sympathetic with those who thought different. But perhaps that weakness was also a strength. God will be my judge.

Appendix H

Pastors

West Side Church (Short-term Name) and Warren Street Mennonite Church

Years of service	Pastor	Other information and status as of 2010–2012
1923 to 1930	Simon S. Yoder	May 5, 1879–Sept 3, 1943; see note 27 in chapter 4.
1930 to 1934	Lee Lantz	June 15, 1873–Nov 22, 1970; left WSMC to minister at Mennonite Gospel Mission in Chicago along with wife and daughter, Mary Elizabeth, who later married Floyd Sharp.
1934 to 1942	Emil (E. A.) Sommer	April 2, 1884–Jan 20, 1957; pastored Tiskilwa Mennonite Church, 1949–1952; wife, Lydia (Augspurger), died 1930.
1942, June to Sept	J. Herbert Fretz (summer student from Bluffton College)	Born Jan 10, 1921; retired at Greencroft, Goshen with wife, Helen (Habegger), after a lifetime of church ministry including pastorates in PA (Deep Run West Mennonite Church, 1945–1953), SD (Salem Mennonite Church, 1953– 1963) and IN (Eighth Street, 1963–1968. Currently a member of Eighth Street Mennonite Church, Goshen. Attended POMC numerous times during its final years.
1943, Apr 18 to Aug 15	Robert W. Hartzler	Aug 4, 1919–April 2, 1994; pastored Silver Street 1942–1945 and Eighth Street Mennonite 1945–1962; first wife, Emma (Blosser), had polio; lived for years in iron lung and rocking bed and died 1991; married Josephine Troyer 1992.

Years of service	Pastor	Other information and status as of 2010–2012
1943 to 1945	Ernest J. Bohn	July 31, 1894–Sept 4, 1992; died in Goshen where he retired after serving as pastor in IL, PA, IN, and Ohio. While pastor at Pandora, OH, he also taught at Bluffton College.
1945 to 1947	Alvin J. Regier	April 15, 1916–July 15, 2007; died in Hobart, IN; wife, Viola, died Feb 9, 2002; pastor at Bible Church in Gary; managed and then owned Bible Bookstore which he called his family's ministry; later run by sons and closed in 2010; member of Baptist Church when he died. (*Goshen News*, Oct 4, 2010.)
1947, June to Aug	Burton Yost (summer student from Bluffton)	Burton and Elnore (Rosenberger) Yost are retired educators living in Bluffton, OH; celebrated their sixtieth wedding anniversary in 2009.
1948 to 1955	Harold Thiessen	Moved with family to Donnellson, Iowa, to pastor; pastored the historic Summerfield Church in Illinois 1961–68. Harold died in 1986; his wife, Marie (Zuercher), died April 9, 2005.
1955 to 1960	Elmer Wall	Born October 30, 1929; now retired in Goshen with wife, Winifred, after forty-three years of pastoral ministry in General Conference churches, for many years at North Danvers Mennonite Church at Carlock, IL. Active member of Silverwood Mennonite Church and occasional preacher at POMC 2006–2009.
1961, Jan to Sept	Bernard (Bernie) Wiebe	Retired in Canada; served in many roles in GC church: pastor, president of Freeman Junior College, editor of *The Mennonite*, associate professor of conflict resolution studies at Menno Simons College, Winnipeg, Manitoba, 1989–1999, and the last associate moderator of the General Conference Mennonite Church, 1992–1999. His wife of 43 years, Marge Letkeman, died of cancer in 1999.
1961 to 1962, Jan to Jan	Raymond M. Yoder	March 28, 1914–April 6, 1983; married Frances Schrock; later was a member of Eighth Street, Goshen; a member of Bay Shore Mennonite in Sarasota, FL, at time of death.
1962 to 1965, June to Aug	Myron Krehbiel	July 12, 1930–March 19, 2011; left POMC for mission work in Colombia; later lived in the Midwest and Texas; married Betty Jamieson in 1970 and adopted John; Betty died in car accident in 1982; married Allie Heck in 1996; Allie died in 2009; moved to Sterling, CO, with son Michael before his death.

Appendix H

Years of service	Pastor	Other information and status as of 2010–2012
1965 to 1975, Sept to June	Floyd Quenzer	Born 1939 in Henderson, NE; conference minister in California before retirement; married to Donna Hougland.
1975 to 1982, Sept to June	Ken and Anne Neufeld Rupp (co-pastors)	Ken (April 23, 1941–April 27, 2010) and Anne (b. March 5, 1932) co-pastored the Alexanderwohl Church in KS, 1982–1987; later Anne was a chaplain, taught piano, and wrote Sunday School materials; Ken did computer programming; retired in KS. Anne moved to N. Newton, KS, after Ken's death.
1982	David L. Myers (interim student pastor)	MDiv from AMBS 1991; in 2011 was the Director of the Department of Homeland Security's Center for Faith-based and Neighborhood Partnerships in Chicago.
1982 to 1984, Nov to Feb	Clarence Sink (interim pastor)	Ministered in Church of the Brethren most of his life; also served as interim minister at Forks Mennonite Church for 18 months in 1983 to 1985; died March 3, 1988.
1984 to 1985, Feb to June	John Reeser	Born Dec 8, 1943; grew up in Meadows Church; founder and pastor of North Penn Christian Fellowship, Lansdale, PA in 2012.
1986, Feb to June	Virgil M. Gerig (interim pastor)	Died March 13, 2006 in Goshen where he retired after serving as pastor in Smithville and Pandora, OH, Freeman, SD, and Hively Ave in Elkhart. He and his wife, Mary Kay (Ramseyer), also served in Lesotho.
1986 to 1998	Barry Schmell	Pastor of Maplewood Mennonite Church, Ft. Wayne. In addition to the three birth children mentioned in the text, in 2008 Barry and his wife, Deb, adopted two daughters from the Philippines named Ellen and LenLen.
1998 to 2000	John King (interim pastor)	Retired in Goshen with wife, Edith, after serving in pastoral ministry for fifty-one years in Ohio, Nebraska and Indiana. Member of Waterford Mennonite Church.
2000 to 2004	Robin K. La Rue	Living in Ft. Wayne, IN; began work as a hospital chaplain in 2004.
2002 to 2006	Michael Miller (youth pastor)	Director SWAP (Students With A Purpose) 2006–2012. Continues to serve with Bible Memory Program in Ohio and Indiana; lead mission trips, both stateside and foreign; preach in churches, schools, and at youth rallies.
2004 to 2005, Sept to Dec	Eugene Bontrager (interim pastor)	In 2012 serves as interim pastor at Forks Mennonite Church and assists families with financial strategies through World Group Securities and Investment Advisors International. Married to Barb (Frye); 4 adult children; had been pastor of Forks 1985–1996, and wrote the congregation's sesquicentennial history, published in 2007.

Years of service	Pastor	Other information and status as of 2010–2012
2006 to 2009, May to Nov	Rachel Nafziger Hartzler	Served as short-term pastor of Asheville Mennonite Fellowship in North Carolina January to June 2010. Now lives in Goshen, Indiana, and works as spiritual director, retreat leader, and writer.
2006, Sept 1 to Nov 30	Matt Gingerich (youth pastor)	Works with Five Star Investment Group and involved in lay youth ministry and prayer ministry at Riverside Church in Three Rivers, MI. Married to Shelly.

Appendix I

Church Members

CHARTER MEMBERS OF WARREN STREET MENNONITE CHURCH, 1923

This list was found in 2009 in the POMC pastor's office
in a locked file marked "Church History"
(Notations in parentheses from J. O. Yoder and Rachel Kreider)

J. Elvyn Blough
Bertha (Kauffman) Blough (Mrs. J. Elvyn)
Paul Blough (Sam's brother)
Samuel Blough (Paul's brother)
Ruth Blough (Mrs. Samuel)
Lester Breniser
Thomas G. Evans
Pearl Evans (Mrs. Thomas)
Russel Evans (son of Thomas and Pearl)
Daniel B. Friesner
Inez Friesner (Mrs. Daniel)
Esther Friesner (daughter of Daniel and Inez)
Freed Hershberger
Nina Hershberger (Mrs. Freed)
Lois Hershberger (daughter of Freed and Nina)
Elmer Hostetler

Osie Hostetler (Mrs. Elmer)
Rebecca Hostetler (step grandmother of Treva Schrock)
Henry Karch
Amanda Karch (Mrs. Henry)
Violet Karch (daughter of Henry and Amanda)
Ella Kauffman (widow of Rudolph, mother of Bertha Blough)
Bernice Kauffman (daughter of Ella, twin of Bertha)
Rollo Kauffman (son of Ella)
Ora S. Kauffman
Ida Kauffman (Mrs. Ora)
Ferne Kauffman (daughter of Ora and Ida)
Verne Kauffman (daughter of Ora and Ida)

Paul Kauffman (son of Ora and Ida)

Orene Kauffman (daughter of Ora and Ida)

John L. Kauffman

Bertha Kefarber

Vernon Kurtz

Grace Kurtz (Mrs. Vernon)

Silas J. Litwiller

Ella Litwiller (Mrs. Silas)

Lillian Litwiller (daughter of Silas and Ella)

J. Earnest Litwiller (son of Silas and Ella)

Chancey Mickem

Lorna Mickem (Mrs. Chancey)

Mary Mickem (daughter of Chancey and Lorna)

D. Walter Miller

Mabel Miller (Mrs. D. Walter)

Gerald Miller (son of D. Walter and Mabel)

Geraldine Miller (daughter of D. Walter and Mabel)

Jerry J. Miller

Edwin G. Miller

Lavona Miller (Mrs. Edwin)

Ella Miller

Daniel Moser

Phebe Moser (Mrs. Daniel)

Frank Parish

Hattie Parish (Mrs. Frank)

Elsie Plank (Mrs. Melvin; sister of Sam Blough)

Ira Schrock

Fanny Schrock (Mrs. Ira)

Lucile Schrock (daughter of Ira and Fanny)

Glen Schrock (son of Ira and Fanny)

Treva Schrock Steele (step granddaughter of Rebecca Hostetler)

Ellsworth ("Ellis") A. Troyer

Elva Troyer (Mrs. Ellsworth)

Arla Troyer (daughter of Ellis and Elva)

Clyde Troyer (son of Ellis and Elva)

Cletus Troyer (son of Ellis and Elva)

Elmer Walter

Barbara Walter (Mrs. Elmer)

Kathryn Walter (daughter of Elmer and Barbara)

John H. Walters

Katie Walters (Mrs. John)

Emma Yoder

Levi R. Yoder

Wilma Grace Yoder (Mrs. Levi)

Rubye Ruth Yoder (daughter of Levi and Wilma)

Noah G. Yoder

Olen Yoder

Barbara Yoder (Mrs. Olen)

Vera Yoder (daughter of Olen and Barbara)

Simon S. Yoder (pastor)

Sarah Yoder (Mrs. Simon)

Ferne Yoder (daughter of Simon and Sarah)

Ruby Yoder (daughter of Simon and Sarah)

Mable Yoder (daughter of Simon and Sarah)

Samuel Yoder (son of Simon and Sarah)

PLEASANT OAKS MENNONITE CHURCH ACTIVE MEMBERS IN 1965

"Church members whose loyalty and dedication
made the Pleasant Oaks Church building a reality"

John and Doneta Burkhardt

Freed and Nina
Hershberger

Donald and Doris Hershberger

Myron and Jean Krehbiel

Kenneth and Sally Miller

Beulah Mockler

Donald and Marlene Mockler

Tom and Sandra Tahara

Lois (Buchtel) Tyson

Robert and Doris Wortinger

J. O. and Leona Yoder

Olen (senior) and Barbara Yoder

Raymond and Frances Yoder

PLEASANT OAKS MENNONITE CHURCH ACTIVE MEMBERS IN NOVEMBER 2009

Connie Beachy

Gerri Beachy

Doneta Burkhardt

Rachel Nafziger Hartzler

Don Hershberger

Doris Hershberger

Glen Horner

Thelma Horner

Ben Kauffman

Gertrude Kauffman

Eileen Miller

Grant Miller

Mike Miller

Robin Tahara Miller

Ruth Miller

Darlene Mishler

Jim Mishler

Dale Schlabach

Viv Schlabach

Nan Stalter (an active non-member)

Bill Swartzendruber

Jan Swartzendruber

Anne Yoder

Brian Yoder

Elnora Yoder

Juanita Yoder

Junior Olen Yoder

Leona Yoder

Paul Yoder

Richard Yoder

Shirley Yoder

Appendix J

Warren Street Mennonite Church

"BOYS IN CAMP"
December 13, 1942

Sgt. Clyde E. Troyer
Hgt. Co. 1st Bn.
327 Glider Inf.
Fort Briggs, N.C.

Mr. Lowell Troyer
C.P.S. Camp # 67
Downey, Idaho

Sgt. Cletus D. Troyer
Co. B 113th Med. Bn.
A. P. O. 38
Carrabelle, Fla.

Pfc. Kenneth B. Troyer
Co. K 152nd Inf.
113th Med. CO.
Camp Shelby, Miss.

Sgt. Herbert C. Troyer
Medical Detachment
Dale Mabry Field
Tallahassee, Fla.

Mr. Lotus Troyer
C.P.S. Camp # 28
Medaryville, Ind.

Chris Bowers T. M.
U.S. Naval Hospital
Brooklyn, N.Y.
Ward E. 5

Corp. Calvin Hershberger
Med. Dot.
Sheppard Field, Tex.

Sgt. Ernest Blough
853 3rd Co.
Barracks 3 U
Camp Carson, Colo.

Pvt. Keith Plank
920th Sqd. AAFRTC
ASN33340192
Atlantic City, N.J.

Pfc. Orla E. Hostetler 3516320
Battery B. 158th F
A.P.O. 45
Pine Camp, N.Y.

"NAMES AND ADDRESSES OF BOYS GONE FROM OUR CHURCH"
(date not given)

Sgt. Ernest D. Blough
35251709 853 Ord. H.G.M.
A.P.O. No. 4915
% P.M., New York, N.Y.

Chris Bowers T.M. 2/c
U.S. Naval Torpedo Sta.
New Port, R. I.

S 2/c Lloyd McCreary
U.S.S. P.O. 469
New York City

Pfc. Orla Hostetler 35169320
"B" B' try, 158th F.A. Bn.
A.P.O. 700, % Postmaster
New York, N.Y.

Sgt. Clyde E. Troyer
35043586—Hdq Co. 1st Bn.
#27th Glider Inf. APO 472
% Postmaster, New York City

Pvt. Keith Plank
3rd A-F 314B, Hg.
Drew Field, Fla.

Sgt. Cletus D. Troyer
35175498- - Co. B, 113th Med.
38th Inf. Div. A. P.O. 38
Camp Livingston, La.

S/Sgt. Herbert C. Troyer
15th Altitude Training Unit
Dale Mabry Field
Tallahassee, Fla.

Cpl. Robert J. Blough
35764676 30th Training Grp.
Jefferson Bks., Mo.

Corp. Calvin Hershberger
Med. Detachment 6
Sheppard Field, Tex.

Pvt. Donald Hershberger
35549351 i87 Harmon Gen. Hosp
Longview, Tex.

Pvt. Paul B. Kauffman
18th R.E.T.L.W.G. Det. B.
C.W.S. Sch. A.A.B.
Kearns, Utah

Lotus Troyer
Box A, Ypsilanti, Mich.

Lowell Troyer
Box A, Ypsilanti, Mich.

Husbands of Girls [who were]
members of Warren St. Church

Cpl. Harold Ulrich 35549352
Hg. Btry. 282 F. A. Bn.
Camp Rucker, Ala.

Cpl. Gordon W. Holdread
477 Q.M. Regt. (Trk)
3556105 A. P.O. 475 Co. E.
% Seattle, Wash.

Pvt. Richard Max Stump
35548362 Co. B. 17 Inf.
A.P.O. 7 U.S. Army
% San Francisco, Cal.

Alden J. Plank, S 2/c, USNR
894-60-60 Plat. 1952, Bks. 101
Camp Peary, Va.

John W. Burkhardt A.R.M. 2/c
205 Fleet
% P.M. New York, N.Y.

Pvt. John A. Wyland
Co. T 3 T L A T 310 Inf.
Camp Butner, N.C

Appendix K

Baptisms At Pleasant Oaks Mennonite Church

1966:	Burton Crapo
1967:	Judy Hershberger, Denise Mockler, Dennis Mockler, Stephen Mockler, Terrence Tahara
May 18, 1969:	James Edward Sutton, Dallas Ernsberger, Randall Christy
Dec 21, 1970:	Robin Tahara, Bruce Miller
1971:	Victoria Mockler, Joellen Yoder
1972:	Richard Bright
1974:	Kent Miller
1975:	Timothy Tahara, Shirley Quenzer, Edward Pleaz Miller
Mar 28, 1976:	Robert Rupert, Joyce Rupert
June 6, 1976:	Cathy Hershberger, Michael Miller, Cynthia Mockler, David Mockler, Richard Yoder
July 25, 1976:	Sherry Yoder, Debra Burkhardt
June 1, 1980:	Keith Gingerich, Deann Kauffman, Cynthia Miller, Jonathan Miller, Gayle Rheinheimer, Mary K. Yoder
May 17, 1981:	Tambrey Rupert, Robert Rupert, Jr.
Apr 3, 1983:	Susan Diane Miller, Donald Andrew Miller, Craig Rheinheimer, Michael Anthony Hurst, Cory Lee Hochstetler , Amy VonGunten, Robert Zook, Randall Miller
May 1983:	Darren Berkey, Gordon Hochstetler, Steve Johnson, Jody Miller
May 19, 1983:	Steve Miller
July 22, 1984:	William Crapo, Robert Crapo
Feb 10, 1985:	Ann Herschberger, Terry Herschberger
Feb 8, 1987:	Janet Ebersol, Steve Ebersol, Denise Risser, Deanna Risser, Ken Rychener, Douglas VonGunten, Tami Schlabach, Timothy Troyer

Appendix K

May 29, 1988:	Timothy Ebersol, Ricki Schlabach, Paul Wingeart, Anthony Yoder, Jason Yoder
May 4, 1989:	Jodi Rychener, Matthew Troyer, Heather Wingeart, Amy Jo Yoder
May 14, 1989:	Barbara Haarer
June 3, 1990:	Camila Beachy, Kathy Renee Miller, Stacy Miller, Eric Risser, Peter VonGunten, Anita Yoder, Russell Yoder
May 19, 1991:	Nathan Pletcher, Jason Wogoman, Douglas Troyer, Robin Yoder
Nov 17, 1991:	Jeffery Wogoman
May 30, 1993:	Andrea Springer
May 22, 1994:	Vicki Wise
May 19, 1996:	Tanya Christy, Melanie Jones, Todd Pletcher, Jennifer Springer, Rachel Stalter, Anika Wedel
May 18, 1997:	Chelsea Haarer, Kyle Herschberger, Lee Herschberger, Rebekah Schmell, Derek Jackson, Lori Jackson, Michelle Jones, Ryan Smeltzer, Alison Troyer, Brett Miller
Dec 7, 1997:	Sol Miller, Robin Miller, Martin Yoder
Feb 6, 2000:	Austin Miller, Evan Stahley, Laura Renaud, Brittany Yoder, Natalie Stalter
Apr 21, 2002:	Jackson Hooley, Jordan Hooley, Jeramiah Morgan, Katelyn Stahley, Brian Yoder
Sept 18, 2005:	Matthew Gingerich, Rosemary Morgan, Jeffery Troyer
Sept 13, 2009:	Grant Tetsuo Miller

Appendix L

Funerals and Memorial Services of Pleasant Oaks Members

(Pastors also officiated at numerous services for nonmembers.)

Name	Birth and death dates	Date of funeral/memorial service and officiant(s)
Jean Noffsinger Krehbiel	Sept 22, 1936–Apr 11, 1965	April 15; first worship service at POMC with Vernon F. Miller and Wilbur Yoder officiating
Timothy Leon Krehbiel	Dec 1, 1964–Apr 11, 1965	April 15; double funeral with mother
Lloyd Mockler	Nov 18, 1904–Dec 11, 1968	At POMC
Levi R. Yoder	Mar 3, 1877–Nov 10, 1969	Nov 12 at Miller Funeral Home, officiated by James Parker, Stone Lake Church of God
Barbara Mishler Yoder	Aug 26,1888–Oct 14, 1970	Oct 16 at POMC with Floyd Quenzer and Paul Goering, Eighth Street pastor
Laura Elsie Showalter	Sept 29, 1893–June 1, 1971	
Amzie K. Miller	1906–Aug 21, 1972	
Freed Hershberger	March 31, 1889–Aug 3, 1973	Aug 6 at POMC with Floyd Quenzer officiating
Kenneth Neer	Oct 14, 1904–Dec 10, 1974	
Ora S. Kauffman	Oct 28, 1874– March 24, 1975	March 25 at POMC with Floyd Quenzer officiating
Addie M. (Lina) Miller	April 19, 1895–May 7, 1977	May 10 at Walley-Mills-Zimmerman Funeral Home in Elkhart with Ken Rupp officiating
Martha Schmidt Peters	Sept 1, 1915–July 2, 1977	A service on July 5 at Yoder Culp Funeral Home with Ken and Anne Rupp officiating; funeral and burial in Kansas

Appendix L

Name	Birth and death dates	Date of funeral/memorial service and officiant(s)
Andrew J. Gingerich	Sept 16, 1906–Dec 8, 1977	Dec 10 at POMC with Ken Rupp officiating
Morris E. Buchtel	Sept 9, 1911–June 2, 1980	June 3 at Miller Funeral Home with Ken Rupp officiating
Nina Horner Hershberger	Oct 9, 1889–Dec 30, 1981	Jan 2, 1982 at Miller Funeral Home with Ken Rupp officiating
Olen Yoder (senior)	Nov 14, 1888–May 24, 1984	May 26 at Yoder Culp Funeral Home with John Reeser officiating
Charlotte Weldy Hurst	Jan 1, 1944–Nov 8, 1985	Nov 12 memorial service at College Mennonite Church, Goshen with Bob Detweiler, Steve Chupp and John Reeser officiating
Arwilda Showalter	Sept 12, 1921–June 7, 1987	
Lois Hershberger Buchtel Tyson	Nov 26, 1911–Sept 27, 1990	at POMC with Barry Schmell officiating
Lynn Devon Rheinheimer	May 8, 1946–Oct 28, 1993	Oct 31 at Shore MC with Barry Schmell officiating
Burton Crapo	May 14, 1925–Jan 13, 1995	Jan 16 at POMC with Barry Schmell officiating
Mary Wineland Troyer	Mar 13, 1914–July 14, 1996	at POMC with Barry Schmell officiating
Beulah Christner Mockler	Mar 16, 1905–Sept 24, 1996	at POMC with Barry Schmell officiating
Abe Peters	Sept 22, 1916–Dec 22, 1996	Dec 26 at POMC with Barry Schmell officiating
Anna Marguerite Deal	Apr 14, 1917–May 1, 1997	at POMC with Barry Schmell officiating
Marlene Baker Mishler Mockler	Feb 26, 1935–Feb 10, 1998	Feb 13 memorial service at Middlebury Church of Brethren; Barry Schmell officiating; meal at POMC
Ken VonGunten	July 13, 1939–Sept 1, 2002	Sept 5 memorial service at First Mennonite Church with Robin La Rue officiating
Emma Schmucker Miller Peters	Jan 15, 1921–Oct 20, 2003	Oct 24 at POMC with Robin La Rue officiating
Lowell O. Troyer	Mar 17, 1912–Sept 14, 2004	Sept 17 at POMC with Eugene Bontrager officiating
Sanford Yoder	July 1, 1912–Feb 25, 2005	Feb 28 at POMC with Eugene Bontrager and John King officiating
Tom Tetsuo Tahara	May 5, 1929–June 4, 2006	June 9 at Middlebury Church of the Brethren with Rachel Nafziger Hartzler and Eugene Bontrager officiating; meal at POMC
Sandra Buchtel Tahara	Aug 8, 1933–July 5, 2007	July 10 at Middlebury Church of the Brethren with Rachel Nafziger Hartzler and Eugene Bontrager officiating; meal at POMC

Name	Birth and death dates	Date of funeral/memorial service and officiant(s)
Marvin J. Miller	Apr 18, 1928–June 9, 2008	June 14 at Miller-Stewart Funeral Home in Middlebury with Rachel Nafziger Hartzler officiating; meal at POMC
Doneta Hershberger Burkhardt*	Jan 13, 1924–Feb 5, 2010	Feb 8 at Greencroft (Goshen) with Linford Martin and Pamela Yoder officiating
James Mishler*	July 9, 1938–Feb 5, 2010	Feb 9 at Shore Mennonite Church with Jeremy Helmuth officiating

*Two POMC members died after the final worship service at POMC and before the legal work of reuniting with First Mennonite Church was complete.

Appendix M

Memorial Gifts At Warren Street and Pleasant Oaks

Date	Gift	In Memory of
1952	Lectern; given to Menno-Hof in 2009	Melvin Plank
1960	Communion table that remains in the Pleasant Oaks sanctuary	Josephine (Mrs. Amzie) Miller, (Marsha Miller Mockler's mother)
1965	Piano in sanctuary	"Dedicated to the glory of God and in memory of the faith shown us by Jean Krehbiel"
1970	Brass candle holders and candle lighter/snuffer	Barbara Mishler Yoder given by her daughter, Vera Bickel
1985	Wooden plaque with words: I am the resurrection and the life; hand carved by John Mishler	Charlotte Hurst
1986	Stained glass windows in west foyer	Andrew and Aloma Gingerich given by their children
1992	Copies of *Hymnal Worship Book*	Lois Hershberger Buchtel Tyson (mother of Sandra Tahara) given by Sandra and Tom Tahara
1992	Copies of *Hymnal Worship Book*	Delila Yoder (mother of Lois Miller) given by Lois Miller
1993	Pew Bibles	Lynn Rheinheimer
1998	Preschool laminator and playground equipment	Marlene Baker Mishler Mockler
2002	Musical Instruments	Ken VonGunten
2006	Copies of *Sing the Journey* and library books	Sanford Yoder
2009	Wooden plaque with words: Jesus said Believe in me; hand carved by John Mishler	Marvin Miller

Appendix N

Communication Protocol Document

A HEALTHY CONGREGATION IS one which makes decisions and deals with its differences in an open environment which is respectful of persons, and is committed to including all and to working toward the best interests of the whole congregation. As our congregation works to fulfill our Vision and become a part of God's Mission here in Middlebury, we also seek to become a healthy congregation, working together in the spirit of unity and peace (Ephesians 4:1–3). Toward that end we would like to help create an open system at Pleasant Oaks Mennonite Church, as opposed to a closed one, and to have everyone commit themselves to behaviors and processes which will cultivate such a system.

A. Identifying a Closed and Open System

Tendencies of a Closed System:	Tendencies of an Open System:
• Information does not flow freely	• Free flow of information
• Some have information; others don't	• Everyone has as much pertinent information as possible
• Decisions are made behind the scenes by small groups with no accountability	• The system is flexible
• The system resists change	• Parts are responsive and accountable to each other and work for the good of the whole
• Persons who try to change the system are marginalized	
• Secrets flourish	• Each person's voice is important in decision making

B. Principles which lie behind an open system:

1. Genuine respect for each other as persons who are created in the image of God and who are temples of God's Spirit

2. A willingness to speak our truth in love and with language that honors the other person

3. Lovingly engaging in direct dialog, open debate and careful listening

4. A willingness to see things from another's perspective

5. A genuine concern for the well being of the whole group

C. Public Conduct: Ways to conduct ourselves publicly in church business meetings and work at decision-making:

D.

1. Acceptable:

   a. Come to meetings having read the materials provided before the meeting

   b. Come prepared to discuss openly and freely, speaking only for yourself

   c. Come prepared to listen respectfully to other perspectives and to try to achieve consensus

2. Unacceptable:

   a. Lobbying or organizing groups to push for one position or another
   Response: The congregation needs to name this when it happens. Individuals need to speak for themselves.

   b. Those representing a minority position pushing to revisit, reverse, control, or otherwise undermine decisions
   Response: Those in the minority need to accept the majority decision graciously and be a part of the body.

3. What you can expect from leadership:

   a. Full information in advance of meetings; everybody receives the same information

   a. A call for simple majority vote (except in calling new pastors)

   b. No secret ballots

   c. Opportunity and encouragement for free and open dialog

   d. Work toward consensus where possible

E. Personal Conduct: How we conduct ourselves personally in and between meetings:

F.

1. Acceptable:

   a. Use "I" language instead of "you" language

      • "I" language permits me to claim my feelings, to address the concern as it affects me and to take responsibility for my own perceptions of the issue.

- Using "you" language communicates an attitude of criticism, judgment, and blaming and creates a defensiveness within the hearer.

b. Speak directly with the person with whom we may have a difference of opinion or misunderstanding, asking for clarification when necessary.

c. Listen carefully to what the other person is saying to make sure information and feelings were heard accurately.

2. Unacceptable:

a. Passing judgment on people based on incomplete or inaccurate information.

Response: Be sure information is correct by going directly to the person involved. If you hear others doing this, encourage them to speak directly to the person involved.

b. Triangling: Occurs in situations of conflict between two people when the anxiety level rises, when one of the two goes to a third person, and that third person allows the other to be irresponsible in the way he communicates. Triangling can take a variety of different forms:

- Lobbying: Attempting to get a third party to take my side when I'm in conflict with another person, to try to drive a wedge between that person and the third party

- Gossiping: Repeating information that you heard about someone else to a third party

- Scapegoating: Placing blame on another person for one's own or the group's problems

Response: If you sense yourself triangling, you need to go directly to the person with whom you have the conflict. If you are the person being addressed, don't listen to it; encourage direct dialog.

c. Serving as a spear carrier for someone else, carrying someone else's agenda
Response: Voice your own opinions clearly and forcefully, and be sure you speak for yourself. When you encounter someone you think is speaking on behalf of another, ask simply "Is this your agenda?"

d. Purporting to speak for "others" in the congregation when you are really voicing your own personal concerns.
Response: Be sure you are speaking only for yourself. When you encounter someone claiming to speak for others, ask who these others are. Suggest that you can only respond to persons if you know who they are and can talk directly with them; we can't be responsible to respond to phantom voices or persons. Let others speak for themselves.

e. Petty criticism and gossip

Response: Treat others as you would wish to be treated. When you encounter someone voicing criticism or gossip, don't listen to it or encourage it; and don't pass it on.

   f. Verbal assaults, angry outbursts, comments which destroy or demean another

Response: If you are tempted to respond in anger, excuse yourself from the conversation and take the time to calm down. When you hear someone expressing anger in these ways, express your own willingness to listen when the other person has regained composure.

3. What you can expect from leadership:

   a. We will listen carefully to your concerns—both positive and negative.

   b. We will respond to you. This doesn't mean that we will automatically do what you ask, but we will let you know we have heard and received your concern and will consider it.

   c. We will keep confidences but not secrets by:

- keeping information confidential which is personal and private

- openly sharing information which pertains to congregational life

   d. We will investigate rumors.

   e. We will deal directly and firmly with conflict and with inappropriate behaviors.

G. Group Conflict: When we don't agree:

Conflict itself isn't necessarily bad. In fact, healthy congregations will have differences of opinions and perspectives. However, how we deal with our differences does matter. Some principles to keep in mind in working at our differences:

1. Stick to the issues. Don't personalize differences.

2. As much as possible, try to identify areas of agreement so that real differences are identified for further exploration.

3. Try to identify the principles behind the different perspectives. Ask of each: What really is at stake? What really matters?

4. All parties should keep in mind the interests and concerns of the whole group. Approach differences in a collaborative, creative, problem-solving mode. Attempt as much as possible to explore mediating positions or "third ways" which hopefully take into account the genuine interests and concerns of all positions.

5. After votes are taken, minorities should be prepared to accept the wish of the majority and to support the outcome of the vote.

H. Personal Conflict: When we don't agree:

It is inevitable that in congregational life (as in work, family, or community life) differences and conflicts will emerge between individuals. When they arise the following principles and procedures should be pursued:

1. Individuals should deal with their differences directly with each other as quickly as possible, not allowing them to fester.

2. If you are experiencing unresolved conflict with another member of the congregation and are genuinely interested in resolving it, it is appropriate to talk with the pastor for counsel on how to work at it and/or to serve as a mediator in approaching the person with whom you have a conflict.

3. Avoid triangling (see above). Rather, apply the principles of Matthew 18:

   a. Go directly to that person and ask to talk one-on-one.

   b. If the person is not responsive, then ask someone else who is neutral to accompany you to help mediate the conflict with that person.

   c. If the problem still persists, then it is appropriate to share this concern with the larger body. However, in this last, most dramatic step, it is encouraged that you work with the pastors as to the most appropriate way of engaging the larger group.

   d. Note: There are some situations in which it is appropriate to forego the first step in the Matthew process. One example would be when a person feels very intimidated by the one with whom there is conflict. Sometimes it is appropriate, also, to write out one's concerns, so long as it is done respectfully and with opportunity for follow-up communication.

4. At times we may have to agree to disagree. Even then, we need to treat one another with respect, charity and grace, as we would wish others would treat us. It is helpful to pray for another person with whom you have differences and/or conflicts; not to change them, but to wish them God's blessings. Above all, do no harm.

In asking you to affirm this protocol, we are asking for more than a vote of approval. We are asking for a strong commitment on your part to uphold it yourself and to help call others to accountability, including the leadership.

Initiated by Pleasant Oaks Mennonite Church Board in 2008.

Appendix O

Sample Letter Sent on Church Letterhead in Early November 2009

Dear John,

Greetings from Pleasant Oaks Mennonite Church. I am writing on behalf of the congregation to inform you that our discernment process of the last eight months has led to the congregation deciding to re-unite with First Mennonite Church of Middlebury (203 E. Lawrence St.), the congregation from which we came 86 years ago. This has been an exciting journey, mixed at times with sadness. The details are not all worked out, but this transition is in process.

I have been asked by the POMC Deacon Council to contact you about your membership with us. I don't think you and I have met, but I have been pastor of the congregation since May, 2006. It has been a joy to be part of POMC for these three and one-half years, but I am now being called elsewhere.

According to our records, you have been a member here since being baptized on May 16, 1993. You are now encouraged to take your membership to the congregation where you currently worship. I will be happy to write a formal letter of transfer for you to take to your present congregation. If you are involved in a congregation that does not keep a membership list, you can simply withdraw from Pleasant Oaks or I can send you a letter of transfer for you to hold in case you sometime join a congregation that requests a church letter.

If you are not involved in another congregation, we encourage you to again find a congregation for worship, fellowship, and mutual care. We invite you to join the majority of the active POMC members who will take their membership to the new fellowship that will result from the re-uniting of Pleasant Oaks Mennonite Church and First Mennonite Church of Middlebury. The lead pastor for the new congregation will be Linford Martin, current lead pastor of FMC, who can be reached at 574–825–5135. (The FMC associate pastor is Pamela Yoder who is presently on sabbatical.)

If you choose to not be involved in a church at this time, you may withdraw your membership or request a letter to keep until such a time that you join another congregation.

Please respond in person; by telephone (574–825–2784) or email (pomchurch@ verizon.net) by November 16, 2009. My last day in the office will be November 20. We would very much like to hear from you. If we don't hear from you by November 16, we will reluctantly remove your name from the membership list.

> May the peace of Christ fill you and make you whole,
> Rachel Nafziger Hartzler, pastor
> Pleasant Oaks Mennonite Church
> P.O. Box 447; 13307 C.R. 16
> Middlebury, IN 46540

Appendix P

Ending, Thanksgiving, and Blessing

Pleasant Oaks Mennonite Church
Middlebury, Indiana
November 22, 2009

Leader: Along with Sarah and Abraham, Ruth and Naomi, Paul and Barnabas, we are sojourners, situated in a given place only for a season. We are forever being drawn near and led forth by the Holy Spirit.

People: Both in laying hold and in letting go we recognize God's goodness in forming us and leading us.

Leader: For everything there is a season—a time to keep and a time to let go. Now is the letting go. For three and one-half years, Rachel Nafziger Hartzler has served as our pastor. She has offered her gifts to us and worked for the up-building of the church here at Pleasant Oaks. She has served us well.

People: We express our deep gratitude to you, Rachel, for your presence in our midst. Your influence on our faith and our discipleship will not leave us at your departure. You have enriched our lives and our life together by offering to us from your own life and your own giftedness. As you go, we ask your forgiveness for any mistakes or ways we may have hurt you. Grateful for what you mean to us, we release you from your ministerial duties here and the carrying of our lives in a pastoral way.

Rachel: I forgive you and accept your gratitude, trusting that our time together and our parting are a part of the unfolding of God in our midst. I ask your forgiveness for mistakes I have made. I am grateful for you and for the time we have had together. I offer my blessing and encouragement for the continuing ministry of each of you, and for the ministry of this beloved congregation within the context on a new congregation formed by the re-uniting of Pleasant Oaks Mennonite Church and First Mennonite Church of Middlebury. I release you from turning to me and depending on me in a pastoral way. May God bless you in your new pastoral relationships with Linford Martin and Pamela Yoder.

People: We forgive you and we will appreciate your prayers for the ongoing transition to becoming a new congregation with First Mennonite, and for the ministry of the new congregation that is emerging. You are a valued part of us and of the Pleasant Oaks Story.

Lois: Your sisters and brothers in Central District offer you their blessing. You have been a vital part of our conference life together. Our memory of you as a congregation, your effort and toil, your devotion and courage, your faith and commitment will be treasured. We look back with thanks on your great and quiet gifts to us and pray God's blessing on your future life with new brothers and sister of our Mennonite faith. We release you from your commitments to Central District Conference and entrust you to the strong and tender hands of God and God's people of First Mennonite Church and Indiana-Michigan Conference. We offer our gratitude for your pastoral leadership, Rachel, for caring for and tending these believers, for standing on the shore of what was and helping the congregation find the shores of a new land.

Leader: God is bringing all of us into a good land, a land of brooks, of fountains and springs, a land of wheat and barley, of vines and fig trees and pomegranates, a land of olive trees and honey, a land in which you will eat bread without scarcity, in which you will lack nothing, a land whose stones are iron, and out of whose hills you can dig copper. And you shall eat and be full, and you shall bless God for the good land that is given to you. (Deuteronomy 8)

Lois: Be of good courage and receive the words of our Lord. Lifting up his hands and blessing his disciples, Jesus said: "I am with you always, even to the end of the age."

All: Eternal God who, like a Mother, broods over her children, we commend one another into your care as we move now into new directions. We give thanks for cherished memories, for spiritual refreshment shared together, for a renewed sense of who we are and are meant to be. We ask for the comfort of the Holy Spirit who intervenes for us with sighs too deep for words. And we trust that you are guiding all of us, in this parting, for the work of the Gospel. Through the name of the Risen Christ we pray. Amen.[1]

---

1. Adapted from various sources and written by Joan Yoder Miller and Lois Johns Kaufmann

Appendix Q

Books on Homosexuality by Mennonite Writers

Geddert, Timothy J. *All Right Now: Finding Consensus on Ethical Questions*. Herald Press, 2008.

King, Michael. *Fractured Dance: Gadamer and a Mennonite Conflict over Homosexuality*. Pandora Press U.S., 2001.

———, Editor. *Stumbling Toward a Genuine Conversation on Homosexuality*. Cascadia, 2007.

Kreider, Roberta Showalter. *From Wounded Hearts: Faith Stories of Lesbian, Gay, Bisexual and Transgender People and Those Who Love Them*. Gaithersburg, Md.: Chi Rho Press, 1998.

———. *Together in Love: Faith Stories of Gay, Lesbian, Bisexual and Transgender Couples*. Kulpsville, Pa.: Strategic Press, 2002.

Kraus, C. Norman. *On Being Human: Sexual Orientation and the Image of God*. Wipf and Stock, 2011.

———, Editor. *To Continue the Dialogue: Biblical Interpretation and Homosexuality*. Living Issues Discussion Series, 2001.

Thiessen Nation, Mark and Ted Grimsrud. *Reasoning Together: A Conversation on Homosexuality*. Herald Press, 2008.

Showalter, Ann. *Touched by Grace: From Secrecy to New Life*. Cascadia, 2006.

Swartley, Willard M. *Homosexuality: Biblical Interpretation and Moral Discernment*. Herald Press, 2003.

Appendix R

An Invitation to the Congregations of Central District Conference

A Congregational Peace Pledge:
A call to intentionally encounter the realities of war

Goal: To invite congregations and conferences to commit to the actions delineated in the proposal

Whereas: We believe that peace is the will of God, that God created the world in peace, that God's will is most fully revealed in Jesus Christ, who is our peace and the peace of the whole world, and that as Christians we are called to follow the path of Jesus and his call to live as peacemakers; we thus believe that we are called to engage the violence of war and injustice in the world that largely leaves us untouched.

1. When we have opportunity for personal contact with those who suffer, compassion is planted, and out of this compassion comes our responses. Examples of showing compassion are encounters: with the hungry in soup kitchens, the homeless in a tornado's wake, or with prisoners. Warfare, on the other hand, causes hurt in ways that Mennonites are not as likely to confront on a regular basis.

2. Historically war was an inescapable reality forcing hard choices on U.S. Mennonites. During the Civil War men had to choose whether they would fight, hire substitutes, pay commutation fees, or face punishments. In World War I some Mennonites drafted into the military refused to wear the uniform or carry guns, while others became stretcher-bearers for the army. There was no possibility of alternative service. Some were court-martialed, imprisoned, and suffered mistreatment. In World War II, the Korean War, and the Vietnam War young

Mennonites could claim conscientious objector status and engage in alternative service if they could defend their convictions convincingly. In recent years the government has adopted a volunteer army and ended the use of the draft. This has radically changed the relationship of civilians to war and in particular has changed the dynamics for pacifists wishing to witness faithfully to the issues of war.

3. Men and women around us volunteer to fight multiple wars simultaneously; Mennonites may avoid scenes of violent conflict, demands to bear arms, or having to justify their pacifism. Can we continue to be a peace church if we remain insulated from the reality of war and the need to witness to this reality?

Therefore, be it resolved:

That Central District Conference invites congregations, who wish to be intentional about the reality of war, its victims, and the hard questions it asks of nonviolent followers of Jesus, to commit themselves each year to actions such as the following:

- For each 100 members in the congregation, send one member on a delegation to a conflict zone with Christian Peacemaker Teams, Witness for Peace, Fellowship of Reconciliation, Mennonite Central Committee (MCC), Mennonite Mission Network, or other organizations dedicated to providing a nonviolent presence internationally or locally. The congregation is encouraged to pay partial funding for the trip and support the member's efforts to raise the remaining funds. Congregations with less than 100 members may pool resources into a common fund to support one of their members. After the trip the congregation will assist the member with sharing about his/her experiences with the congregation and other local audience.

- Sponsor at least one event each year that asks youth to question participation in war. Examples can include education of the congregation's youth group, counter-recruitment efforts in local schools, and/or provide a counter-presence when military recruiters visit local schools.

- Bring at least one speaker to the congregation each year who has worked at peace building with victims of war, is a former combatant who knows the experience of having inflicted harm on others, or did alternative service during a previous war. The Oasis of Hope Community in Newport News (757–775–8101), the TWOW (Transforming the Wounds of War) program at EMU's Center for Justice and Peacebuilding (http://www.emu.edu/cjp/pti/twow), or the MCC Peace Office are possible sources of speakers.

Affirmed by delegates June 22, 2012

Appendix S

WSMC and POMC Membership and Attendance Records and Summaries

Year	Membership and attendance
1923	83 (records vary between 70 and 100)
1926	81
1932	115 (active and inactive members); 93 (average attendance)
1934	113 (active and inactive members); 85 (average attendance)
1936	"membership stable; losses and gains equal"
1942	80 (active); 19 (inactive)
1947	88 (active and inactive)
1948	62 (active); 21 (inactive)

Year	Members (active and inactive)[A]	Members[B]	Children—not members
1956	59		
1957	63	65	20
1958	71	59	22
1959	65	64	23
1960	66	64	23
1061	65		
1962	36 active; 24 inactive	67	30
1963	35 active; 22 inactive	59	39
1964	38 active; 20 inactive	58	
1965	13 households	29	22
1966	55 active and inactive	32	22

A. This data is from church yearbooks.

B. Data in this column and the next column (children—not members) is from conference reports in archives at Bluffton University.

Appendix S

Year	Members (active and inactive)[A]	Average attendance	Average attendance of children
1966	55	49	
1967	67	52	
1968	80	78	
1969	103	104	
1970	117	100	
1971	120	108	
1972	119	96	
1973	119	90	
1974	118	90	
1975	115	85	
1976	114	90	
1977	117	85	
1978	109	79	
1979	107	91	
1980			
1981	125	92	
1982	123		
1983	135		
1984	130		
1985	130		
1986	125	74	
1987	126	80	
1988	142	93	
1989	144	100	25
1990	152	100	25
1991	149	113[B]	25
1992	149	117	29[C]
1993	149	118[D]	27
1994	158	107	25
1995	155	101	26
1996	162	107	26
1997		97	24
1998		78	
1999		55	
2000		60	
2001		61	
2002		59	

WSMC and POMC Membership and Attendance Records and Summaries

Year	Members (active and inactive)[A]	Average attendance	Average attendance of children
2003		51	
2004		41	
2005		37	
2006		36	
2007		31	
2008		27	
2009		36.5	

A. Data in this and the following tables is from church records maintained by office secretaries and pastors Barry Schmell, Eugene Bontrager, and Rachel Nafziger Hartzler.

B. The greatest number of people recorded for a Sunday morning worship service was 168 on November 10, 1991. The greatest number of visitors (fifty-two) was recorded for that Sunday also. The highest monthly average attendance was 135 in November 1991 and April 1993.

C. The greatest number of children recorded for a Sunday was forty-eight on December 20, 1992.

D. The overall highest yearly average attendance was 118 in 1993.

AVERAGE MONTHLY ATTENDANCE AT PLEASANT OAKS MENNONITE CHURCH, 1986–2009

Year	Average	Jan.	Feb.	Mar.	April	May	June	July	Aug.	Sept.	Oct.	Nov.	Dec.
1986	74	83	66	85	70	77	68	62	79	76	64	80	80
1987	80	78	84	79	85	78	74	65	84	67	90	84	92
1988	93	86	87	100	97	99	90	87	83	94	93	99	101
1989	100	105	95	100	90	101	108	74	97	97	108	108	118
1990	100	94	99	105	104	101	119	84	95	91	90	106	108
1991	113	119	112	121	110	123	98	94	96	118	119	135	115
1992	117	123	115	98	129	124	112	107	102	118	117	126	133
1993	118	128	105	126	135	124	109	96	107	127	120	133	105
1994	107	104	116	106	108	114	95	86	98	116	122	111	113
1995	101	93	105	93	110	104	91	86	94	110	101	108	116
1996	107	96	95	98	125	124	115	100	87	110	108	118	107
1997	97	101	99	110	98	111	103	70	83	91	103	95	97
1998	78	79	92	88	92	94	79	70	71	66	64	72	67
1999	55	58	58	54	58	56	54	52	47	58	57	41	66
2000	60	58	62	60	71	56	58	53	63	58	55	61	66

2001	61	59	63	62	63	62	64	53	60	60	56	57	69
2002	59	58	65	62	59	60	55	55	60	56	56	57	69
2003	51	58	48	56	60	51	52	41	50	56	47	47	43
2004	41	45	43	51	33	38	39	39	48	44	30	42	38
2005	37	37	37	39	34	36	37	33	36	43	35	37	34
2006	36	29	31	38	29	43	37	38	37	35	31	39	40
2007	31	31	22	34	36	32	34	32	33	29	30	27	32
2008	27	25	21	26	26	28	27	28	41	27	26	27	25
2009	32	25	23	21	26	24	25	24	31	69	54	80	
Overall	74	74	73	76	77	78	73	64	70	76	74	79	80

Appendix T

Peace be with you
PLEASANT OAKS   77 77D

"Peace be with you!" Je - sus said,___ and dis - played his hands__ and
"Peace be with you!" Je - sus said;___ "I send you as God___ sends
"Peace be with you!" Hear the call:___ new cre - a - tion is___ be -

side,___ Fri - day's dread - ful wounds that bled as u -
me: ri - sing from___ a - mong the dead, live to
gun!___ Ev - 'ry crea - ture, great and small, lift your

pon___ the cross he died.___ Now and through all time he stands
set___ cre - a - tion free." ___ Then he breathed u - pon___ his friends
hearts__ to God as one.___ Earth and cos - mos, raise your voice,

where his true___ dis - ci - ples meet,___ hol - ding out___ his
and the Spi - rit moved with - in___ with au - thor - i -
ev - 'ry thing__ that draws a breath,___ sing and dance__ with

woun-ded hands, Sun - day's signs___ of death's___ de - feat.___
ty God sends: pow - er, e - ven o - ver sin.___
God! Re - joice! Christ has con - quered sin___ and death!___

Text: ©2007 Adam M.L. Tice
Tune: ©2007 Chris Ángel

Bibliography

100th Anniversary 1854–1954: Maple Grove Mennonite Church (Topeka, Indiana). Sixteen-page booklet, 1954.

Augsburger, Myron. *Pilgrim Aflame*. Scottdale, PA: Herald Press, 1967, 2005.

Beck, Ervin, ed. *College Mennonite Church 1903–2003*. Nappanee, IN: Evangel Press, 2003.

Bender, Harold S. "Elkhart Institute (Elkhart, Indiana, USA)." *GAMEO*[1], 1956. http://www.gameo.org/encyclopedia/contents/elkhart_institute_elkhart_indiana_usa.

———. "Funk, John Fretz (1835–1930)." *GAMEO*, 1956. http://www.gameo.org/encyclopedia/contents/F868ME.html.

———. "John F. Funk and Brother." *GAMEO*, 1956. http://www.gameo.org/encyclopedia/contents/F867ME.html.

———. "Mennonite Church General Conference." *GAMEO*, 1956. http://www.gameo.org/encyclopedia/contents/M46611ME.html.

———. "Mennonite Publishing Company (Elkhart, Indiana, USA)." *GAMEO*, 1957, http://www.gameo.org/encyclopedia/contents/M467080.html.

Bender, Harold S. and Beulah Stauffer Hostetler. "Mennonite Church (MC)." *GAMEO*, 1989. http://www.gameo.org/encyclopedia/contents/M46610ME.html.

Bender, Harold S. and Cornelius Krahn. "Literary Societies." *GAMEO*, 1955. http://www.gameo.org/encyclopedia/contents/L583.html.

Bender, Harold S., Cornelius Krahn, Nanne van der Zijpp, and Marlene Kropf. "Sunday School." *GAMEO*, 1989. http://www.gameo.org/encyclopedia/contents/S8437ME.html.

Bender, Harold S. and Richard D. Thiessen. "Mennonitische Rundschau, Die (Periodical)." *GAMEO*, 2007. http://www.gameo.org/encyclopedia/contents/M4720.html.

Bloom, Harry E., publisher. "Middlebury Should be 100 Per Cent (*sic*) Patriotic." *Middlebury Independent*, Vol. XXXII, April 5, 1918.

Bontrager, Ellis. *History of Bonneyville Mennonite Church*. Unpublished student paper for Mennonite History with J. C. Wenger, AMBS, 1982.

Bontrager, Eugene and Mary Bontrager Owens, ed. *Forks Mennonite Church: Sesquicentennial History 1857–2007*. Published by Forks at Middlebury Graphic Arts, 2007.

Boshart, David. "Becoming a United Church in a World of Division: A Biblical View of Christian Unity." Presentation at Central Plains Mennonite Conference, March 12, 2011. http://www.centralplainsmc.org/:/Events/Unity%20Conference%202011/Becoming%20a%20United%20Church.pdf.

---

1. *GAMEO* is *Global Anabaptist Mennonite Encyclopedia Online*.

Bush, Perry. *Dancing with the Kobzar: Bluffton College and Mennonite Higher Education 1899–1999*. Studies in Anabaptist and Mennonite History, no. 38. Telford, PA: Pandora Press US, 2000.

Coffman, Barbara F. "Coffman, John S. (1848–1899)." *GAMEO*, 1953. http://www.gameo.org/encyclopedia/contents/coffman_john_s._1848_1899.

Coffman, Vinetta. "Shore Mennonite Church (Shipshewana, Indiana, USA)." *GAMEO*, 1958. http://www.gameo.org/encyclopedia/contents/shore_mennonite_church_shipshewana_indiana_usa.

"Dordrecht Confession of Faith (Mennonite, 1632)." *GAMEO*, 1632. http://www.gameo.org/encyclopedia/contents/D674.html.

Dyck, Cornelius J. *An Introduction to Mennonite History: A Popular History of the Anabaptists and the Mennonites*. Scottdale, PA: Herald Press, 1967, 1981, 1993.

———. "President of Mennonite Biblical Seminary." In *The Work is Thine, O Christ: In Honor of Erland Waltner*, 13–23. Edited by June Alliman Yoder. Elkhart, IN: Institute of Mennonite Studies, 2002.

Eash, Brent. "Bonneyville Mennonite Chapel: A Church History." Unpublished Goshen College student paper for John Oyer's class, 1978. In Mennonite Historical Library, Goshen, Indiana.

Erb, Paul and Leonard Gross. "Kauffman, Daniel (1865–1944)." *GAMEO*, 1989. http://www.gameo.org/encyclopedia/contents/K386ME.html.

Estes, Steven R. *From Mountains to Meadows: A Century of Witness of the Meadows Mennonite Church, 1890–1990*. Published by Historical Committee of the Meadows Mennonite Church, 1990.

———. *A Goodly Heritage: A History of the North Danvers Mennonite Church*. Newton, KS: Mennonite Press, Inc.,1982.

———. *A Goodly Heritage II: Our Journey Continues*. Newton, KS: Mennonite Press, Inc., 2009.

———. *A Heritage of Faith: The Ninetieth Anniversary History of the Silver Street Mennonite Church, 1892–1982*. Booklet for services of worship, October 31, 1982.

———. "Hartzler, Raymond Livingston (1893–1988)." *GAMEO*, 1988. http://www.gameo.org/encyclopedia/contents/H3824.html.

Fretz, J. Herbert. "Oberholtzer, John H. (1809–1895)." *GAMEO*, 1987. http://www.gameo.org/encyclopedia/contents/O363.html.

Fretz, J. Winfield, "Reflections at the End of a Century." *Mennonite Life II,* July 1947, 33–34.

Friesen, Abraham. *Reformers, Radicals, Revolutionaries: Anabaptism in the Context of the Reformation Conflict*. Elkhart, IN: Institute of Mennonite Studies, 2012.

General Conference Mennonite Church. "Our Common Confession." *GAMEO*, 1896. http://www.gameo.org/encyclopedia/contents/O9.html.

———. "Statement of Doctrine (1941)." *GAMEO*, 1941. http://www.gameo.org/encyclopedia/contents/S7273.html.

Gingerich, Alice Kauffman. *Life and Times of Daniel Kauffman*. Scottdale, PA: Herald Press, 1954.

Gingerich, Ken, ed. *First News and Views, Centennial Edition*. Published for members and friends of First Mennonite Church, Middlebury, Indiana, 2004.

Gingerich, Melvin. *Mennonite Attire through Four Centuries*. Breinigsville, PA: The Pennsylvania German Society, 1970.

———. "West Point Mennonite Church (Lee County, Iowa, USA)." *GAMEO*, 1959. http://www.gameo.org/encyclopedia/contents/W4746.html.

Glick, Maggie. *Looking Back . . . Going Forward: Topeka Mennonite Church, 1898–1998*. Fuller Design, 1998.

Glick, Sally Weaver. *In Tune with God: The Art of Congregational Discernment*. Scottdale, PA: Herald Press, 2004.

Graber, Daniel J. "Silver Street Mennonite Church (Clinton Township, Indiana, USA)." *GAMEO*, 1959. http://www.gameo.org/encyclopedia/contents/silver_street_mennonite_church.

Graber, Ellis. "Zion Mennonite Church (Souderton, Pennsylvania, USA)." *GAMEO*, 1959. http://www.gameo.org/encyclopedia/contents/Z57752.html.

Graber, Marge. *Vision, Faith, Service: The Story of Camp Friedenswald, 1950–2000*. Elkhart, Indiana: Franklin Press, 2001.

Gratz, Delbert. "Ramseyer, Lloyd L. (1899-1977)." *GAMEO*, 1990. http://www.gameo.org/encyclopedia/contents/R367.html.

Hartzler, John Ellsworth. *Education among the Mennonites of America*. Danvers IL: The Central Mennonite Publishing Board, 1925.

Hershberger, Galen. "A Study of the Schism of the First Mennonite Church in Middlebury, 1962." Unpublished Goshen College student paper for John A. Lapp's class, 1974. In Mennonite Historical Library, Goshen, Indiana.

Hershberger, Guy. *The Mennonite Church in the Second World War*. Scottdale, PA: Mennonite Publishing House, 1951.

Hershey, Mary Jane. "A Study of the Dress of the (Old) Mennonites of the Franconia Conference 1700–1952." *Pennsylvania Folklife*, Summer 1958, 26–27.

Hiebert, Paul. *Anthropological Reflections on Missiological Issues*. Grand Rapids, MI: Baker Books, 1994.

Homan, Gerlof D. "Orie Benjamin Gerig: Mennonite Rebel, Peace Activist, International Civil Servant, and American Diplomat, 1894–1976." *The Mennonite Quarterly Review*, October 1999. http://www.goshen.edu/mqr/pastissues/oct99homan.html.

Horsch, John. *Menno Simons: His Life, Labors, and Teachings*. Scottdale, PA: Mennonite Publishing House,1916. "Menno Simons' Attitude Towards the Munsterites." http://www.mennosimons.net/horsch13.html.

Hostetler, John Andrew. *God Uses Ink: The Heritage and Mission of the Mennonite Publishing House After Fifty Years*. Scottdale, PA: Herald Press, 1958.

Johns, Ira S. "Clinton Frame Mennonite Church (Goshen, Indiana, USA)." *GAMEO*, 1954.

Juhnke, James C. "Historical Contexts for MC-GC Integration: Franconia Conference Split (1847) and Russian Migration (1874)." In *Without Spot or Wrinkle: Reflecting Theologically on the Nature of the Church*, edited by Karl Koop and Mary H. Schertz, 26–37. Elkhart, IN: Institute of Mennonite Studies, 2000.

———. "Mob Violence and Kansas Mennonites in 1918." *Kansas Collection: Kansas Historical Quarterlies* in http://www.kancoll.org/khq/1977/77_3_juhnke.htm.

———. "Preparation of a Leader: Erland Waltner from Dakota to Elkhart." In *The Work is Thine, O Christ: In Honor of Erland Waltner*, edited by June Alliman Yoder, 3–12. Elkhart, IN: Institute of Mennonite Studies, 2002.

———. *Vision, Doctrine, War: Mennonite Identity and Organization in America 1890–1930*. Vol. 3, The Mennonite Experience in America. Scottdale, PA: Herald Press, 1989.

Kanagy, Conrad. *Road Signs for the Journey: A Profile of Mennonite Church USA*. Scottdale, PA: Herald Press, 2007.

Kauffman, Daniel. *The Conservative Viewpoint: A Message to Members of the Mennonite Church*. Scottdale: Mennonite Publishing House, 1918.

———, ed. *Bible Doctrine: A Treatise on the Great Doctrines of the Bible pertaining to God, Angels, Satan, the Church and the Salvation, Duties and Destiny of Man*. Scottdale: PA: Mennonite Publishing House, 1914.

———, ed. *Doctrines of the Bible: A Brief Discussion of the Teachings of God's Word*. Scottdale: PA: Mennonite Publishing House, 1928.

———. "The General Mennonite Convention at Berne, Indiana." *Gospel Herald*. August 28, 1913, 338.

———. *Manual of Bible Doctrines: Setting Forth the General Principles of the Plan of Salvation, Explaining the Symbolical Meaning and Practical Use of the Ordinances Instituted by Christ and His Apostles, and Pointing Out Specifically some of the Restrictions which the New Testament Scriptures Enjoin upon Believers*. Elkhart, IN: Mennonite Publishing Company, 1898.

Kauffman, Gary and Wanda Kauffman Hoffman. *Brick by Brick: The Story of Clinton Brick Mennonite Church, 1854–2004*. Goshen, IN: Clinton Brick Mennonite Church, 2004.

Kauffman, J. Howard and Leland Harder. *Anabaptists four Centuries Later: A Profile of Five Mennonite and Brethren in Christ Denominations*. Scottdale, PA: Herald Press, 1975.

Kauffman, Minerva. "Devotional Covering." *Gospel Herald*, August 12, 1923, 429.

Kauffmann, Nancy. "Sanctuary: Where we maintain the unity of the Spirit." In *Vision*, Spring 2010.

Kaufman, Edmund G. and Henry Poettcker. "General Conference Mennonite Church (GCM)." *GAMEO*, 1990. http://www.gameo.org/encyclopedia/contents/G4647ME.html.

Keim, Albert N. *Harold S. Bender, 1897–1962*. Scottdale, PA: Herald Press, 1998.

Klaassen, Walter. "Church Discipline and the Spirit in Pilgram Marpeck." In *De Geest in bet Geding*. Edited by Irvin B. Horst, A Jong, D. Tjeenk, 180. Willink: Tjeenk, 1978.

Klaassen, Walter and William Klassen. *Marpeck: A Life of Dissent and Conformity*. Scottdale, PA: Herald Press, 2008.

Kniss, Fred. *Disquiet in the Land: Cultural Conflict in American Mennonite Communities*. New Brunswick, NJ: Rutgers University Press, 1997.

Koop, Karl. "Requisite Conditions for Identity and Vision." In *Anabaptist Visions for the New Millennium: A Search for Identity*, 19–22. Edited by Dale Schrag and James Juhnke. Waterloo, ON: Pandora Press, 2000.

Krahn, Cornelius. "Freeland Seminary (Collegeville, Pennsylvania, USA)." *GAMEO*, 1956. http://www.gameo.org/encyclopedia/contents/freeland_seminary_collegeville_pennsylvania_usa.

——— and John D. Rempel. "Ordinances." *GAMEO*, 1989. http://www.gameo.org/encyclopedia/contents/O745ME.html.

Kraybill, Donald B., Steven M. Nolt and David L. Weaver-Zercher. *Amish Grace: How Forgiveness Transcended Tragedy*. Jossey-Bass, 2010.

Krehbiel, June Galle. "Leader looks back on a time of change: Retiring MC USA director writes the story of merging two denominations." *Mennonite Weekly Review*. http://www.mennoworld.org/2009/12/7/leader-looks-back-time-change/?page=3.

Kreider, Rachel Weaver. *The History of the Eighth Street Mennonite Church, 1913–1978*. Unpublished manuscript held in the Mennonite Historical Library, Goshen College, 1978.

Kroeker, Wally. *An Introduction to the Russian Mennonites*. Intercourse, PA: Good Books, 2005.

Lapp, John A. "Page, Alice Thut (1872–1951) and William B. (1871–1945)." *GAMEO*, 1987. http://www.gameo.org/encyclopedia/contents/P348.html.

Loewen, Harry and Steven Nolt. *Through Fire and Water: An Overview of Mennonite History—Revised Edition*. Scottdale, PA: Herald Press, 2010.

Loewen, Howard John. *One Lord, One Church, One Hope, and One God: Mennonite Confessions of Faith in North America*. Elkhart, IN: Institute of Mennonite Studies, 1985.

MacMaster, Richard K. *Land, Piety, Peoplehood: The Establishment of Mennonite Communities in America, 1683–1790*. Scottdale, PA: Herald Press, 1985.

Mennonite Church. "Christian Fundamentals (Mennonite Church, 1921)." *GAMEO*, 1921. http://www.gameo.org/encyclopedia/contents/C4798.html.

———. *Confession of Faith in a Mennonite Perspective*. Scottdale, PA: Herald Press, 1995. http://www.mennolink.org/doc/cof.

———. "The Nurture and Evangelism of Children (Mennonite Church, 1955)." *GAMEO*, 1955. http://www.gameo.org/encyclopedia/contents/N88ME.html.

Merton, Thomas. *Hidden Ground of Love: The Letters on Religious Experience and Social Concerns*. Edited by William H. Shannon. Toronto, ON: Collins Publishers, 1985.

Middlebury History Book Committee of the Friends of the Library. *Middlebury: The Town Beautiful, 1836–1986*. Goshen, IN: News Printing Company, 1986.

Middlebury Independent. "Churches Have Important Place in History of the Community," June 18, 1936, 4.

Middlebury Independent. "Middlebury Should be 100 Per Cent (*sic*) Patriotic." Vol. XXXII, April 5, 1918.

Miller, Ernest. *Daniel D. Miller: A Biographical Sketch by One of his Sons*. Scottdale, PA: Mennonite Publishing House, 1957.

Miller, Marlin E. "Inerrancy of Scripture." *GAMEO*, 1989. http://www.gameo.org/encyclopedia/contents/I553ME.html.

Miller, Peggy Reiff. "Coming of Age on a Cattle Boat: The Mennonite Seagoing Cowboys." *The Mennonite*, January 10, 2006, 14–17.

Miller, Susan Fisher. *Culture for Service: A History of Goshen College, 1894–1994*. Goshen, IN: Goshen College, 1994.

———. "One remarkable year: 1903-1904." *Goshen College Bulletin*, June 2003. http://www.goshen.edu/news/bulletin/03june/01_year.php.

Murray, Stuart. *Church after Christendom*. "Belonging, Believing, Behaving," chapter 1. http://www.anabaptistnetwork.com/node/260.

———. *The Naked Anabaptist: The Bare Essentials of a Radical Faith*. Scottdale, PA: Herald Press, 2010.

Neff, Christian. "Ban (1953)." *GAMEO*, 1953. http://www.gameo.org/encyclopedia/contents/B36ME.html.

Neff, Christian, John C. Wenger, Harold S. Bender and Howard John Loewen. "Confessions, Doctrinal." *GAMEO*, 1989. http://www.gameo.org/encyclopedia/contents/C6656ME.html.

Neufeld, Henry. "Believe, Behave, Belong (Or how the church has got the art of discipleship backwards for so long)." *Canadian Mennonite*. Volume 13, No. 9, Apr. 27, 2009, 4.

Neufeld, Thomas Yoder. *Ephesians: Believers Church Bible Commentary*. Scottdale, PA: Herald Press, 2002.

Pannabecker, Samuel Floyd. *Faith in Ferment: A History of the Central District Conference.* Newton, KS: Faith and Life Press, 1967.

———. *Open Doors: A History of the General Conference Mennonite Church.* Newton, KS: Faith and Life Press, 1975.

———. "Wadsworth Mennonite School (Wadsworth, Ohio, USA)." *GAMEO,* 1959. http://www.gameo.org/encyclopedia/contents/W154.html.

Preheim, Rich. "History of Indiana-Michigan Conference." Unpublished manuscript, May 30, 2011. Microsoft Word files.

Redekop, Calvin. *Brotherhood and Schism.* Scottdale, PA: Herald Press, 1963.

Rempel, John D. "Biblical and Historical Roots of Mennonite Communion Practice," paper at Bethel College Mennonite Church, Conference on Communion, September 24, 2005.

———. *Jörg Maler's Kunstbuch: Writings of the Pilgram Marpeck Circle.* Kitchener, ON: Pandora Press, 2010.

———, ed. *Minister's Manual.* Scottdale, PA: Herald Press, 1998.

———. "Mennonite Worship: A Multitude of Practices Looking for a Theology." In *Anabaptist Visions for the New Millennium: A Search for Identity,* 159–164. Edited by Dale Schrag and James Juhnke. Waterloo, ON: Pandora Press, 2000.

Rempel, Peter Gerhard. *Forever Summer, Forever Sunday: Peter Gerhard Rempel's Photographs of Mennonites in Russia, 1890–1917.* Edited by John D. Rempel, Hildi Froese Tiessen, and Paul Tiessen. St. Jacobs, ON: Sand Hills Books, 1981.

Rich, Elaine Sommers, ed. *Walking Together in Faith: The Central District Conference 1957–1990.* Newton, KS: Mennonite Press, 1993.

Roth, John D. *Beliefs: Mennonite Faith and Practice.* Scottdale, PA: Herald Press, 2005.

———. *Choosing Against War: A Christian View.* Intercourse, PA: Good Books, 2002.

———. "The Church 'Without Spot or Wrinkle' in Anabaptist Experience." In *Without Spot or Wrinkle: Reflecting Theologically on the Nature of the Church,* edited by Karl Koop and Mary H. Schertz, 7–25. Elkhart, IN: Institute of Mennonite Studies, 2000.

———. *Practices: Mennonite Worship and Witness.* Scottdale, PA: Herald Press, 2009.

———. *Stories: How Mennonites Came to Be.* Scottdale, PA: Herald Press, 2006.

Roxburgh, Alan and Fred Romanuk. *The Missional Leader: Equipping Your Church to Reach a Changing World.* Jossey-Bass, 2006.

Ruth, John. *Maintaining the Right Fellowship: A Narrative Account of Life in the Oldest Mennonite Community in North America.* Herald Press, 1984; Wipf and Stock, 2004.

Salzman, Vinora Weaver. *Day by Day—Year by Year.* Unpublished booklet in Goshen College Mennonite Historical Library, 1982.

Schlabach, Gerald W. *Unlearning Protestantism: Sustaining Christian Community in an Unstable Age.* Brazos, 2010.

Schlabach, Theron F. *Gospel Versus Gospel: Mission and the Mennonite Church, 1863–1944.* Scottdale, PA: Herald Press, 1980.

———. "Nineteenth-century Humility: a Vital Message for Today?" edited transcript of Schlabach's address given at the annual meeting of the Mennonite Historical Association of the Cumberland Valley, November 19, 1996. http://www.mcusa-archives.org/mhb/Schlabach-humility.html.

———. "Reveille for *Die Stillen im Lande*: A Stir Among Mennonites in the Late Nineteenth Century." *The Mennonite Quarterly Review,* July 1977.

———. "The Past in Perspective: History." *College Mennonite Church 1903–2003,* 15–130. Edited by Ervin Beck. Nappanee, IN: Evangel Press, 2003.

———. *Peace, Faith, Nation: Mennonites and Amish in Nineteenth-century America*. Vol. 2, The Mennonite Experience in America. Scottdale, PA: Herald Press, 1988.

Schrock, Elden. *100th Anniversary Edition of the History and a Pictorial Directory of the First Mennonite Church, Nappanee, Indiana*. Booklet in Mennonite Historical Library, 1975.

Schrock (Roth), Elva May. *75th Anniversary Edition of the History of The First Mennonite Church, Nappanee, Indiana*. Booklet in Mennonite Historical Library, 1950.

Smith, C. Henry. "Bluffton College/University (Bluffton, Ohio, USA)." *GAMEO*, 1955. http://www.gameo.org/encyclopedia/contents/B5815.html.

———. *Mennonite Country Boy: The Early Years of C. Henry Smith*. Newton, KS: Faith and Life Press, 1962.

———. *The Story of the Mennonites* (Third edition revised and enlarged by Cornelius Krahn). Newton, KS: Mennonite Publication Office, 1950.

Smith, Willard H. "Byers, Noah E. (1873–1962)." *GAMEO*, 1986. www.gameo.org/encyclopedia/contents/B93.html.

Snyder, C. Arnold. *Anabaptist History and Theology: An Introduction*. Kitchener, ON: Pandora Press, 1995.

———. *Anabaptist History and Theology: Revised Student Edition*. Kitchener, ON: Pandora Press, 1997.

Springer, Joe. *Centennial Chronicles 1903–2003: 101 Vignettes from College Mennonite Church Life*. Goshen, IN: self published, 2004.

Steiner, Susan Clemmer. *Joining the Army That Sheds No Blood*. Wipf and Stock, 2009.

Stoltzfus, Grant M. *Ohio and Eastern Conference, From Colonial Period in Pennsylvania to 1968*. Scottdale, PA: Herald Press, 1969. http://www.mcusa-archives.org/library/omh/index.htm.

Stoner, André Gingerich. "Reattaching the Body Parts." *Mennonite Weekly Review*, April 4, 2011. http://www.mennoweekly.org/2011/4/4/reattaching-body-parts/?page=1.

———. "Who Wants to Hang in There." *Mennonite Weekly Review*, February 20, 2012. http://www.mennoweekly.org/2012/2/20/who-wants-hang-there.

Storms, Everek R. "Brenneman, Daniel (1834–1919)." *GAMEO*, 1953. http://www.gameo.org/encyclopedia/contents/B74215.html.

Stutzman, Ervin Ray. *From Nonresistance to Justice: The Transformation of Mennonite Church Peace Rhetoric 1908–2008*. Scottdale, PA: Herald Press, 2011.

Swartley, Willard M. *Slavery, Sabbath, War and Women*. Scottdale, PA: Herald Press, 1983.

Thomas, Everett. *Johann*. CreateSpace, 2011.

Tickle, Phyllis. *The Great Emergence: How Christianity is Changing and Why*. Grand Rapids, MI: Baker Books, 2008.

Toews, Paul and Harold S. Bender. "Fundamentalism." *GAMEO*, 1989. http://www.gameo.org/encyclopedia/contents/F85ME.html.

Umble, John S. "Central Mennonite Church (Archbold, Ohio, USA)." *GAMEO*, 1953. http://www.gameo.org/encyclopedia/contents/C45903.html.

———. "Hartzler, Jonas S. (1857–1953)." *GAMEO*, 1956. http://www.gameo.org/encyclopedia/contents/hartzler_jonas_s._1857_1953.

———. "Indiana-Michigan Amish Mennonite Conference." *GAMEO*, 1958. http://www.gameo.org/encyclopedia/contents/I5356.html.

VonGunten, Sara Yoder. *Warren Street Mennonite Church, 1923–1964; Pleasant Oaks Mennonite Church 1965–1984*. Non-published notebook, 1984.

Weaver, J. Denny. "Hartzler, John Ellsworth (1879–1963)." *GAMEO*, 1987. http://www. gameo.org/encyclopedia/contents/H382.html.

Weaver, William B. "Central Conference Mennonite Church." *GAMEO*, 1953. http://www. gameo.org/encyclopedia/contents/C458857.html.

———. *History of the Central Conference Mennonite Church*. Danvers, IL: published by the author, 1926. Also online at http://www.archive.org/stream/MN5038ucmf_9/ MN5038ucmf_9_djvu.txt.

——— and Harold S. Bender. "Joseph Stuckey (1825–1902)." *GAMEO*, 1959. http://www. gameo.org/encyclopedia/contents/stuckey_ joseph.

Wenger, John Christian. "First Mennonite Church (Middlebury, Indiana, USA)." *GAMEO*, 1957. http://www.gameo.org/encyclopedia/contents/F5663.html.

———. *J. C.: A Life Sketch*. Goshen, IN: Historical Committee of the Mennonite Church, 1993.

———. "Johns, Daniel J. (1850–1942)." *GAMEO*, 1957. http://www.gameo.org/encyclopedia/ contents/J6460.html.

———. *The Mennonite Church in America: Sometimes called Old Mennonites*. Mennonite History, vol. 2. Scottdale, PA: Herald Press, 1966.

———. *The Mennonites in Indiana and Michigan*. Studies in Anabaptist and Mennonite History, no. 10. Scottdale, PA: Herald Press, 1961.

———. "Miller, Daniel D." *Mennonite Encyclopedia*, vol. 3, 691.

———. "Plain Coat." *GAMEO*, 1959. http://www.gameo.org/encyclopedia/contents/plain_ coat.

———. "Warren Street Mennonite Church (Middlebury, Indiana, USA)." *GAMEO*, 1959. http://www.gameo.org/encyclopedia/contents/W3763.html.

——— and Russell R. Krabill. "Indiana-Michigan Mennonite Conference." *GAMEO,* 2010. http://www.gameo.org/encyclopedia/contents/I5359.html.

——— and C. Arnold Snyder. "Schleitheim Confession." *GAMEO*, 1955, 1990. http://www. gameo.org/encyclopedia/contents/S345ME.html.

Whitmer, Paul E. *The Autobiography of Paul E. Whitmer*. Unpublished document in Goshen College Mennonite Historical Library, February 15, 1952.

———. "Witmarsum Theological Seminary (Bluffton, Ohio, USA)." *GAMEO,* 1959. http:// www.gameo.org/encyclopedia/contents/witmarsum_theological_seminary_bluffton_ ohio_usa.

Yoder, Charles. "History of Middlebury Congregation." Unpublished Goshen College student paper for John C. Wenger's class, undated (about 1952). Mennonite Historical Library, Goshen, Indiana.

Yoder, Elmer S. and Alvin J. Beachy. "Beachy Amish Mennonite Fellowship." *GAMEO*, 2010. http://www.gameo.org/encyclopedia/contents/B435ME.html.

Yoder (Friesen), Genevieve. *The History of Maple Grove Mennonite Church, Topeka, Indiana*. Unpublished Goshen College student paper, undated (about 1935). Mennonite Historical Library, Goshen, Indiana.

Yoder, John Howard, ed. *The Legacy of Michael Sattler*. Classics of the Radical Reformation, vol.1. Scottdale, PA: Herald Press, 1973.

———. *The Politics of Jesus*. Grand Rapids, MI: Eerdmans, (1972), 1994.

Yoder, June Alliman, ed. *The Work is Thine, O Christ: In Honor of Erland Waltner*. Elkhart, IN: Institute of Mennonite Studies, 2002.